COUNTDOWN ARENA

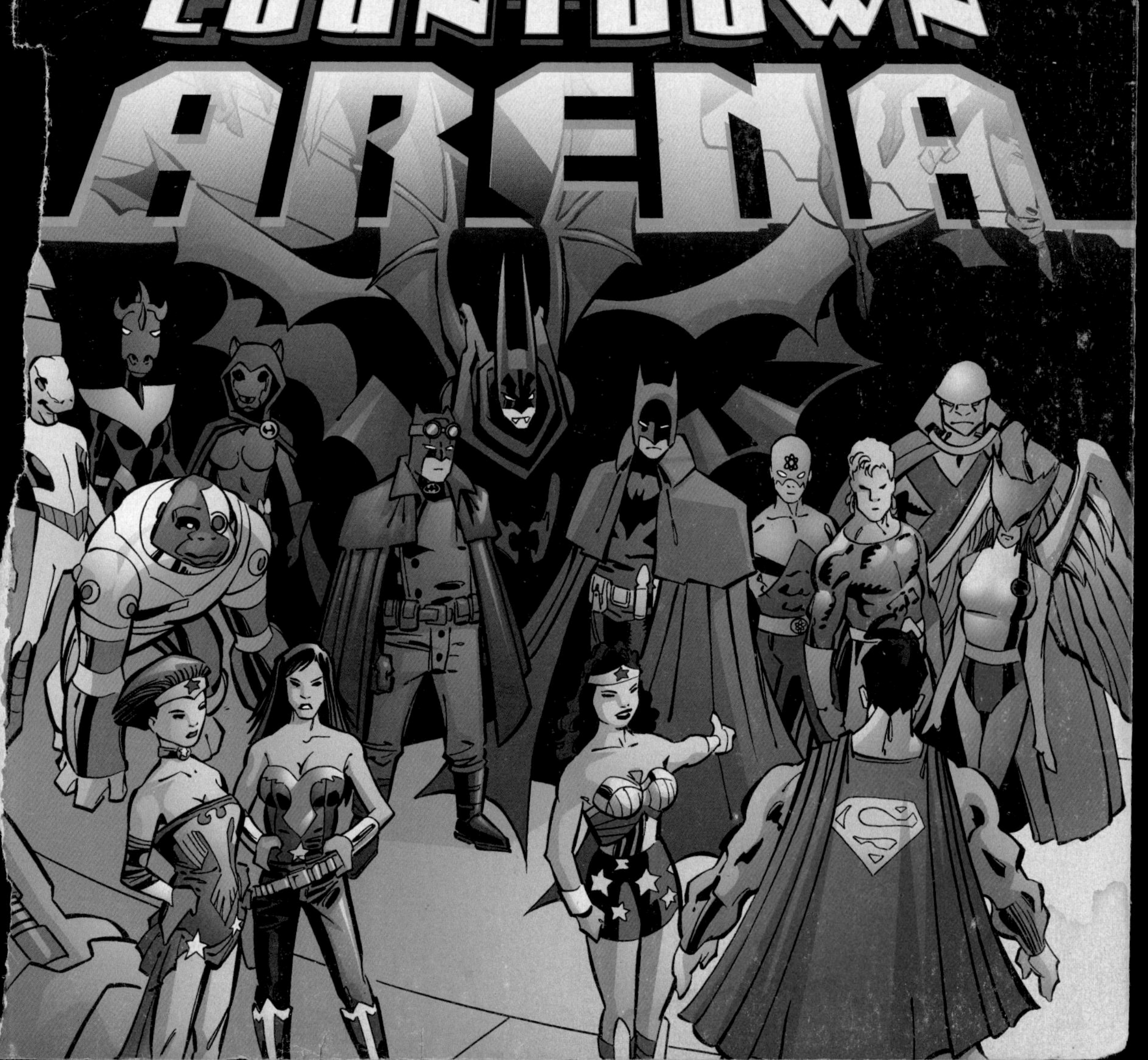

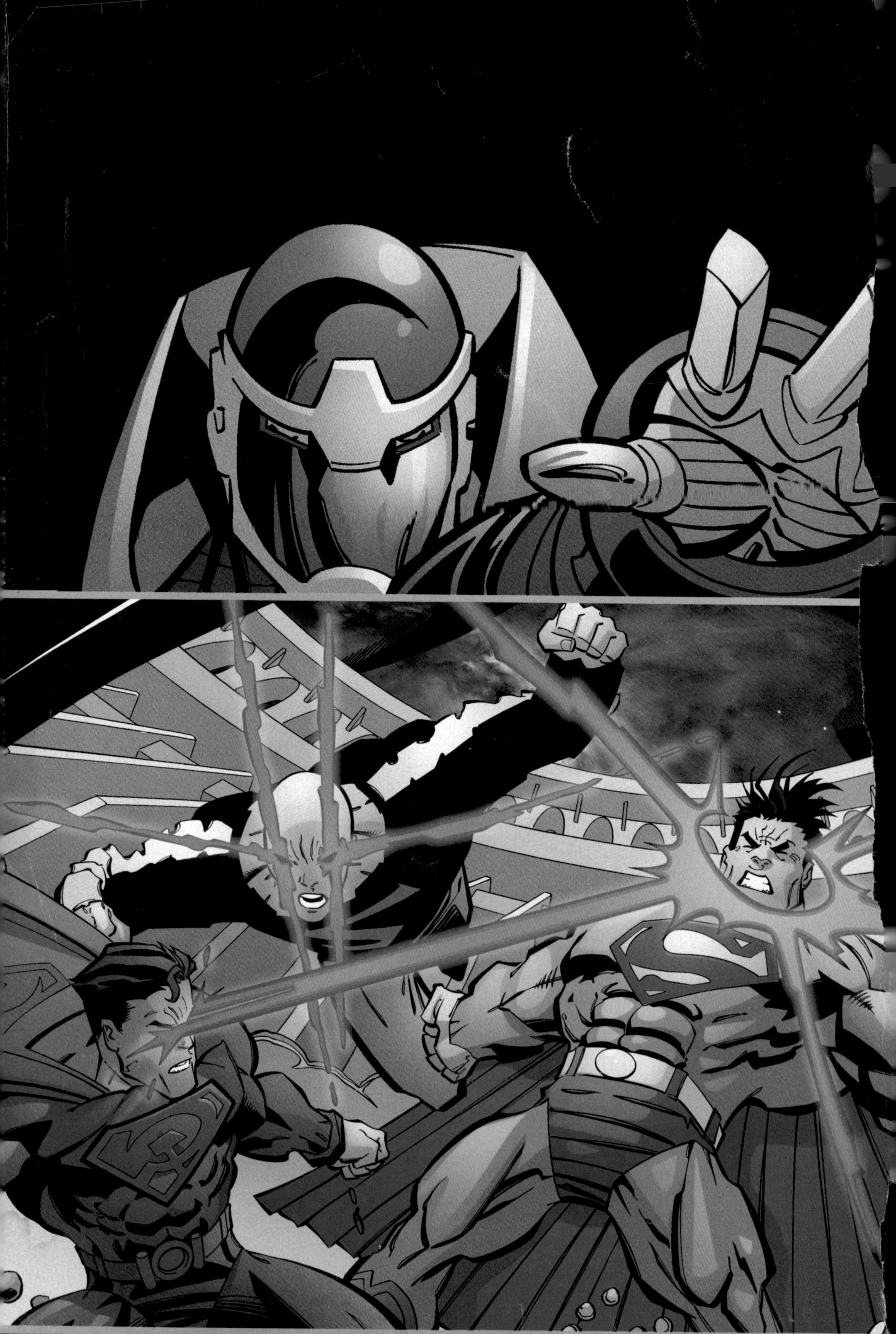

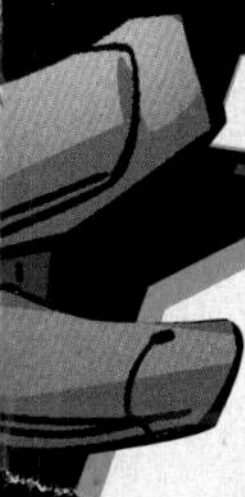

COUNTDOWN ARENA

KEITH CHAMPAGNE
Writer

SCOTT McDANIEL
Penciller

ANDY OWENS
Inker

GUY MAJOR
Colorist

NICK NAPOLITANO
JOHN J. HILL
Letterers

Cover by Scott McDaniel and Andy Owens
Publication design by Joe DiStefano

COUNTDOWN: ARENA
Published by DC Comics. Cover and compilation Copyright © 2008
DC Comics. All Rights Reserved.

DC Comics, 1700 Broadway, New York, NY 10019
A Warner Bros. Entertainment Company
Printed in Canada. First Printing.
ISBN: 978-1-4012-1822-5

THE BLOOD-SOAKED SANDS

COVER ART BY ANDY KUBERT

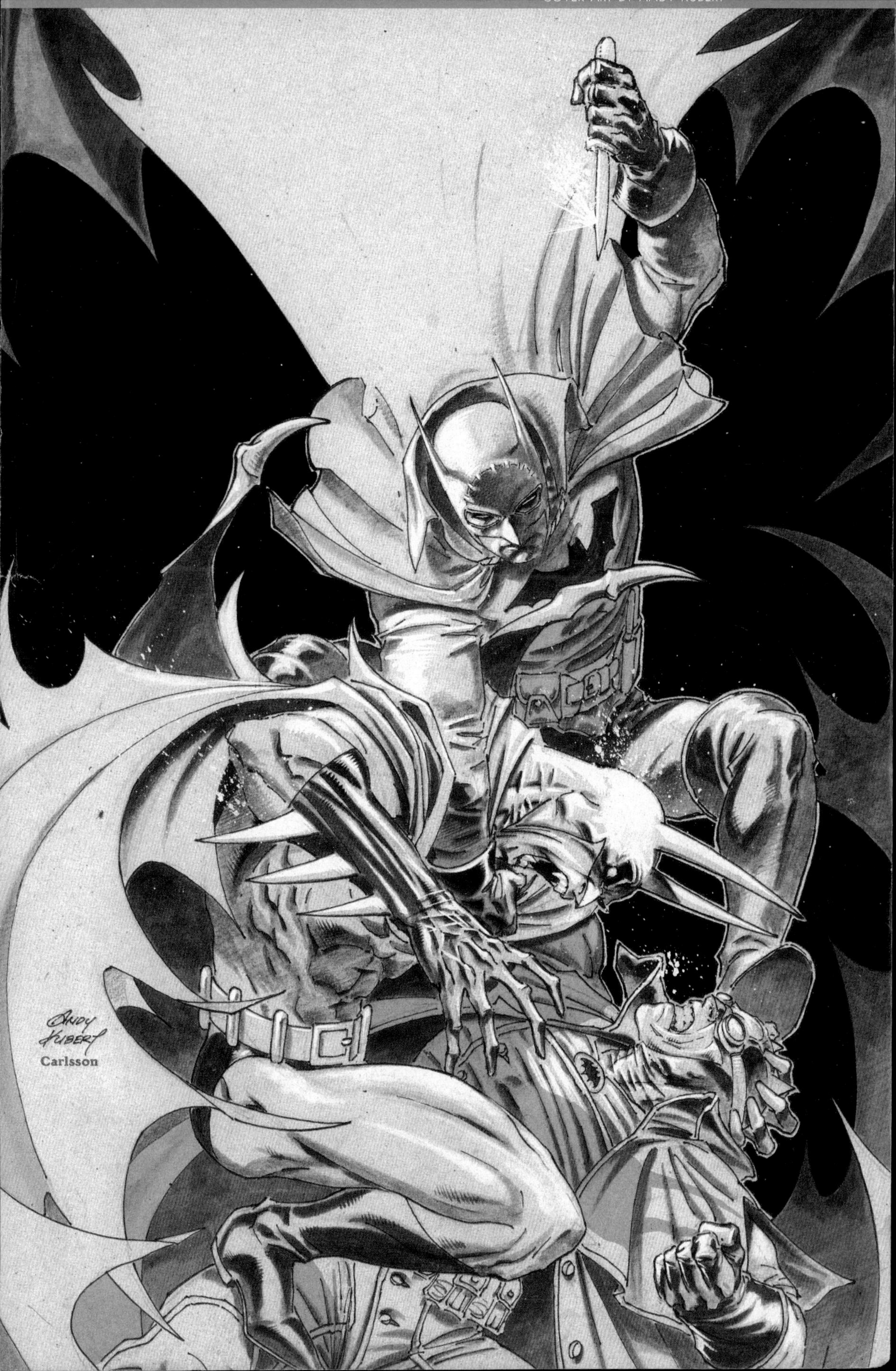
ANDY KUBERT
Carlsson

VARIANT COVER ART BY DALE EAGLESHAM & MICK GRAY

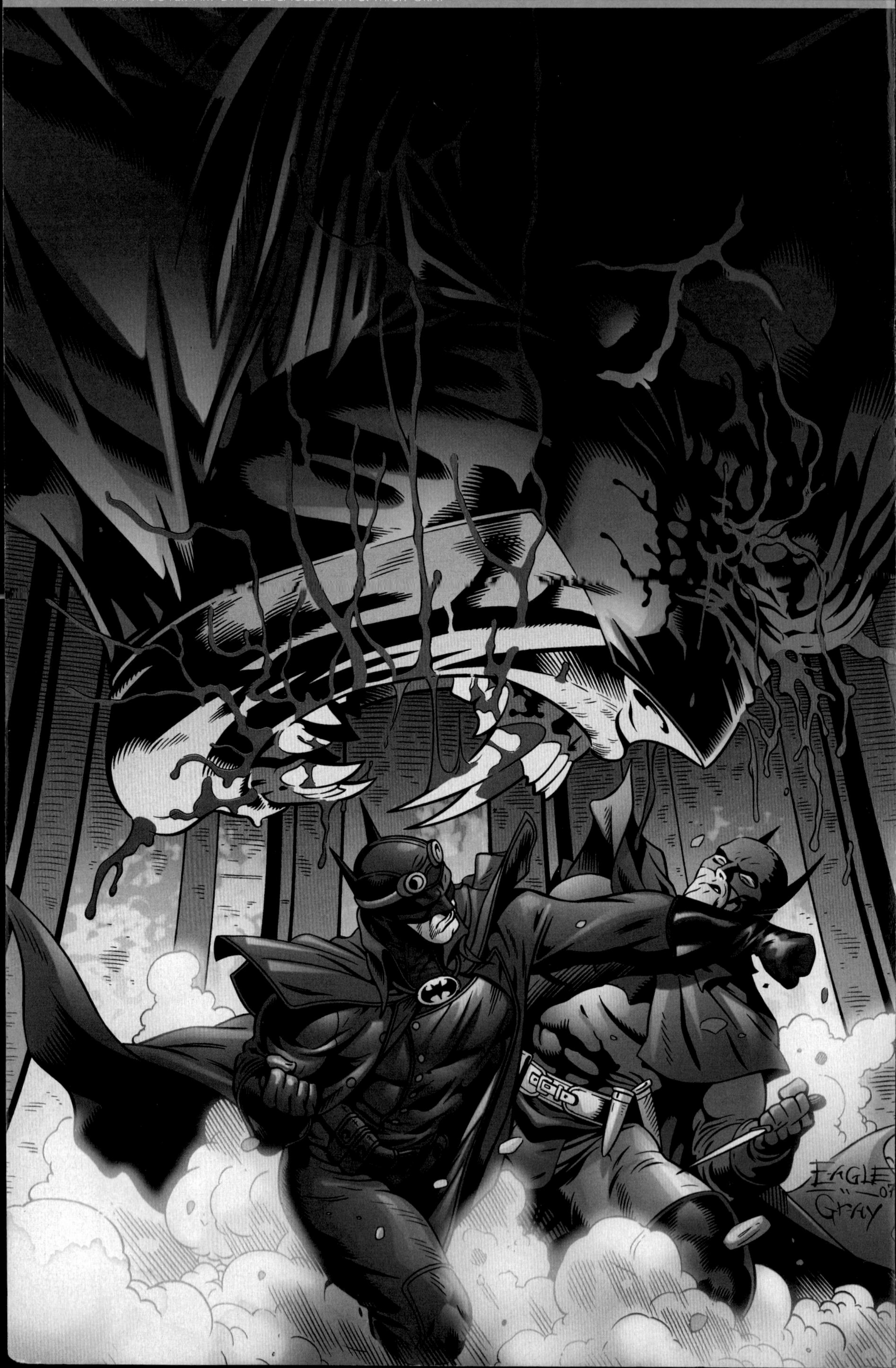
EAGLE
Gray

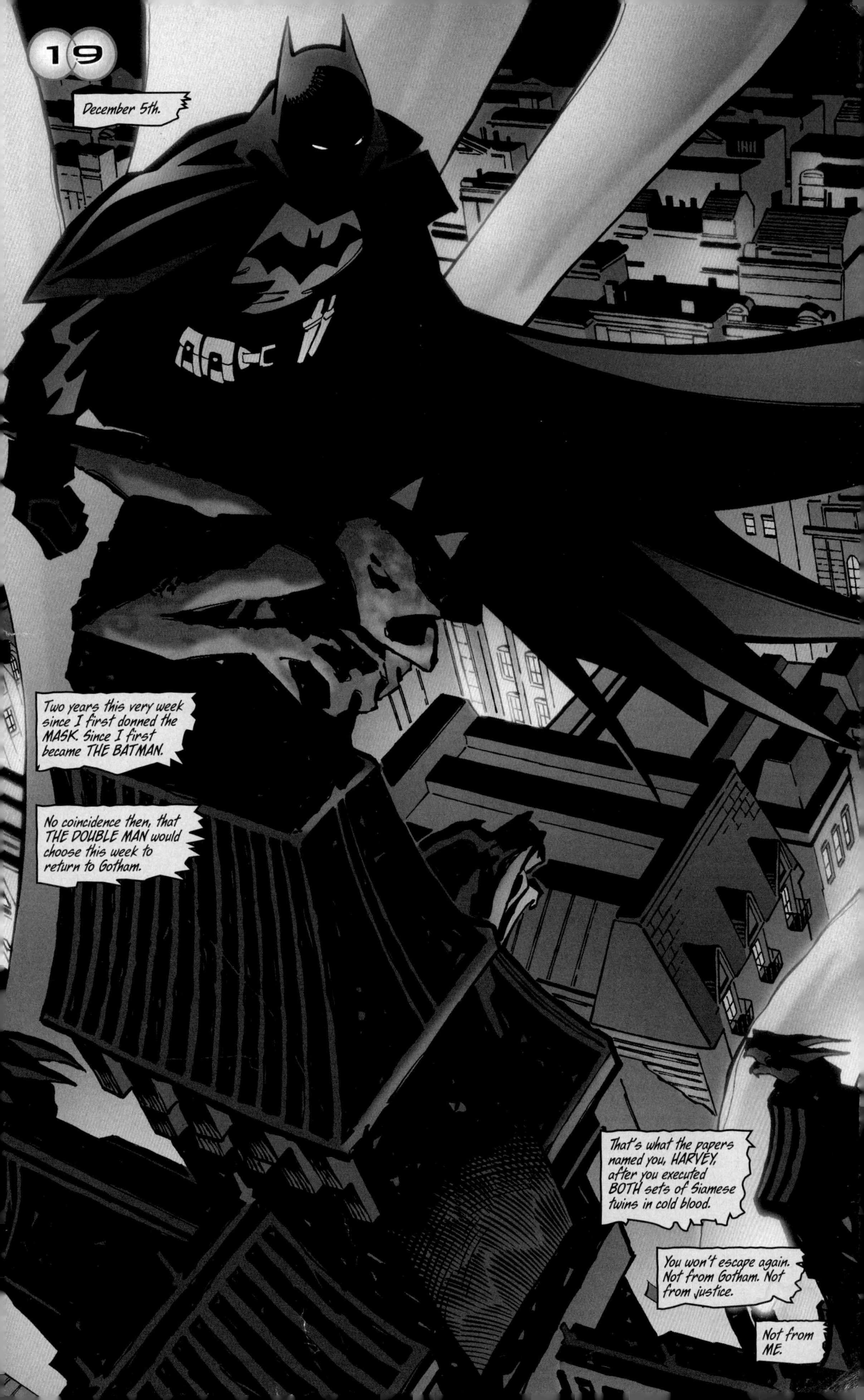
December 5th.
Two years this very week since I first donned the MASK. Since I first became THE BATMAN.
No coincidence then, that THE DOUBLE MAN would choose this week to return to Gotham.
That's what the papers named you, HARVEY, after you executed BOTH sets of Siamese twins in cold blood.
You won't escape again. Not from Gotham. Not from justice.
Not from ME.

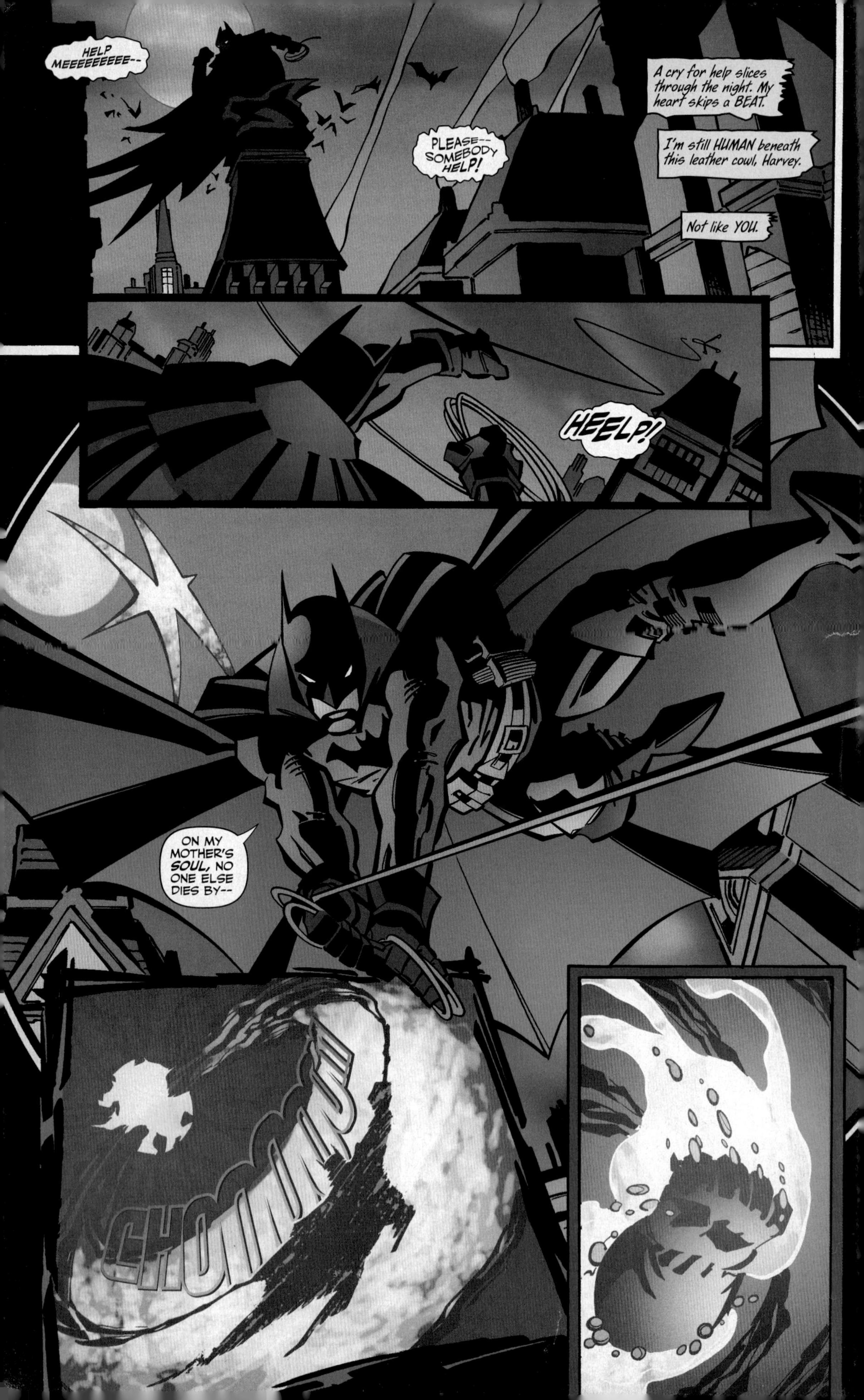

HELP MEEEEEEEEE--
A cry for help slices through the night. My heart skips a BEAT.
PLEASE-- SOMEBODY HELP!
I'm still HUMAN beneath this leather cowl, Harvey.
Not like YOU.
HEELP!
ON MY MOTHER'S SOUL, NO ONE ELSE DIES BY--

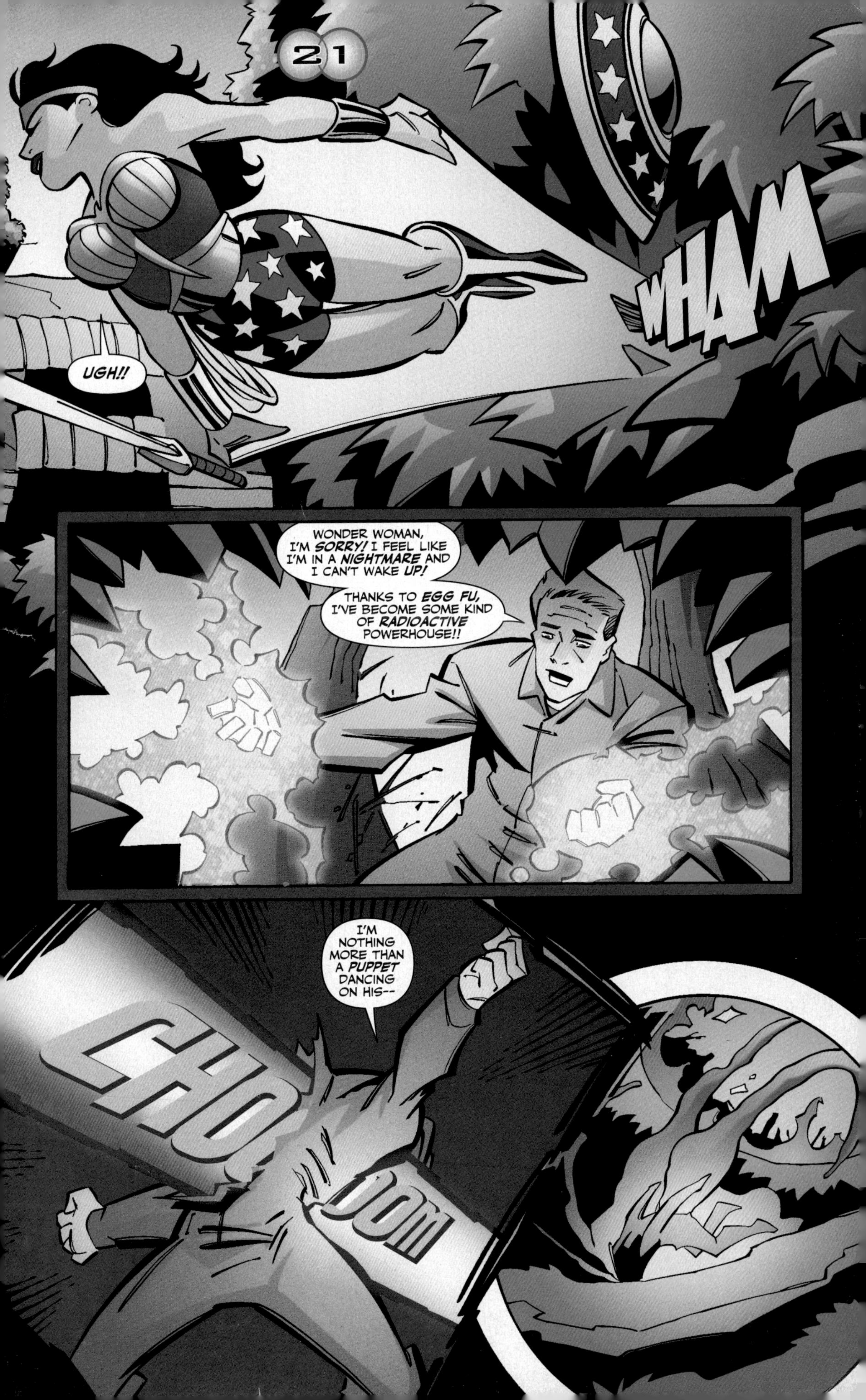
21
WHAM
UGH!!
WONDER WOMAN, I'M SORRY! I FEEL LIKE I'M IN A NIGHTMARE AND I CAN'T WAKE UP!
THANKS TO EGG FU, I'VE BECOME SOME KIND OF RADIOACTIVE POWERHOUSE!!
I'M NOTHING MORE THAN A PUPPET DANCING ON HIS--
CHOOOM

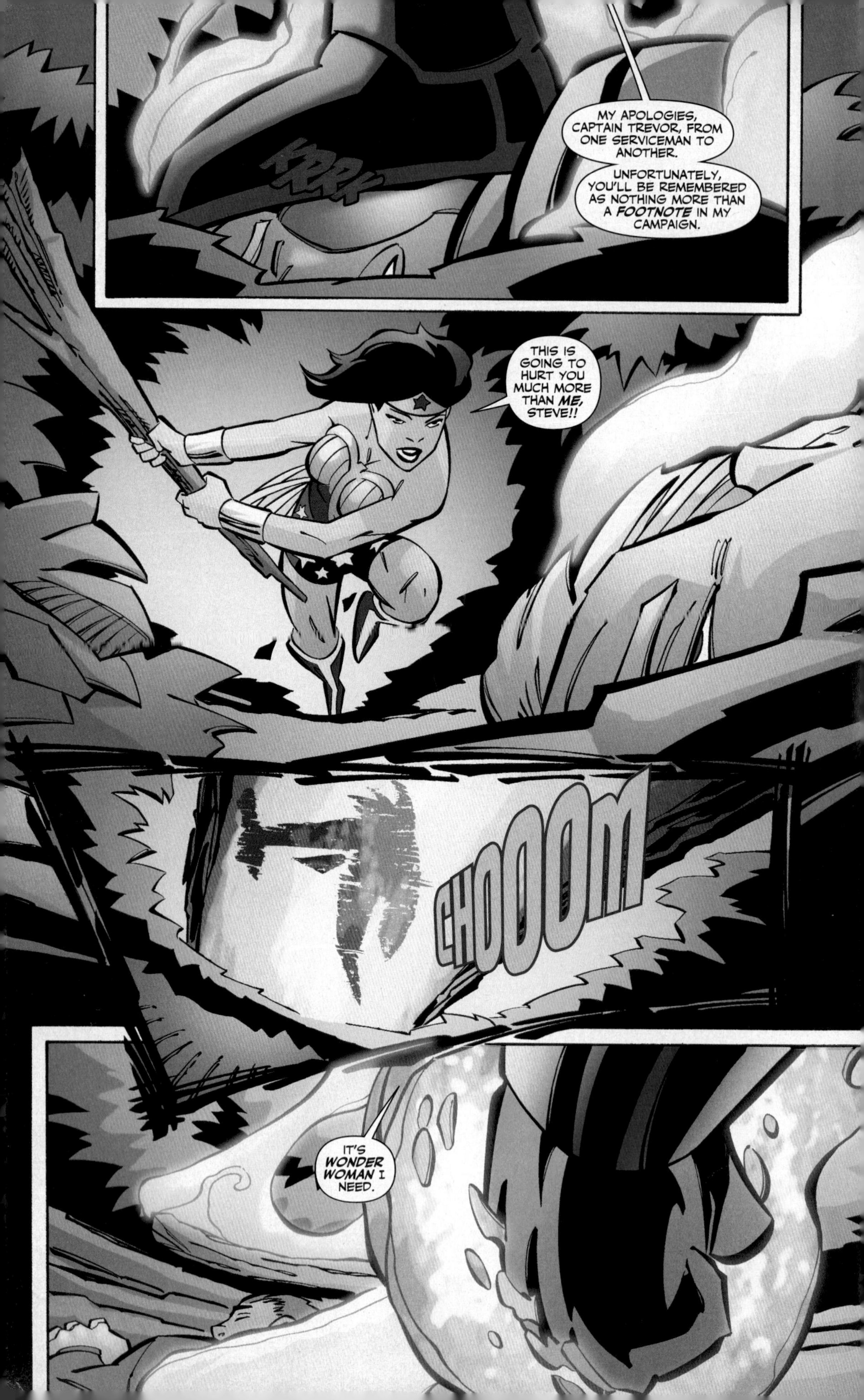
KRRK
MY APOLOGIES, CAPTAIN TREVOR, FROM ONE SERVICEMAN TO ANOTHER.
UNFORTUNATELY, YOU'LL BE REMEMBERED AS NOTHING MORE THAN A *FOOTNOTE* IN MY CAMPAIGN.
THIS IS GOING TO HURT YOU MUCH MORE THAN *ME,* STEVE!!
CHOOOM
IT'S *WONDER WOMAN* I NEED.

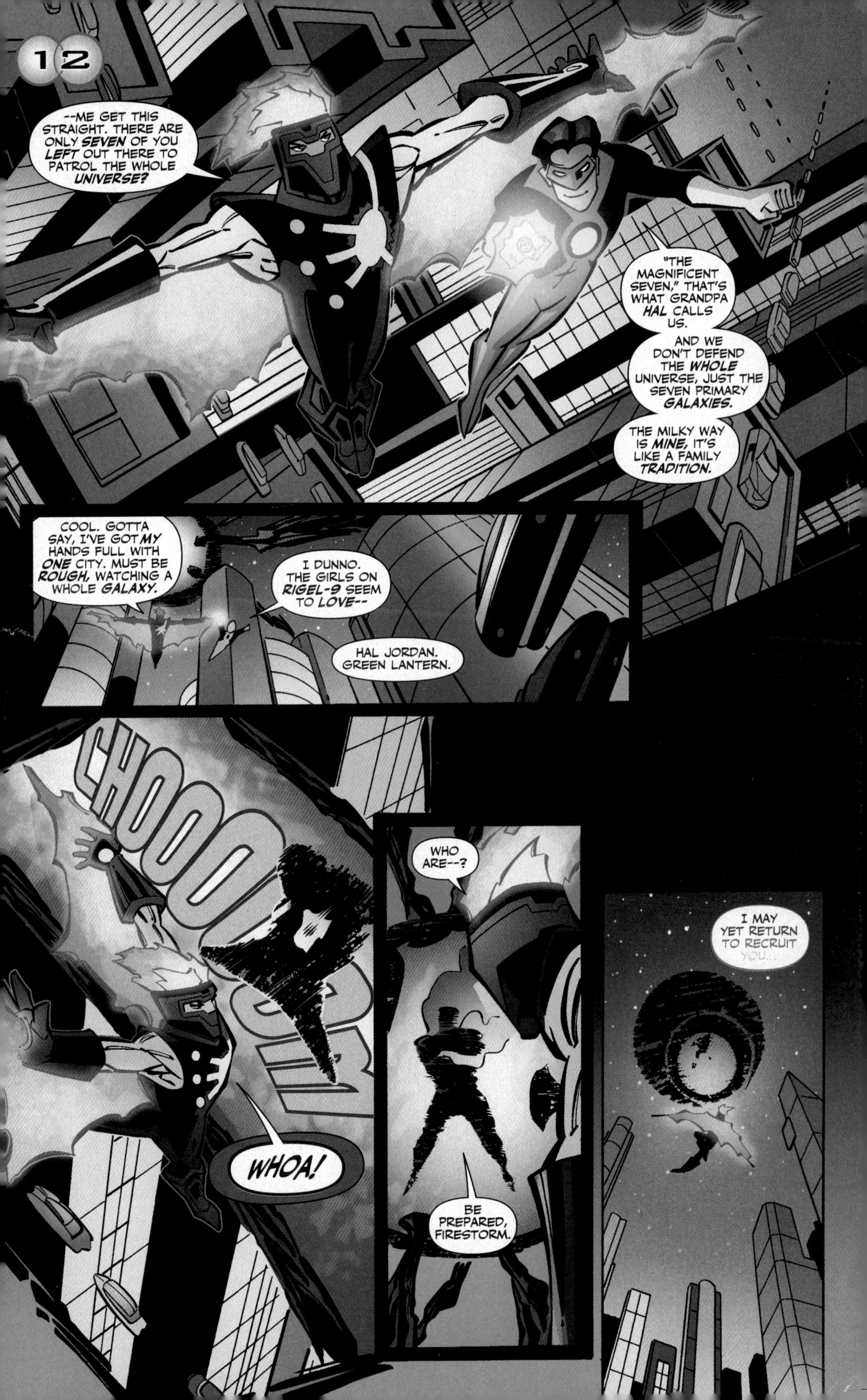
--ME GET THIS STRAIGHT. THERE ARE ONLY SEVEN OF YOU LEFT OUT THERE TO PATROL THE WHOLE UNIVERSE?
"THE MAGNIFICENT SEVEN," THAT'S WHAT GRANDPA HAL CALLS US.
AND WE DON'T DEFEND THE WHOLE UNIVERSE, JUST THE SEVEN PRIMARY GALAXIES.
THE MILKY WAY IS MINE, IT'S LIKE A FAMILY TRADITION.
COOL. GOTTA SAY, I'VE GOT MY HANDS FULL WITH ONE CITY. MUST BE ROUGH, WATCHING A WHOLE GALAXY.
I DUNNO. THE GIRLS ON RIGEL-9 SEEM TO LOVE--
HAL JORDAN. GREEN LANTERN.
CHOOOOM
WHOA!
WHO ARE--?
BE PREPARED, FIRESTORM.
I MAY YET RETURN TO RECRUIT YOU...

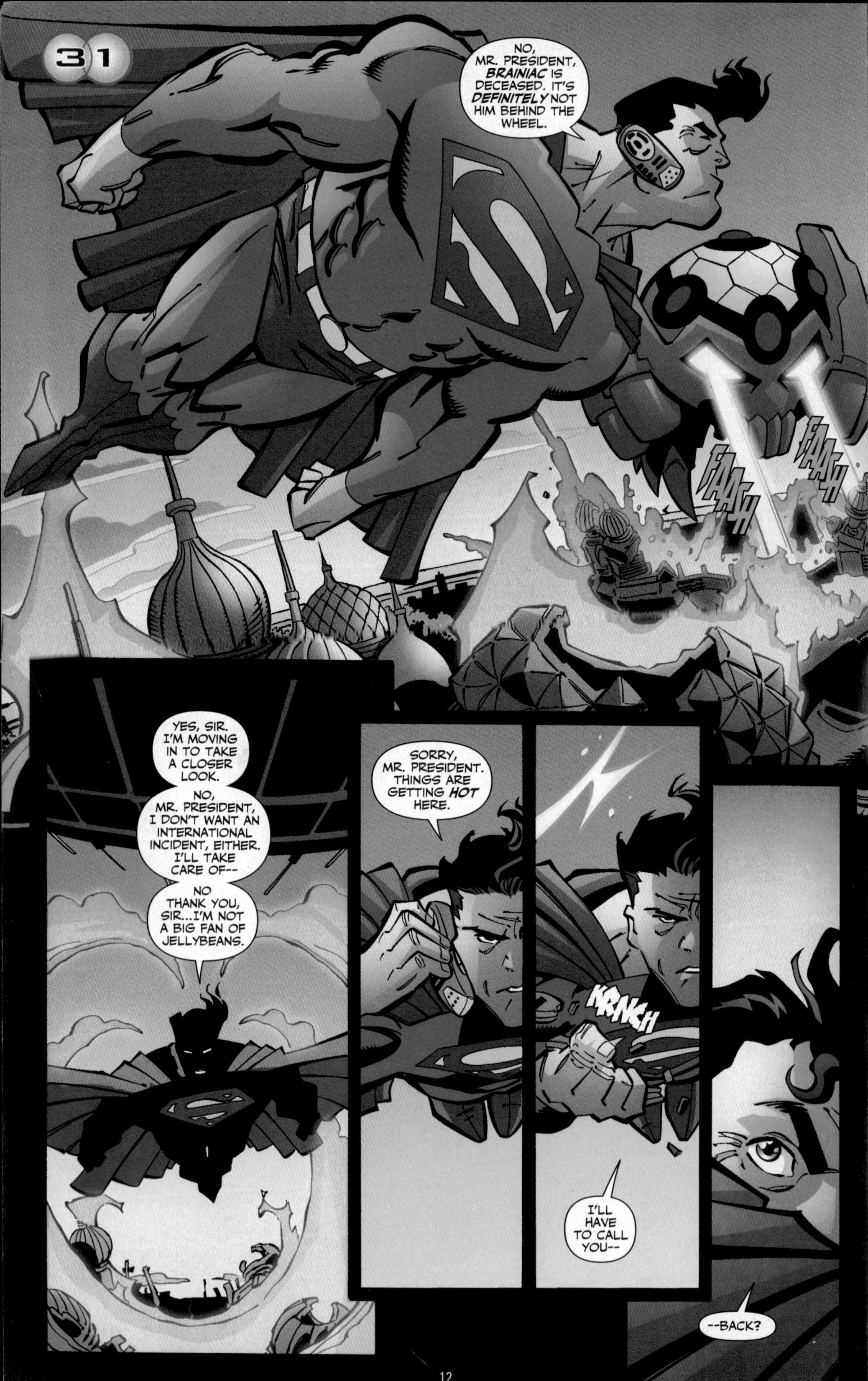
31
NO, MR. PRESIDENT, BRAINIAC IS DECEASED. IT'S DEFINITELY NOT HIM BEHIND THE WHEEL.
FAASH
FAASH
YES, SIR. I'M MOVING IN TO TAKE A CLOSER LOOK.
NO, MR. PRESIDENT, I DON'T WANT AN INTERNATIONAL INCIDENT, EITHER. I'LL TAKE CARE OF--
NO THANK YOU, SIR...I'M NOT A BIG FAN OF JELLYBEANS.
SORRY, MR. PRESIDENT. THINGS ARE GETTING HOT HERE.
KRNCH
I'LL HAVE TO CALL YOU--
--BACK?

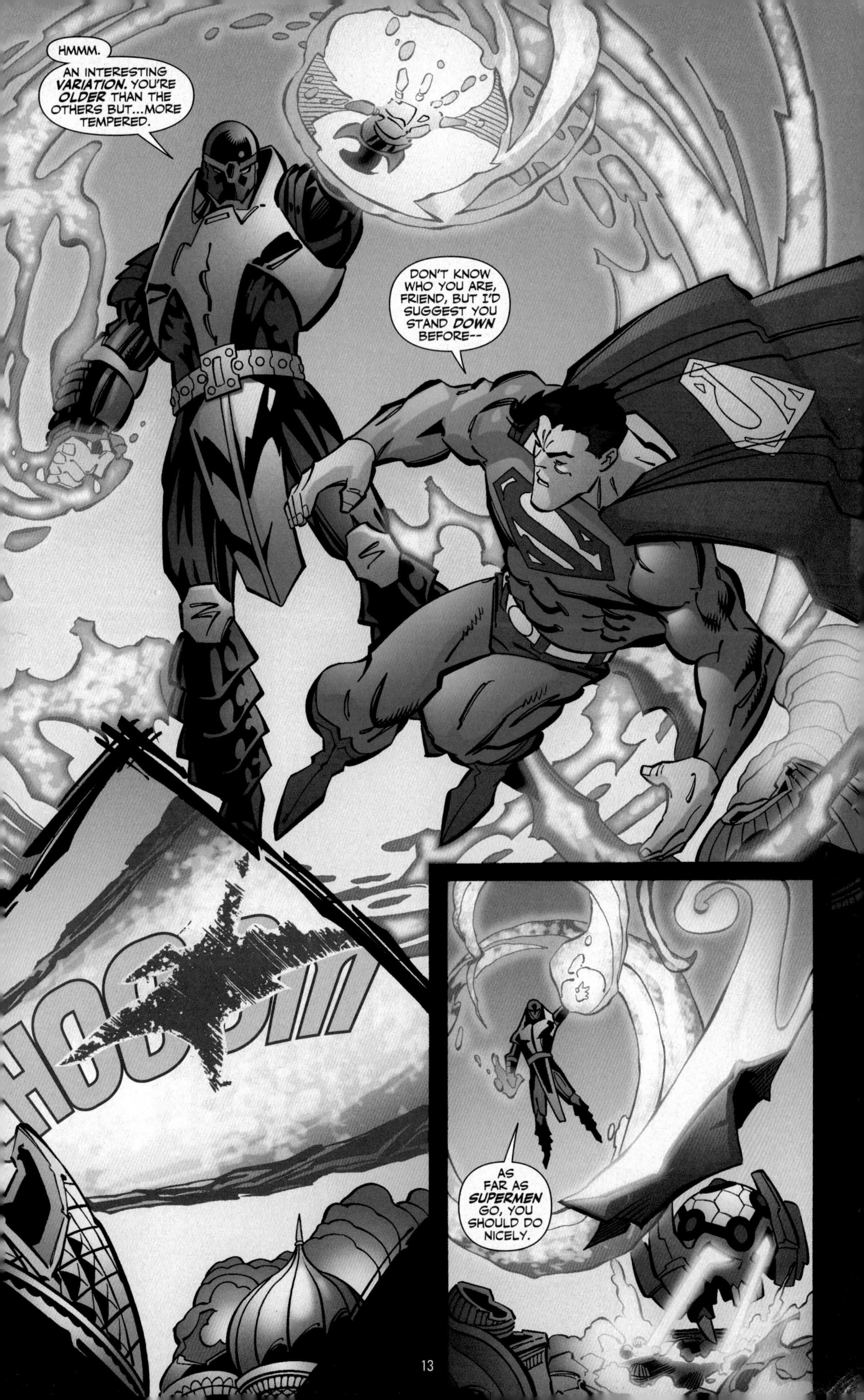
HMMM.
AN INTERESTING VARIATION. YOU'RE OLDER THAN THE OTHERS BUT...MORE TEMPERED.
DON'T KNOW WHO YOU ARE, FRIEND, BUT I'D SUGGEST YOU STAND DOWN BEFORE--
AS FAR AS SUPERMEN GO, YOU SHOULD DO NICELY.

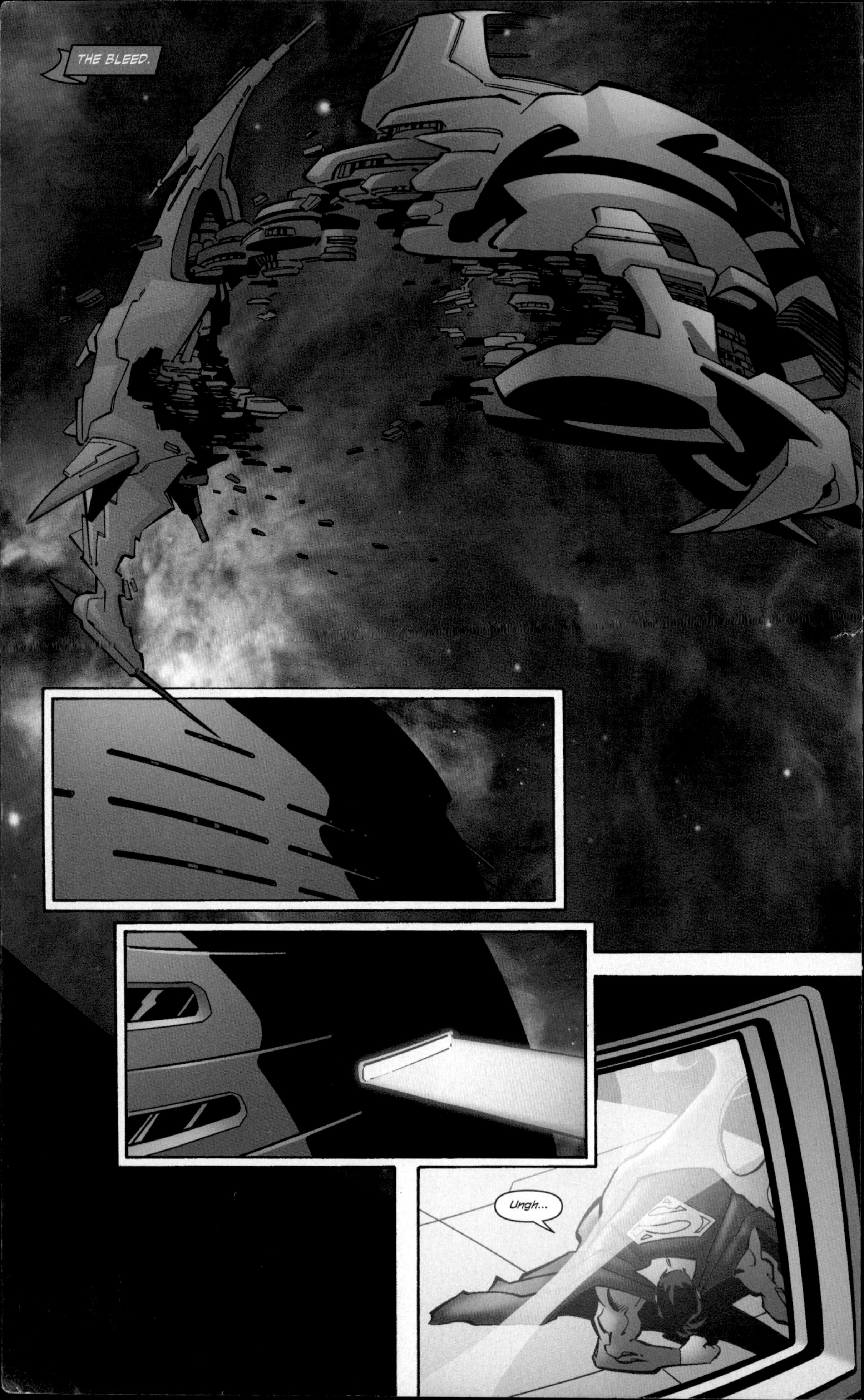
THE BLEED.
Ungh...

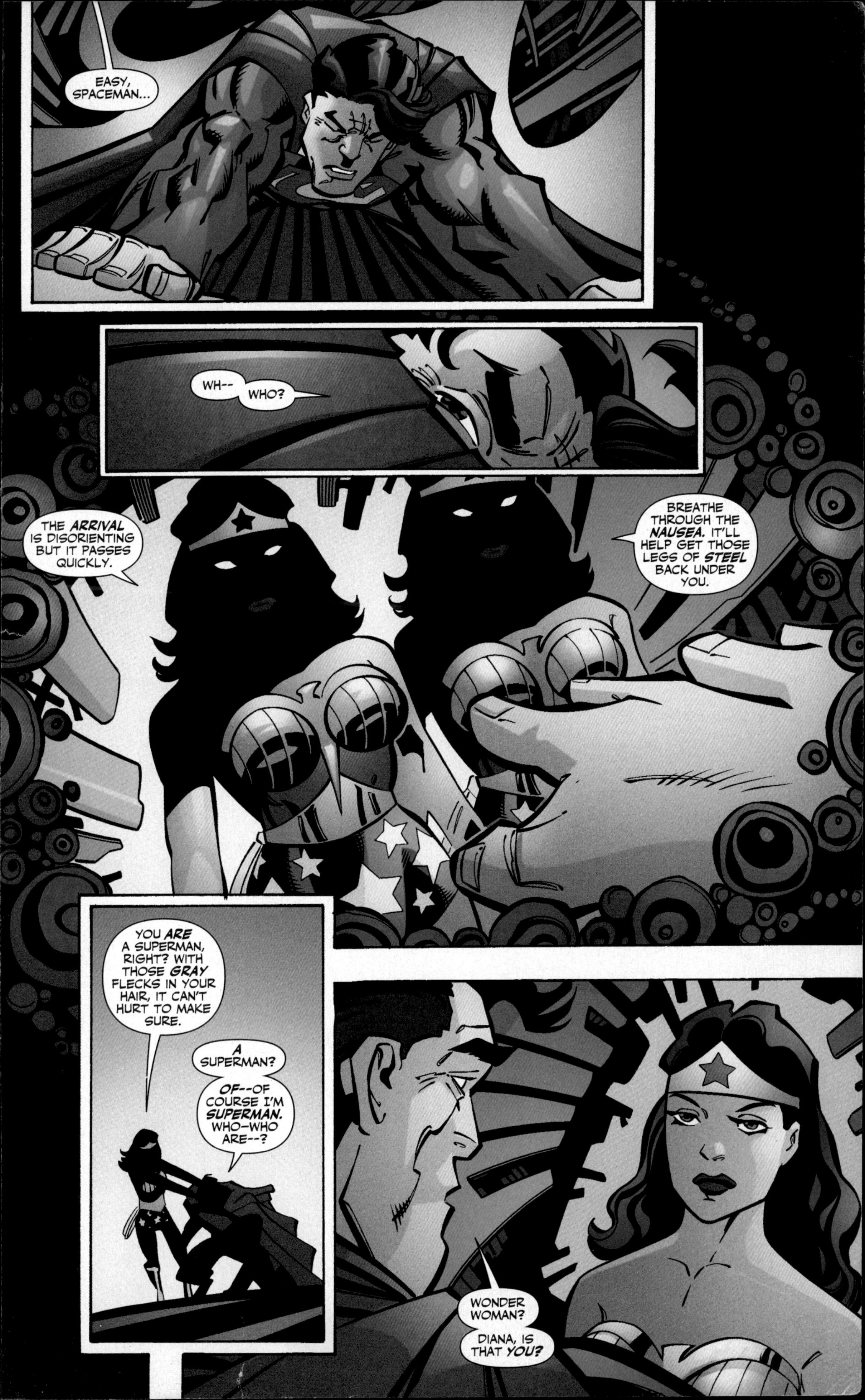
EASY, SPACEMAN...
WH--
WHO?
THE ARRIVAL IS DISORIENTING BUT IT PASSES QUICKLY.
BREATHE THROUGH THE NAUSEA. IT'LL HELP GET THOSE LEGS OF STEEL BACK UNDER YOU.
YOU ARE A SUPERMAN, RIGHT? WITH THOSE GRAY FLECKS IN YOUR HAIR, IT CAN'T HURT TO MAKE SURE.
A SUPERMAN?
OF--OF COURSE I'M SUPERMAN. WHO-WHO ARE--?
WONDER WOMAN?
DIANA, IS THAT YOU?

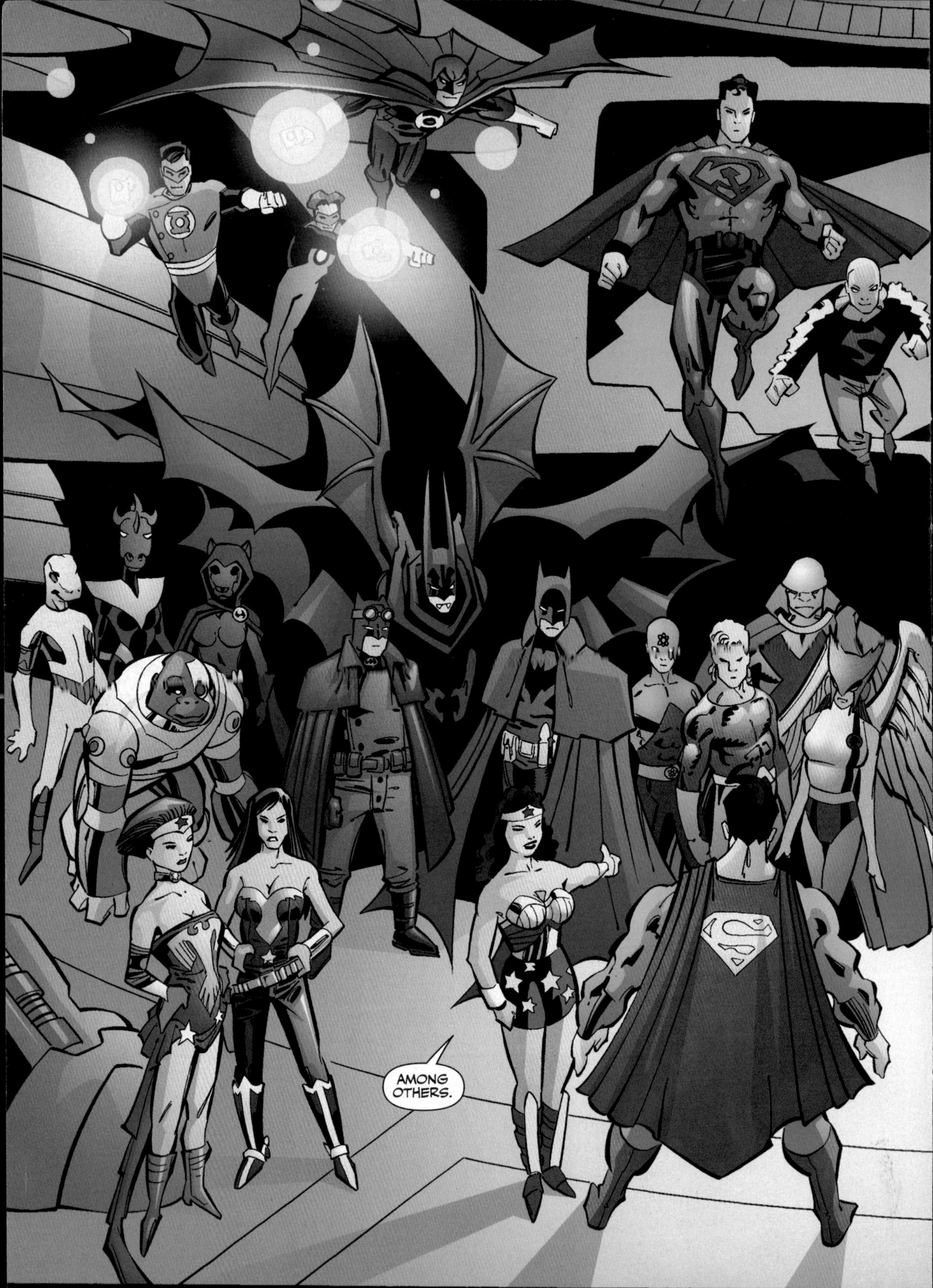
AMONG OTHERS.

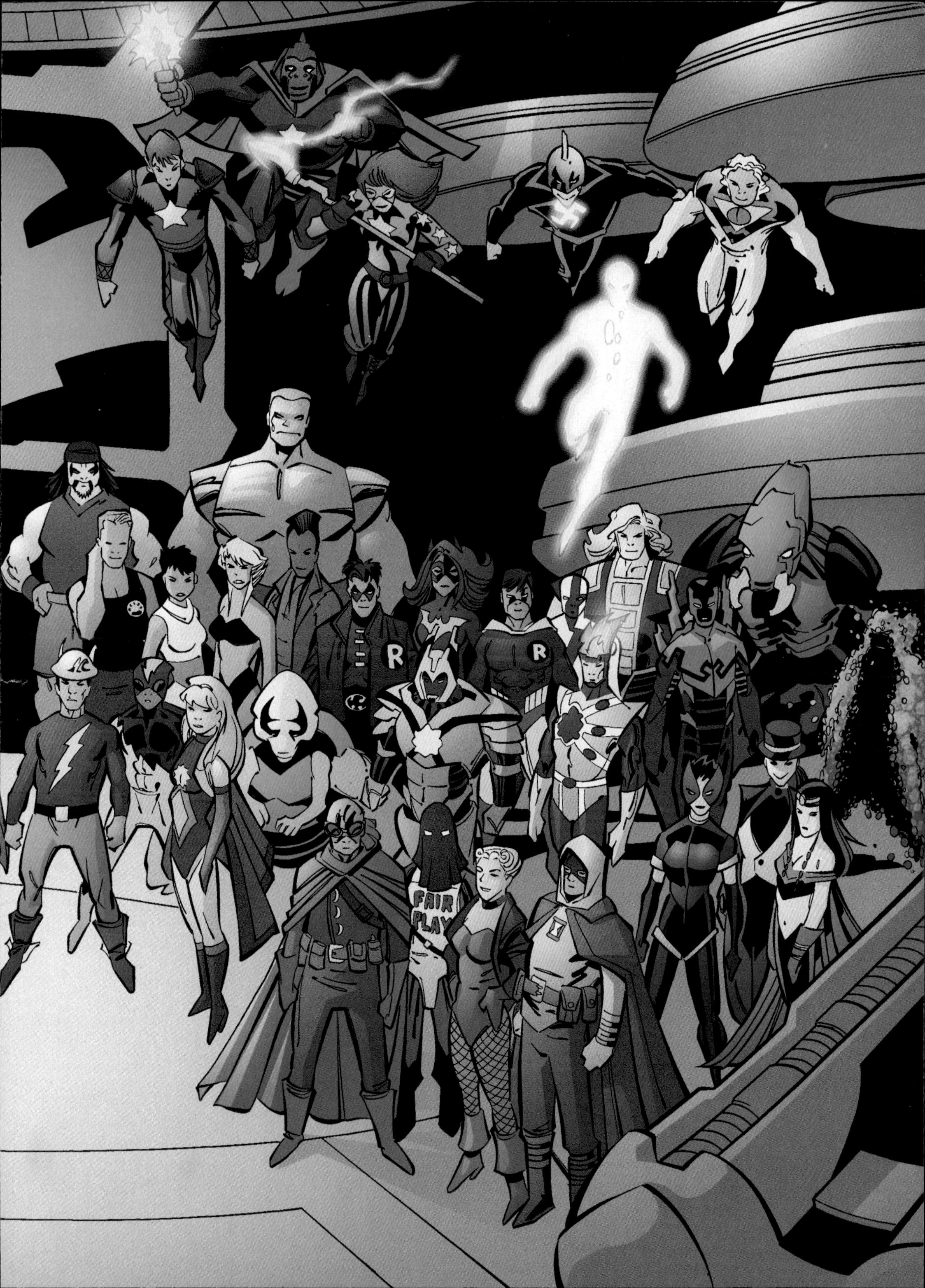
FAIR PLAY

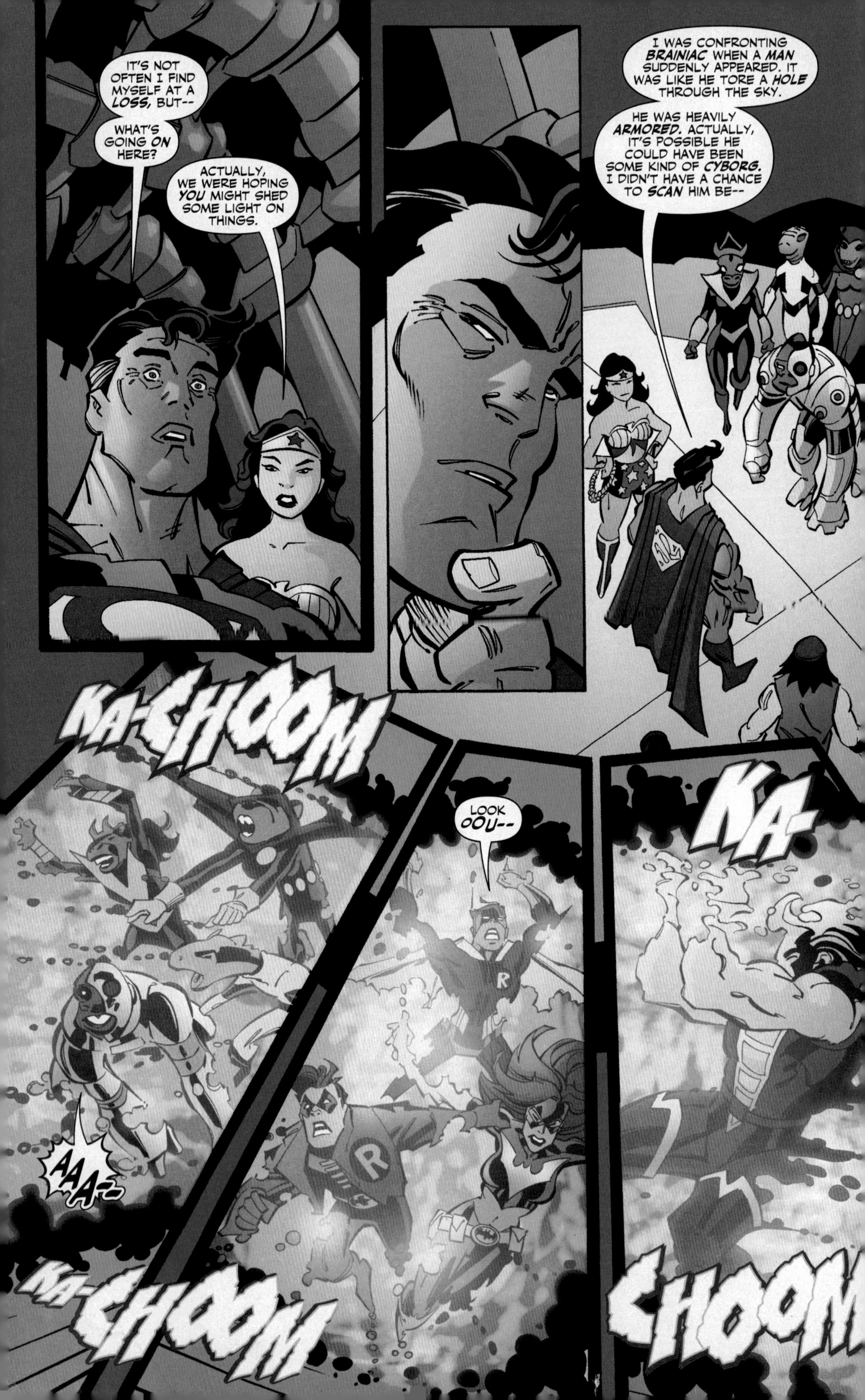
IT'S NOT OFTEN I FIND MYSELF AT A LOSS, BUT--
WHAT'S GOING ON HERE?
ACTUALLY, WE WERE HOPING YOU MIGHT SHED SOME LIGHT ON THINGS.
I WAS CONFRONTING BRAINIAC WHEN A MAN SUDDENLY APPEARED. IT WAS LIKE HE TORE A HOLE THROUGH THE SKY.
HE WAS HEAVILY ARMORED. ACTUALLY, IT'S POSSIBLE HE COULD HAVE BEEN SOME KIND OF CYBORG. I DIDN'T HAVE A CHANCE TO SCAN HIM BE--
KA-CHOOM
AAA
KA-CHOOM
LOOK OOU--
KA-
CHOOM

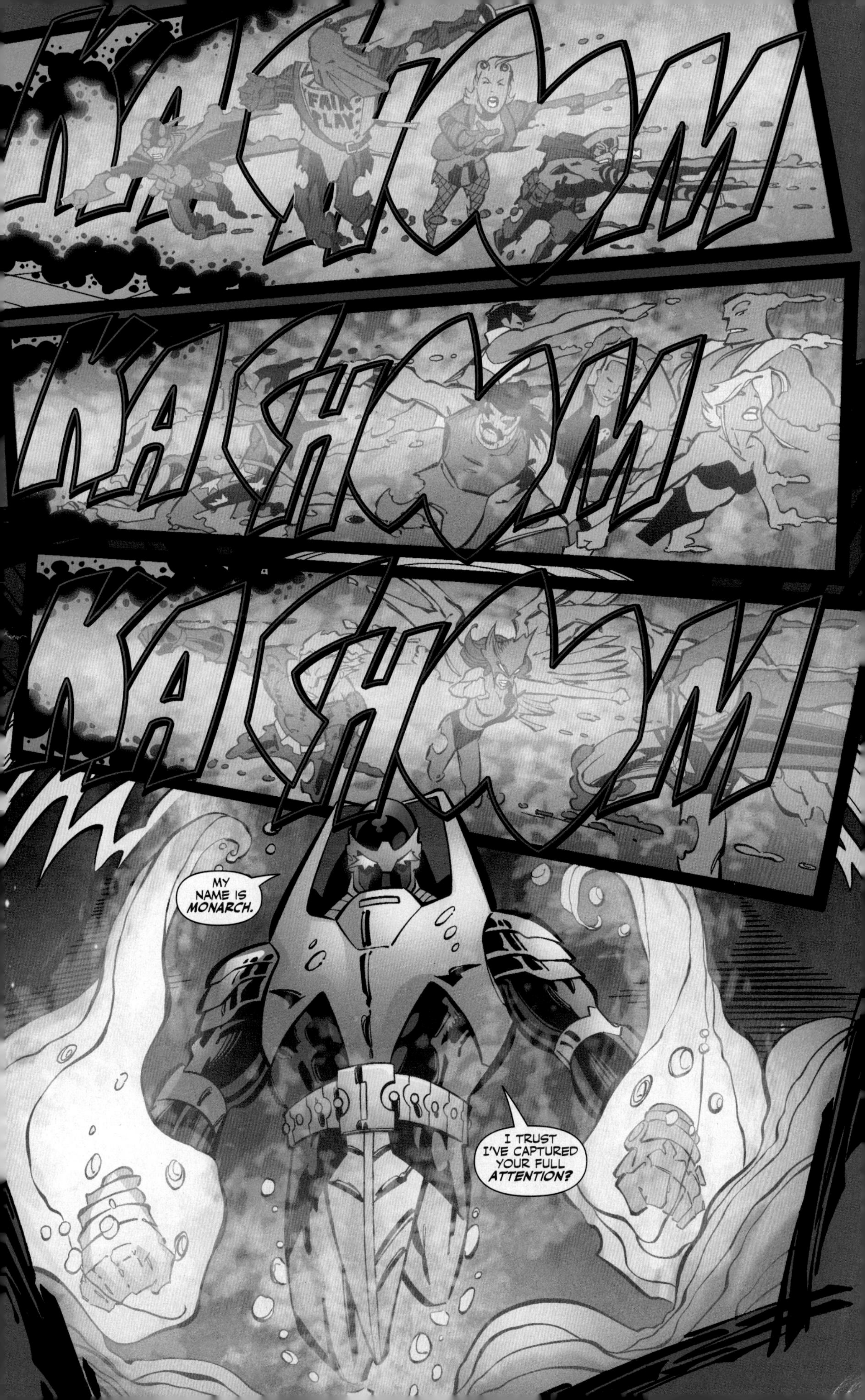
KA-KHOOM
KA-KHOOM
KA-KHOOM
MY NAME IS MONARCH.
I TRUST I'VE CAPTURED YOUR FULL ATTENTION?

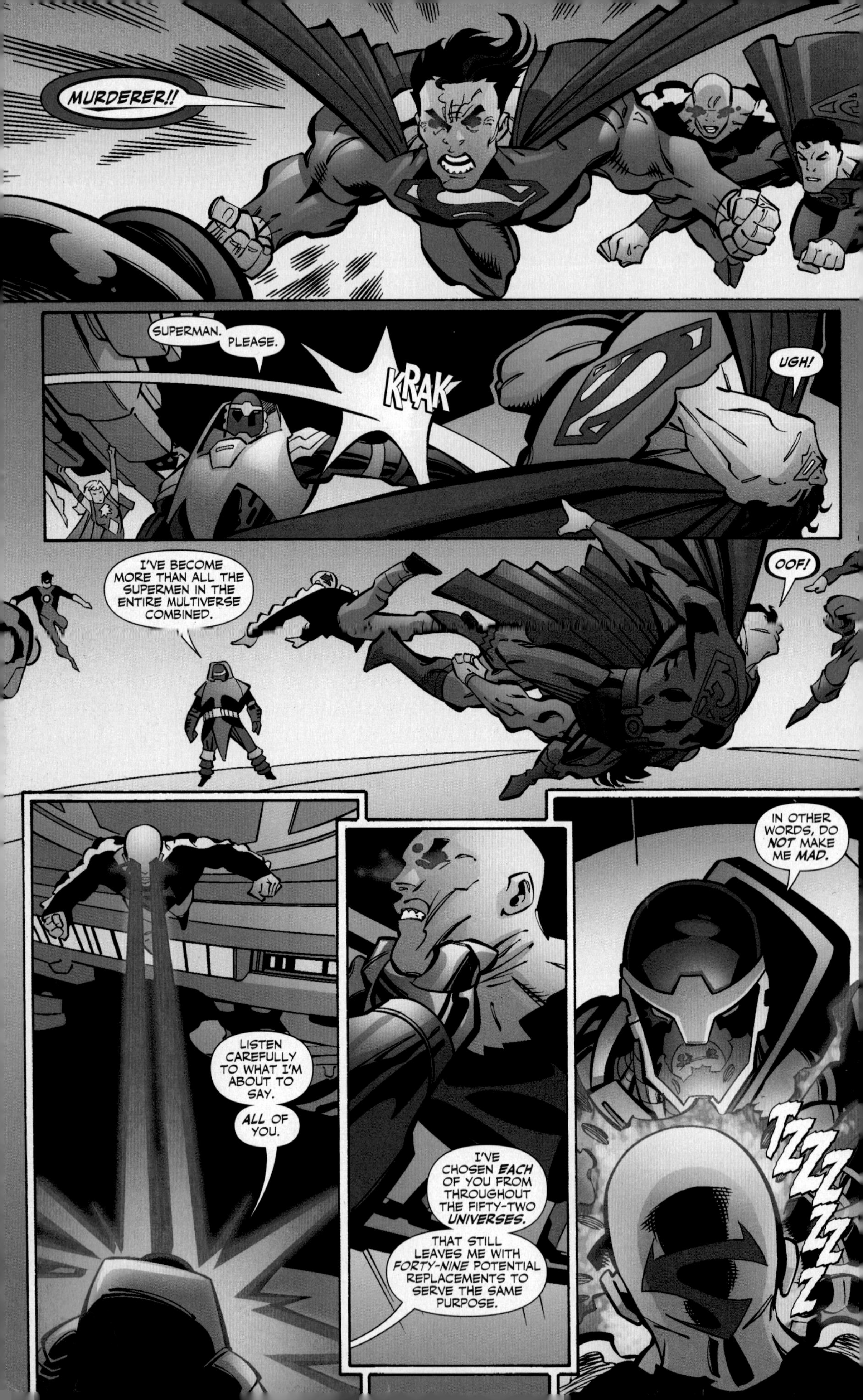
MURDERER!!
SUPERMAN.
PLEASE.
KRAK
UGH!
I'VE BECOME MORE THAN ALL THE SUPERMEN IN THE ENTIRE MULTIVERSE COMBINED.
OOF!
LISTEN CAREFULLY TO WHAT I'M ABOUT TO SAY.
ALL OF YOU.
I'VE CHOSEN EACH OF YOU FROM THROUGHOUT THE FIFTY-TWO UNIVERSES.
THAT STILL LEAVES ME WITH FORTY-NINE POTENTIAL REPLACEMENTS TO SERVE THE SAME PURPOSE.
IN OTHER WORDS, DO NOT MAKE ME MAD.
TZZZZZ

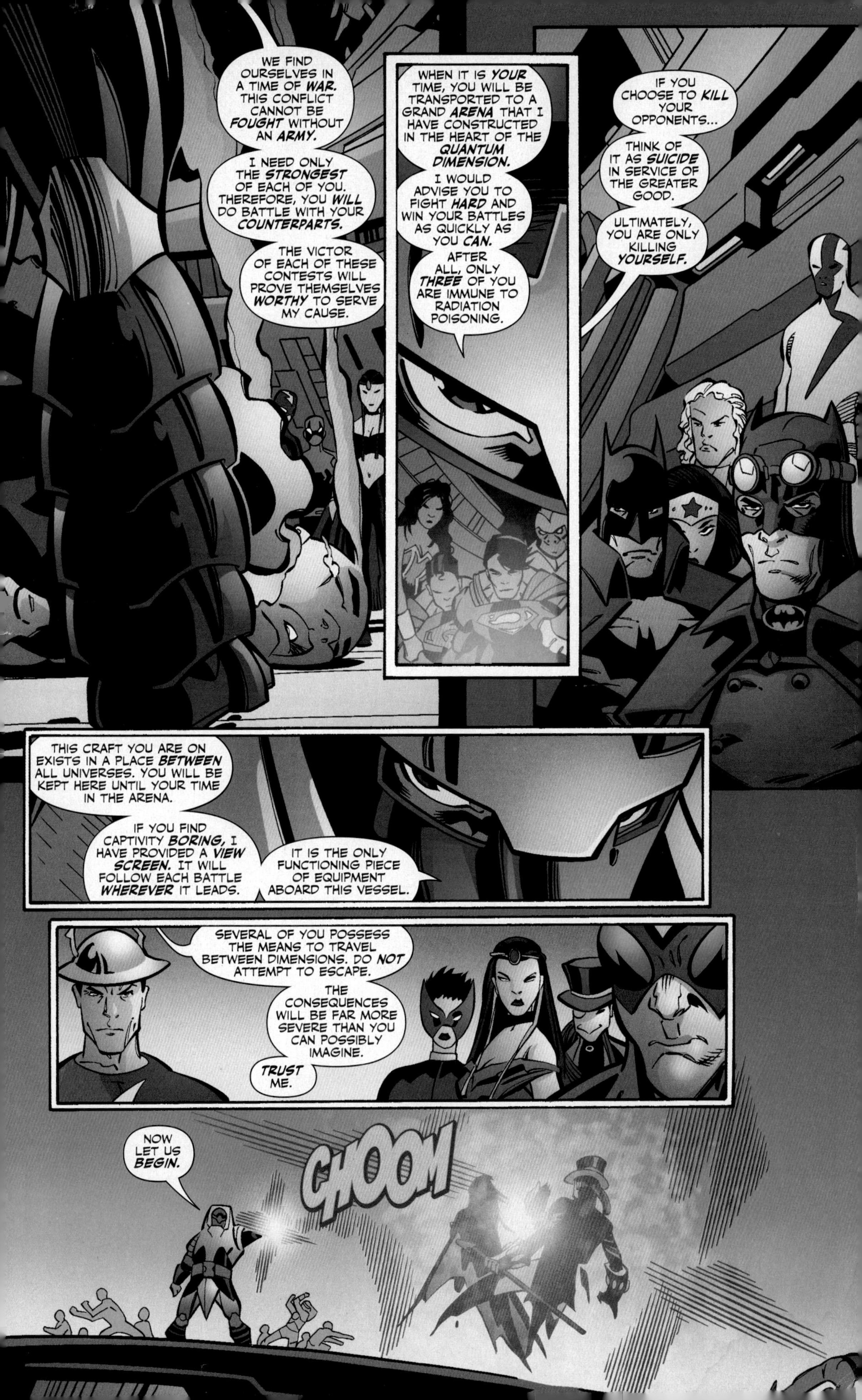
WE FIND OURSELVES IN A TIME OF WAR. THIS CONFLICT CANNOT BE FOUGHT WITHOUT AN ARMY.
I NEED ONLY THE STRONGEST OF EACH OF YOU. THEREFORE, YOU WILL DO BATTLE WITH YOUR COUNTERPARTS.
THE VICTOR OF EACH OF THESE CONTESTS WILL PROVE THEMSELVES WORTHY TO SERVE MY CAUSE.
WHEN IT IS YOUR TIME, YOU WILL BE TRANSPORTED TO A GRAND ARENA THAT I HAVE CONSTRUCTED IN THE HEART OF THE QUANTUM DIMENSION.
I WOULD ADVISE YOU TO FIGHT HARD AND WIN YOUR BATTLES AS QUICKLY AS YOU CAN.
AFTER ALL, ONLY THREE OF YOU ARE IMMUNE TO RADIATION POISONING.
IF YOU CHOOSE TO KILL YOUR OPPONENTS...
THINK OF IT AS SUICIDE IN SERVICE OF THE GREATER GOOD.
ULTIMATELY, YOU ARE ONLY KILLING YOURSELF.
THIS CRAFT YOU ARE ON EXISTS IN A PLACE BETWEEN ALL UNIVERSES. YOU WILL BE KEPT HERE UNTIL YOUR TIME IN THE ARENA.
IF YOU FIND CAPTIVITY BORING, I HAVE PROVIDED A VIEW SCREEN. IT WILL FOLLOW EACH BATTLE WHEREVER IT LEADS.
IT IS THE ONLY FUNCTIONING PIECE OF EQUIPMENT ABOARD THIS VESSEL.
SEVERAL OF YOU POSSESS THE MEANS TO TRAVEL BETWEEN DIMENSIONS. DO NOT ATTEMPT TO ESCAPE.
THE CONSEQUENCES WILL BE FAR MORE SEVERE THAN YOU CAN POSSIBLY IMAGINE.
TRUST ME.
NOW LET US BEGIN.
CHOOM

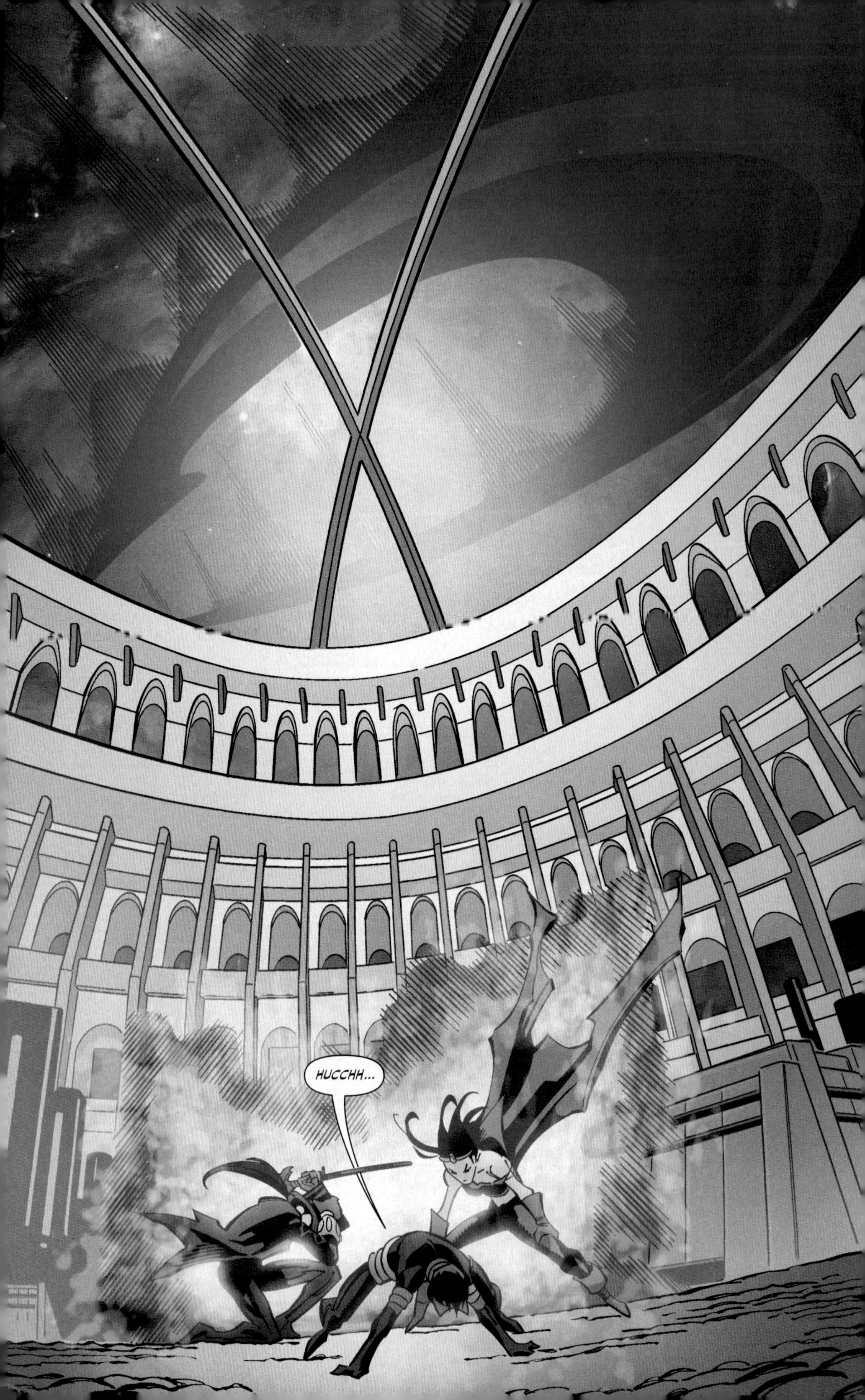
HUCCHH...

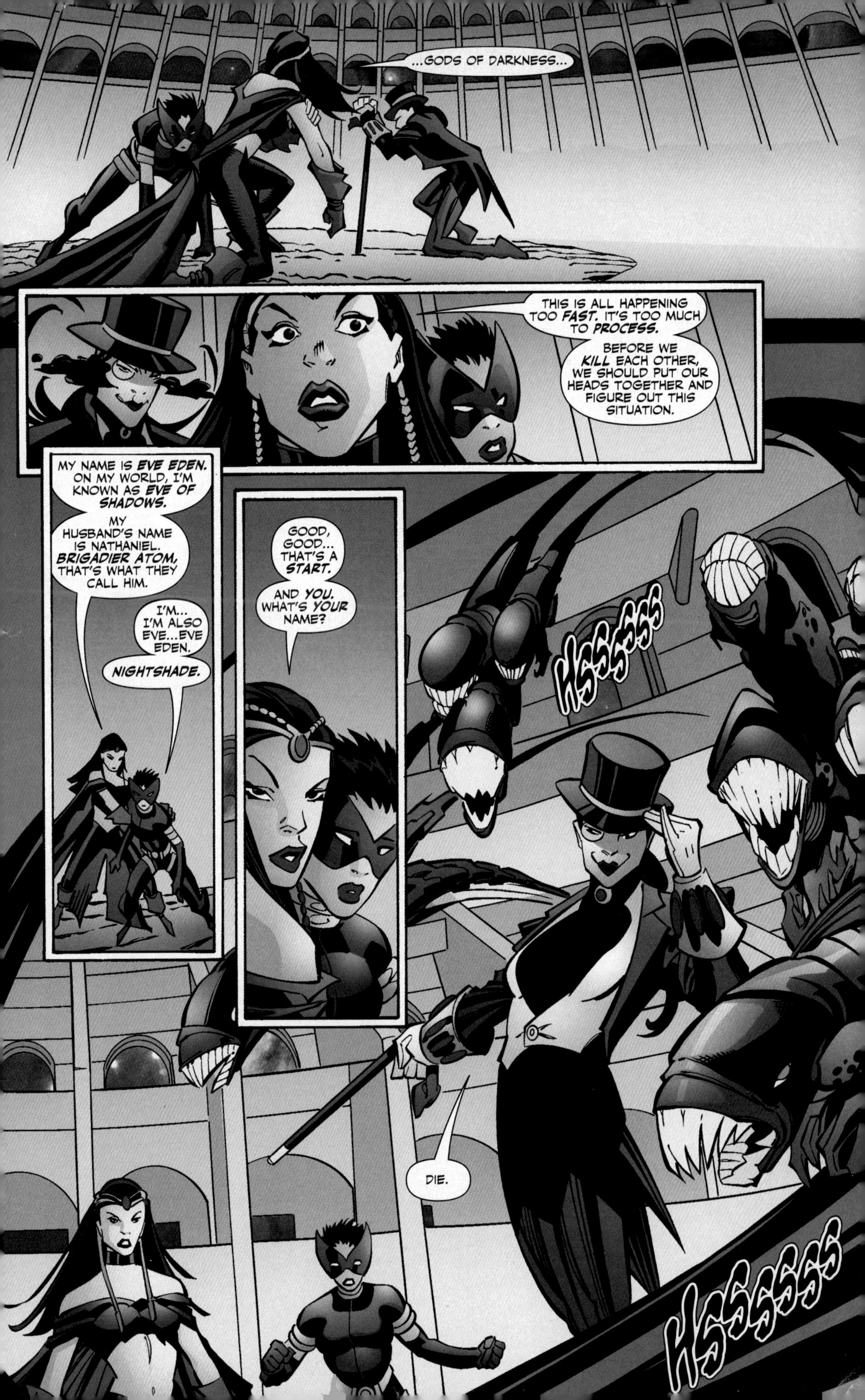
...GODS OF DARKNESS...
THIS IS ALL HAPPENING TOO FAST. IT'S TOO MUCH TO PROCESS.
BEFORE WE KILL EACH OTHER, WE SHOULD PUT OUR HEADS TOGETHER AND FIGURE OUT THIS SITUATION.
MY NAME IS EVE EDEN. ON MY WORLD, I'M KNOWN AS EVE OF SHADOWS.
MY HUSBAND'S NAME IS NATHANIEL. BRIGADIER ATOM, THAT'S WHAT THEY CALL HIM.
I'M... I'M ALSO EVE...EVE EDEN.
NIGHTSHADE.
GOOD, GOOD... THAT'S A START.
AND YOU. WHAT'S YOUR NAME?
HSSSSSS
DIE.
HSSSSSS

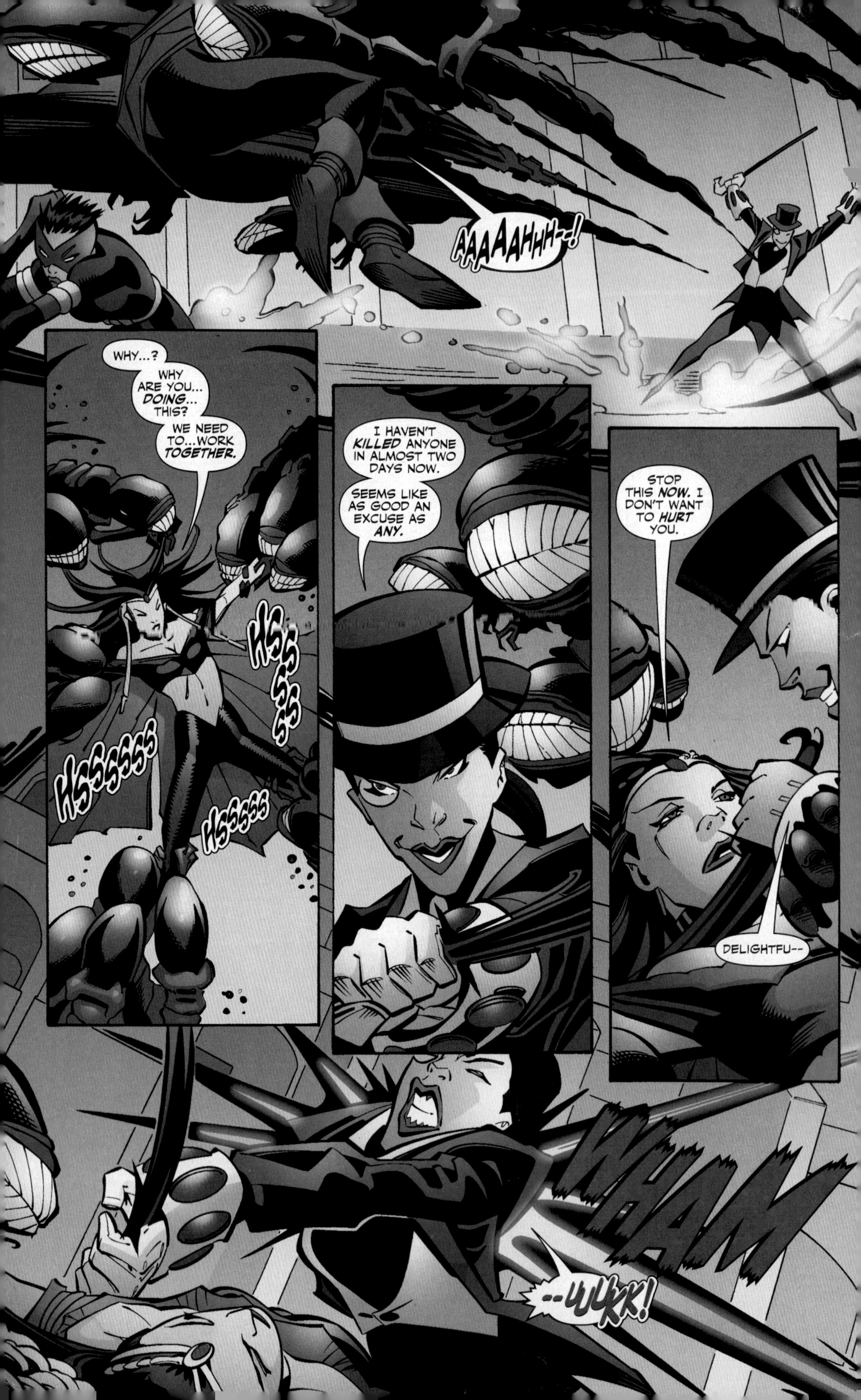
AAAAAHHH--!
WHY...?
WHY ARE YOU... DOING... THIS?
WE NEED TO...WORK TOGETHER.
HSSSSSS
HSSSSS
HSSSSS
I HAVEN'T KILLED ANYONE IN ALMOST TWO DAYS NOW.
SEEMS LIKE AS GOOD AN EXCUSE AS ANY.
STOP THIS NOW. I DON'T WANT TO HURT YOU.
DELIGHTFU--
WHAM
--UUUKK!

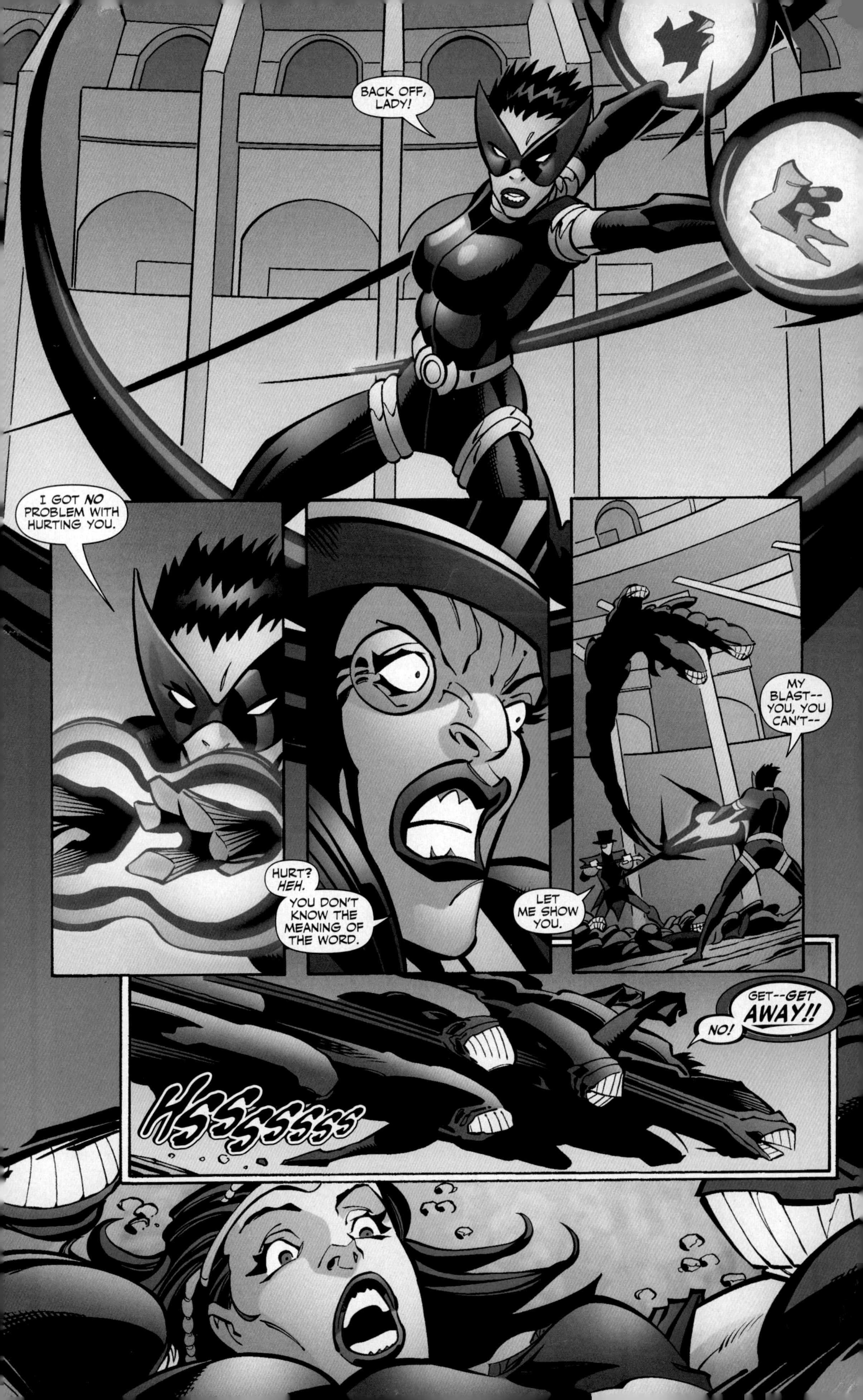
BACK OFF, LADY!
I GOT NO PROBLEM WITH HURTING YOU.
HURT? HEH.
YOU DON'T KNOW THE MEANING OF THE WORD.
LET ME SHOW YOU.
MY BLAST-- YOU, YOU CAN'T--
HSSSSSSS
NO!
GET--GET AWAY!!

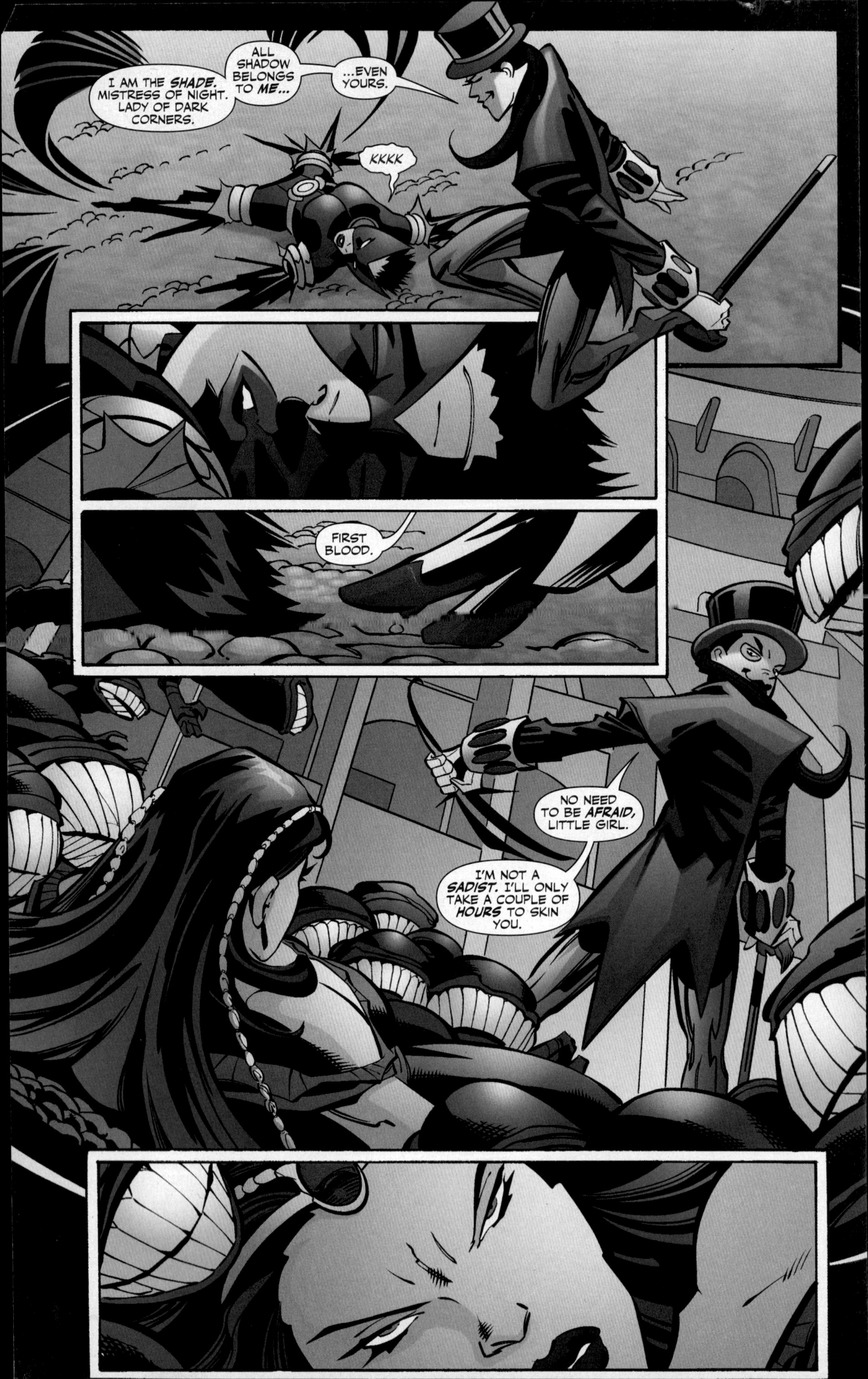
I AM THE SHADE. MISTRESS OF NIGHT. LADY OF DARK CORNERS.
ALL SHADOW BELONGS TO ME...
...EVEN YOURS.
KKKK
FIRST BLOOD.
NO NEED TO BE AFRAID, LITTLE GIRL.
I'M NOT A SADIST. I'LL ONLY TAKE A COUPLE OF HOURS TO SKIN YOU.

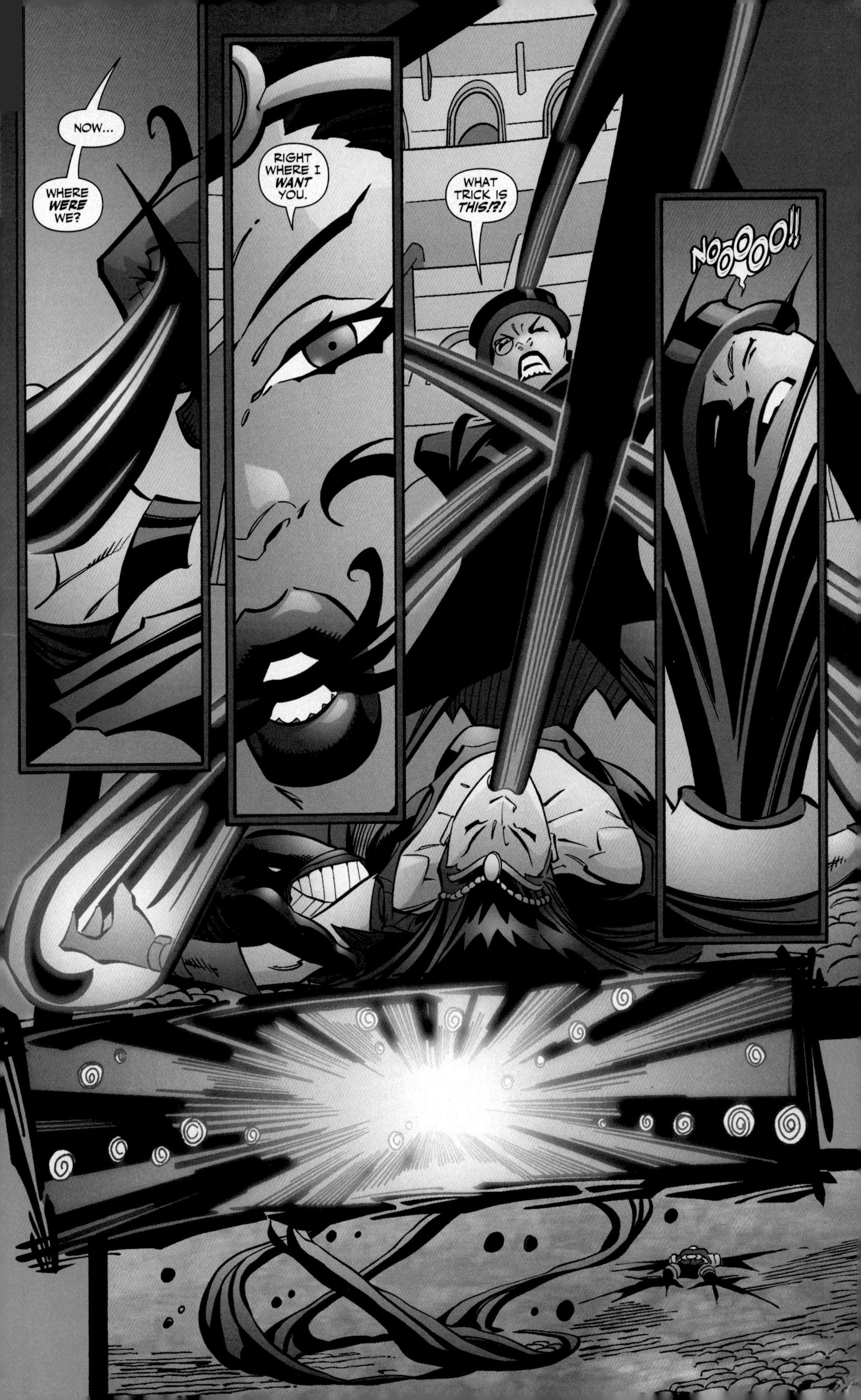
NOW...
WHERE WERE WE?
RIGHT WHERE I WANT YOU.
WHAT TRICK IS THIS!?!
NOOOOOO!!

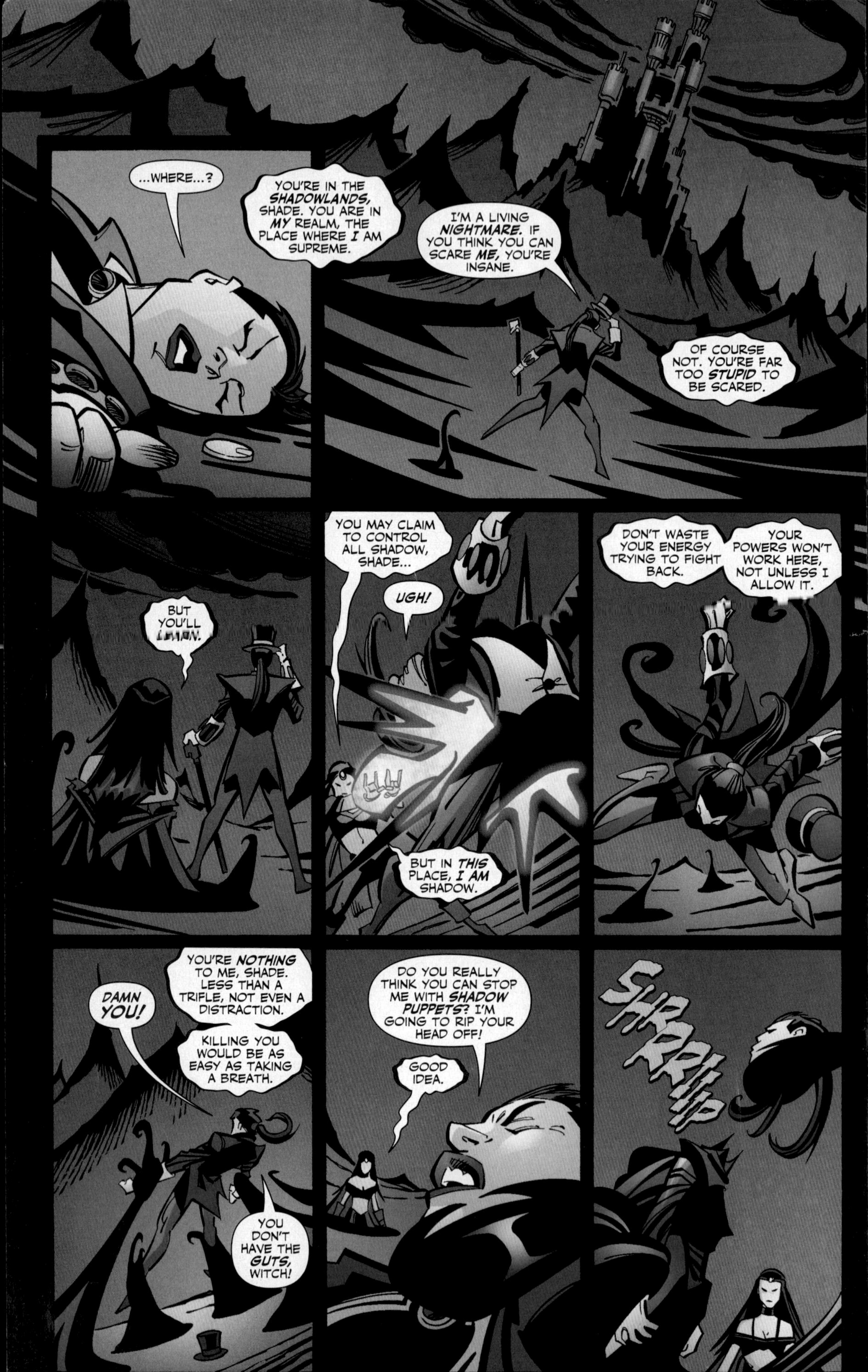

...WHERE...?
YOU'RE IN THE SHADOWLANDS, SHADE. YOU ARE IN MY REALM, THE PLACE WHERE I AM SUPREME.
I'M A LIVING NIGHTMARE. IF YOU THINK YOU CAN SCARE ME, YOU'RE INSANE.
OF COURSE NOT. YOU'RE FAR TOO STUPID TO BE SCARED.
BUT YOU'LL
YOU MAY CLAIM TO CONTROL ALL SHADOW, SHADE...
UGH!
BUT IN THIS PLACE, I AM SHADOW.
DON'T WASTE YOUR ENERGY TRYING TO FIGHT BACK.
YOUR POWERS WON'T WORK HERE, NOT UNLESS I ALLOW IT.
DAMN YOU!
YOU'RE NOTHING TO ME, SHADE. LESS THAN A TRIFLE, NOT EVEN A DISTRACTION.
KILLING YOU WOULD BE AS EASY AS TAKING A BREATH.
YOU DON'T HAVE THE GUTS, WITCH!
DO YOU REALLY THINK YOU CAN STOP ME WITH SHADOW PUPPETS? I'M GOING TO RIP YOUR HEAD OFF!
GOOD IDEA.
SHRRIIP

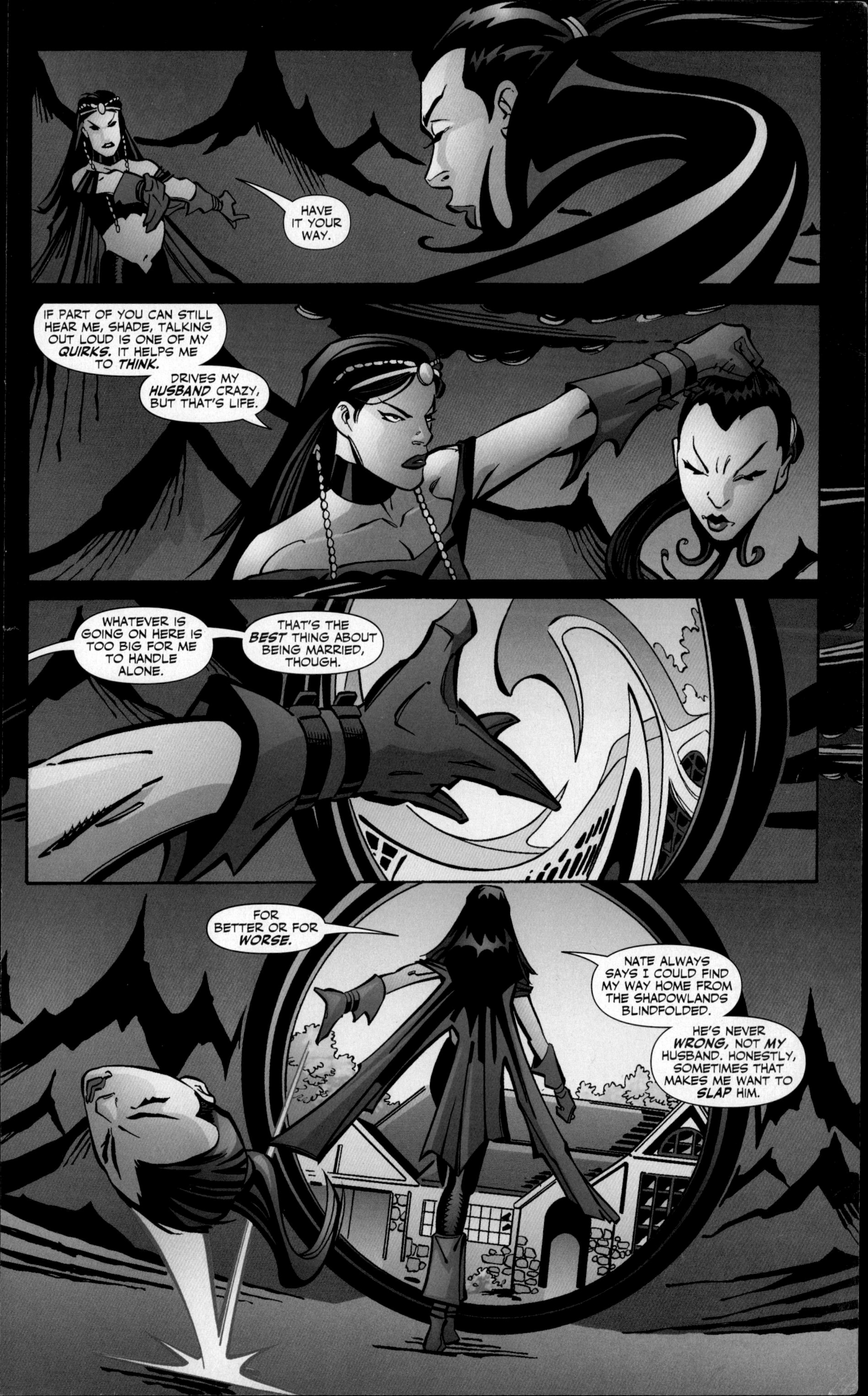
HAVE IT YOUR WAY.
IF PART OF YOU CAN STILL HEAR ME, SHADE, TALKING OUT LOUD IS ONE OF MY QUIRKS. IT HELPS ME TO THINK.
DRIVES MY HUSBAND CRAZY, BUT THAT'S LIFE.
WHATEVER IS GOING ON HERE IS TOO BIG FOR ME TO HANDLE ALONE.
THAT'S THE BEST THING ABOUT BEING MARRIED, THOUGH.
FOR BETTER OR FOR WORSE.
NATE ALWAYS SAYS I COULD FIND MY WAY HOME FROM THE SHADOWLANDS BLINDFOLDED.
HE'S NEVER WRONG, NOT MY HUSBAND. HONESTLY, SOMETIMES THAT MAKES ME WANT TO SLAP HIM.

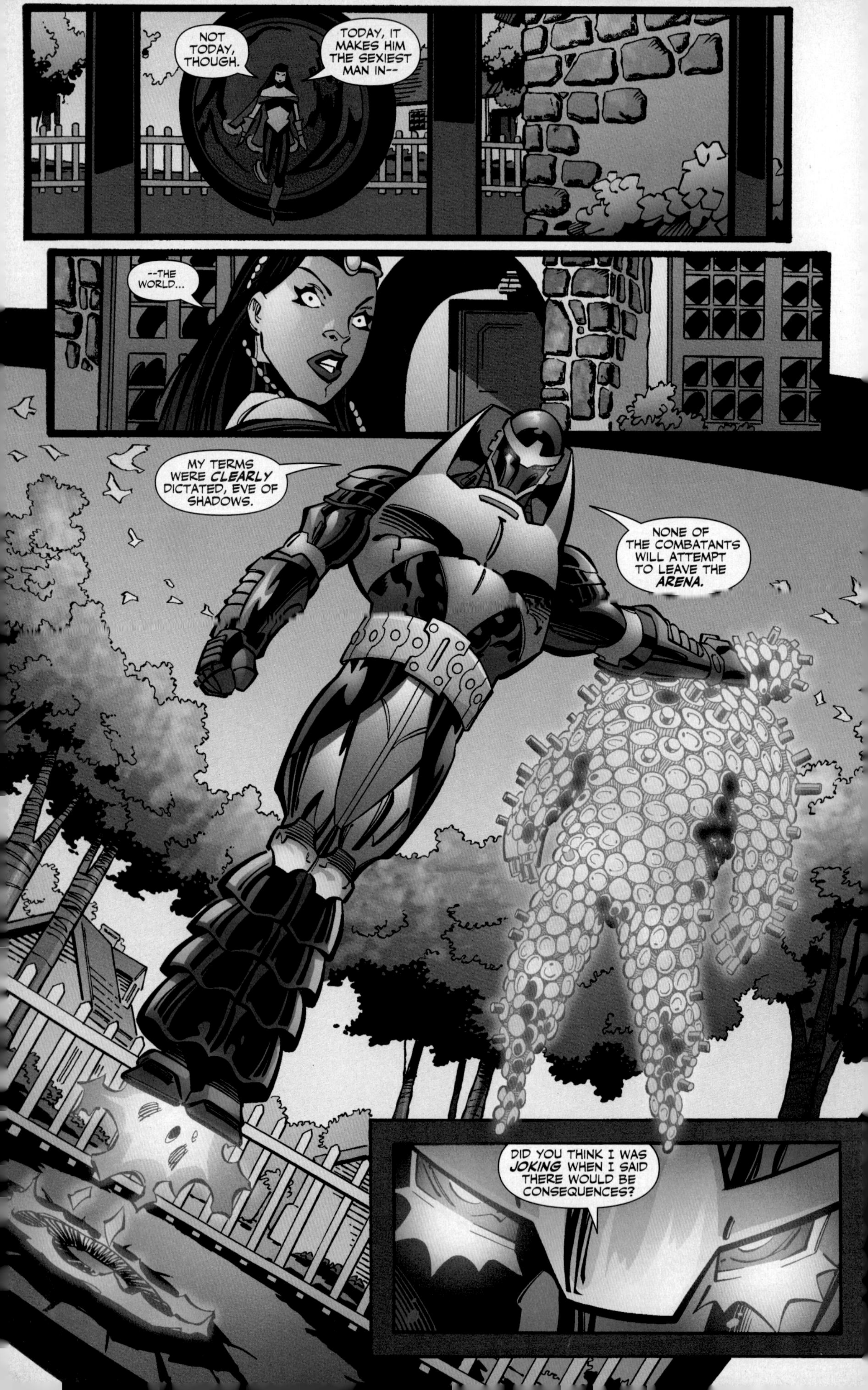
NOT TODAY, THOUGH.
TODAY, IT MAKES HIM THE SEXIEST MAN IN--
--THE WORLD...
MY TERMS WERE CLEARLY DICTATED, EVE OF SHADOWS.
NONE OF THE COMBATANTS WILL ATTEMPT TO LEAVE THE ARENA.
DID YOU THINK I WAS JOKING WHEN I SAID THERE WOULD BE CONSEQUENCES?

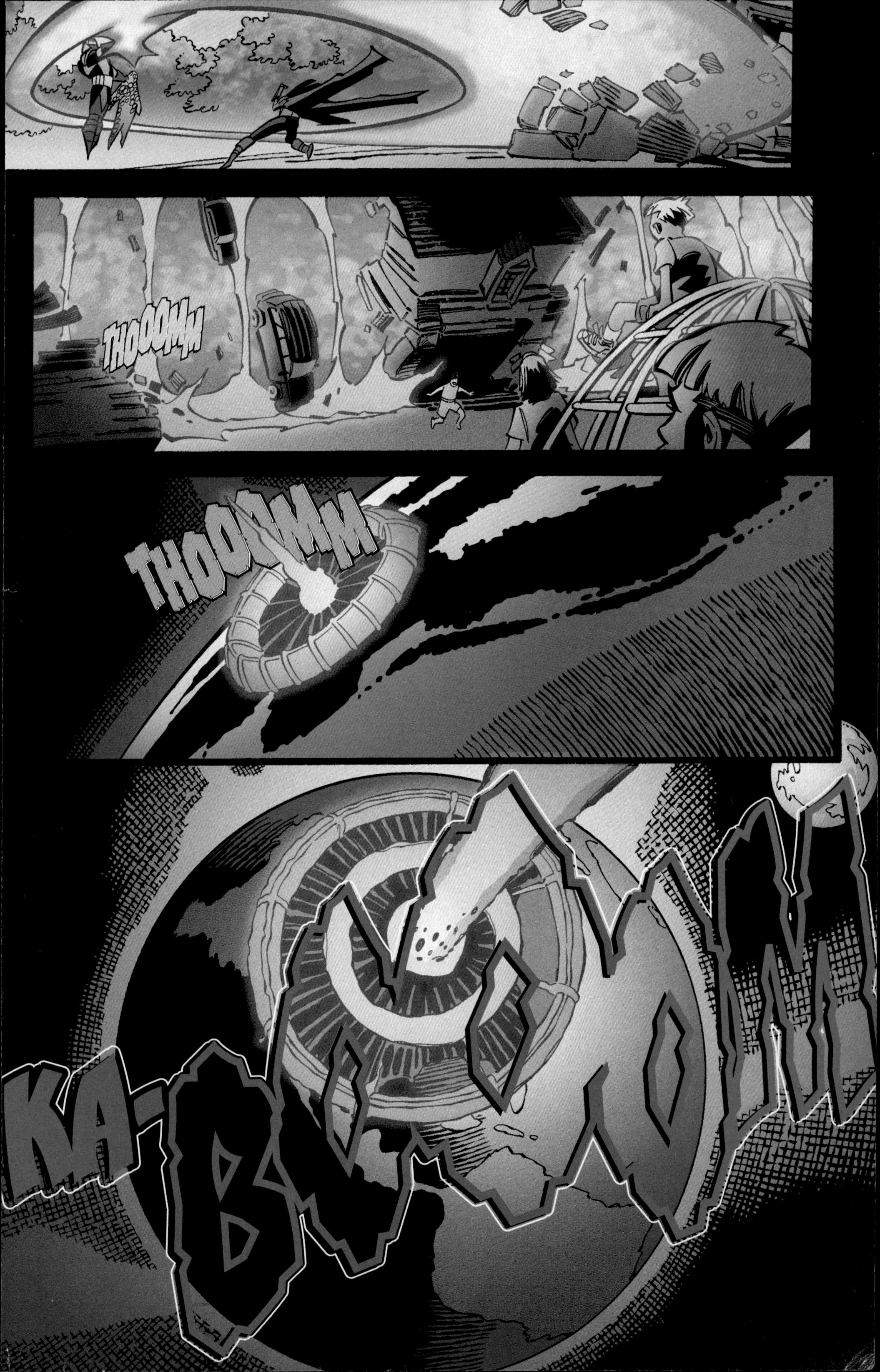
THOOOMM
THOOOMM
KA-BOOOM

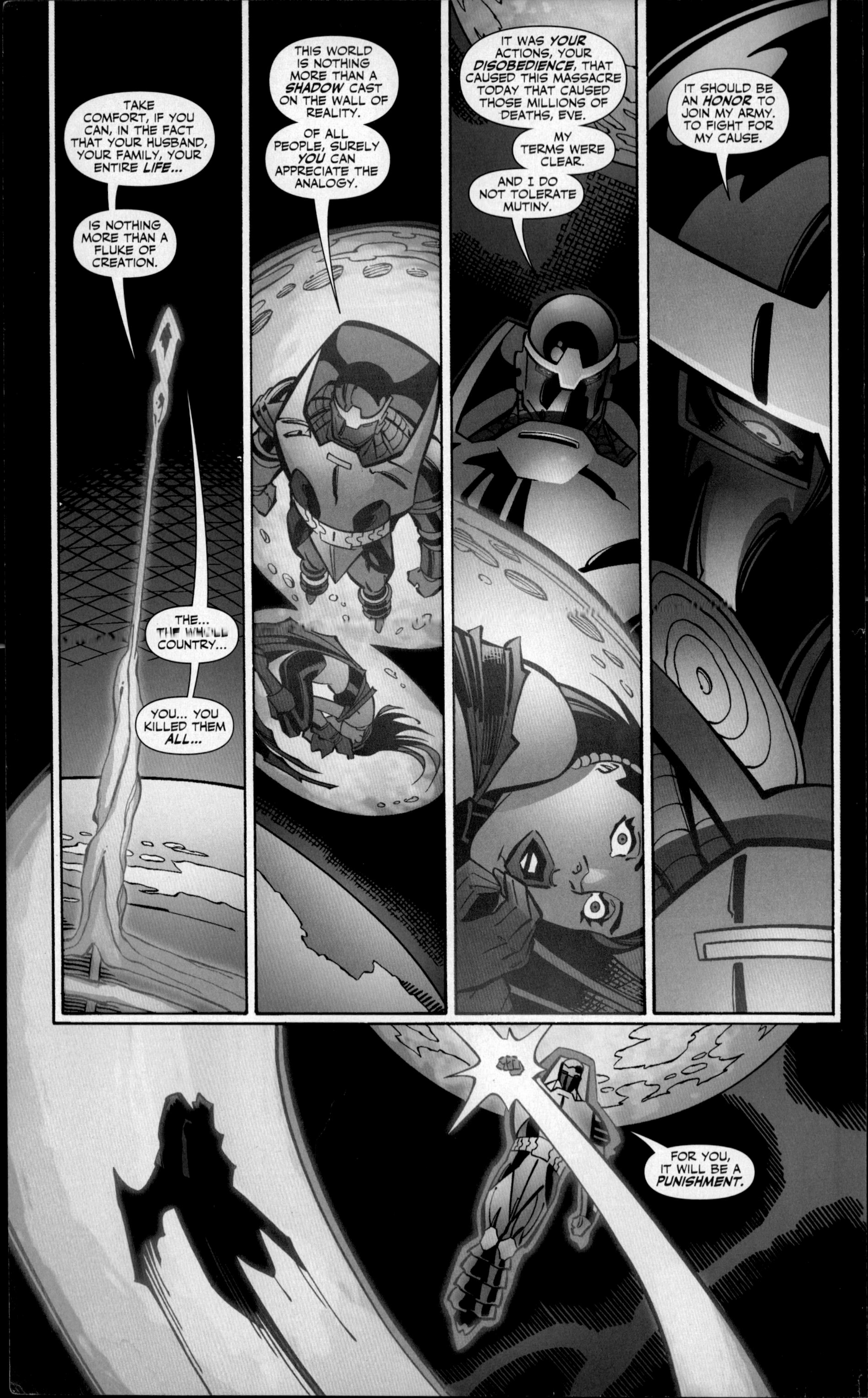
TAKE COMFORT, IF YOU CAN, IN THE FACT THAT YOUR HUSBAND, YOUR FAMILY, YOUR ENTIRE LIFE...
IS NOTHING MORE THAN A FLUKE OF CREATION.
THE... THE WHOLE COUNTRY...
YOU... YOU KILLED THEM ALL...
THIS WORLD IS NOTHING MORE THAN A SHADOW CAST ON THE WALL OF REALITY.
OF ALL PEOPLE, SURELY YOU CAN APPRECIATE THE ANALOGY.
IT WAS YOUR ACTIONS, YOUR DISOBEDIENCE, THAT CAUSED THIS MASSACRE TODAY THAT CAUSED THOSE MILLIONS OF DEATHS, EVE.
MY TERMS WERE CLEAR.
AND I DO NOT TOLERATE MUTINY.
IT SHOULD BE AN HONOR TO JOIN MY ARMY. TO FIGHT FOR MY CAUSE.
FOR YOU, IT WILL BE A PUNISHMENT.

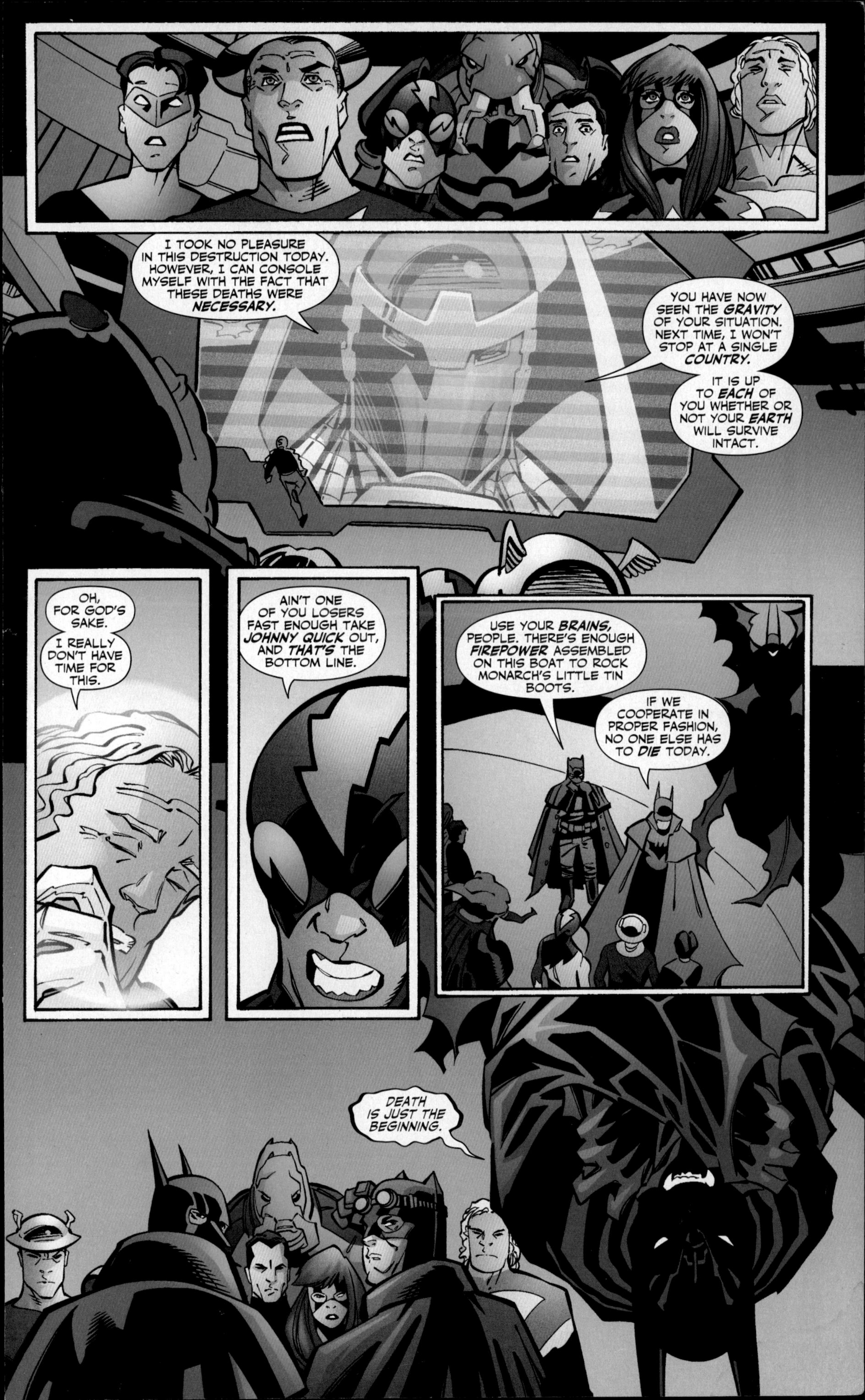
I TOOK NO PLEASURE IN THIS DESTRUCTION TODAY. HOWEVER, I CAN CONSOLE MYSELF WITH THE FACT THAT THESE DEATHS WERE NECESSARY.
YOU HAVE NOW SEEN THE GRAVITY OF YOUR SITUATION. NEXT TIME, I WON'T STOP AT A SINGLE COUNTRY.
IT IS UP TO EACH OF YOU WHETHER OR NOT YOUR EARTH WILL SURVIVE INTACT.
OH, FOR GOD'S SAKE.
I REALLY DON'T HAVE TIME FOR THIS.
AIN'T ONE OF YOU LOSERS FAST ENOUGH TAKE JOHNNY QUICK OUT, AND THAT'S THE BOTTOM LINE.
USE YOUR BRAINS, PEOPLE. THERE'S ENOUGH FIREPOWER ASSEMBLED ON THIS BOAT TO ROCK MONARCH'S LITTLE TIN BOOTS.
IF WE COOPERATE IN PROPER FASHION, NO ONE ELSE HAS TO DIE TODAY.
DEATH IS JUST THE BEGINNING.

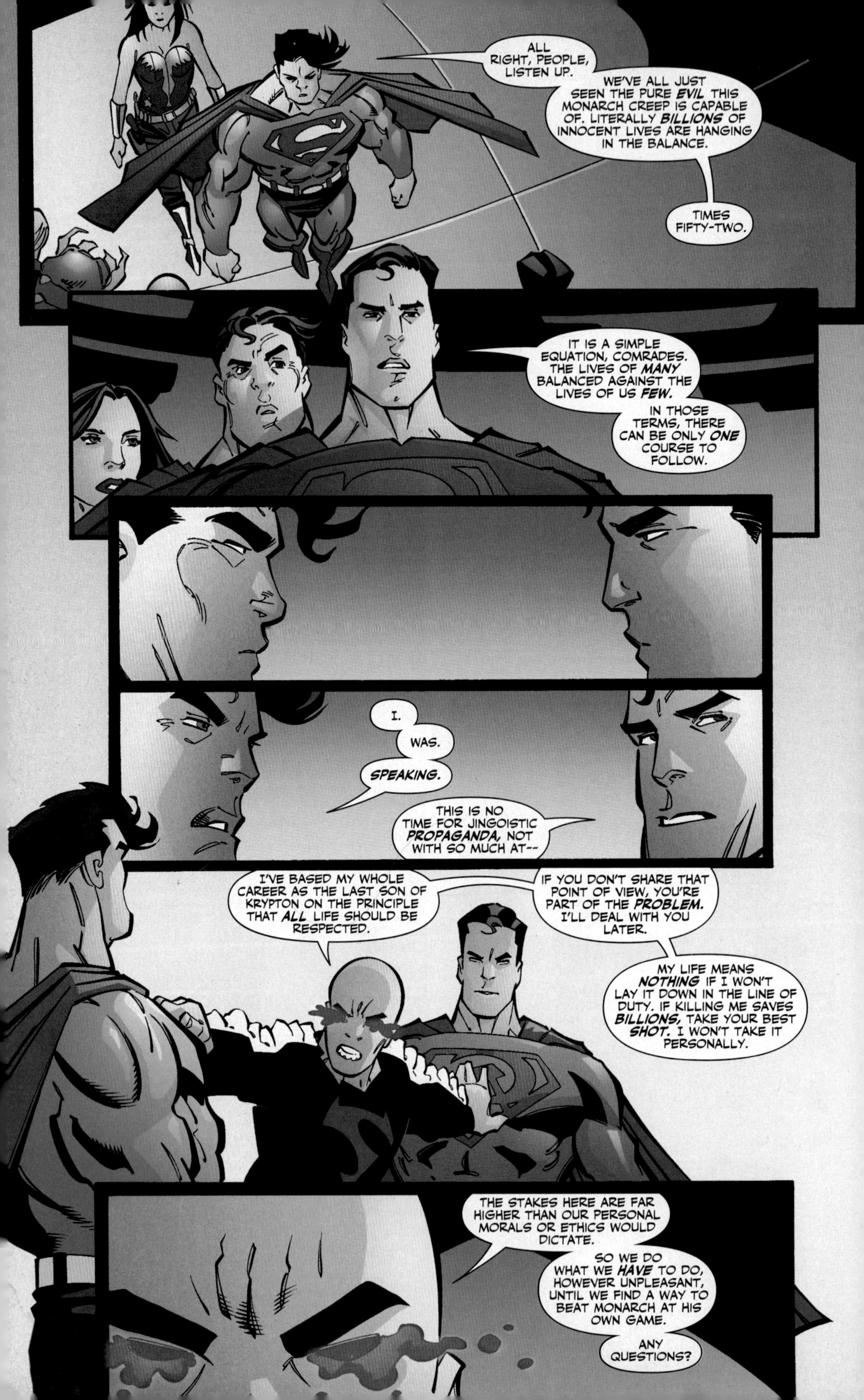
ALL RIGHT, PEOPLE, LISTEN UP.
WE'VE ALL JUST SEEN THE PURE EVIL THIS MONARCH CREEP IS CAPABLE OF. LITERALLY BILLIONS OF INNOCENT LIVES ARE HANGING IN THE BALANCE.
TIMES FIFTY-TWO.
IT IS A SIMPLE EQUATION, COMRADES. THE LIVES OF MANY BALANCED AGAINST THE LIVES OF US FEW.
IN THOSE TERMS, THERE CAN BE ONLY ONE COURSE TO FOLLOW.
I.
WAS.
SPEAKING.
THIS IS NO TIME FOR JINGOISTIC PROPAGANDA, NOT WITH SO MUCH AT--
I'VE BASED MY WHOLE CAREER AS THE LAST SON OF KRYPTON ON THE PRINCIPLE THAT ALL LIFE SHOULD BE RESPECTED.
IF YOU DON'T SHARE THAT POINT OF VIEW, YOU'RE PART OF THE PROBLEM. I'LL DEAL WITH YOU LATER.
MY LIFE MEANS NOTHING IF I WON'T LAY IT DOWN IN THE LINE OF DUTY. IF KILLING ME SAVES BILLIONS, TAKE YOUR BEST SHOT. I WON'T TAKE IT PERSONALLY.
THE STAKES HERE ARE FAR HIGHER THAN OUR PERSONAL MORALS OR ETHICS WOULD DICTATE.
SO WE DO WHAT WE HAVE TO DO, HOWEVER UNPLEASANT, UNTIL WE FIND A WAY TO BEAT MONARCH AT HIS OWN GAME.
ANY QUESTIONS?

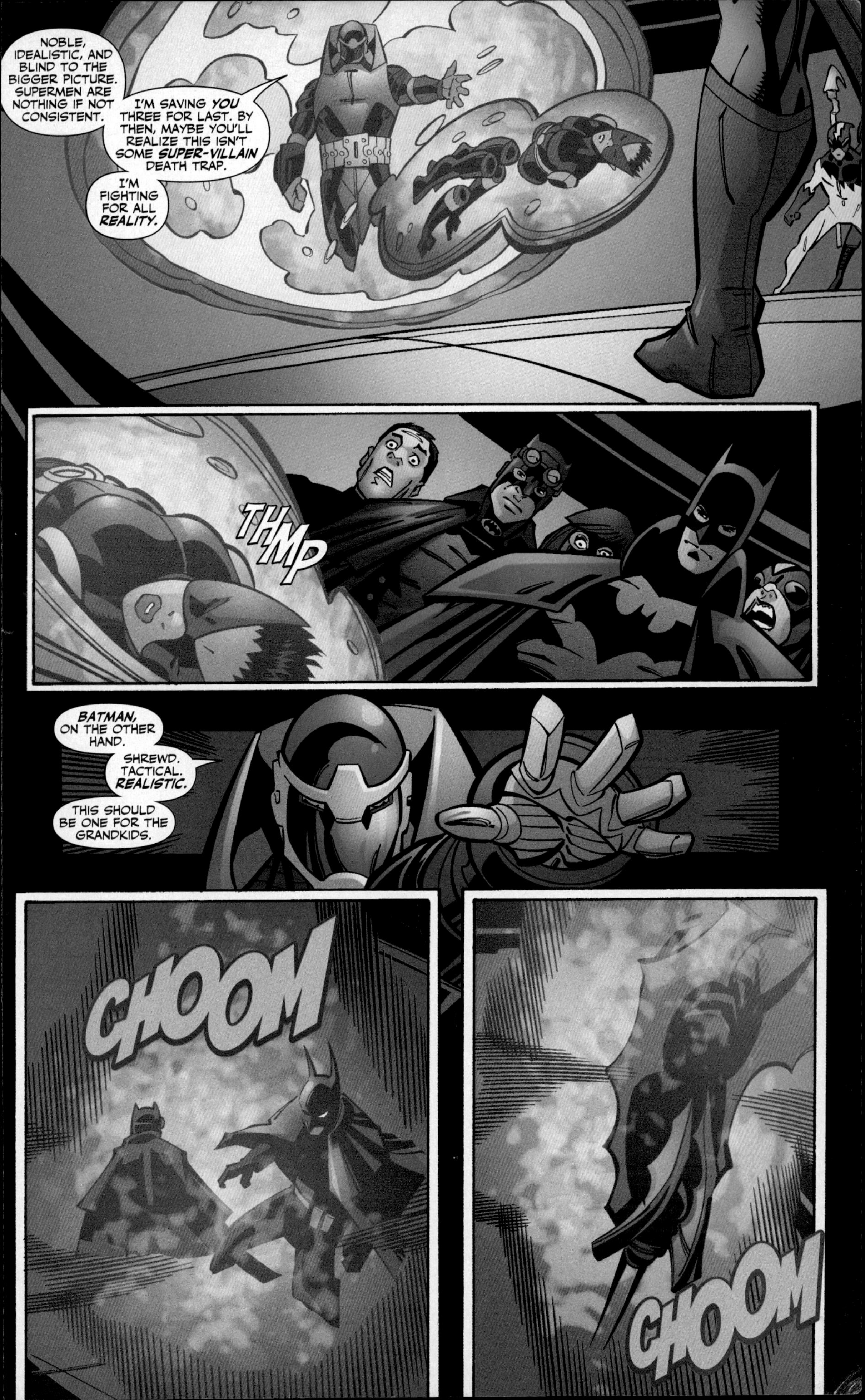
NOBLE, IDEALISTIC, AND BLIND TO THE BIGGER PICTURE. SUPERMEN ARE NOTHING IF NOT CONSISTENT.
I'M SAVING YOU THREE FOR LAST. BY THEN, MAYBE YOU'LL REALIZE THIS ISN'T SOME SUPER-VILLAIN DEATH TRAP.
I'M FIGHTING FOR ALL REALITY.
THMP
BATMAN, ON THE OTHER HAND.
SHREWD. TACTICAL. REALISTIC.
THIS SHOULD BE ONE FOR THE GRANDKIDS.
CHOOM
CHOOM

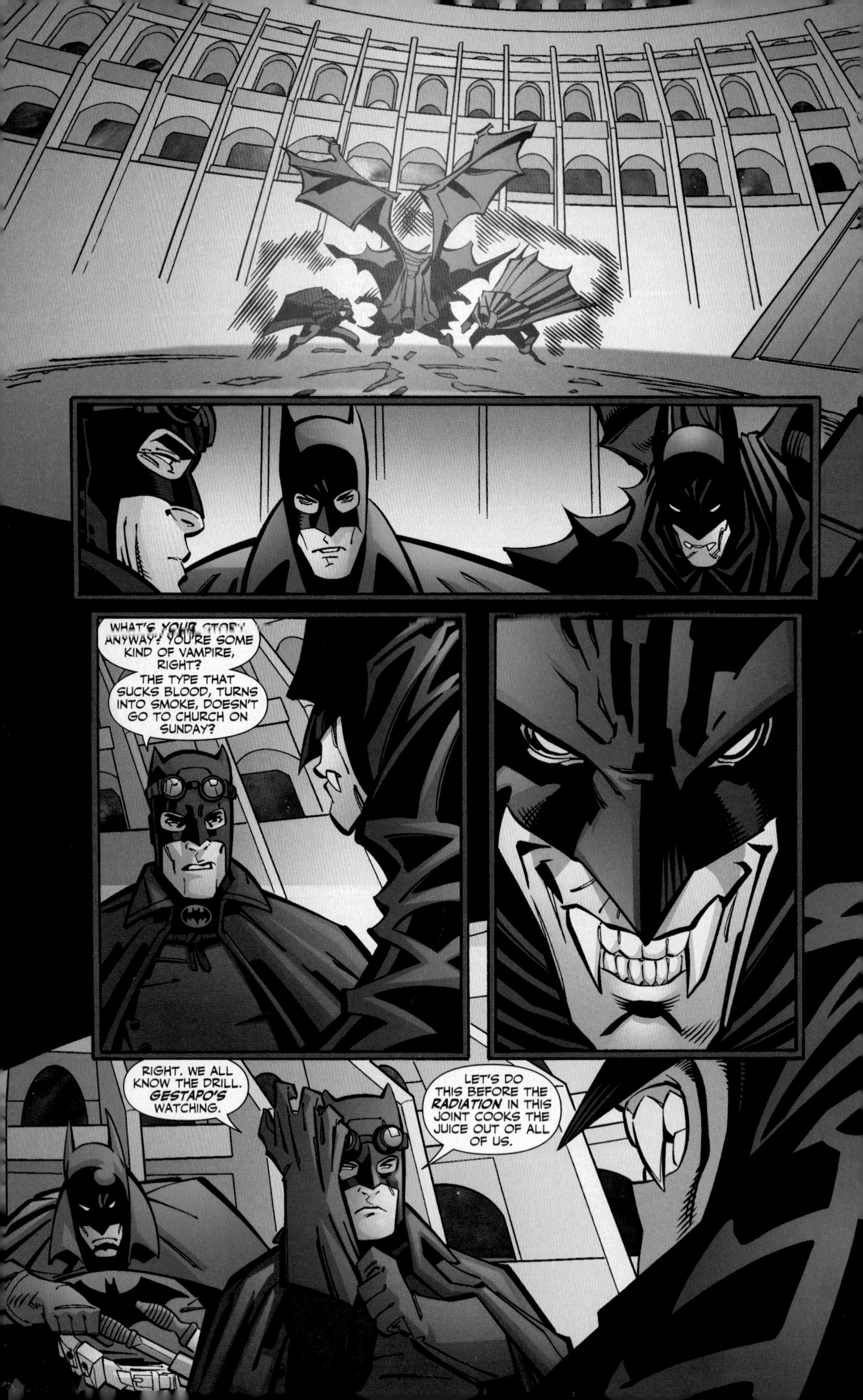
WHAT'S YOUR STORY ANYWAY? YOU'RE SOME KIND OF VAMPIRE, RIGHT?
THE TYPE THAT SUCKS BLOOD, TURNS INTO SMOKE, DOESN'T GO TO CHURCH ON SUNDAY?
RIGHT. WE ALL KNOW THE DRILL. GESTAPO'S WATCHING.
LET'S DO THIS BEFORE THE RADIATION IN THIS JOINT COOKS THE JUICE OUT OF ALL OF US.

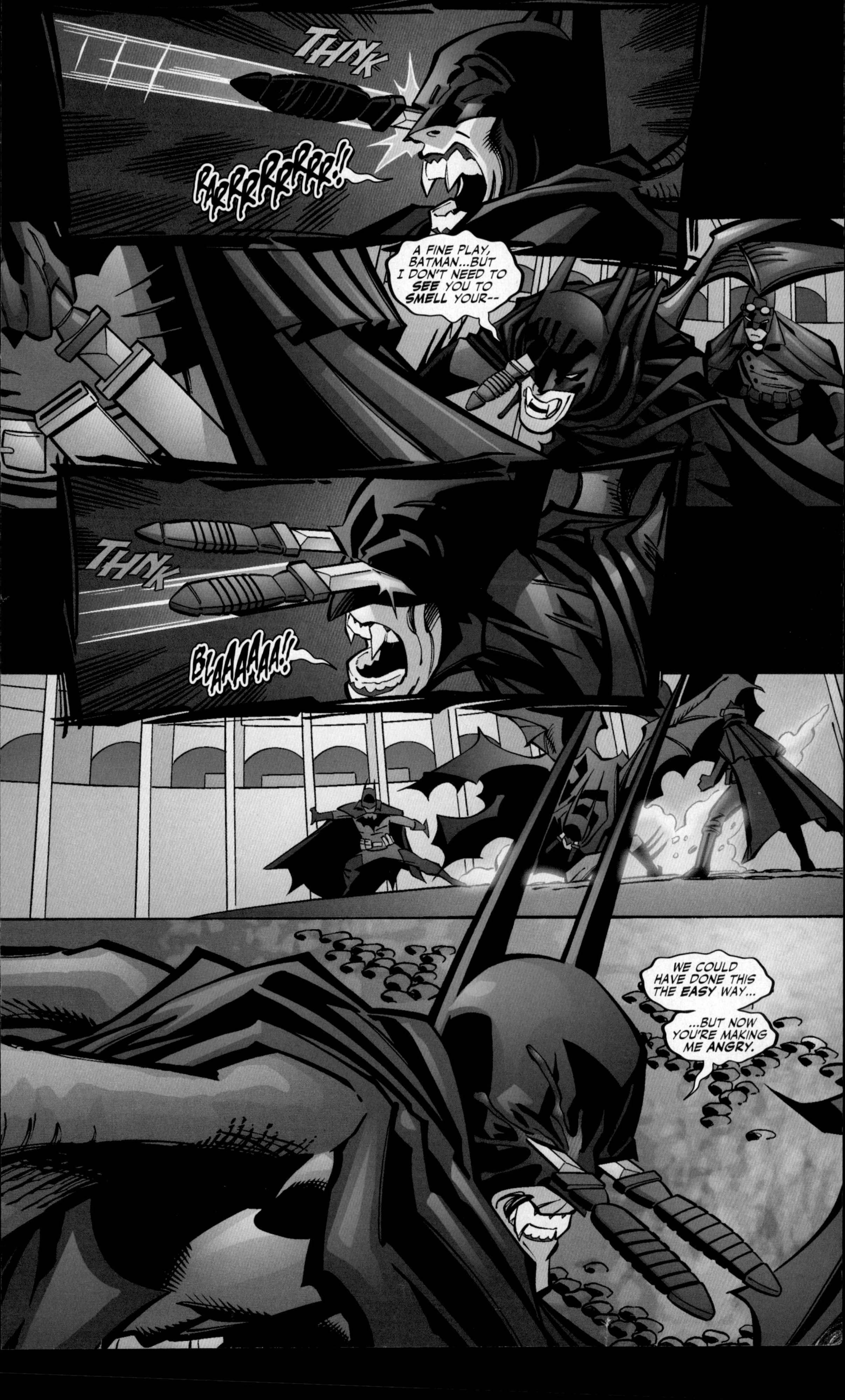
THINK
RAERRRRRR!!
A FINE PLAY, BATMAN...BUT I DON'T NEED TO SEE YOU TO SMELL YOUR--
THINK
BLAAAAAA!!
WE COULD HAVE DONE THIS THE EASY WAY...
...BUT NOW YOU'RE MAKING ME ANGRY.

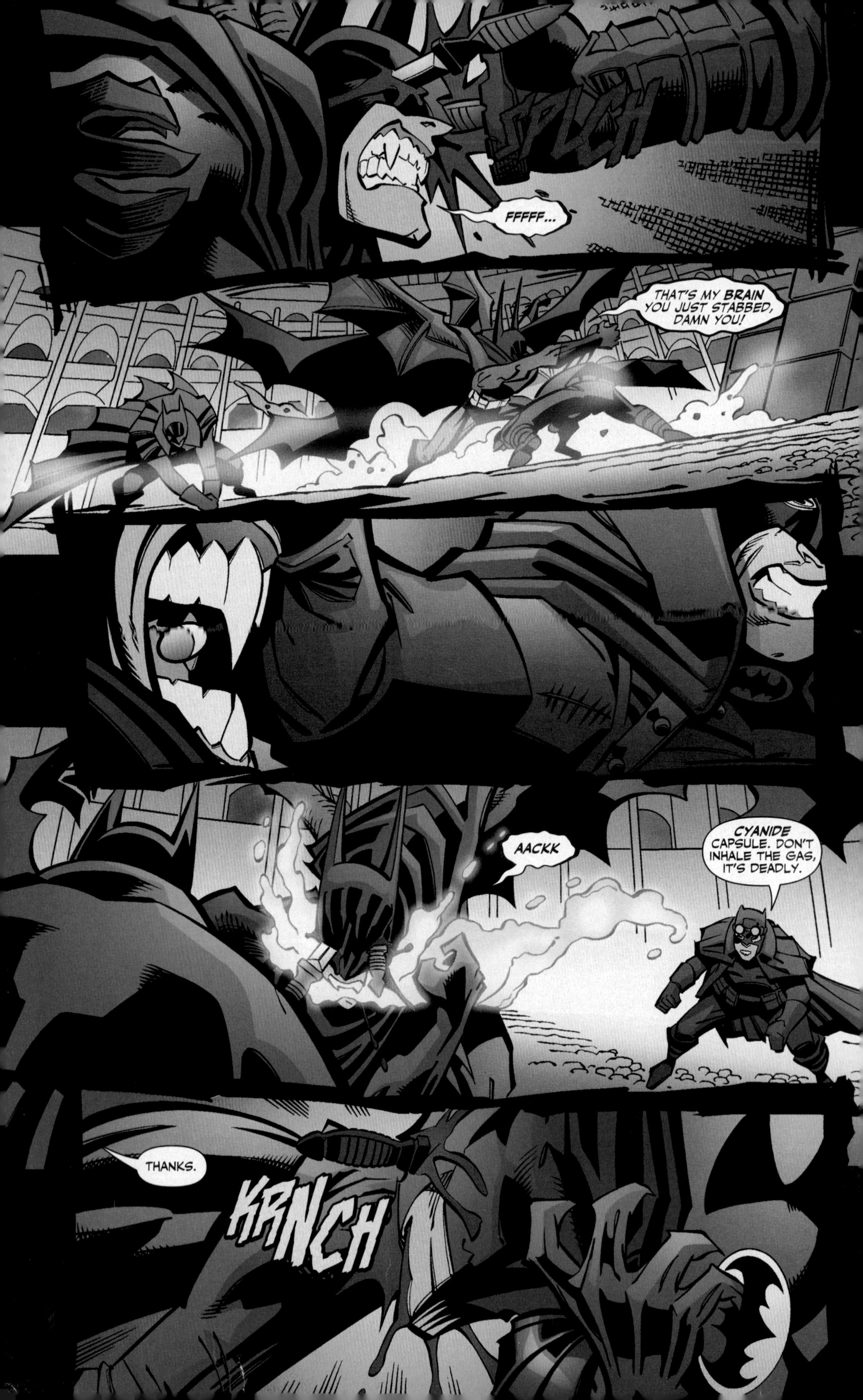
SPLCH
FFFFF...
THAT'S MY BRAIN YOU JUST STABBED, DAMN YOU!
AACKK
CYANIDE CAPSULE. DON'T INHALE THE GAS, IT'S DEADLY.
THANKS.
KRNCH

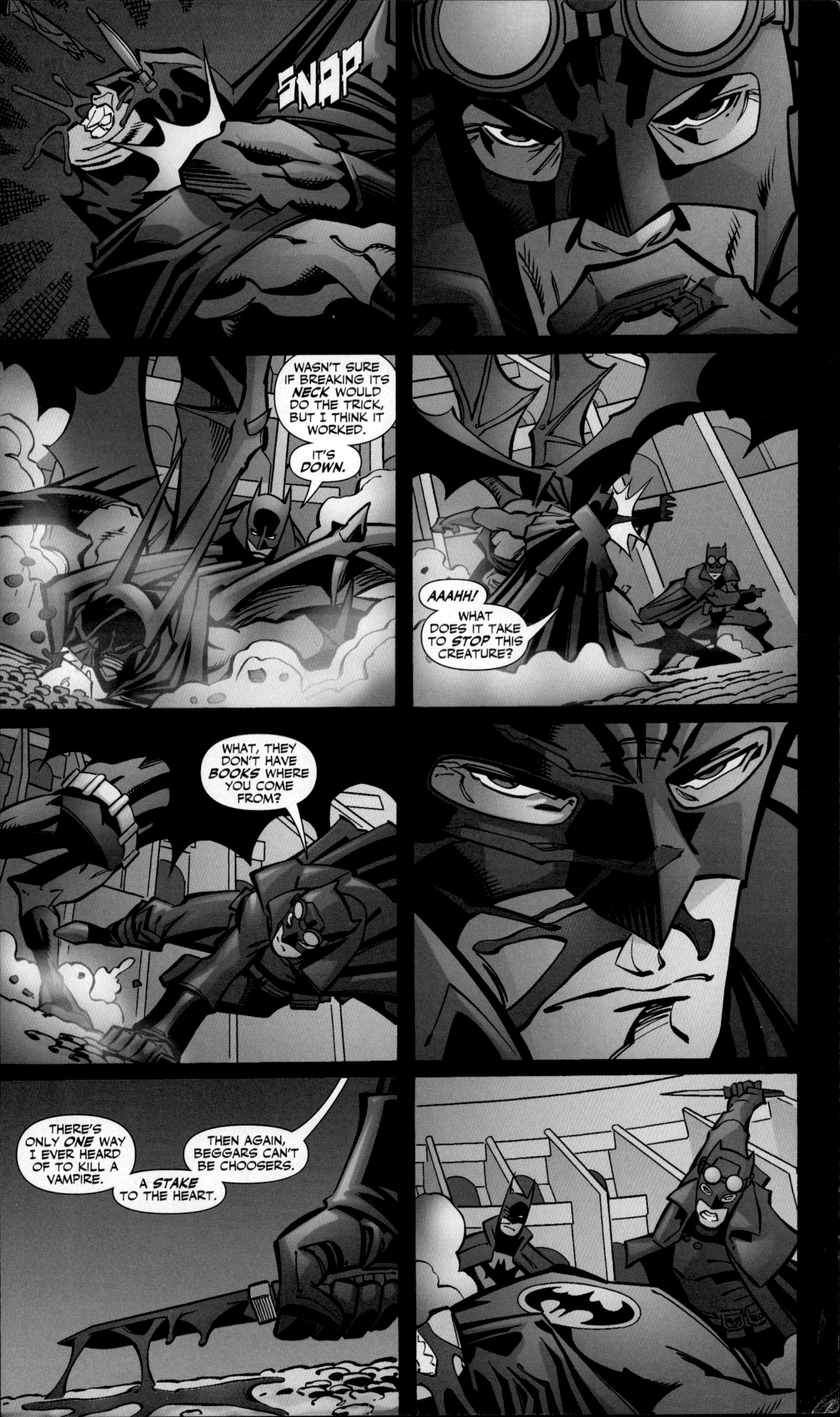
SNAP
WASN'T SURE IF BREAKING ITS NECK WOULD DO THE TRICK, BUT I THINK IT WORKED.
IT'S DOWN.
AAAHH! WHAT DOES IT TAKE TO STOP THIS CREATURE?
WHAT, THEY DON'T HAVE BOOKS WHERE YOU COME FROM?
THERE'S ONLY ONE WAY I EVER HEARD OF TO KILL A VAMPIRE.
A STAKE TO THE HEART.
THEN AGAIN, BEGGARS CAN'T BE CHOOSERS.

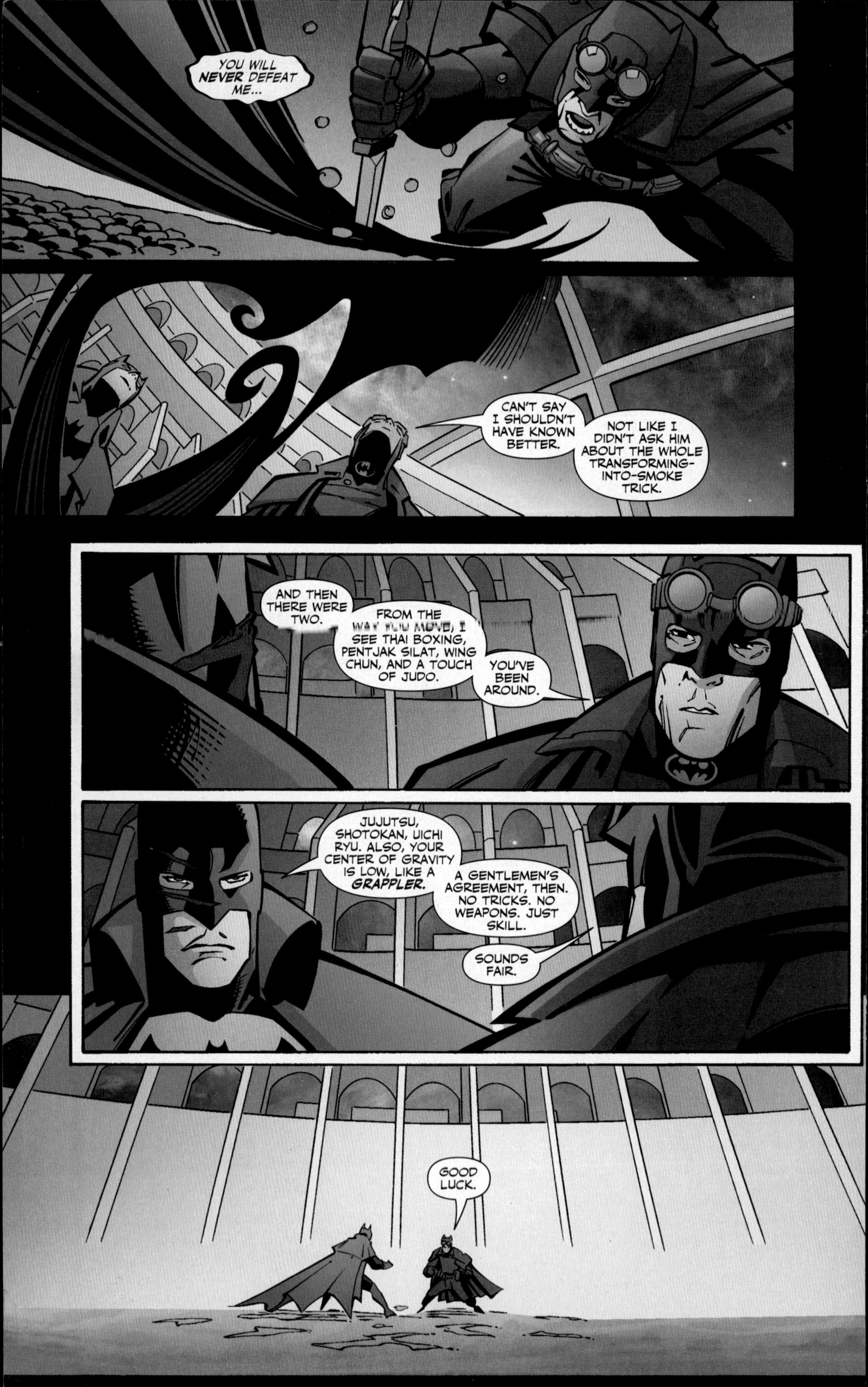
YOU WILL NEVER DEFEAT ME...
CAN'T SAY I SHOULDN'T HAVE KNOWN BETTER.
NOT LIKE I DIDN'T ASK HIM ABOUT THE WHOLE TRANSFORMING-INTO-SMOKE TRICK.
AND THEN THERE WERE TWO.
FROM THE WAY YOU MOVE, I SEE THAI BOXING, PENTJAK SILAT, WING CHUN, AND A TOUCH OF JUDO.
YOU'VE BEEN AROUND.
JUJUTSU, SHOTOKAN, UICHI RYU. ALSO, YOUR CENTER OF GRAVITY IS LOW, LIKE A GRAPPLER.
A GENTLEMEN'S AGREEMENT, THEN. NO TRICKS. NO WEAPONS. JUST SKILL.
SOUNDS FAIR.
GOOD LUCK.

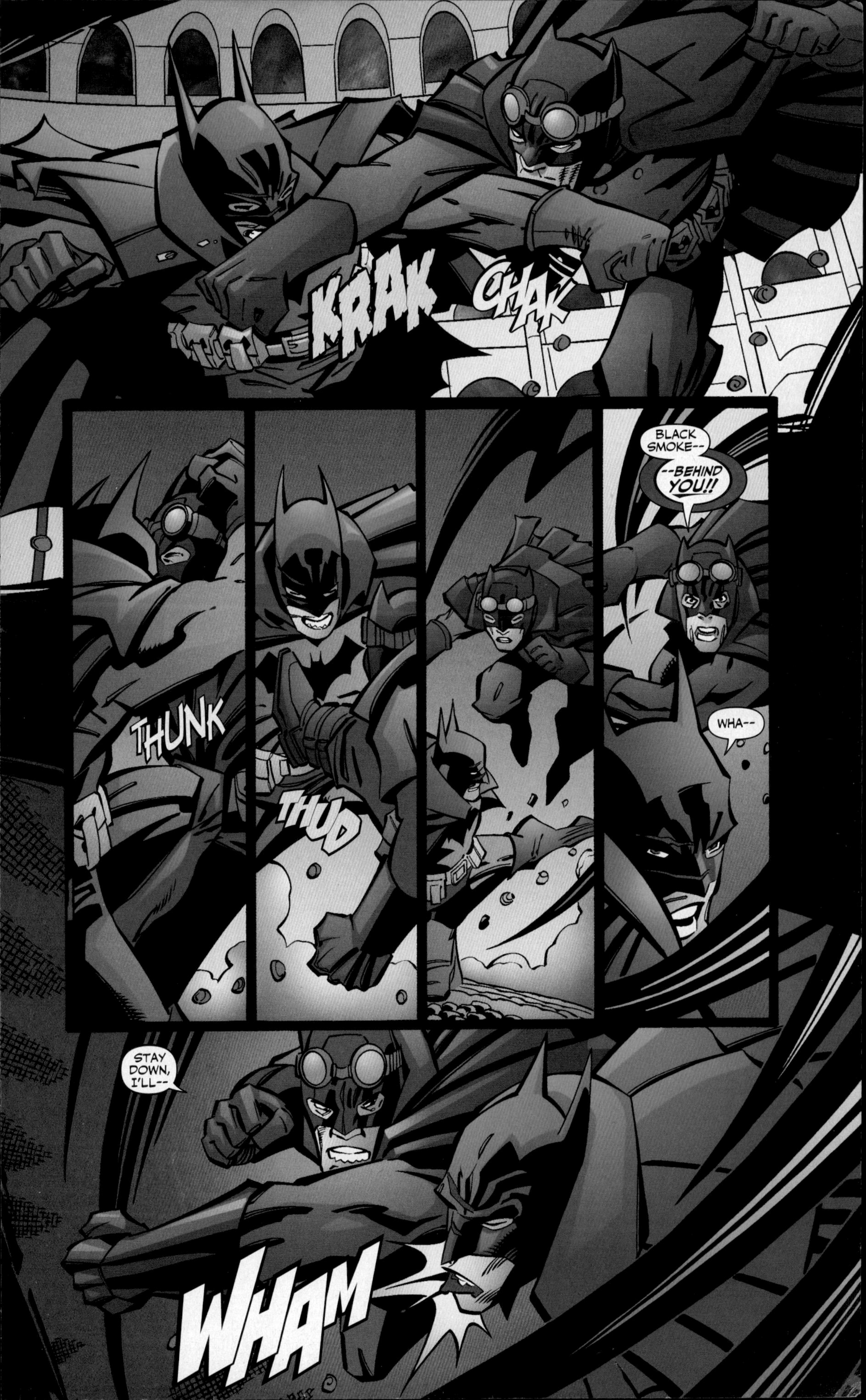

KRAK
CHAK
THUNK
THUD
BLACK SMOKE--
--BEHIND YOU!!
WHA--
STAY DOWN, I'LL--
WHAM

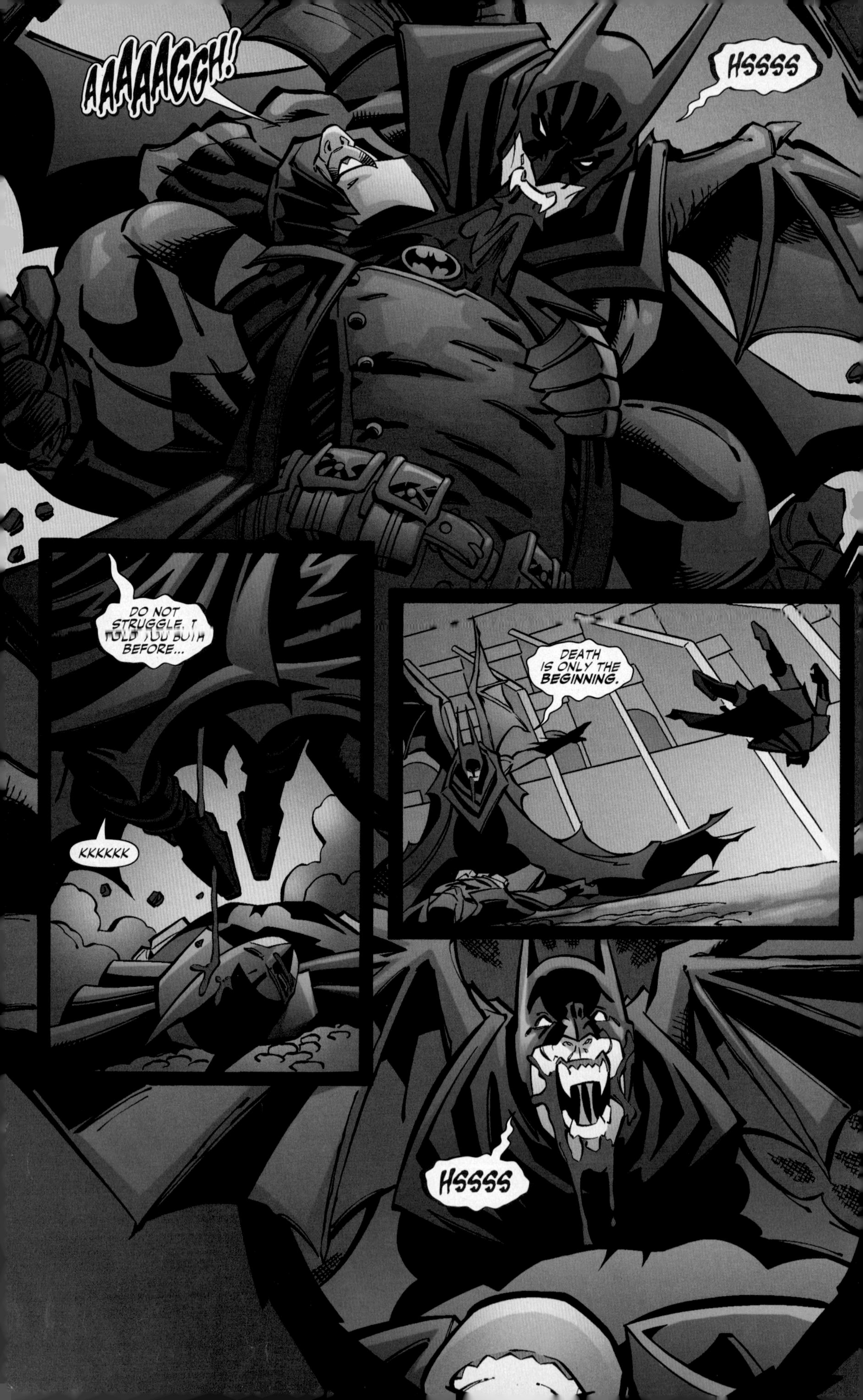
AAAAAGGH!
HSSSS
DO NOT STRUGGLE. I TOLD YOU BOTH BEFORE...
KKKKKK
DEATH IS ONLY THE BEGINNING.
HSSSS

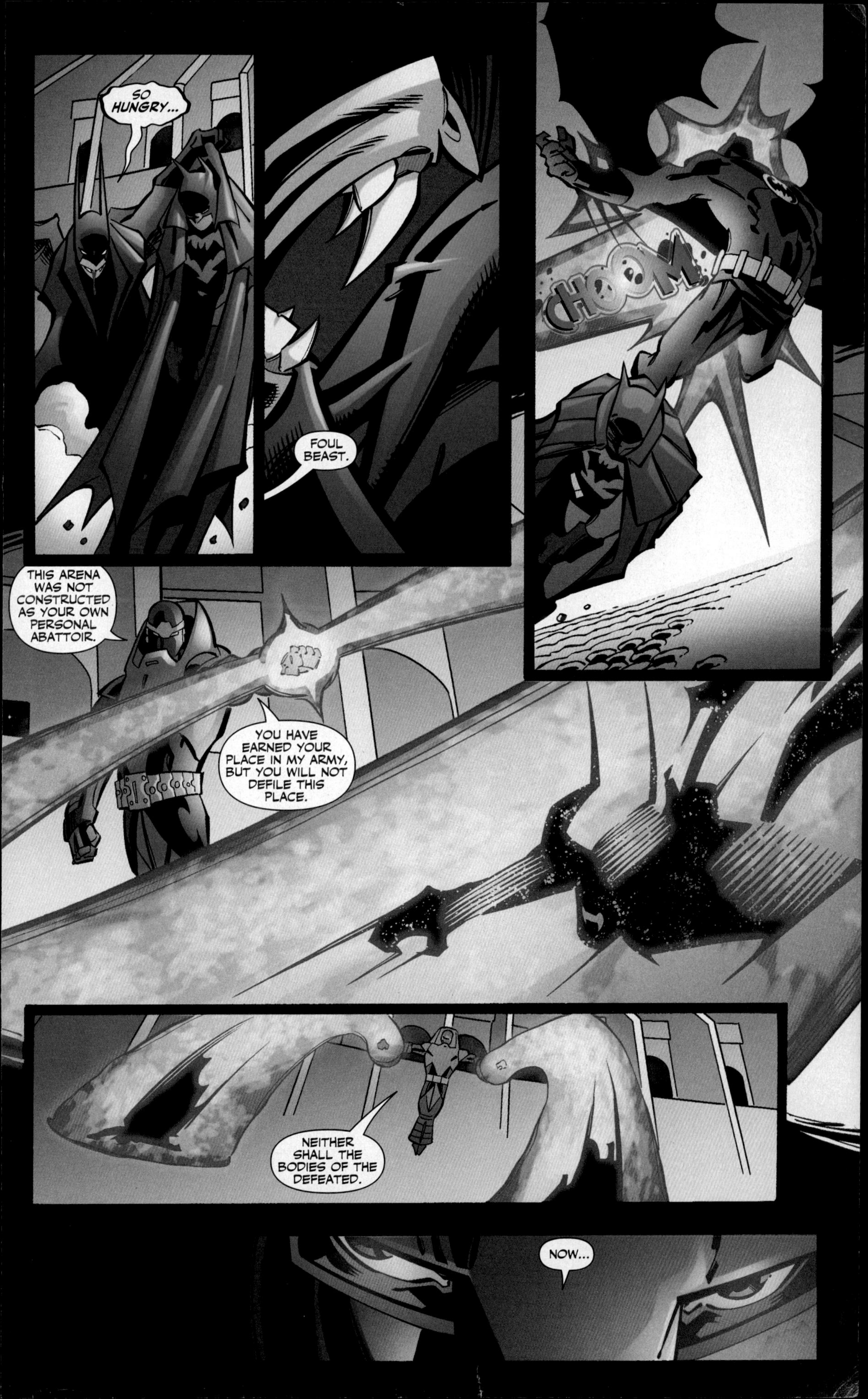
SO HUNGRY...
FOUL BEAST.
CHOOM
THIS ARENA WAS NOT CONSTRUCTED AS YOUR OWN PERSONAL ABATTOIR.
YOU HAVE EARNED YOUR PLACE IN MY ARMY, BUT YOU WILL NOT DEFILE THIS PLACE.
NEITHER SHALL THE BODIES OF THE DEFEATED.
NOW...

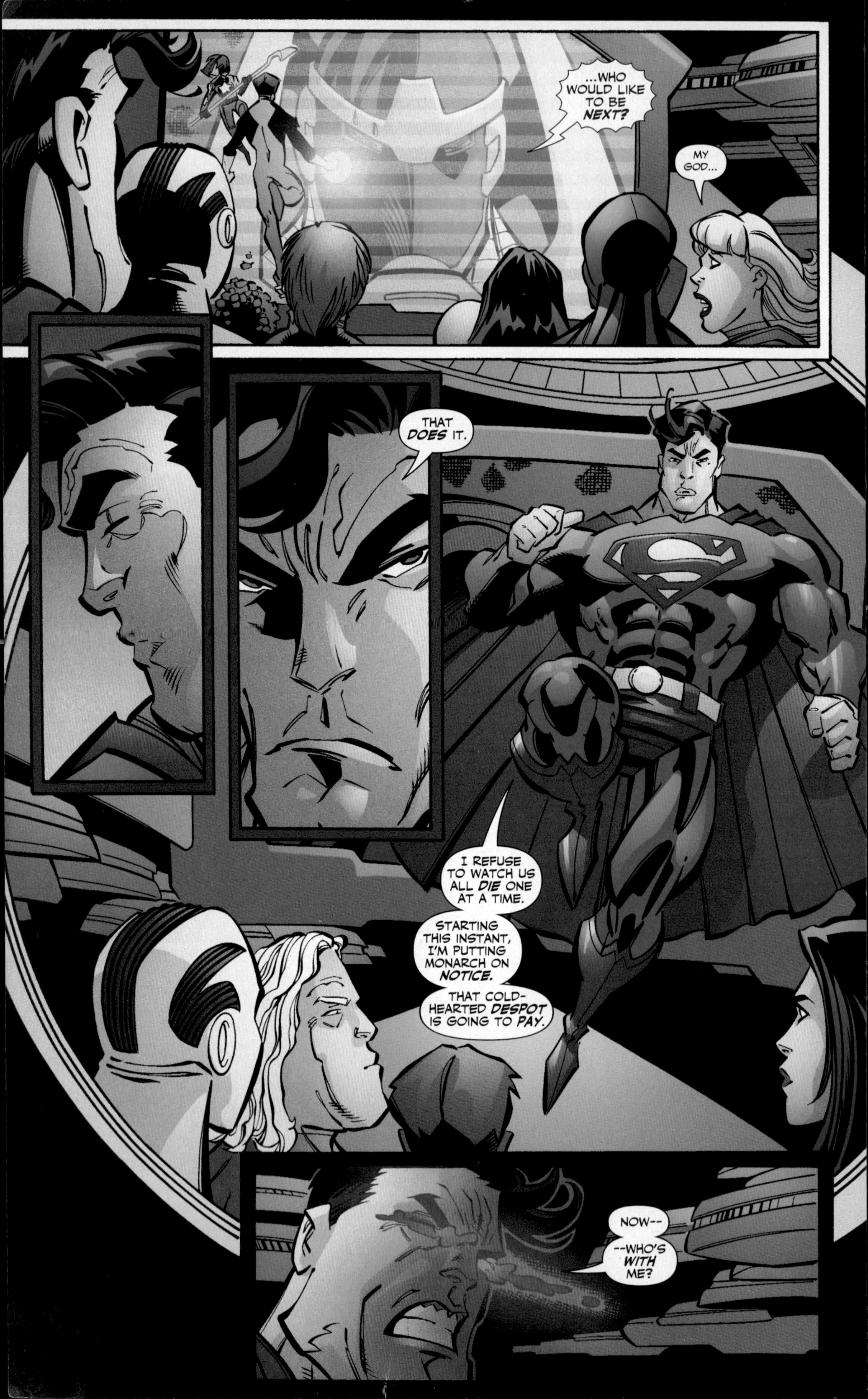
...WHO WOULD LIKE TO BE NEXT?
MY GOD...
THAT DOES IT.
I REFUSE TO WATCH US ALL DIE ONE AT A TIME.
STARTING THIS INSTANT, I'M PUTTING MONARCH ON NOTICE.
THAT COLD-HEARTED DESPOT IS GOING TO PAY.
NOW--
--WHO'S WITH ME?

THE FACE OF DEATH COVER ART BY ANDY KUBERT

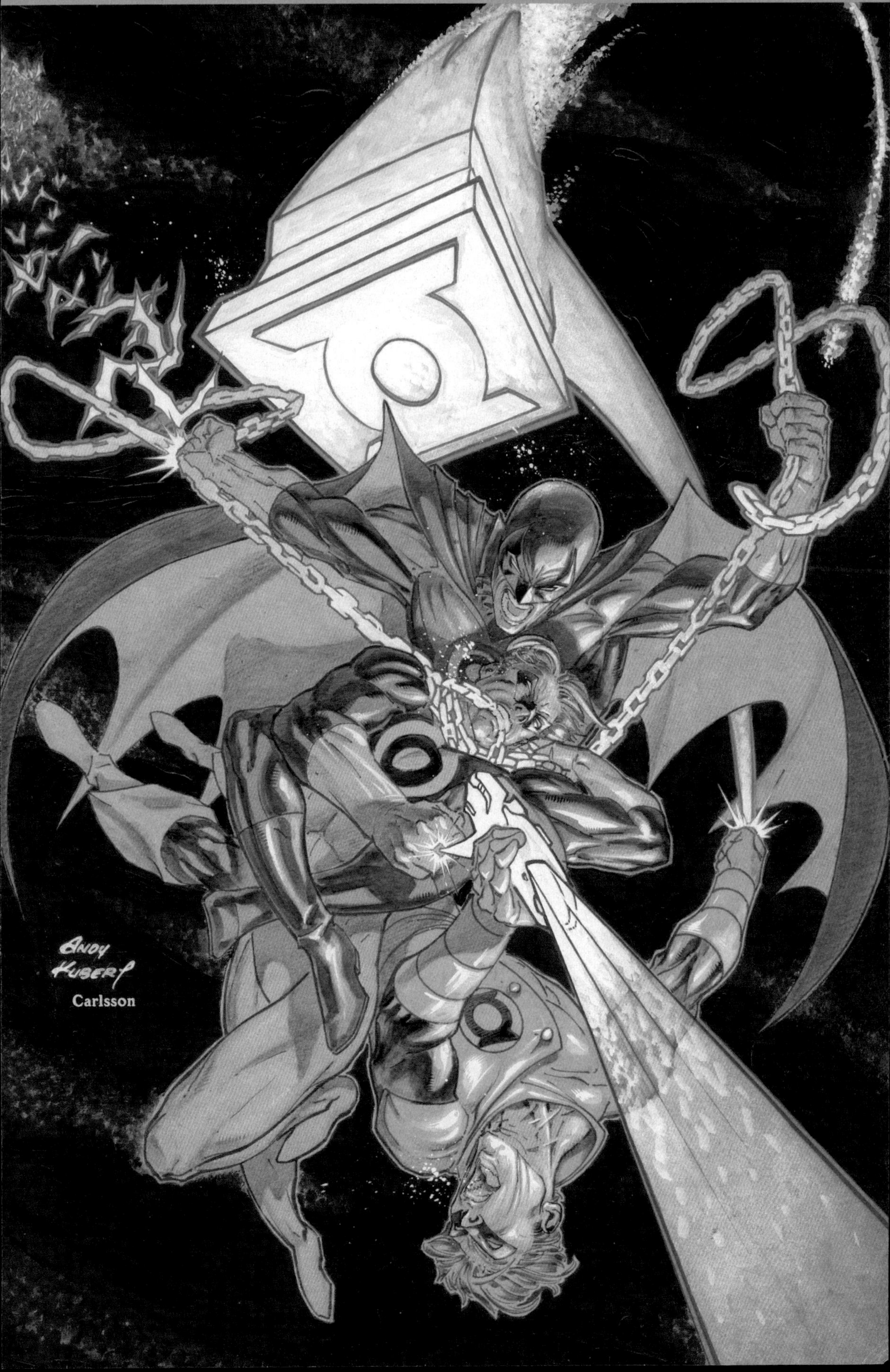

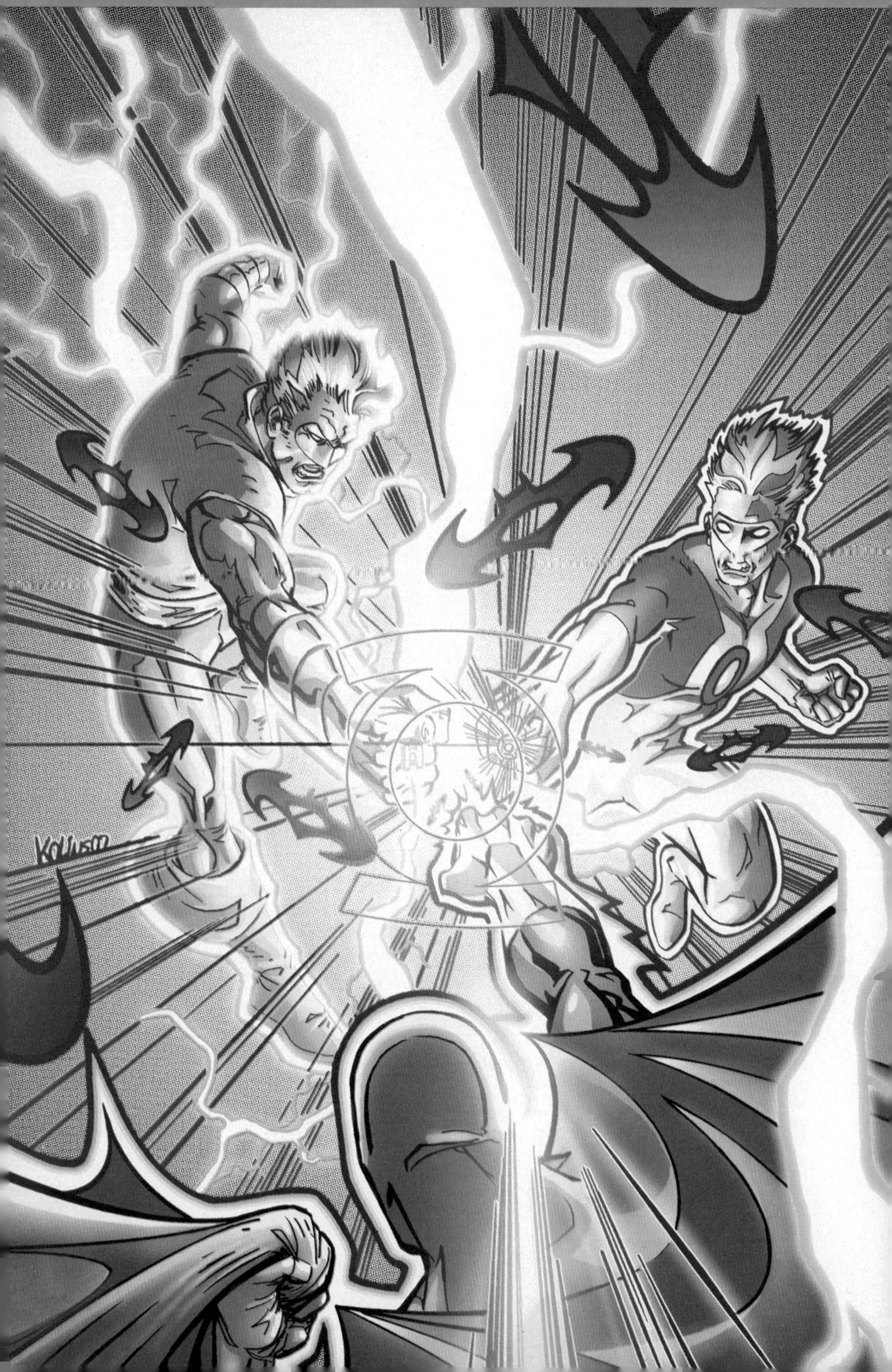

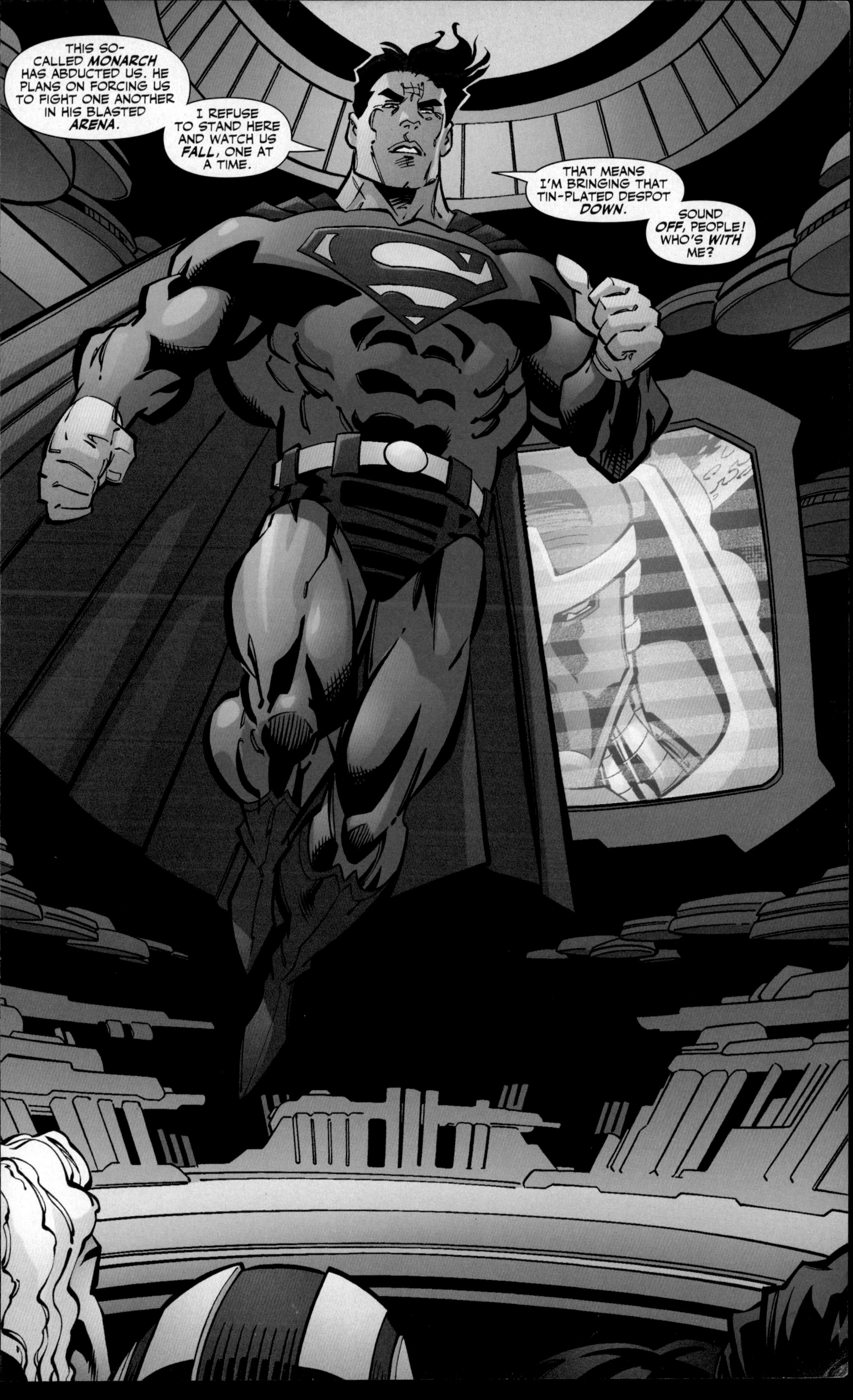

THIS SO-CALLED MONARCH HAS ABDUCTED US. HE PLANS ON FORCING US TO FIGHT ONE ANOTHER IN HIS BLASTED ARENA.
I REFUSE TO STAND HERE AND WATCH US FALL, ONE AT A TIME.
THAT MEANS I'M BRINGING THAT TIN-PLATED DESPOT DOWN.
SOUND OFF, PEOPLE! WHO'S WITH ME?

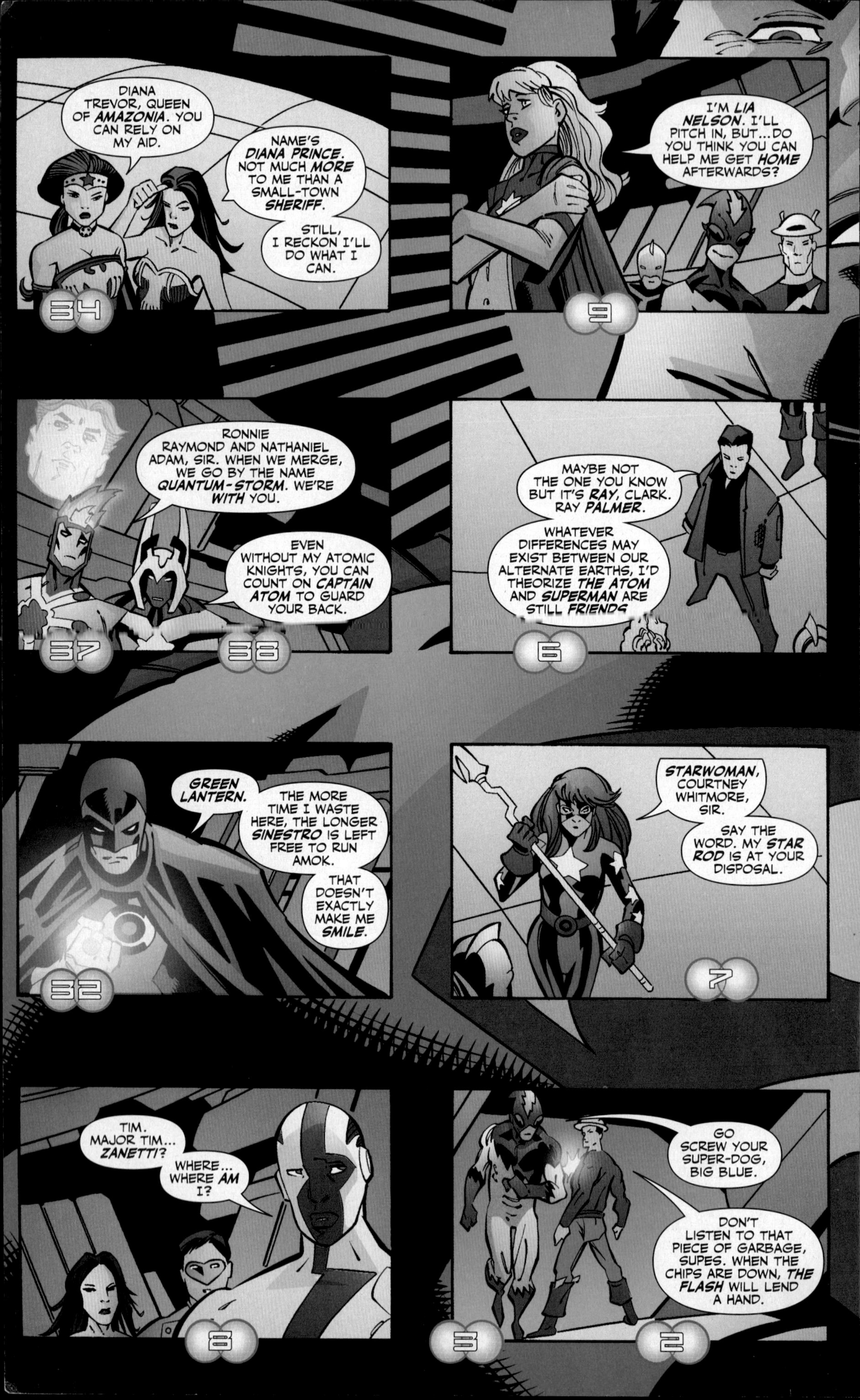
DIANA TREVOR, QUEEN OF AMAZONIA. YOU CAN RELY ON MY AID.
NAME'S DIANA PRINCE. NOT MUCH MORE TO ME THAN A SMALL-TOWN SHERIFF.
STILL, I RECKON I'LL DO WHAT I CAN.
34
I'M LIA NELSON. I'LL PITCH IN, BUT... DO YOU THINK YOU CAN HELP ME GET HOME AFTERWARDS?
9
RONNIE RAYMOND AND NATHANIEL ADAM, SIR. WHEN WE MERGE, WE GO BY THE NAME QUANTUM-STORM. WE'RE WITH YOU.
EVEN WITHOUT MY ATOMIC KNIGHTS, YOU CAN COUNT ON CAPTAIN ATOM TO GUARD YOUR BACK.
37
38
MAYBE NOT THE ONE YOU KNOW BUT IT'S RAY, CLARK. RAY PALMER.
WHATEVER DIFFERENCES MAY EXIST BETWEEN OUR ALTERNATE EARTHS, I'D THEORIZE THE ATOM AND SUPERMAN ARE STILL FRIENDS
6
GREEN LANTERN.
THE MORE TIME I WASTE HERE, THE LONGER SINESTRO IS LEFT FREE TO RUN AMOK.
THAT DOESN'T EXACTLY MAKE ME SMILE.
32
STARWOMAN, COURTNEY WHITMORE, SIR.
SAY THE WORD. MY STAR ROD IS AT YOUR DISPOSAL.
7
TIM. MAJOR TIM... ZANETTI?
WHERE... WHERE AM I?
8
GO SCREW YOUR SUPER-DOG, BIG BLUE.
DON'T LISTEN TO THAT PIECE OF GARBAGE, SUPES. WHEN THE CHIPS ARE DOWN, THE FLASH WILL LEND A HAND.
3
2

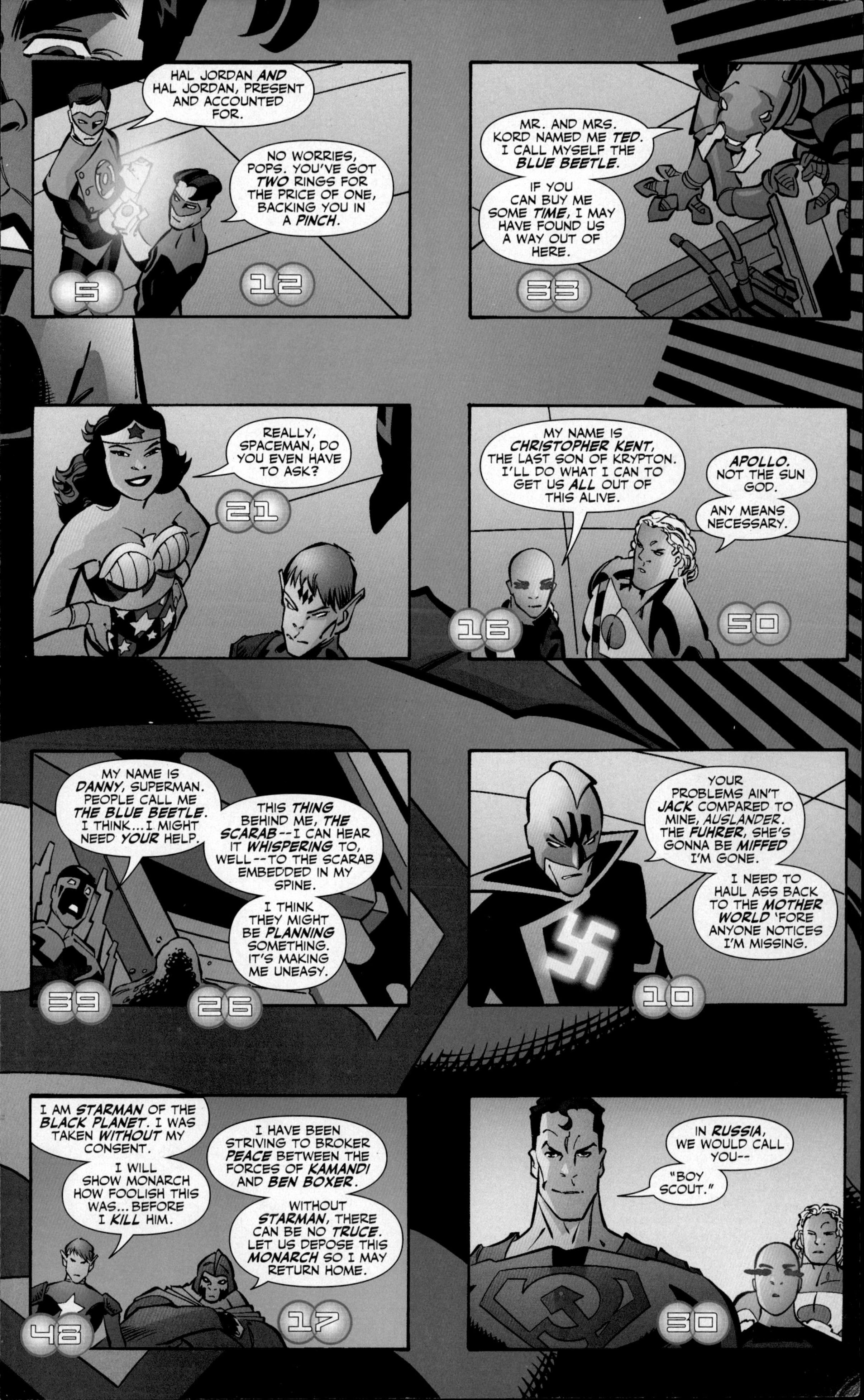
HAL JORDAN AND HAL JORDAN, PRESENT AND ACCOUNTED FOR.
NO WORRIES, POPS. YOU'VE GOT TWO RINGS FOR THE PRICE OF ONE, BACKING YOU IN A PINCH.
5
12
MR. AND MRS. KORD NAMED ME TED. I CALL MYSELF THE BLUE BEETLE.
IF YOU CAN BUY ME SOME TIME, I MAY HAVE FOUND US A WAY OUT OF HERE.
33
REALLY, SPACEMAN, DO YOU EVEN HAVE TO ASK?
21
MY NAME IS CHRISTOPHER KENT, THE LAST SON OF KRYPTON. I'LL DO WHAT I CAN TO GET US ALL OUT OF THIS ALIVE.
APOLLO. NOT THE SUN GOD.
ANY MEANS NECESSARY.
16
50
MY NAME IS DANNY, SUPERMAN. PEOPLE CALL ME THE BLUE BEETLE. I THINK...I MIGHT NEED YOUR HELP.
THIS THING BEHIND ME, THE SCARAB--I CAN HEAR IT WHISPERING TO, WELL--TO THE SCARAB EMBEDDED IN MY SPINE.
I THINK THEY MIGHT BE PLANNING SOMETHING. IT'S MAKING ME UNEASY.
39
26
YOUR PROBLEMS AIN'T JACK COMPARED TO MINE, AUSLANDER. THE FUHRER, SHE'S GONNA BE MIFFED I'M GONE.
I NEED TO HAUL ASS BACK TO THE MOTHER WORLD 'FORE ANYONE NOTICES I'M MISSING.
10
I AM STARMAN OF THE BLACK PLANET. I WAS TAKEN WITHOUT MY CONSENT.
I WILL SHOW MONARCH HOW FOOLISH THIS WAS...BEFORE I KILL HIM.
I HAVE BEEN STRIVING TO BROKER PEACE BETWEEN THE FORCES OF KAMANDI AND BEN BOXER.
WITHOUT STARMAN, THERE CAN BE NO TRUCE. LET US DEPOSE THIS MONARCH SO I MAY RETURN HOME.
48
17
IN RUSSIA, WE WOULD CALL YOU--
"BOY SCOUT."
30

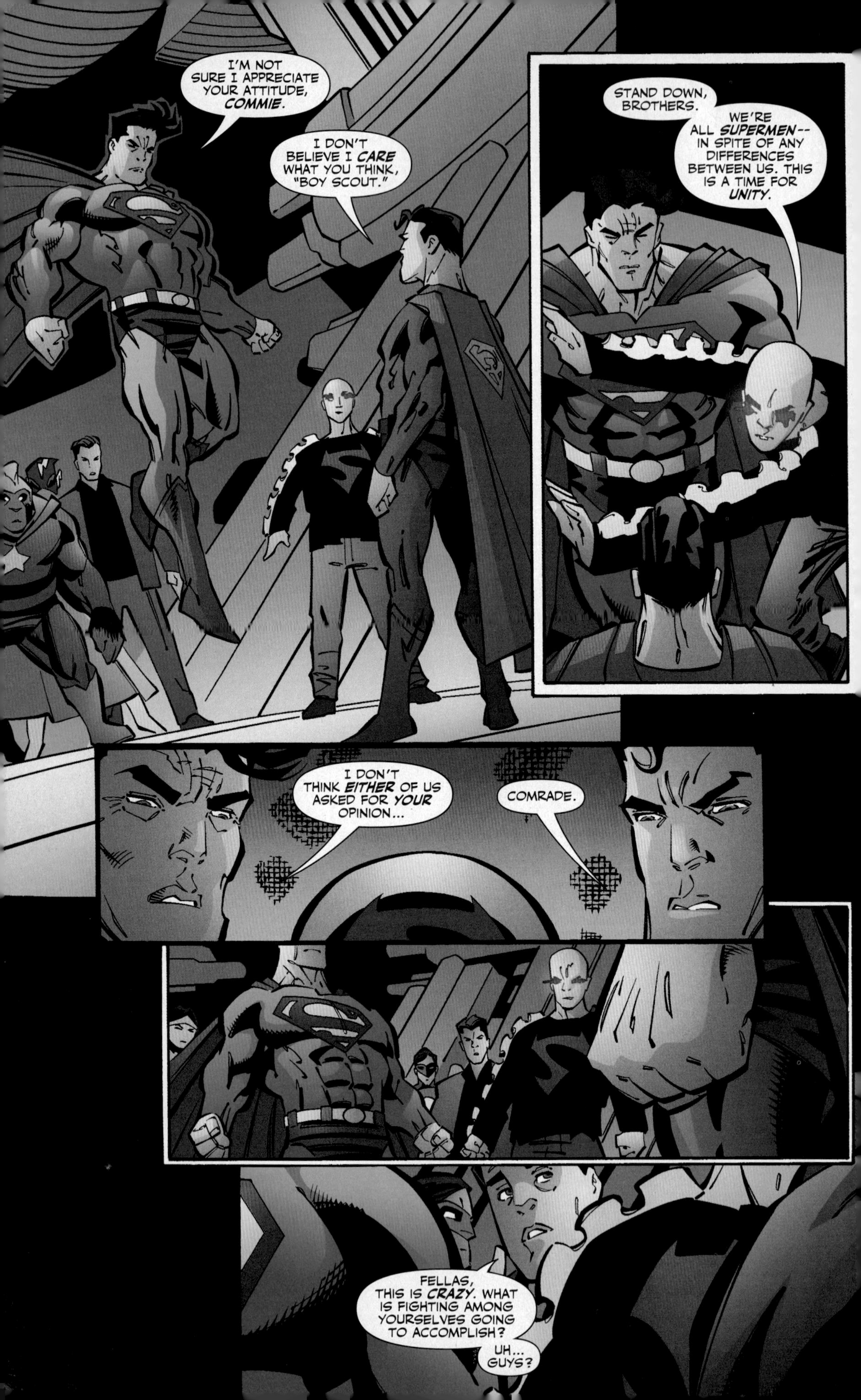
I'M NOT SURE I APPRECIATE YOUR ATTITUDE, COMMIE.
I DON'T BELIEVE I CARE WHAT YOU THINK, "BOY SCOUT."
STAND DOWN, BROTHERS.
WE'RE ALL SUPERMEN-- IN SPITE OF ANY DIFFERENCES BETWEEN US. THIS IS A TIME FOR UNITY.
I DON'T THINK EITHER OF US ASKED FOR YOUR OPINION...
COMRADE.
FELLAS, THIS IS CRAZY. WHAT IS FIGHTING AMONG YOURSELVES GOING TO ACCOMPLISH?
UH... GUYS?

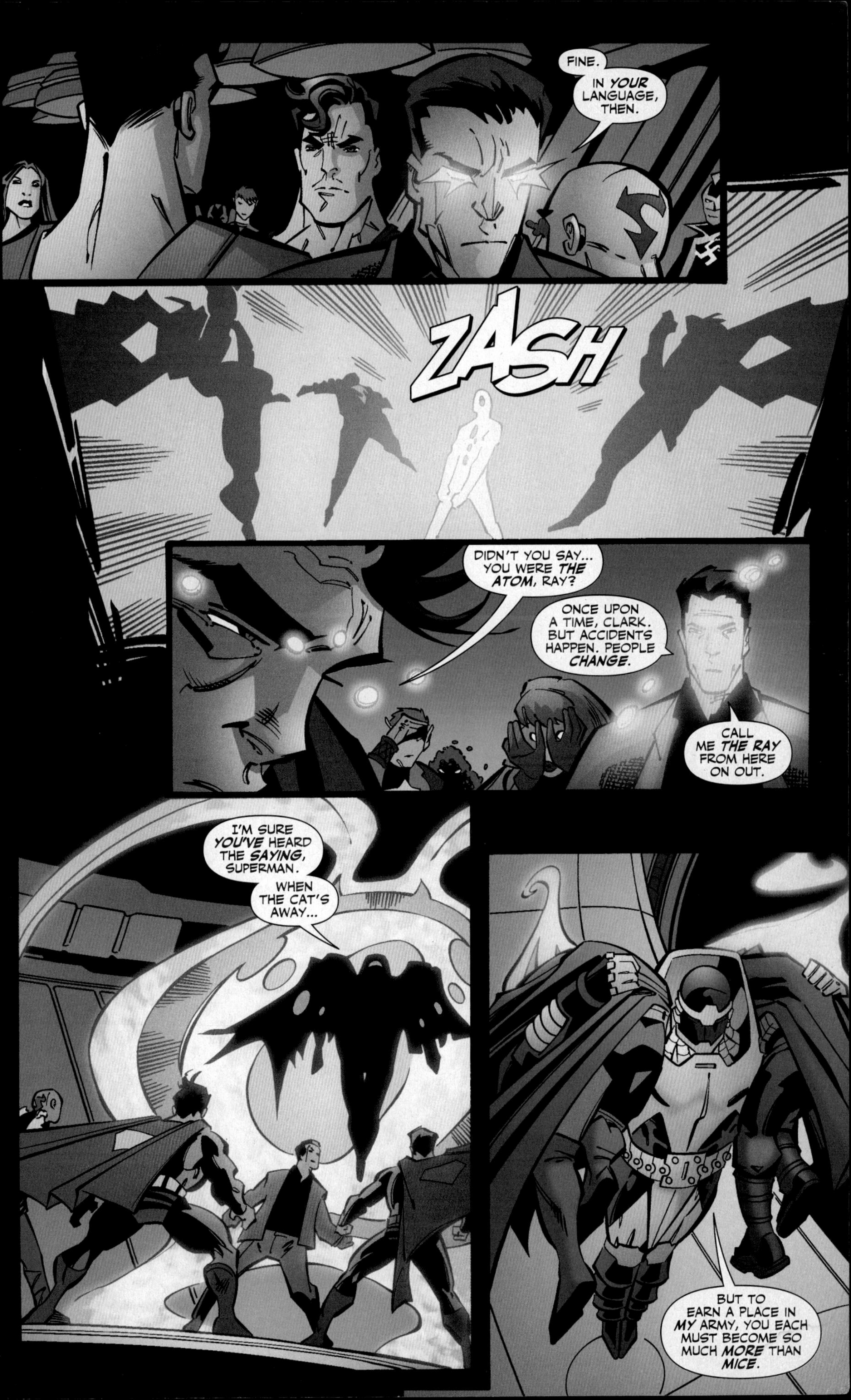
FINE.
IN YOUR LANGUAGE, THEN.
ZASH
DIDN'T YOU SAY... YOU WERE THE ATOM, RAY?
ONCE UPON A TIME, CLARK. BUT ACCIDENTS HAPPEN. PEOPLE CHANGE.
CALL ME THE RAY FROM HERE ON OUT.
I'M SURE YOU'VE HEARD THE SAYING, SUPERMAN.
WHEN THE CAT'S AWAY...
BUT TO EARN A PLACE IN MY ARMY, YOU EACH MUST BECOME SO MUCH MORE THAN MICE.

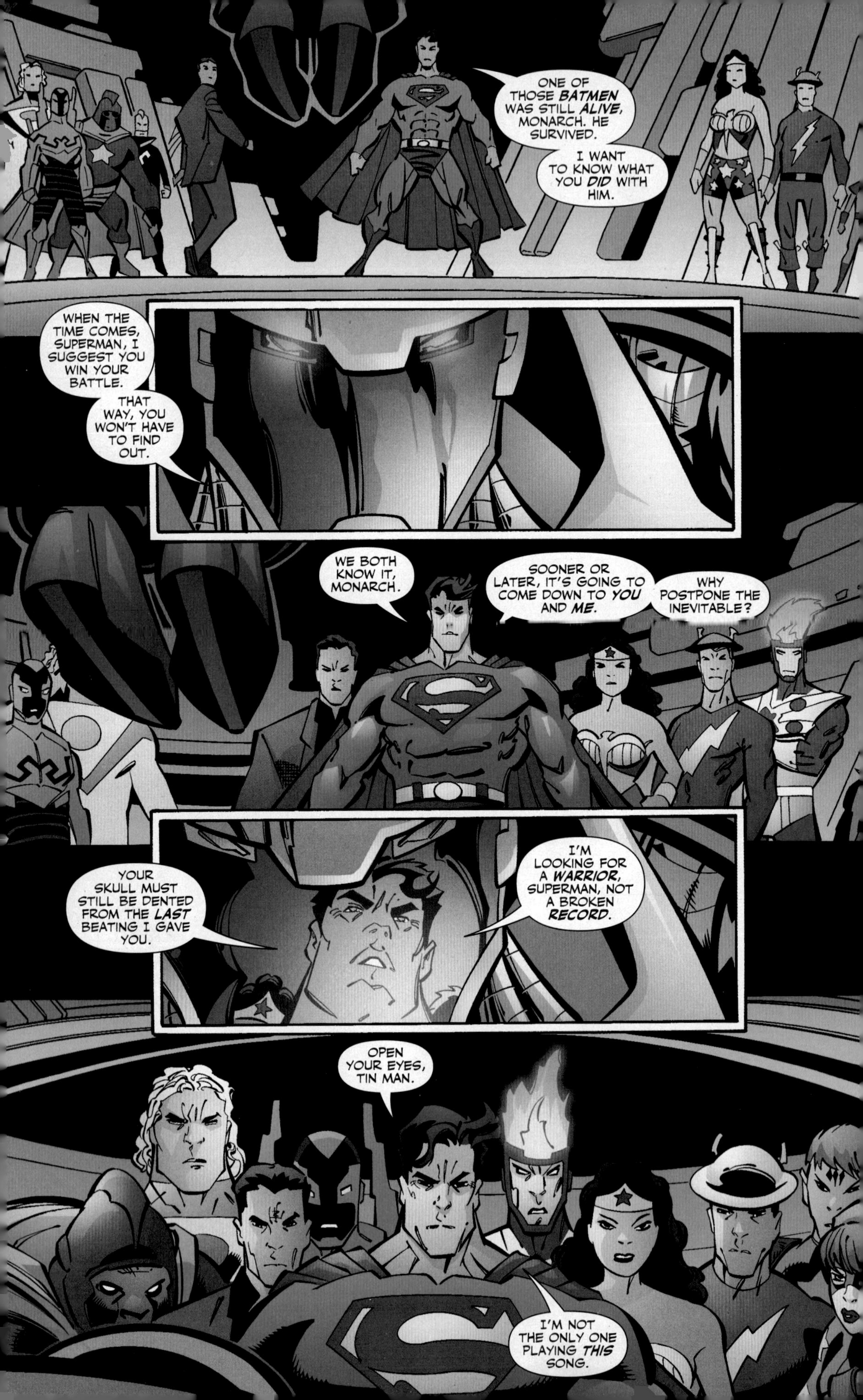
ONE OF THOSE BATMEN WAS STILL ALIVE, MONARCH. HE SURVIVED.
I WANT TO KNOW WHAT YOU DID WITH HIM.
WHEN THE TIME COMES, SUPERMAN, I SUGGEST YOU WIN YOUR BATTLE.
THAT WAY, YOU WON'T HAVE TO FIND OUT.
WE BOTH KNOW IT, MONARCH.
SOONER OR LATER, IT'S GOING TO COME DOWN TO YOU AND ME.
WHY POSTPONE THE INEVITABLE?
YOUR SKULL MUST STILL BE DENTED FROM THE LAST BEATING I GAVE YOU.
I'M LOOKING FOR A WARRIOR, SUPERMAN, NOT A BROKEN RECORD.
OPEN YOUR EYES, TIN MAN.
I'M NOT THE ONLY ONE PLAYING THIS SONG.

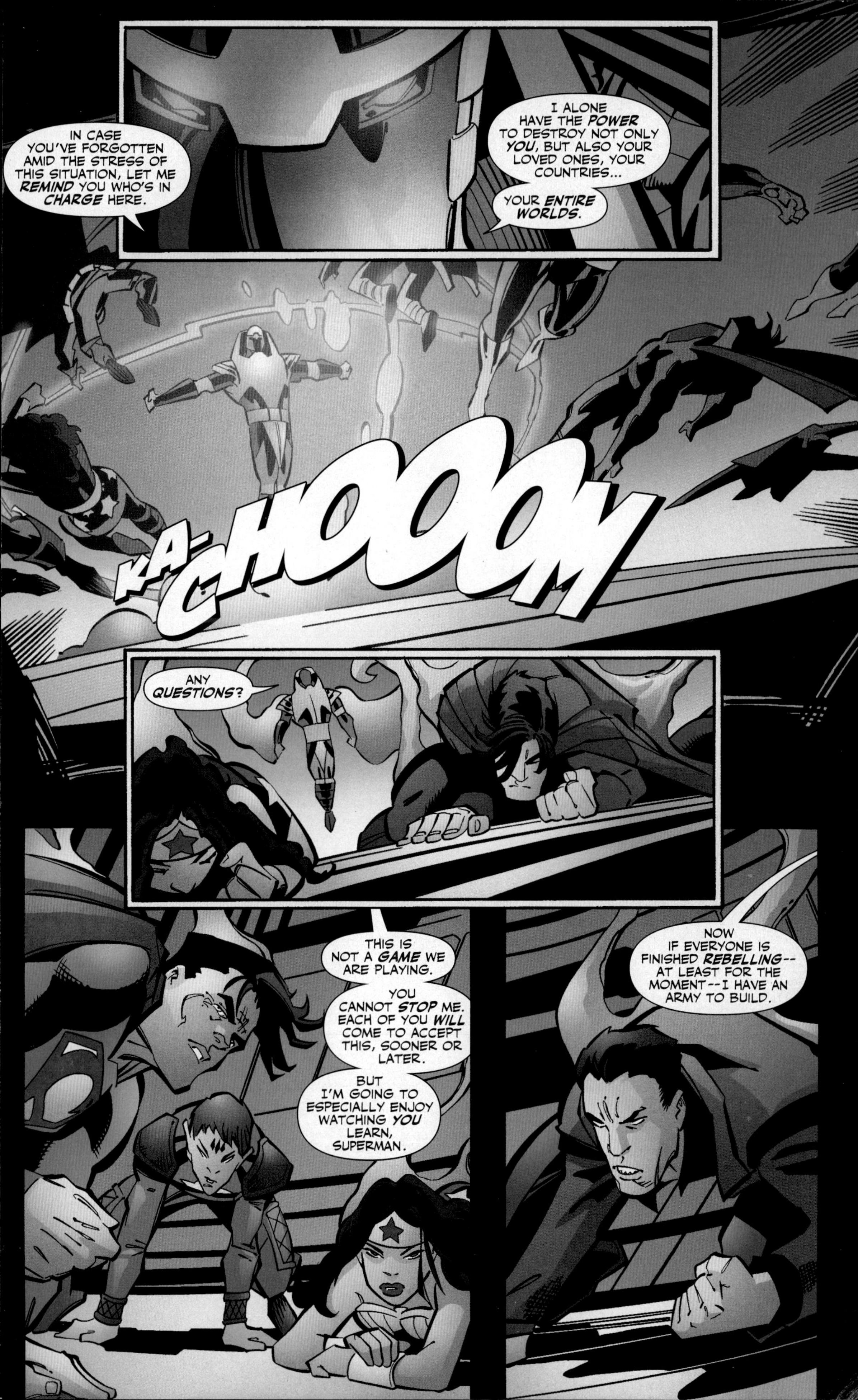
IN CASE YOU'VE FORGOTTEN AMID THE STRESS OF THIS SITUATION, LET ME REMIND YOU WHO'S IN CHARGE HERE.
I ALONE HAVE THE POWER TO DESTROY NOT ONLY YOU, BUT ALSO YOUR LOVED ONES, YOUR COUNTRIES...
YOUR ENTIRE WORLDS.
KA-CHOOOM
ANY QUESTIONS?
THIS IS NOT A GAME WE ARE PLAYING.
YOU CANNOT STOP ME. EACH OF YOU WILL COME TO ACCEPT THIS, SOONER OR LATER.
BUT I'M GOING TO ESPECIALLY ENJOY WATCHING YOU LEARN, SUPERMAN.
NOW IF EVERYONE IS FINISHED REBELLING-- AT LEAST FOR THE MOMENT--I HAVE AN ARMY TO BUILD.

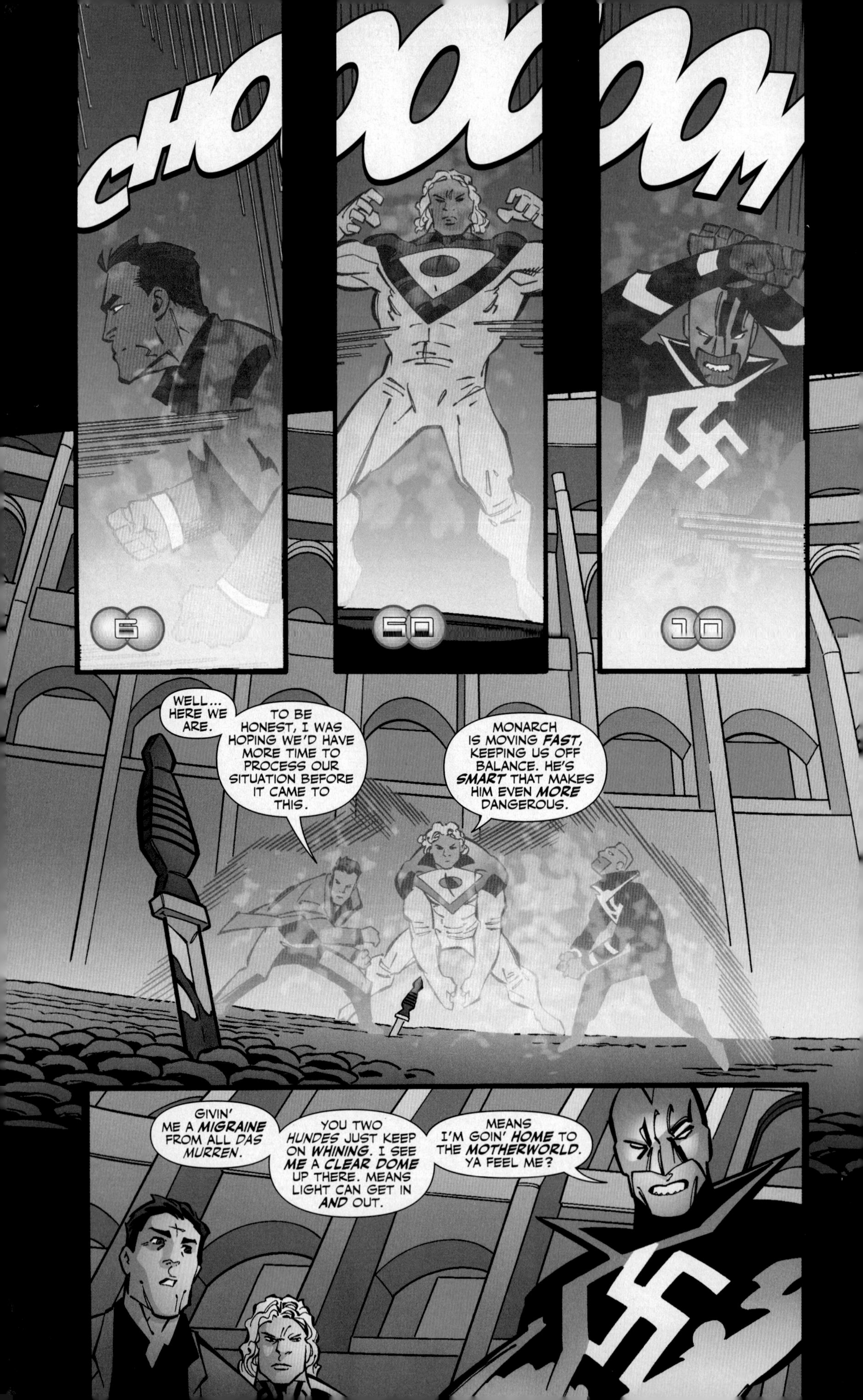
CHOOOOOOM
6
50
10
WELL... HERE WE ARE.
TO BE HONEST, I WAS HOPING WE'D HAVE MORE TIME TO PROCESS OUR SITUATION BEFORE IT CAME TO THIS.
MONARCH IS MOVING FAST, KEEPING US OFF BALANCE. HE'S SMART THAT MAKES HIM EVEN MORE DANGEROUS.
GIVIN' ME A MIGRAINE FROM ALL DAS MURREN.
YOU TWO HUNDES JUST KEEP ON WHINING. I SEE ME A CLEAR DOME UP THERE. MEANS LIGHT CAN GET IN AND OUT.
MEANS I'M GOIN' HOME TO THE MOTHERWORLD. YA FEEL ME?

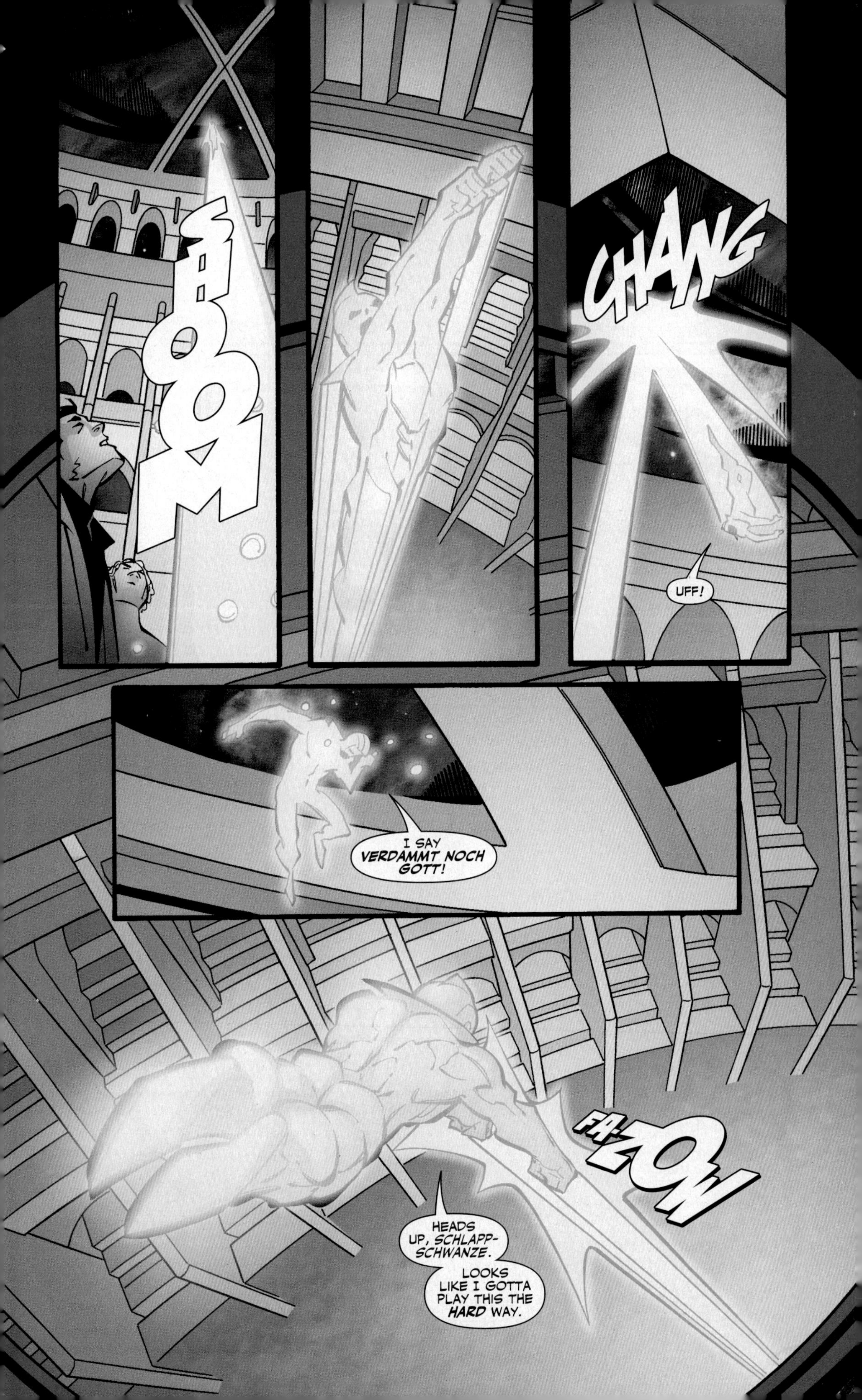
SHOOOM
CHANG
UFF!
I SAY VERDAMMT NOCH GOTT!
FA-ZOOM
HEADS UP, SCHLAPP-SCHWANZE.
LOOKS LIKE I GOTTA PLAY THIS THE HARD WAY.

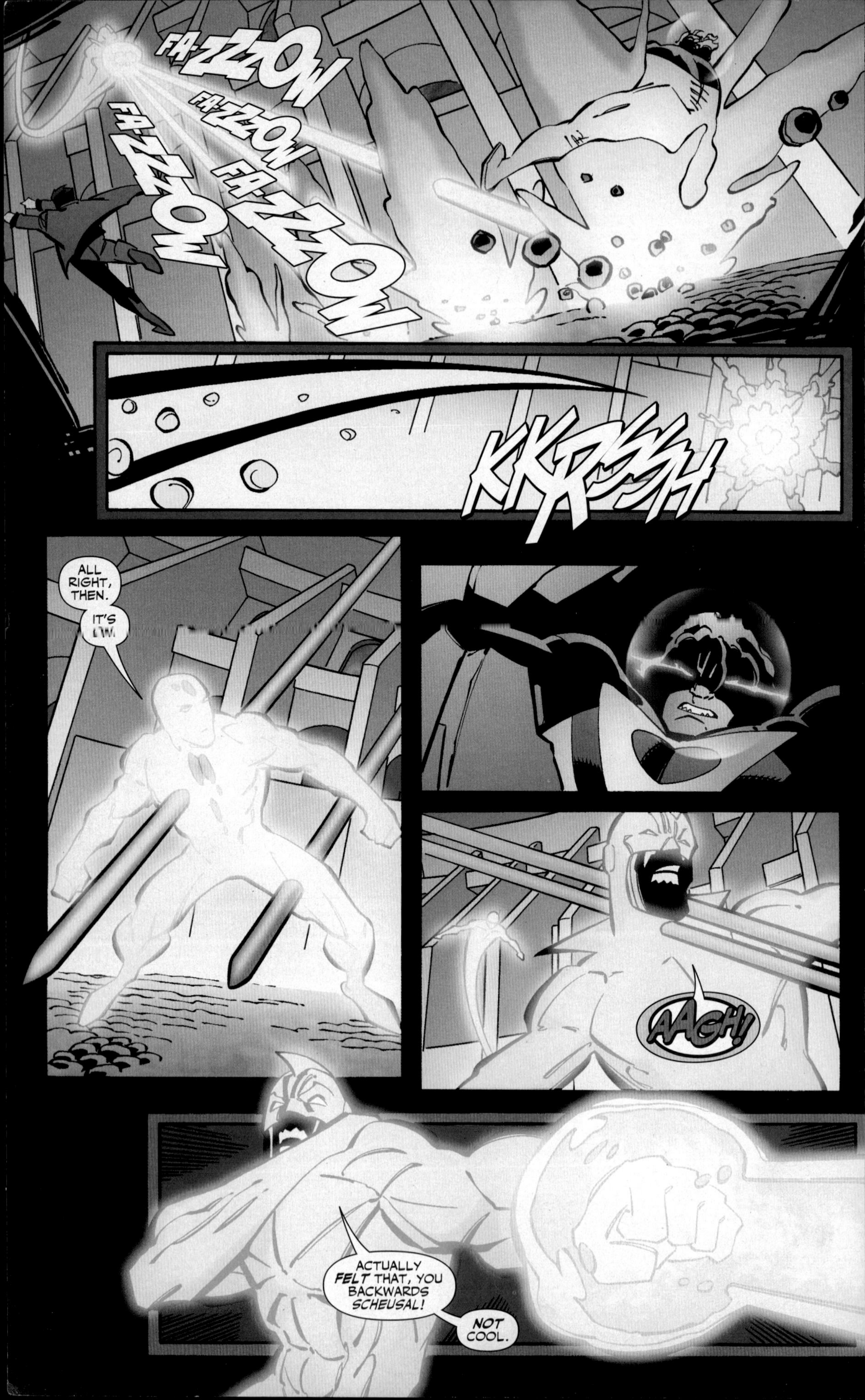
FA-ZZOW
FA-ZZOW
FA-ZZOW
FA-ZZOW
KKRSSH
ALL RIGHT, THEN.
IT'S
AACH!
ACTUALLY FELT THAT, YOU BACKWARDS SCHEUSAL!
NOT COOL.

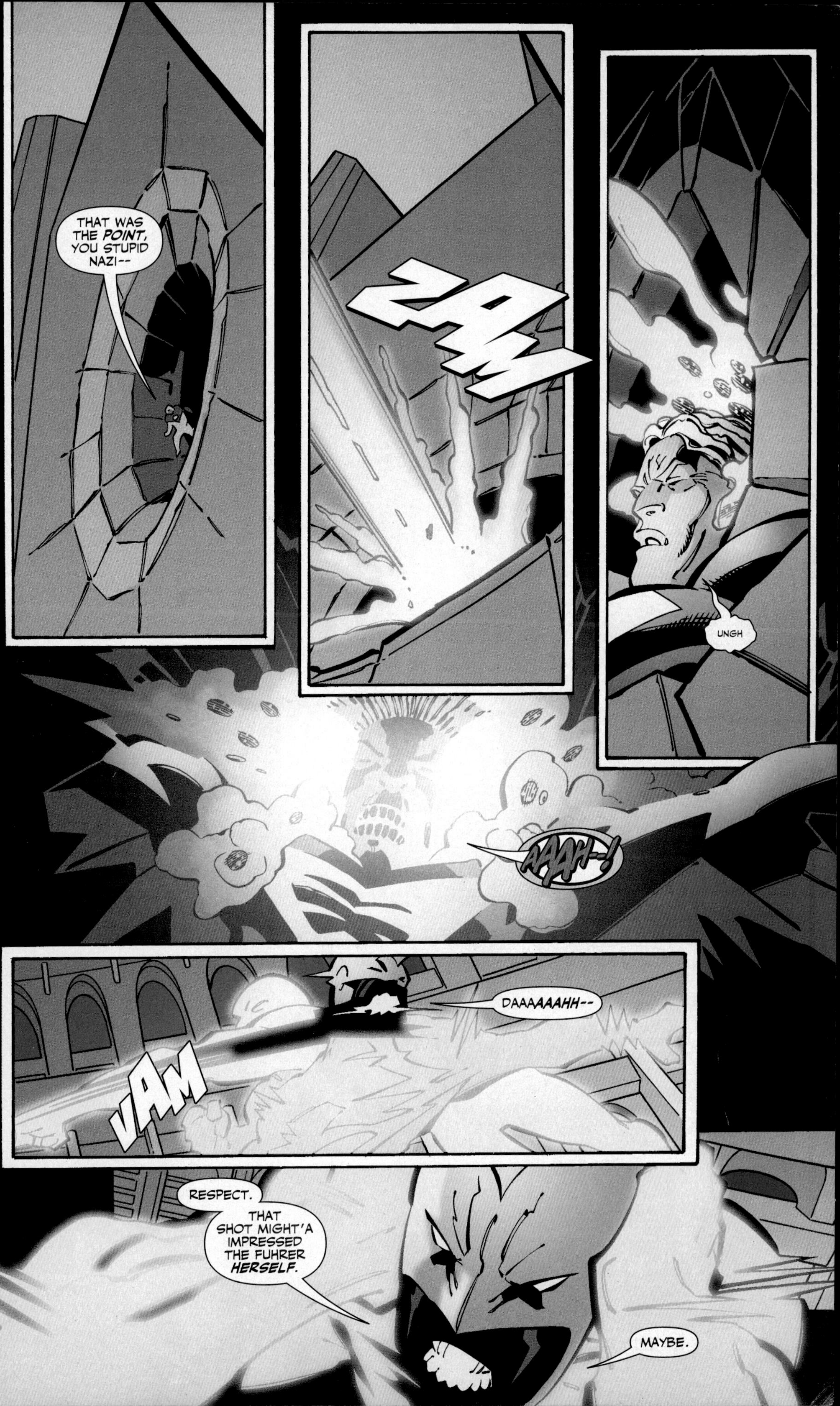
THAT WAS THE POINT, YOU STUPID NAZI--
ZAM
UNGH
AAAH--!
DAAAAAAHH--
VAM
RESPECT.
THAT SHOT MIGHT'A IMPRESSED THE FUHRER HERSELF.
MAYBE.

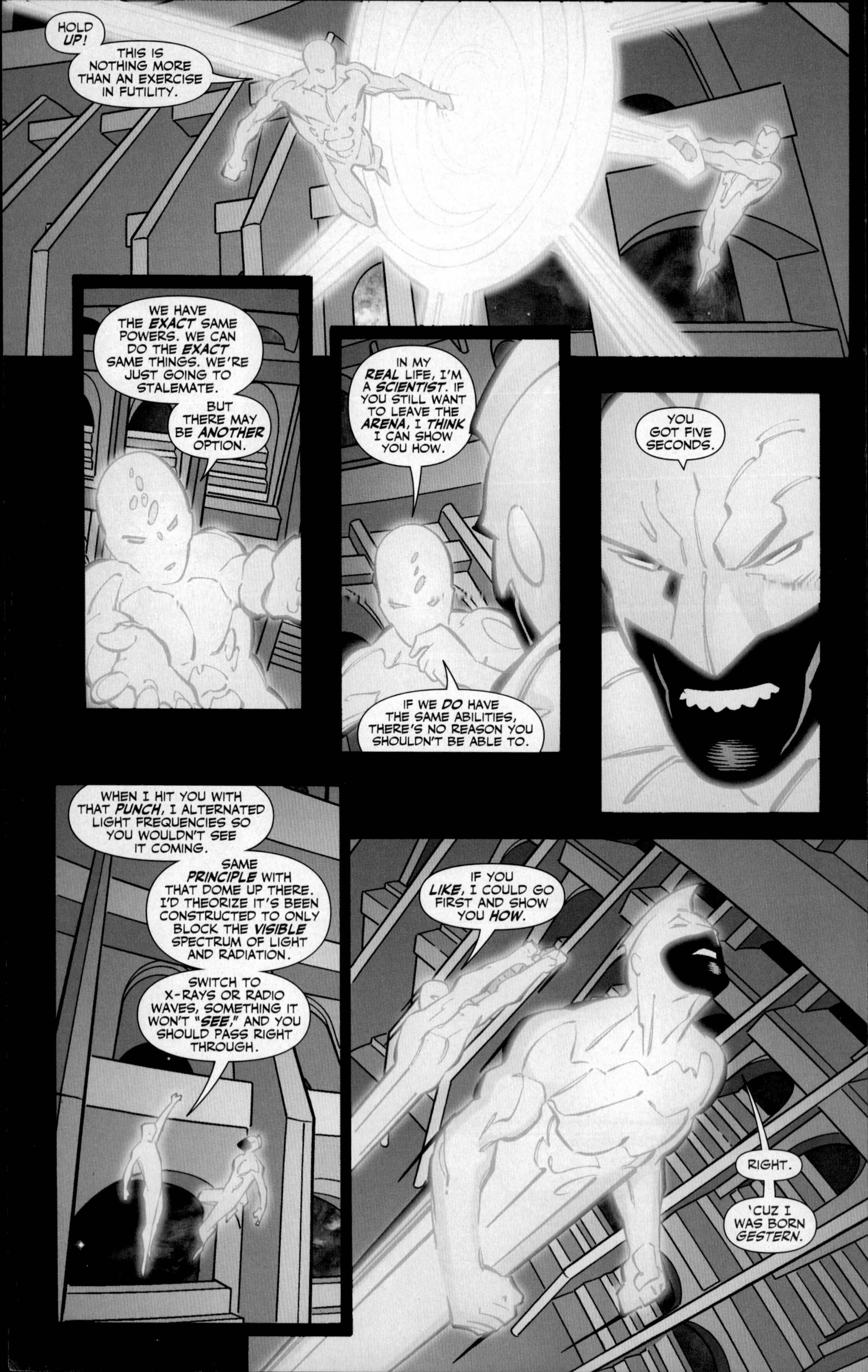
HOLD UP!
THIS IS NOTHING MORE THAN AN EXERCISE IN FUTILITY.
WE HAVE THE EXACT SAME POWERS. WE CAN DO THE EXACT SAME THINGS. WE'RE JUST GOING TO STALEMATE.
BUT THERE MAY BE ANOTHER OPTION.
IN MY REAL LIFE, I'M A SCIENTIST. IF YOU STILL WANT TO LEAVE THE ARENA, I THINK I CAN SHOW YOU HOW.
IF WE DO HAVE THE SAME ABILITIES, THERE'S NO REASON YOU SHOULDN'T BE ABLE TO.
YOU GOT FIVE SECONDS.
WHEN I HIT YOU WITH THAT PUNCH, I ALTERNATED LIGHT FREQUENCIES SO YOU WOULDN'T SEE IT COMING.
SAME PRINCIPLE WITH THAT DOME UP THERE. I'D THEORIZE IT'S BEEN CONSTRUCTED TO ONLY BLOCK THE VISIBLE SPECTRUM OF LIGHT AND RADIATION.
SWITCH TO X-RAYS OR RADIO WAVES, SOMETHING IT WON'T "SEE," AND YOU SHOULD PASS RIGHT THROUGH.
IF YOU LIKE, I COULD GO FIRST AND SHOW YOU HOW.
RIGHT.
'CUZ I WAS BORN GESTERN.

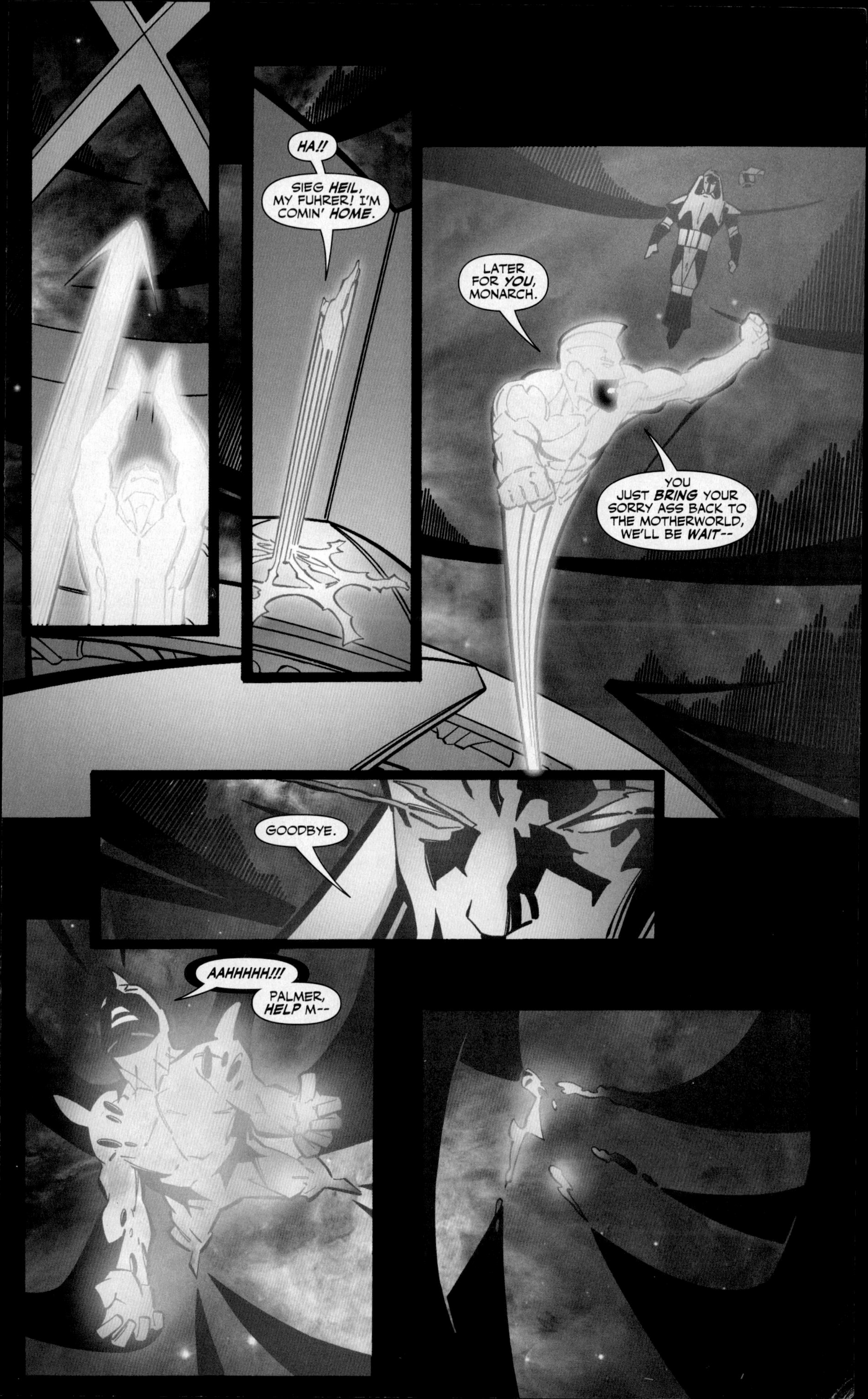
HA!!
SIEG HEIL, MY FUHRER! I'M COMIN' HOME.
LATER FOR YOU, MONARCH.
YOU JUST BRING YOUR SORRY ASS BACK TO THE MOTHERWORLD, WE'LL BE WAIT--
GOODBYE.
AAHHHHH!!!
PALMER, HELP M--

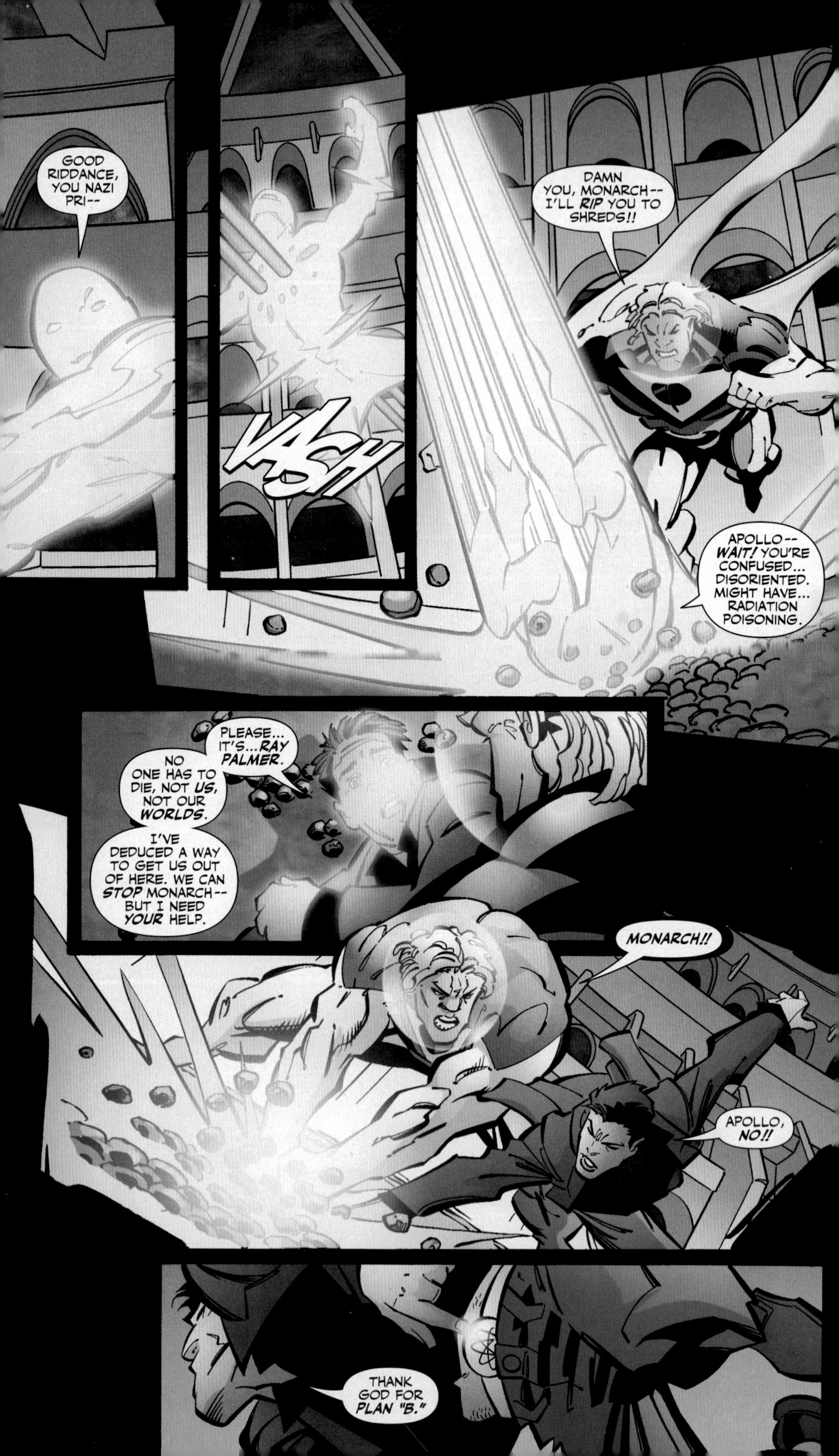
GOOD RIDDANCE, YOU NAZI PRI--
VASH
DAMN YOU, MONARCH-- I'LL *RIP* YOU TO SHREDS!!
APOLLO-- *WAIT!* YOU'RE CONFUSED... DISORIENTED. MIGHT HAVE... RADIATION POISONING.
PLEASE... IT'S... *RAY PALMER*.
NO ONE HAS TO DIE, NOT *US*, NOT OUR *WORLDS*.
I'VE DEDUCED A WAY TO GET US OUT OF HERE. WE CAN *STOP* MONARCH-- BUT I NEED *YOUR* HELP.
MONARCH!!
APOLLO, *NO!!*
THANK GOD FOR *PLAN "B."*

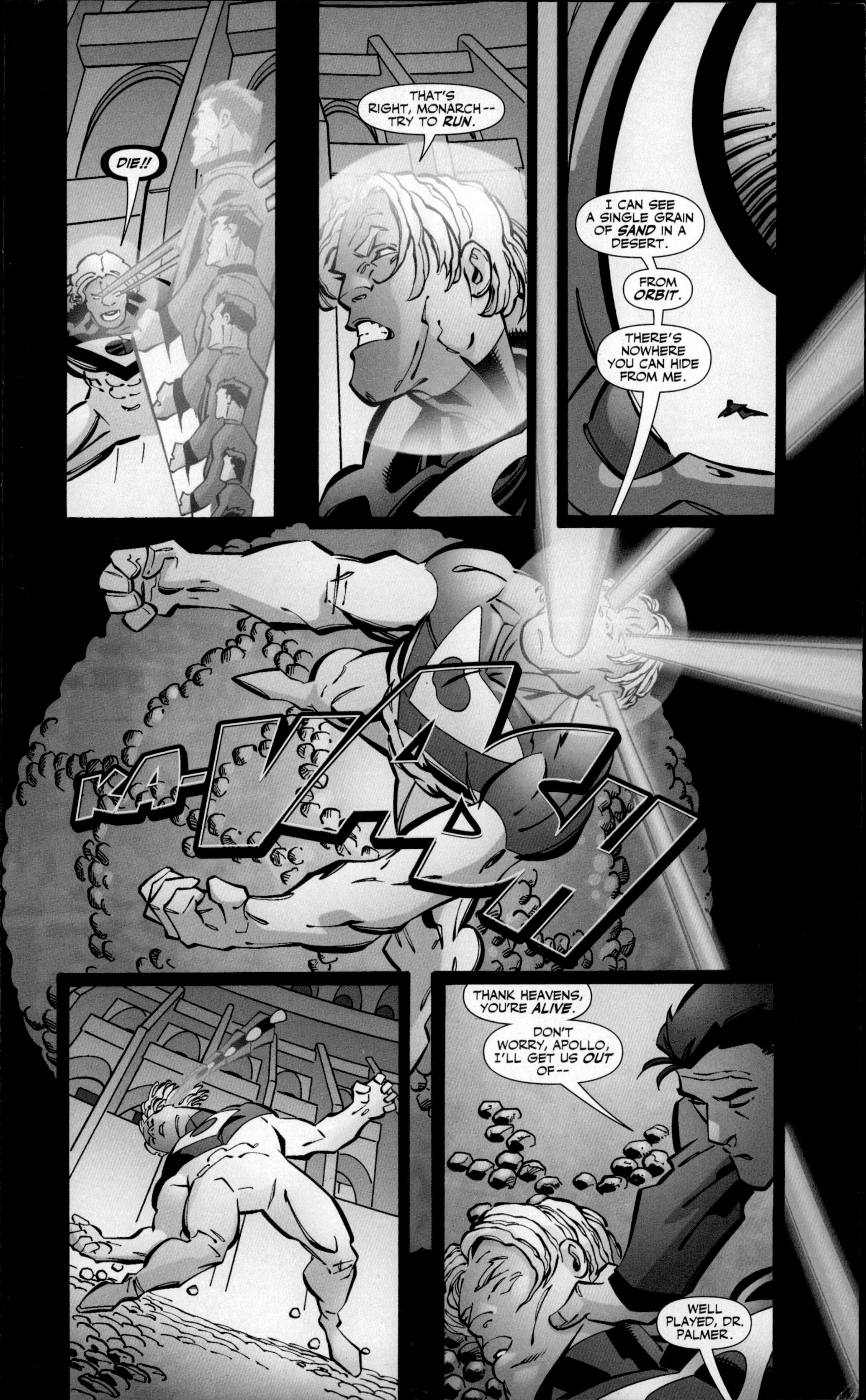
DIE!!
THAT'S RIGHT, MONARCH-- TRY TO RUN.
I CAN SEE A SINGLE GRAIN OF SAND IN A DESERT.
FROM ORBIT.
THERE'S NOWHERE YOU CAN HIDE FROM ME.
KA-VASH
THANK HEAVENS, YOU'RE ALIVE.
DON'T WORRY, APOLLO, I'LL GET US OUT OF--
WELL PLAYED, DR. PALMER.

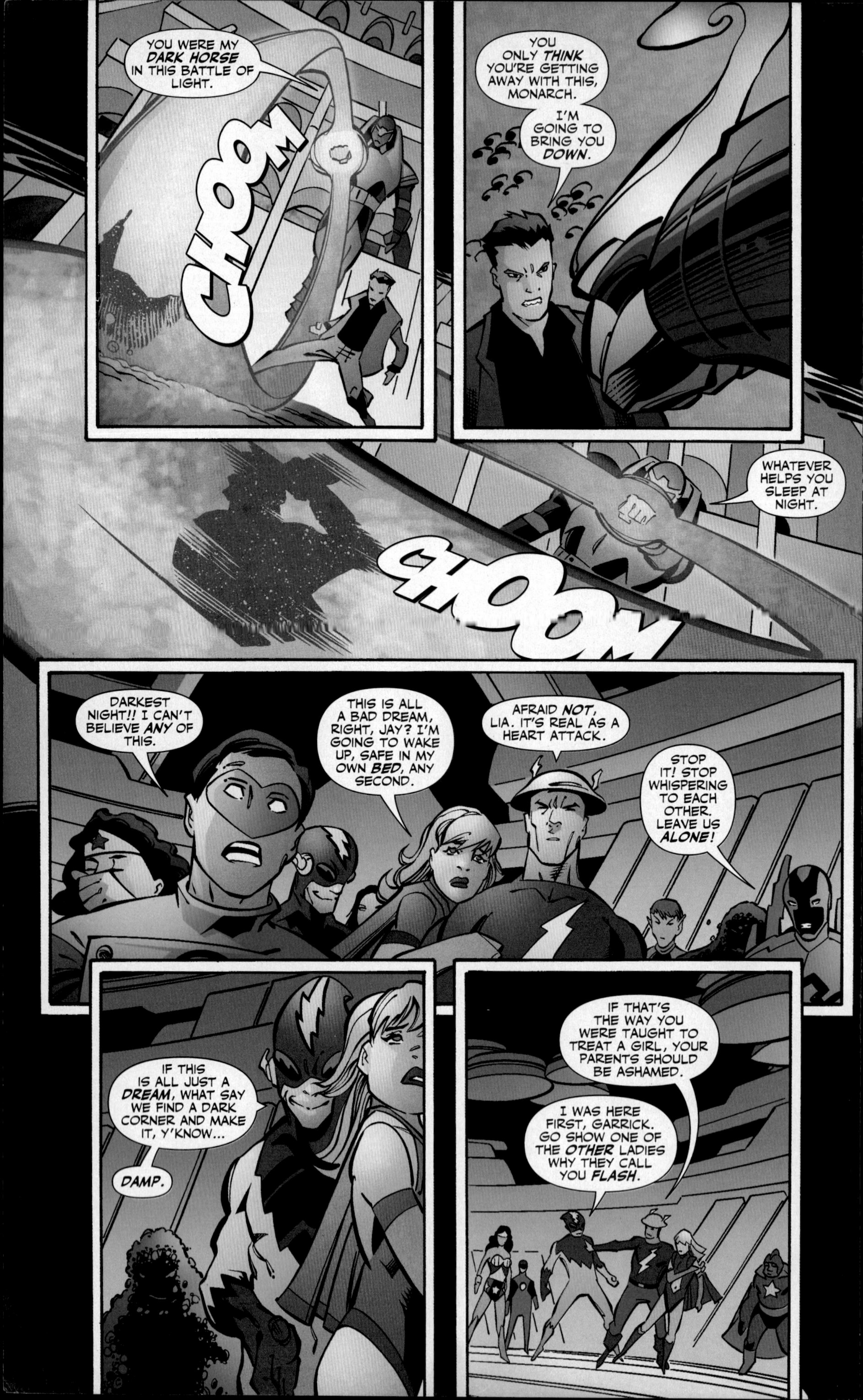
YOU WERE MY DARK HORSE IN THIS BATTLE OF LIGHT...
CHOOM
YOU ONLY THINK YOU'RE GETTING AWAY WITH THIS, MONARCH.
I'M GOING TO BRING YOU DOWN.
WHATEVER HELPS YOU SLEEP AT NIGHT.
CHOOM
DARKEST NIGHT!! I CAN'T BELIEVE ANY OF THIS.
THIS IS ALL A BAD DREAM, RIGHT, JAY? I'M GOING TO WAKE UP, SAFE IN MY OWN BED, ANY SECOND.
AFRAID NOT, LIA. IT'S REAL AS A HEART ATTACK.
STOP IT! STOP WHISPERING TO EACH OTHER. LEAVE US ALONE!
IF THIS IS ALL JUST A DREAM, WHAT SAY WE FIND A DARK CORNER AND MAKE IT, Y'KNOW...
DAMP.
IF THAT'S THE WAY YOU WERE TAUGHT TO TREAT A GIRL, YOUR PARENTS SHOULD BE ASHAMED.
I WAS HERE FIRST, GARRICK. GO SHOW ONE OF THE OTHER LADIES WHY THEY CALL YOU FLASH.

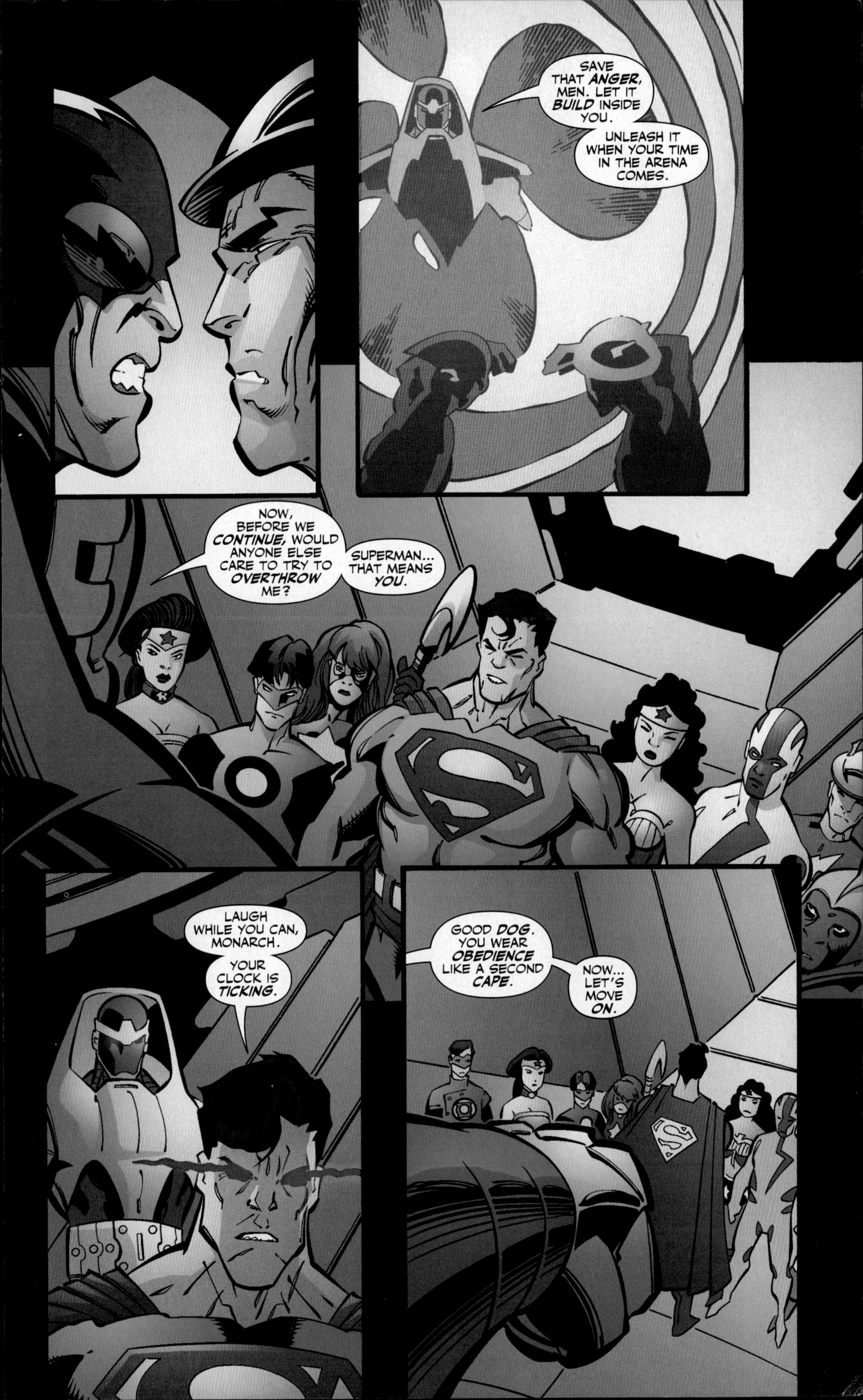
SAVE THAT ANGER, MEN. LET IT BUILD INSIDE YOU.
UNLEASH IT WHEN YOUR TIME IN THE ARENA COMES.
NOW, BEFORE WE CONTINUE, WOULD ANYONE ELSE CARE TO TRY TO OVERTHROW ME?
SUPERMAN... THAT MEANS YOU.
LAUGH WHILE YOU CAN, MONARCH.
YOUR CLOCK IS TICKING.
GOOD DOG. YOU WEAR OBEDIENCE LIKE A SECOND CAPE.
NOW... LET'S MOVE ON.

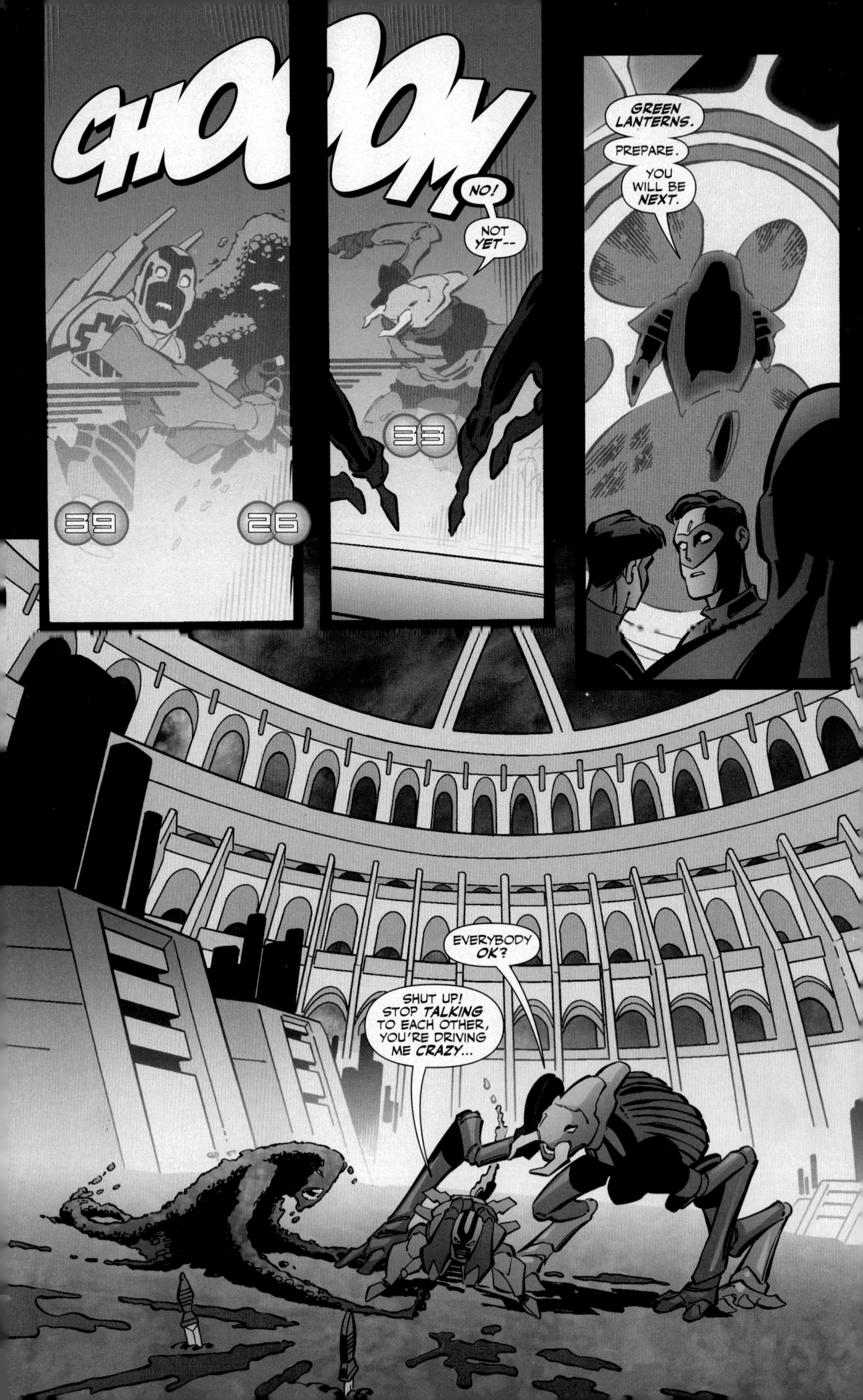
CHOOOOM
39
26
NO!
NOT YET--
33
GREEN LANTERNS.
PREPARE.
YOU WILL BE NEXT.
EVERYBODY OK?
SHUT UP! STOP TALKING TO EACH OTHER, YOU'RE DRIVING ME CRAZY...

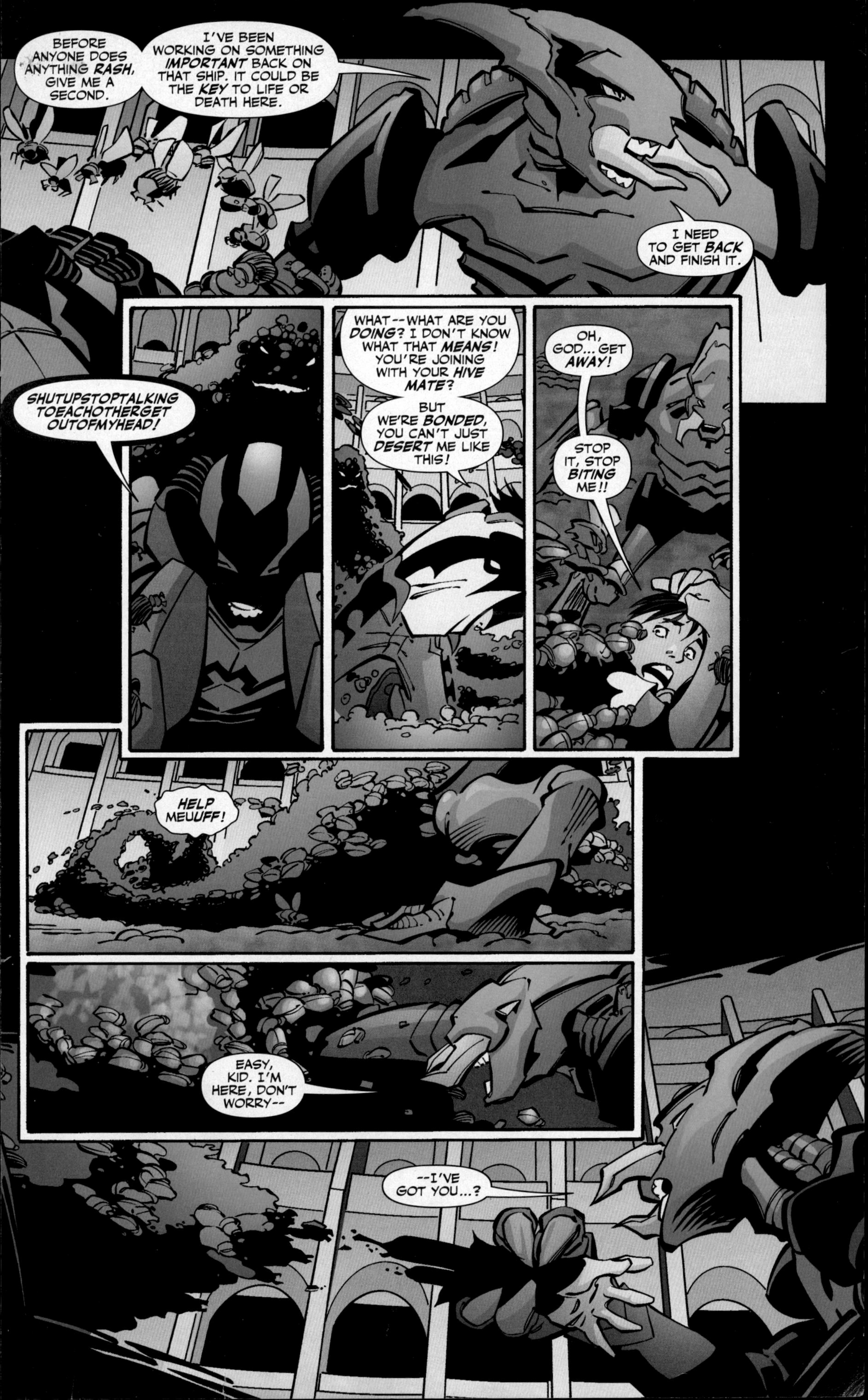
BEFORE ANYONE DOES ANYTHING RASH, GIVE ME A SECOND.
I'VE BEEN WORKING ON SOMETHING IMPORTANT BACK ON THAT SHIP. IT COULD BE THE KEY TO LIFE OR DEATH HERE.
I NEED TO GET BACK AND FINISH IT.
SHUTUPSTOPTALKING TOEACHOTHERGET OUTOFMYHEAD!
WHAT--WHAT ARE YOU DOING? I DON'T KNOW WHAT THAT MEANS! YOU'RE JOINING WITH YOUR HIVE MATE?
BUT WE'RE BONDED, YOU CAN'T JUST DESERT ME LIKE THIS!
OH, GOD... GET AWAY!
STOP IT, STOP BITING ME!!
HELP MEUUFF!
EASY, KID. I'M HERE, DON'T WORRY--
--I'VE GOT YOU...?

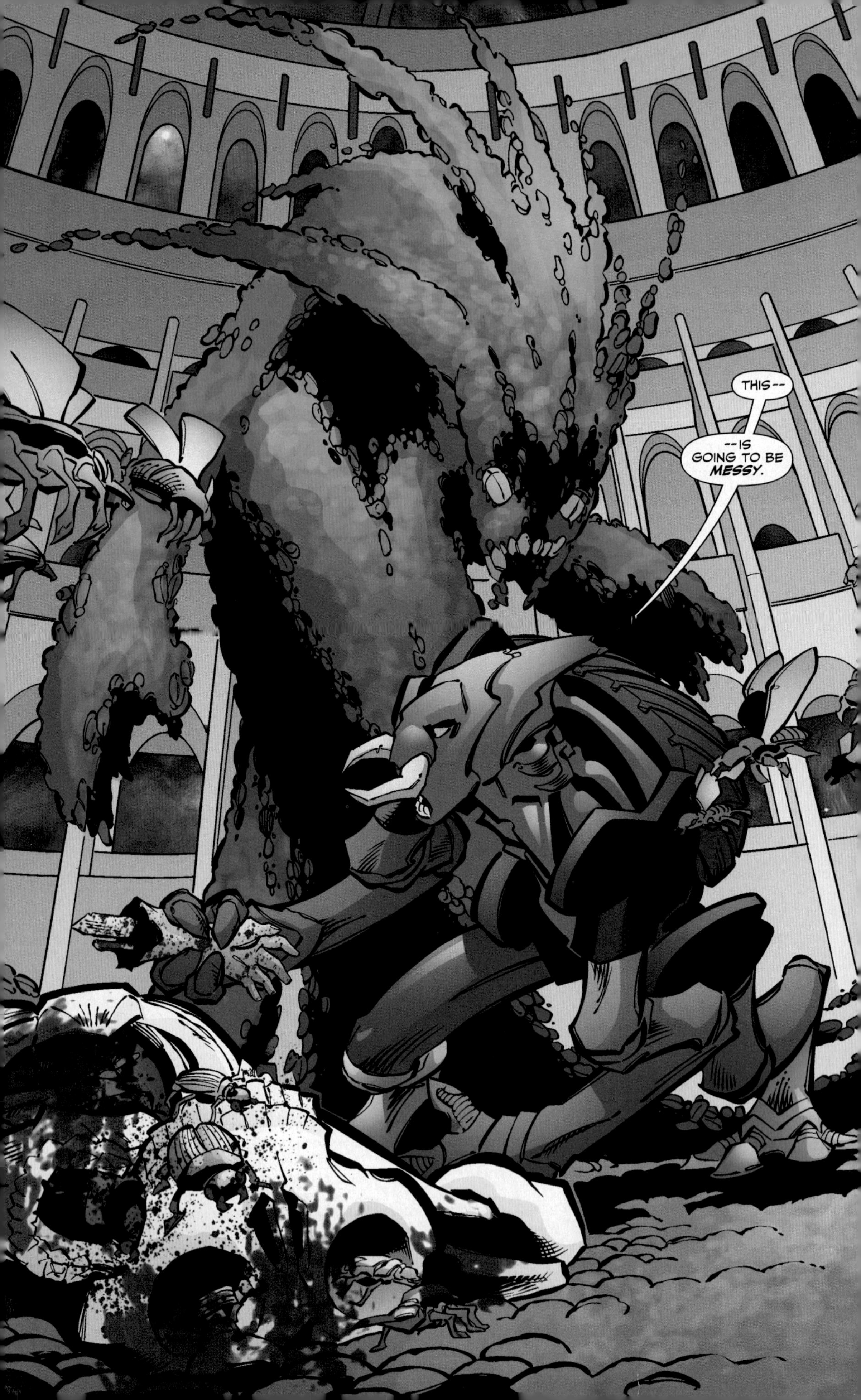
THIS--
--IS GOING TO BE *MESSY*.

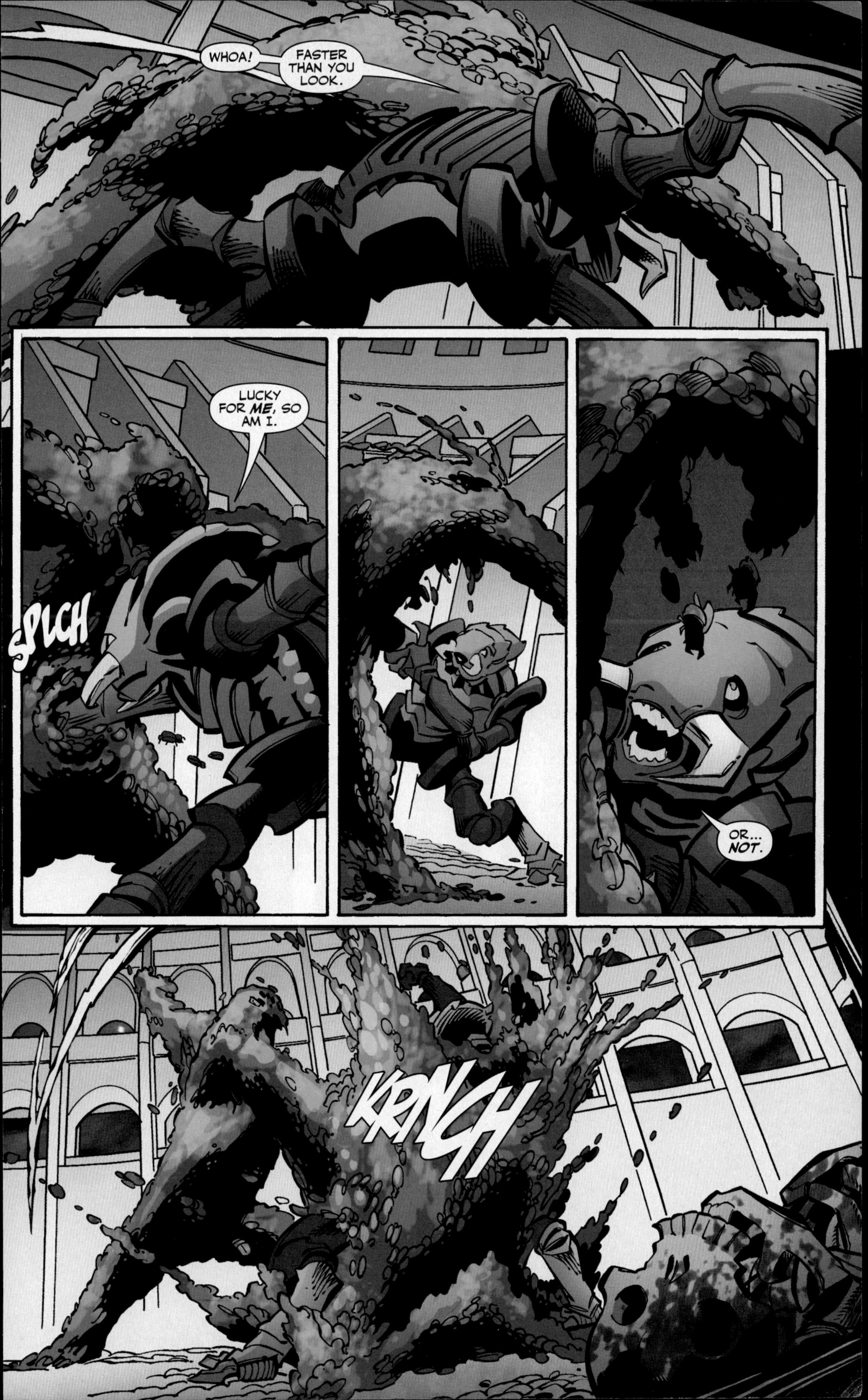
WHOA!
FASTER THAN YOU LOOK.
LUCKY FOR ME, SO AM I.
SPLCH
OR... NOT.
KRNCH

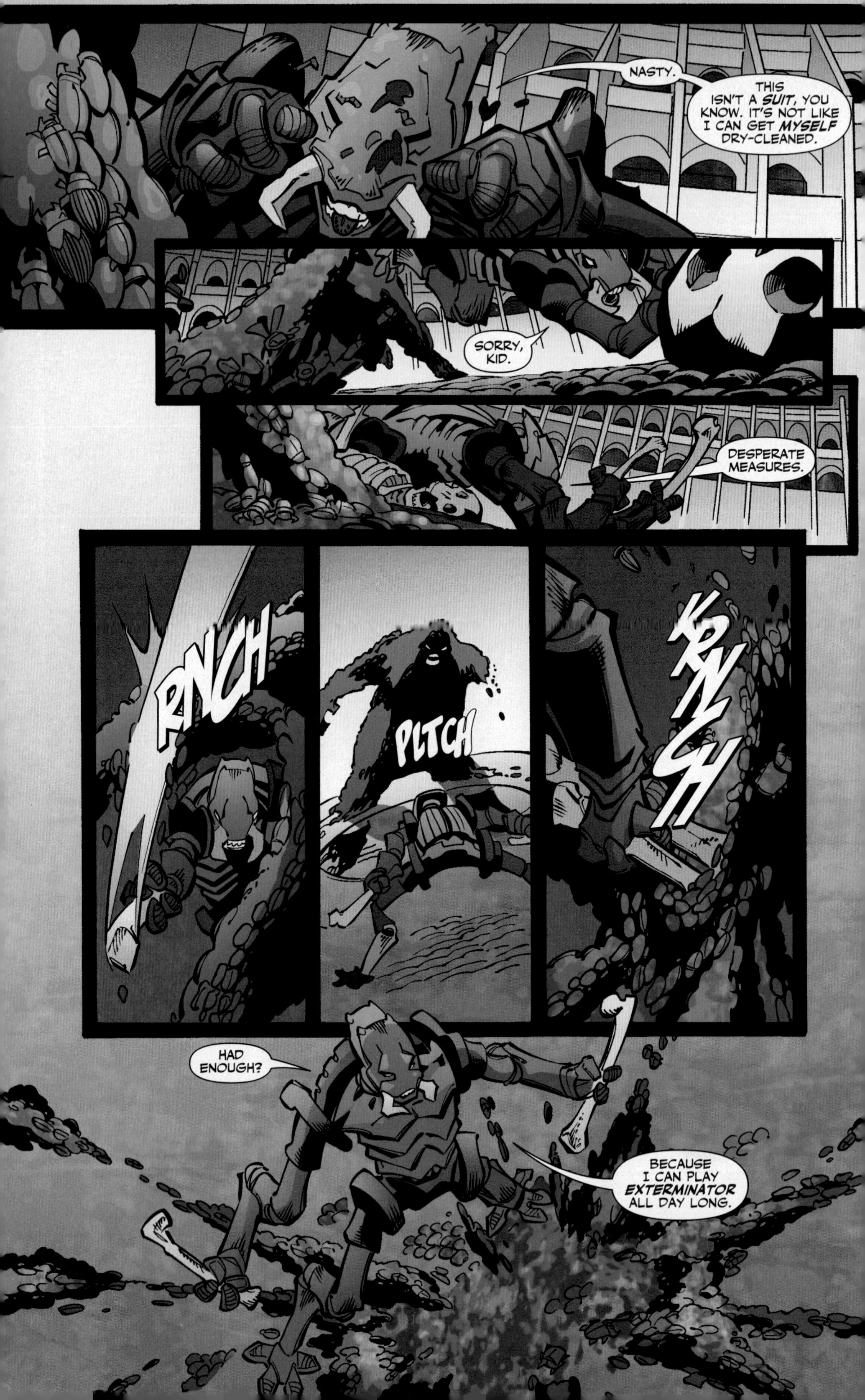
NASTY.
THIS ISN'T A SUIT, YOU KNOW. IT'S NOT LIKE I CAN GET MYSELF DRY-CLEANED.
SORRY, KID.
DESPERATE MEASURES.
RNCH
PLTCH
KRNCH
HAD ENOUGH?
BECAUSE I CAN PLAY EXTERMINATOR ALL DAY LONG.

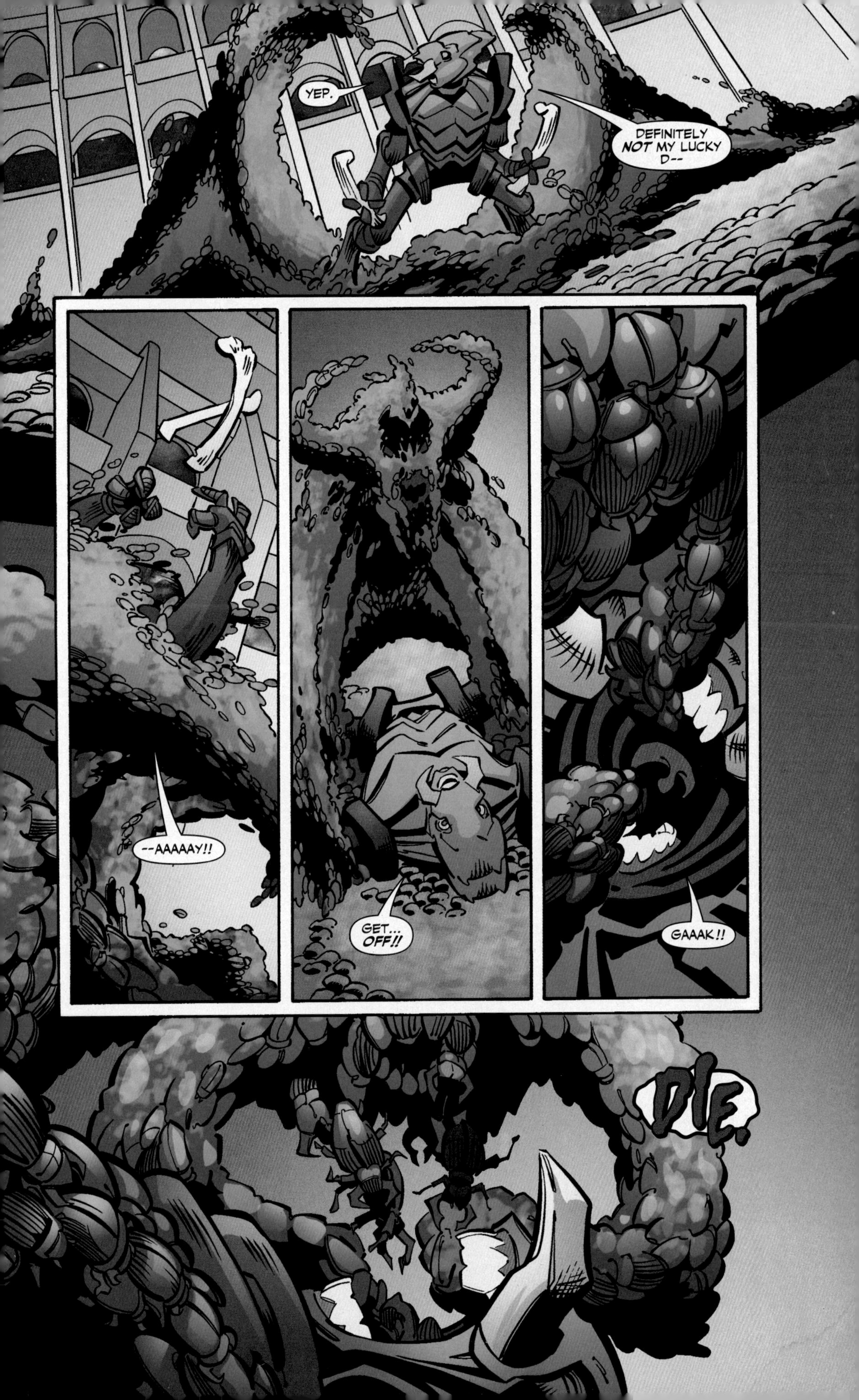
YEP.
DEFINITELY NOT MY LUCKY D--
--AAAAAY!!
GET... OFF!!
GAAAK!!
DIE.

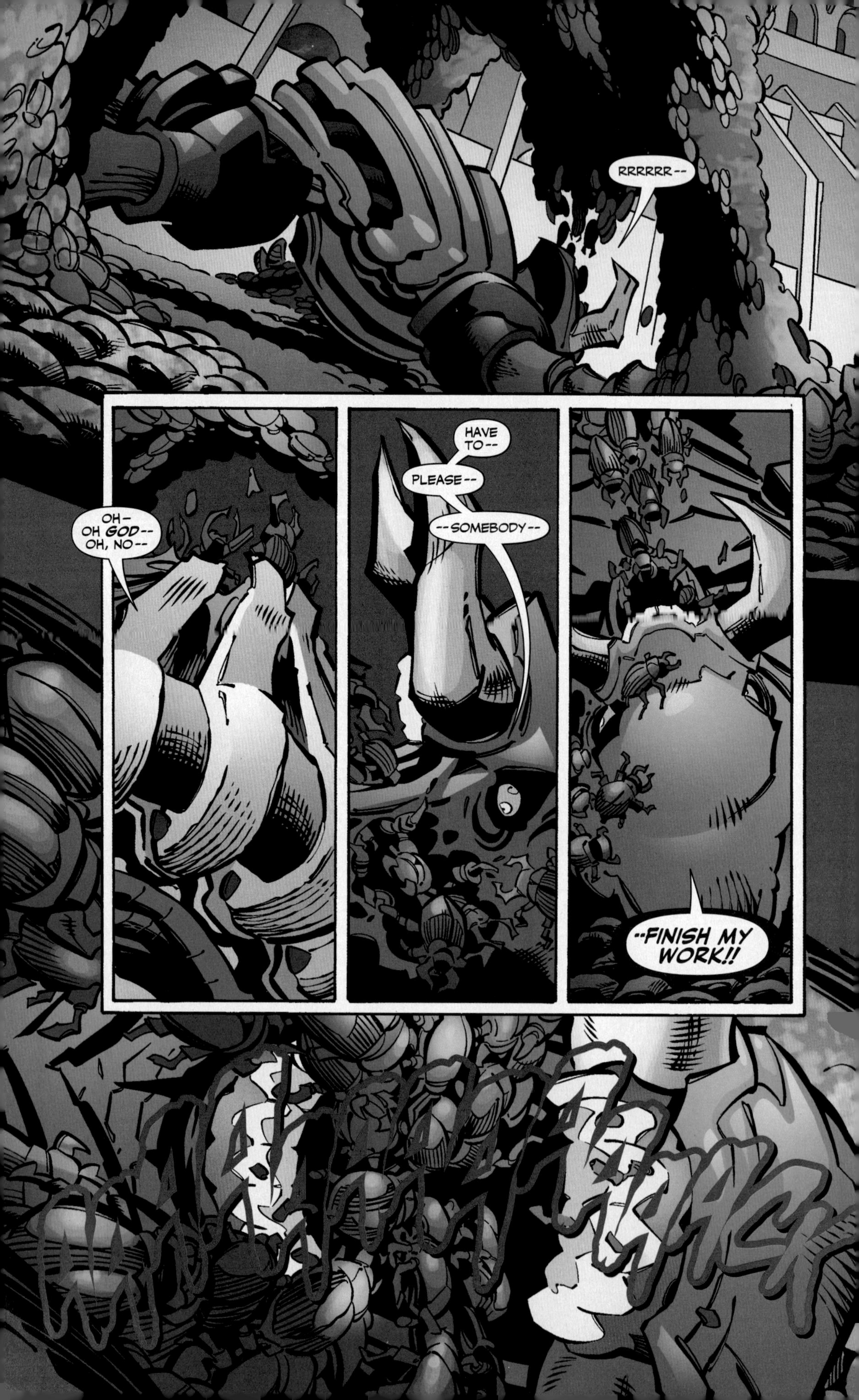

RRRRRR--
OH--
OH GOD--
OH, NO--
HAVE TO--
PLEASE--
--SOMEBODY--
--FINISH MY WORK!!

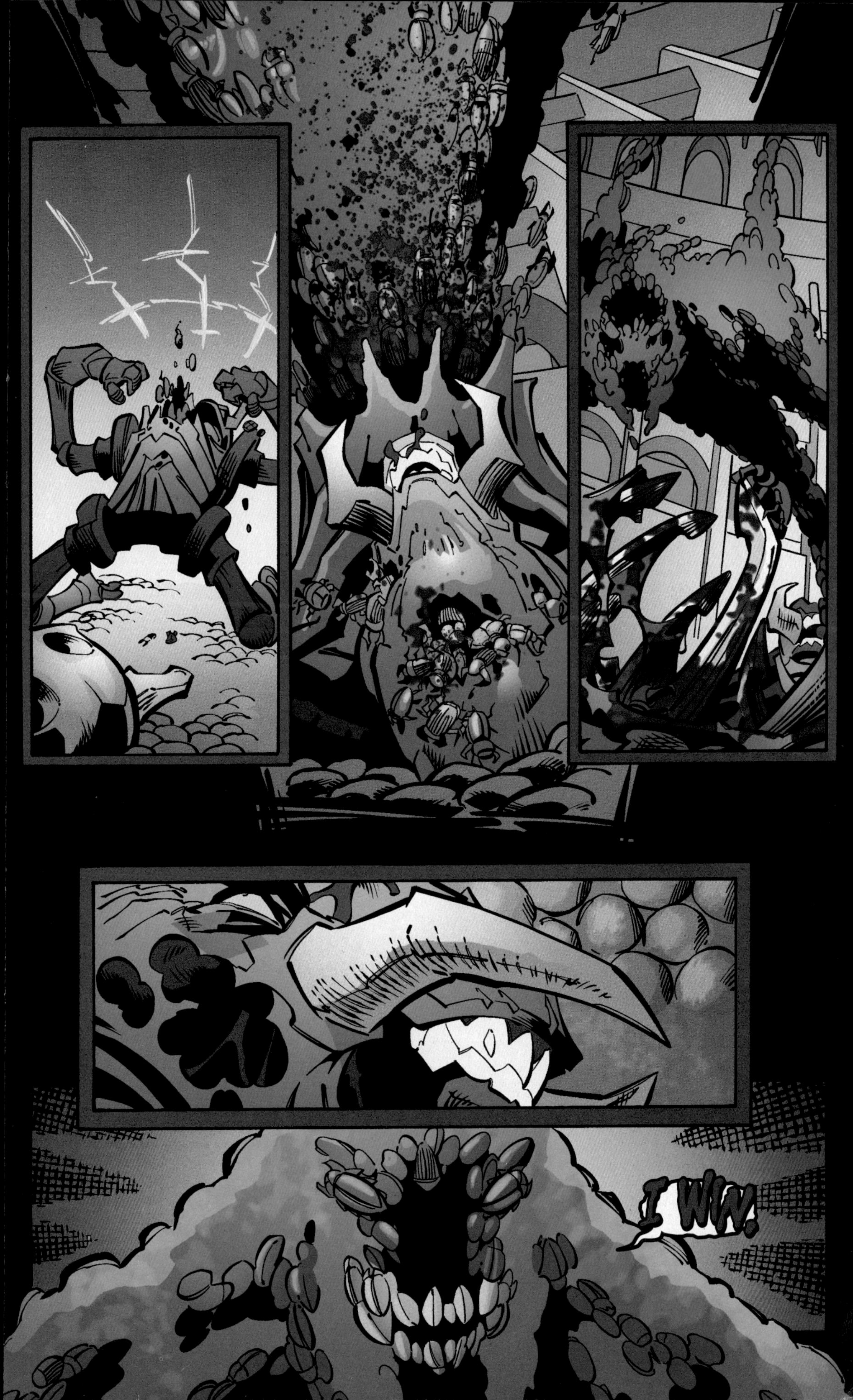
I WIN!

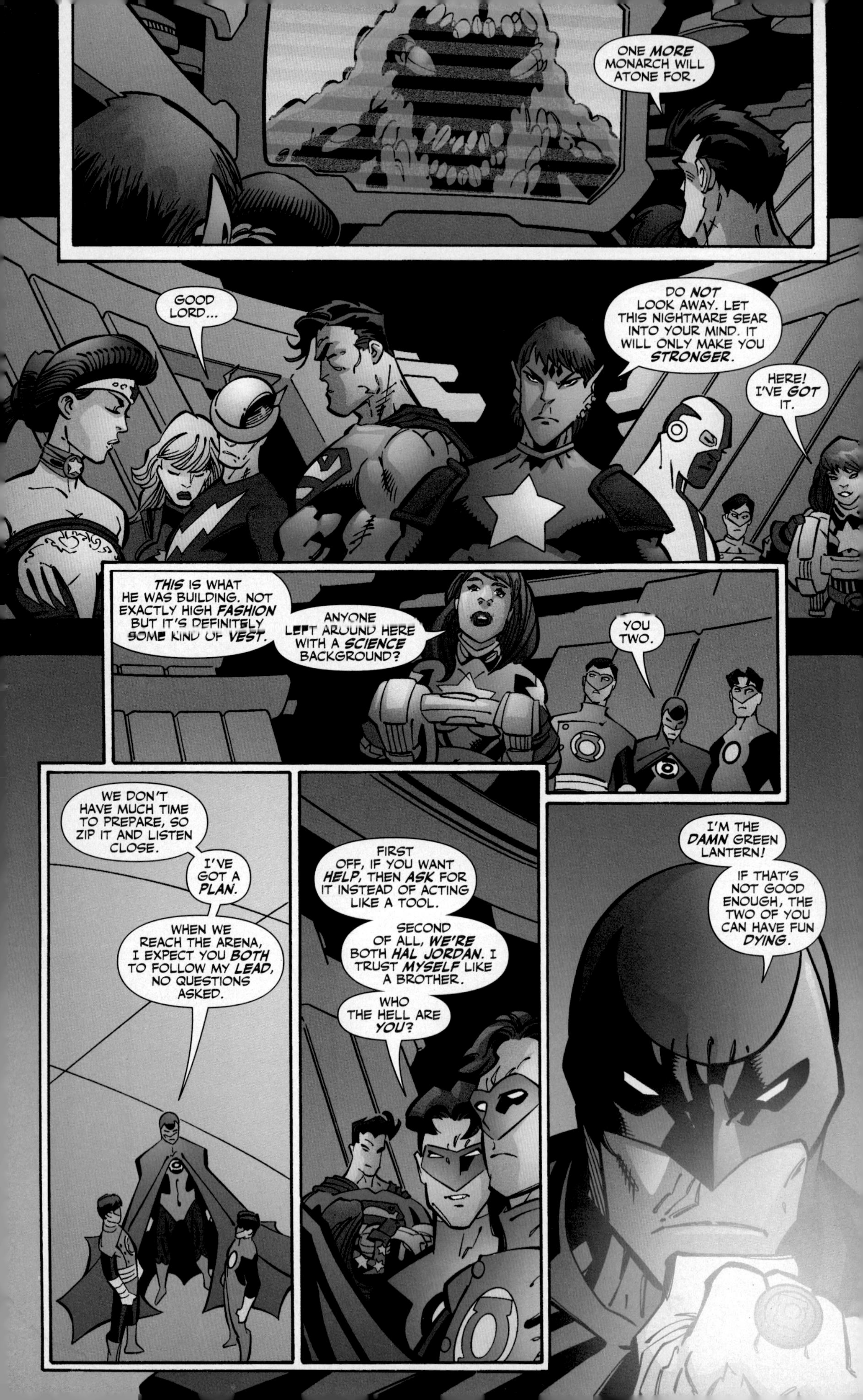
ONE MORE MONARCH WILL ATONE FOR.
GOOD LORD...
DO NOT LOOK AWAY. LET THIS NIGHTMARE SEAR INTO YOUR MIND. IT WILL ONLY MAKE YOU STRONGER.
HERE! I'VE GOT IT.
THIS IS WHAT HE WAS BUILDING. NOT EXACTLY HIGH FASHION BUT IT'S DEFINITELY SOME KIND OF VEST.
ANYONE LEFT AROUND HERE WITH A SCIENCE BACKGROUND?
YOU TWO.
WE DON'T HAVE MUCH TIME TO PREPARE, SO ZIP IT AND LISTEN CLOSE.
I'VE GOT A PLAN.
WHEN WE REACH THE ARENA, I EXPECT YOU BOTH TO FOLLOW MY LEAD, NO QUESTIONS ASKED.
FIRST OFF, IF YOU WANT HELP, THEN ASK FOR IT INSTEAD OF ACTING LIKE A TOOL.
SECOND OF ALL, WE'RE BOTH HAL JORDAN. I TRUST MYSELF LIKE A BROTHER.
WHO THE HELL ARE YOU?
I'M THE DAMN GREEN LANTERN!
IF THAT'S NOT GOOD ENOUGH, THE TWO OF YOU CAN HAVE FUN DYING.

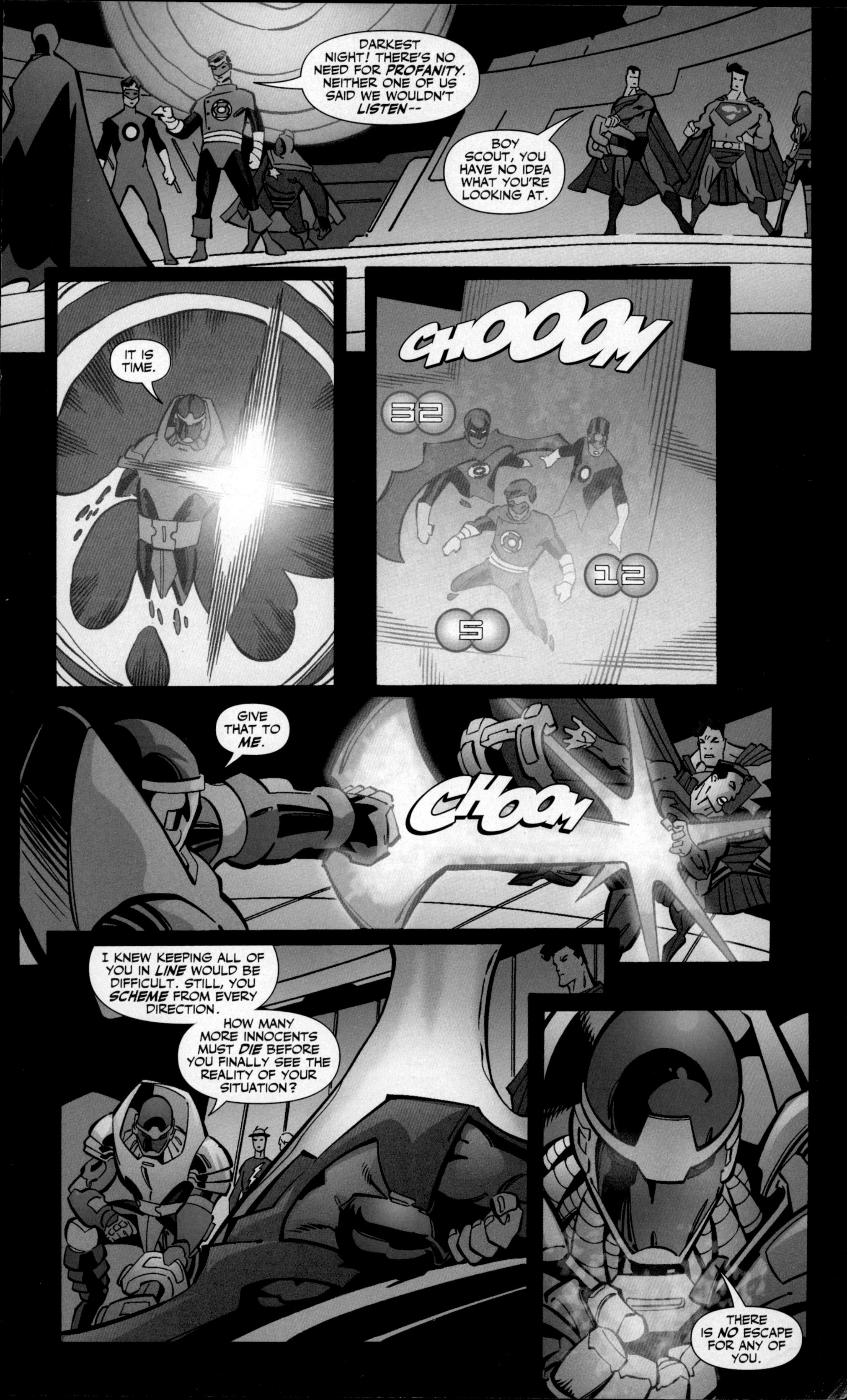
DARKEST NIGHT! THERE'S NO NEED FOR *PROFANITY*. NEITHER ONE OF US SAID WE WOULDN'T *LISTEN*--
BOY SCOUT, YOU HAVE NO IDEA WHAT YOU'RE LOOKING AT.
IT IS TIME.
CHOOOOM
32
12
5
GIVE THAT TO *ME*.
CHOOM
I KNEW KEEPING ALL OF YOU IN *LINE* WOULD BE DIFFICULT. STILL, YOU *SCHEME* FROM EVERY DIRECTION.
HOW MANY MORE INNOCENTS MUST *DIE* BEFORE YOU FINALLY SEE THE REALITY OF YOUR SITUATION?
THERE IS *NO* ESCAPE FOR ANY OF YOU.

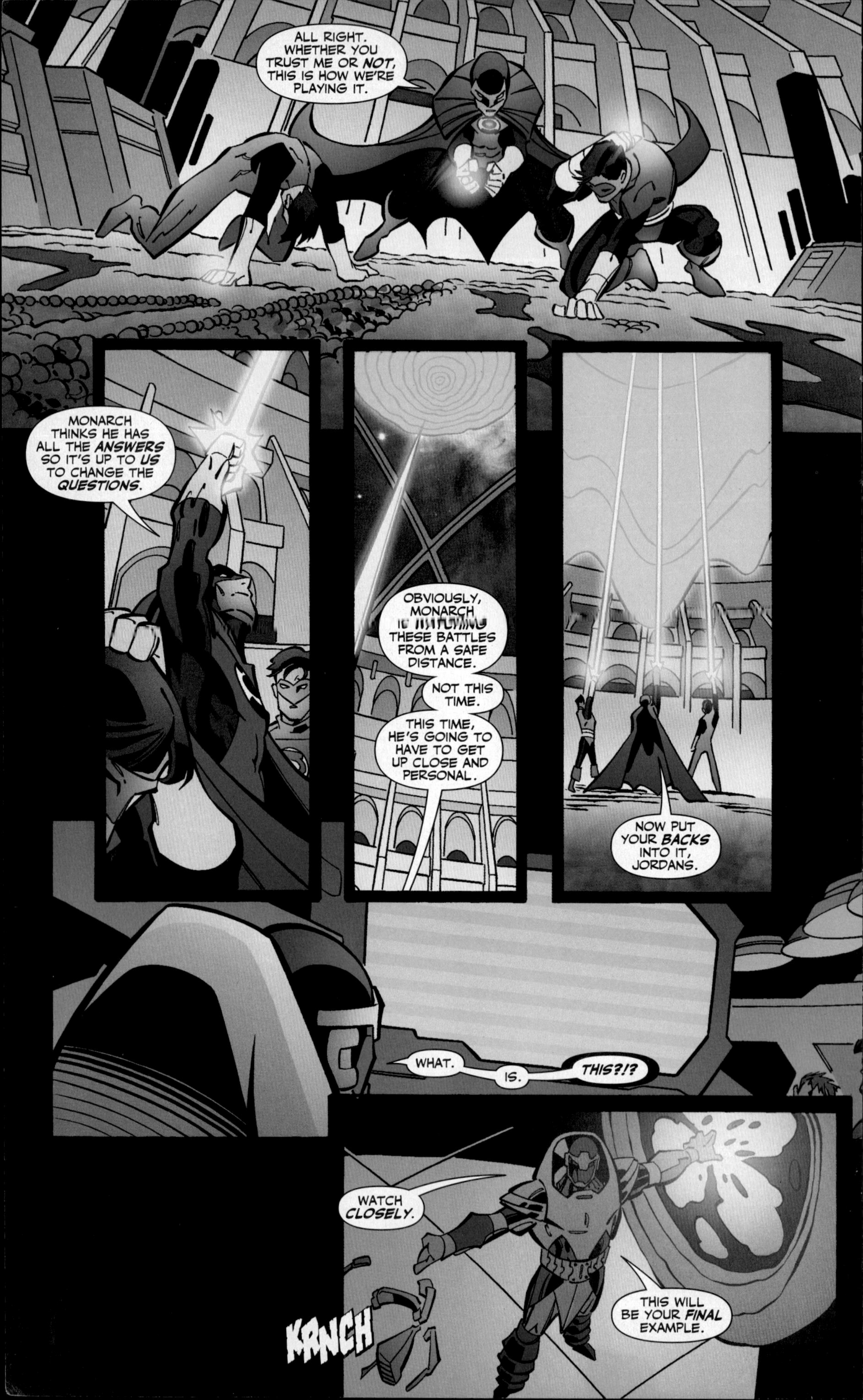

ALL RIGHT. WHETHER YOU TRUST ME OR *NOT*, THIS IS HOW WE'RE PLAYING IT.
MONARCH THINKS HE HAS ALL THE *ANSWERS* SO IT'S UP TO *US* TO CHANGE THE *QUESTIONS*.
OBVIOUSLY, MONARCH THESE BATTLES FROM A SAFE DISTANCE.
NOT THIS TIME.
THIS TIME, HE'S GOING TO HAVE TO GET UP CLOSE AND PERSONAL.
NOW PUT YOUR *BACKS* INTO IT, JORDANS.
WHAT.
IS.
THIS?!?
WATCH *CLOSELY*.
THIS WILL BE YOUR *FINAL* EXAMPLE.
KRNCH

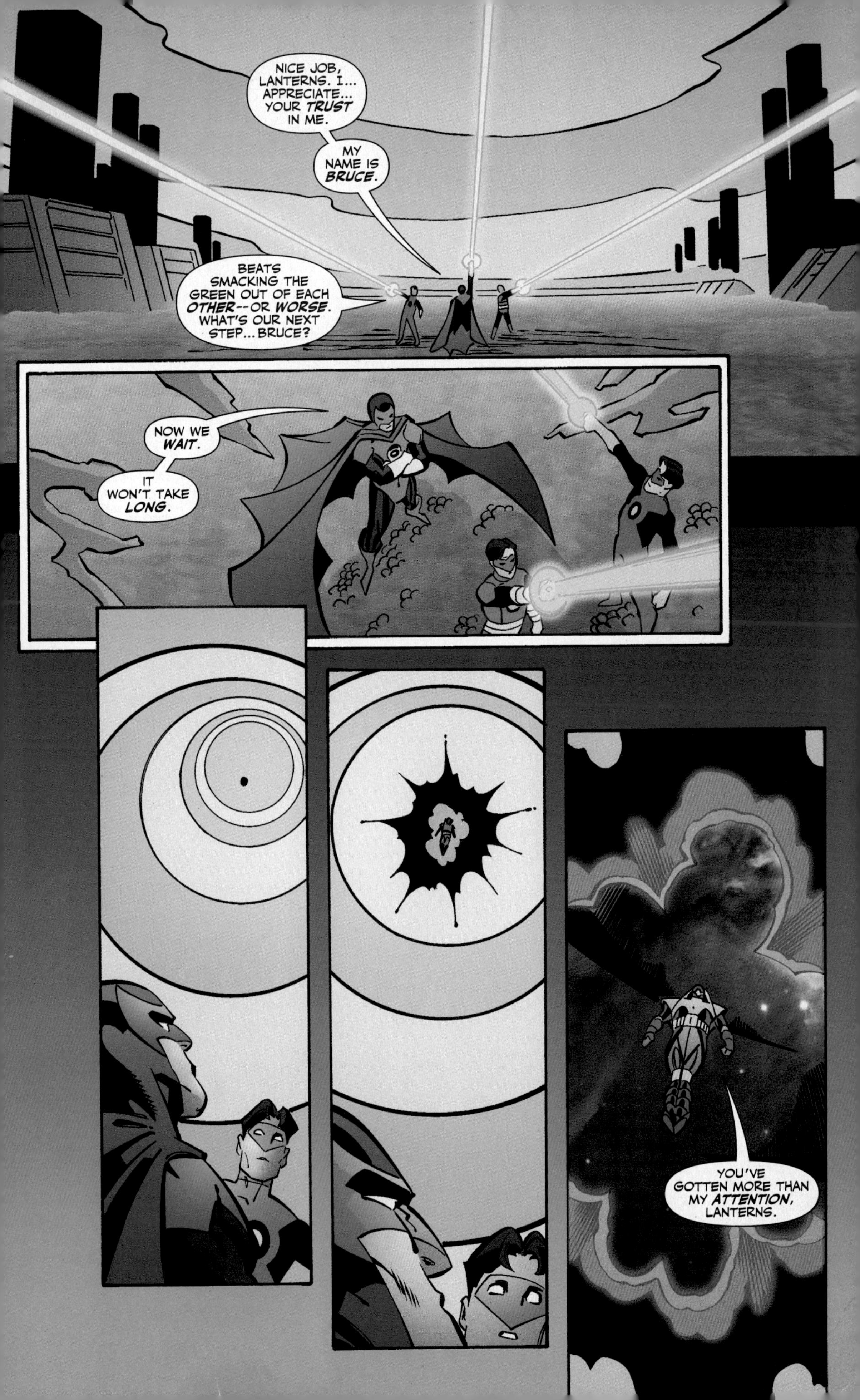
NICE JOB, LANTERNS. I... APPRECIATE... YOUR TRUST IN ME.
MY NAME IS BRUCE.
BEATS SMACKING THE GREEN OUT OF EACH OTHER--OR WORSE. WHAT'S OUR NEXT STEP...BRUCE?
NOW WE WAIT.
IT WON'T TAKE LONG.
YOU'VE GOTTEN MORE THAN MY ATTENTION, LANTERNS.

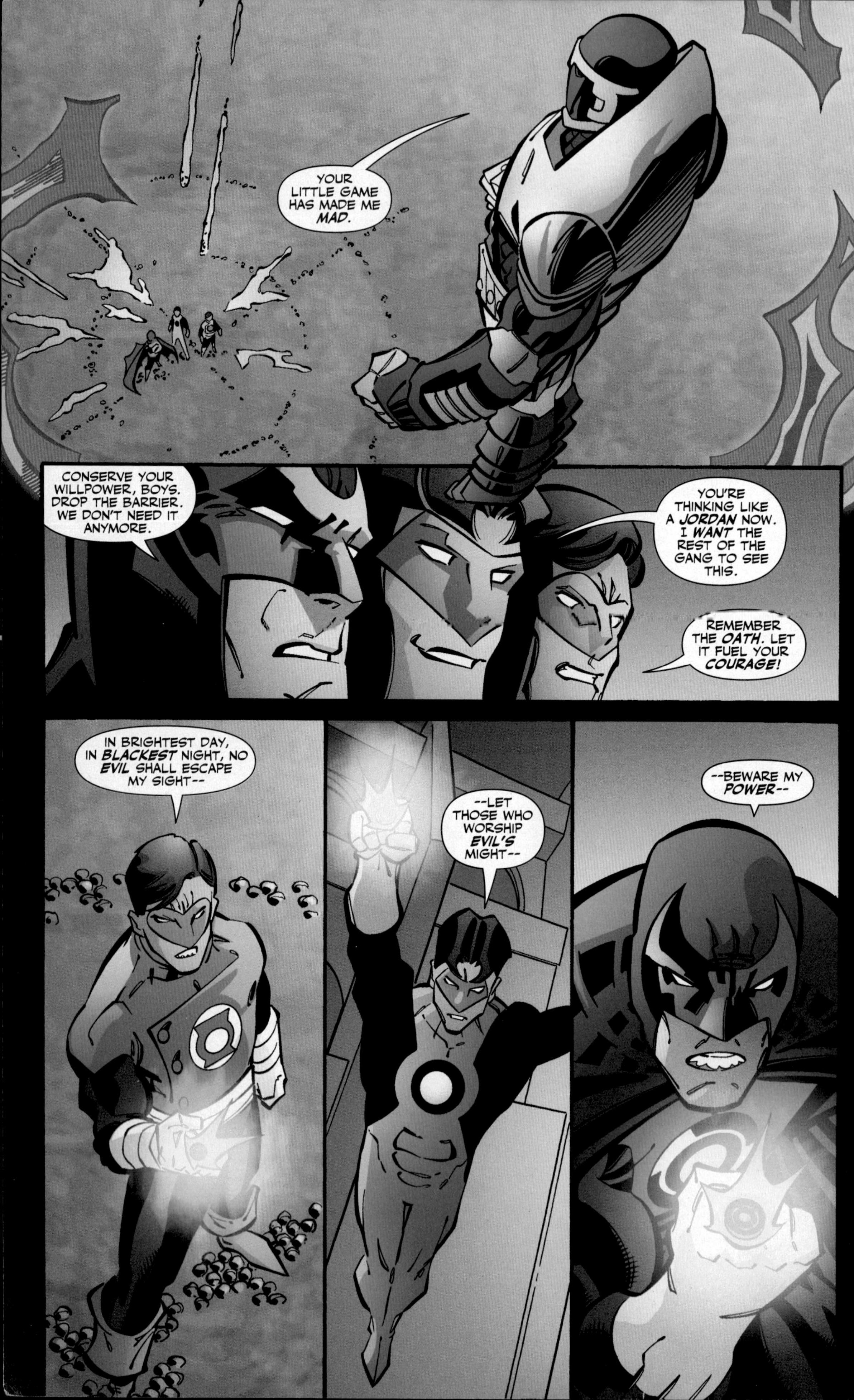
YOUR LITTLE GAME HAS MADE ME MAD.
CONSERVE YOUR WILLPOWER, BOYS. DROP THE BARRIER. WE DON'T NEED IT ANYMORE.
YOU'RE THINKING LIKE A JORDAN NOW. I WANT THE REST OF THE GANG TO SEE THIS.
REMEMBER THE OATH. LET IT FUEL YOUR COURAGE!
IN BRIGHTEST DAY, IN BLACKEST NIGHT, NO EVIL SHALL ESCAPE MY SIGHT--
--LET THOSE WHO WORSHIP EVIL'S MIGHT--
--BEWARE MY POWER--

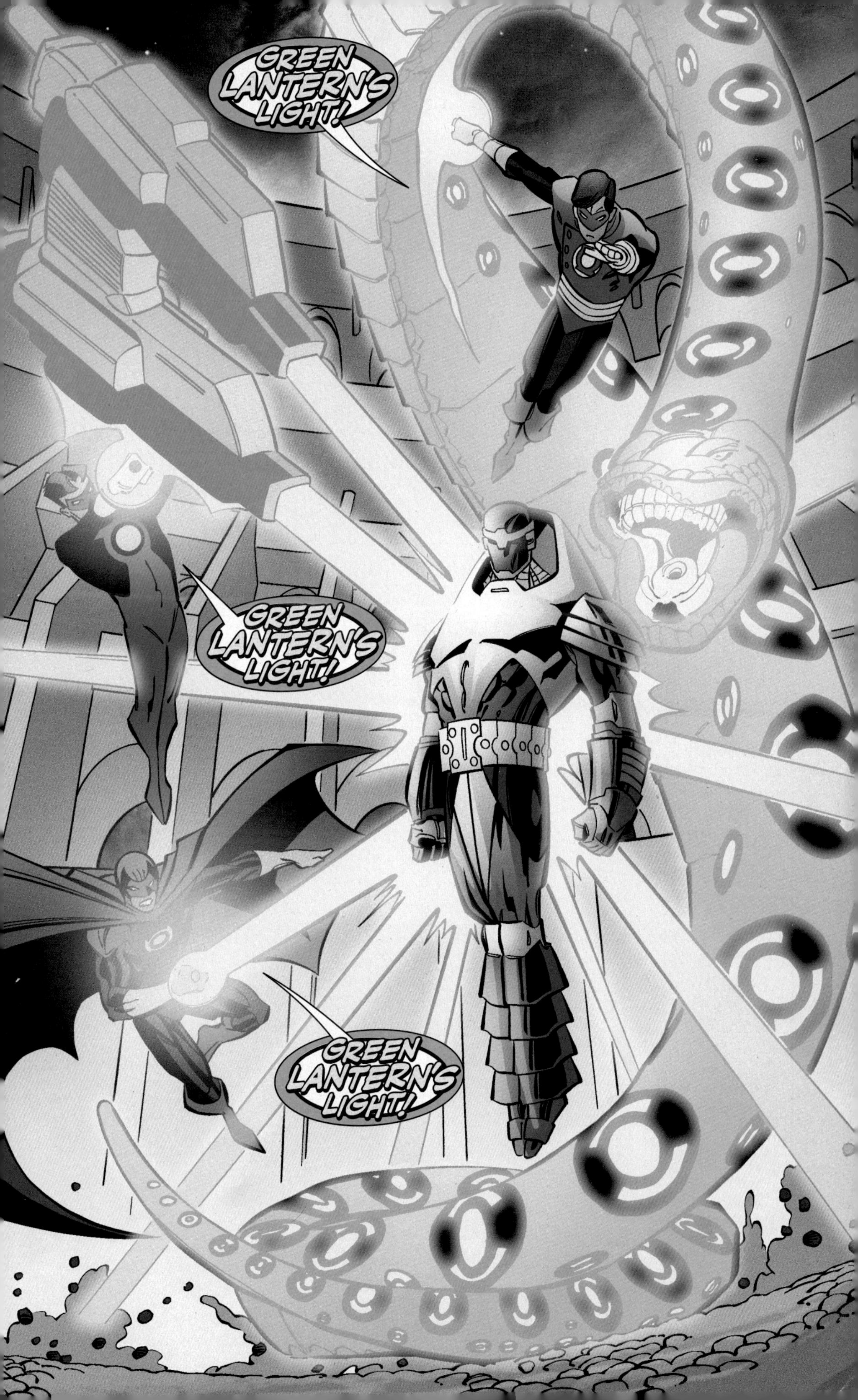
GREEN LANTERN'S LIGHT!
GREEN LANTERN'S LIGHT!
GREEN LANTERN'S LIGHT!

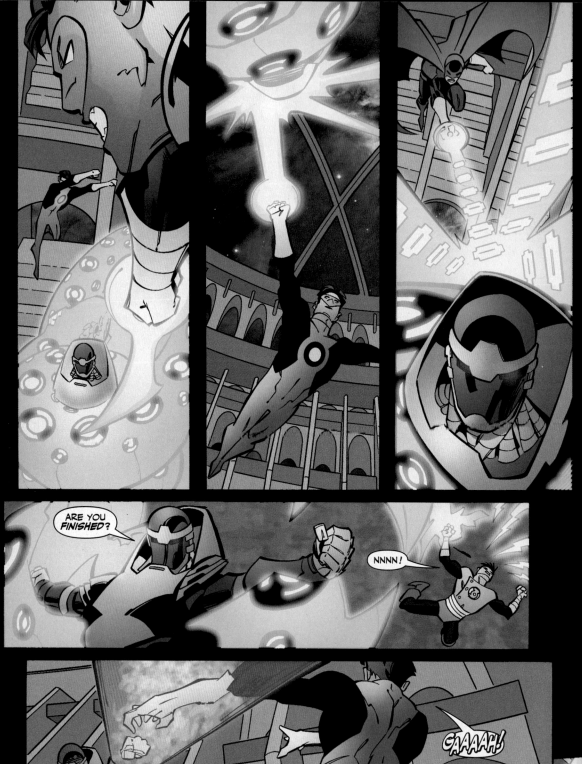

ARE YOU
FINISHED?

NNNN!

GAAAAH!

...MY
ARM...IT'S
GONE...

SUCK IT
UP AND FOCUS
YOUR WILL. USE
YOUR RING TO
MAKE ANOTHER
ONE.

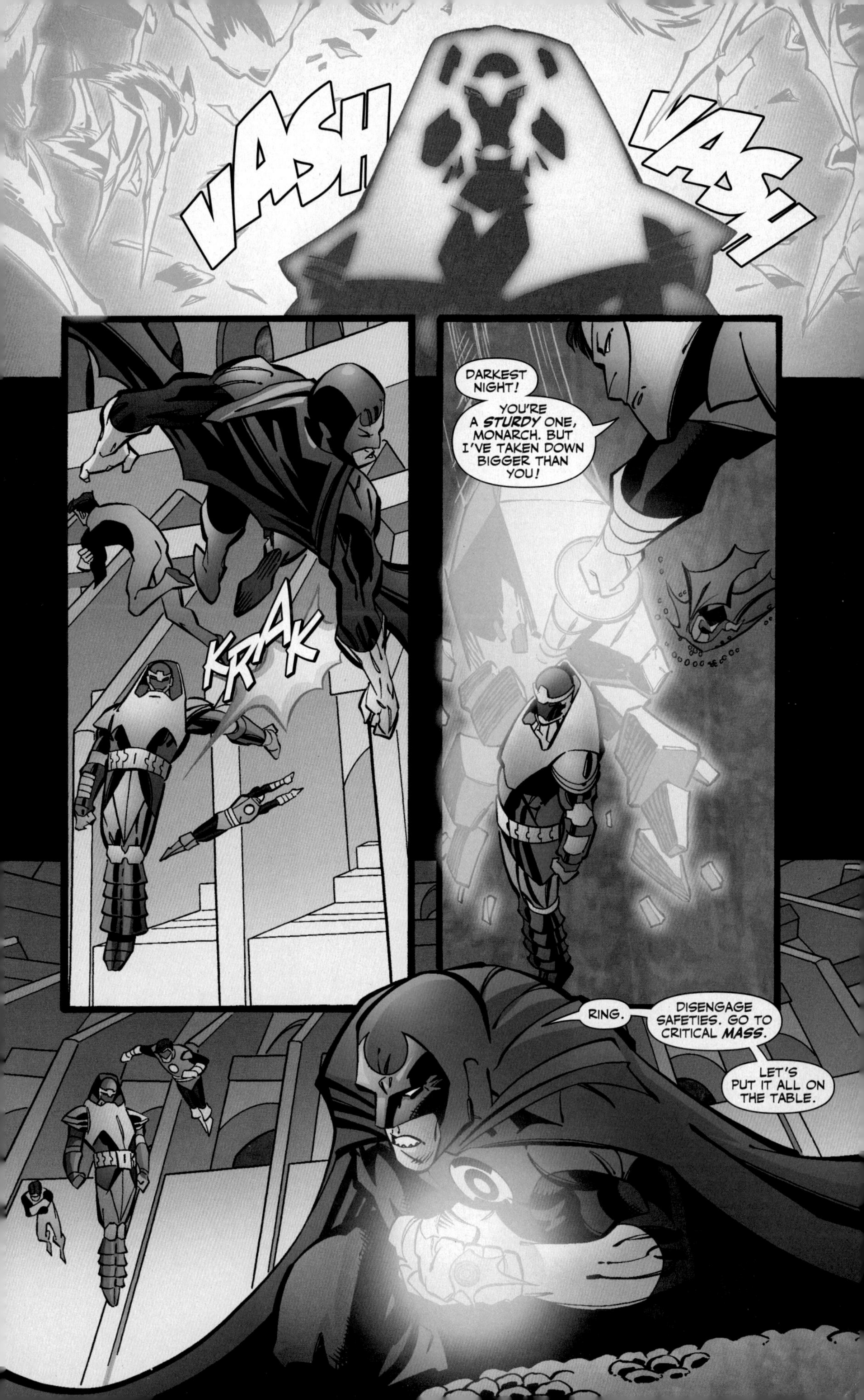
VASH VASH
KRAK
DARKEST NIGHT!
YOU'RE A **STURDY** ONE, MONARCH. BUT I'VE TAKEN DOWN BIGGER THAN YOU!
RING.
DISENGAGE SAFETIES. GO TO CRITICAL **MASS**.
LET'S PUT IT ALL ON THE TABLE.

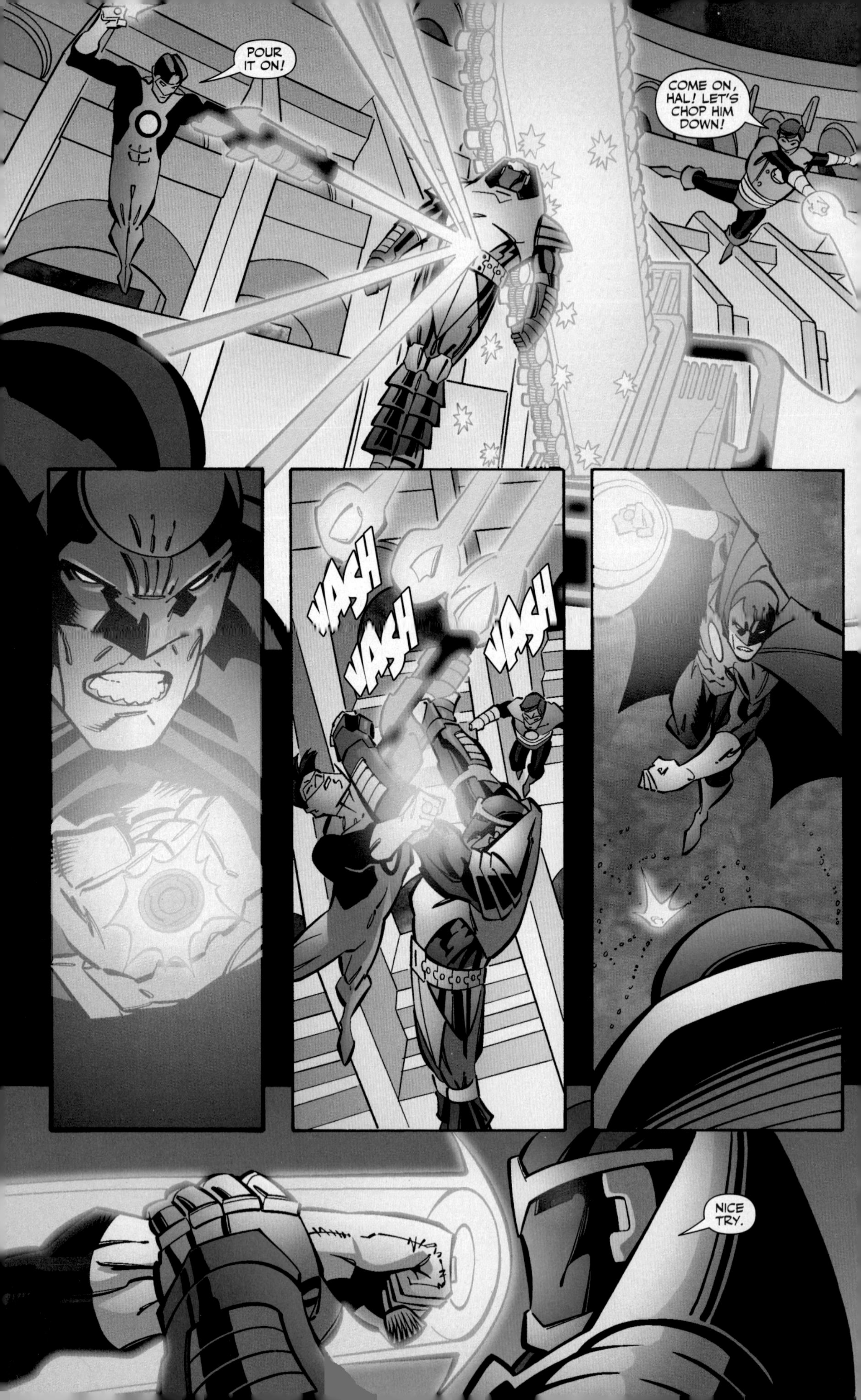

POUR IT ON!
COME ON, HAL! LET'S CHOP HIM DOWN!
VASH
VASH
VASH
NICE TRY.

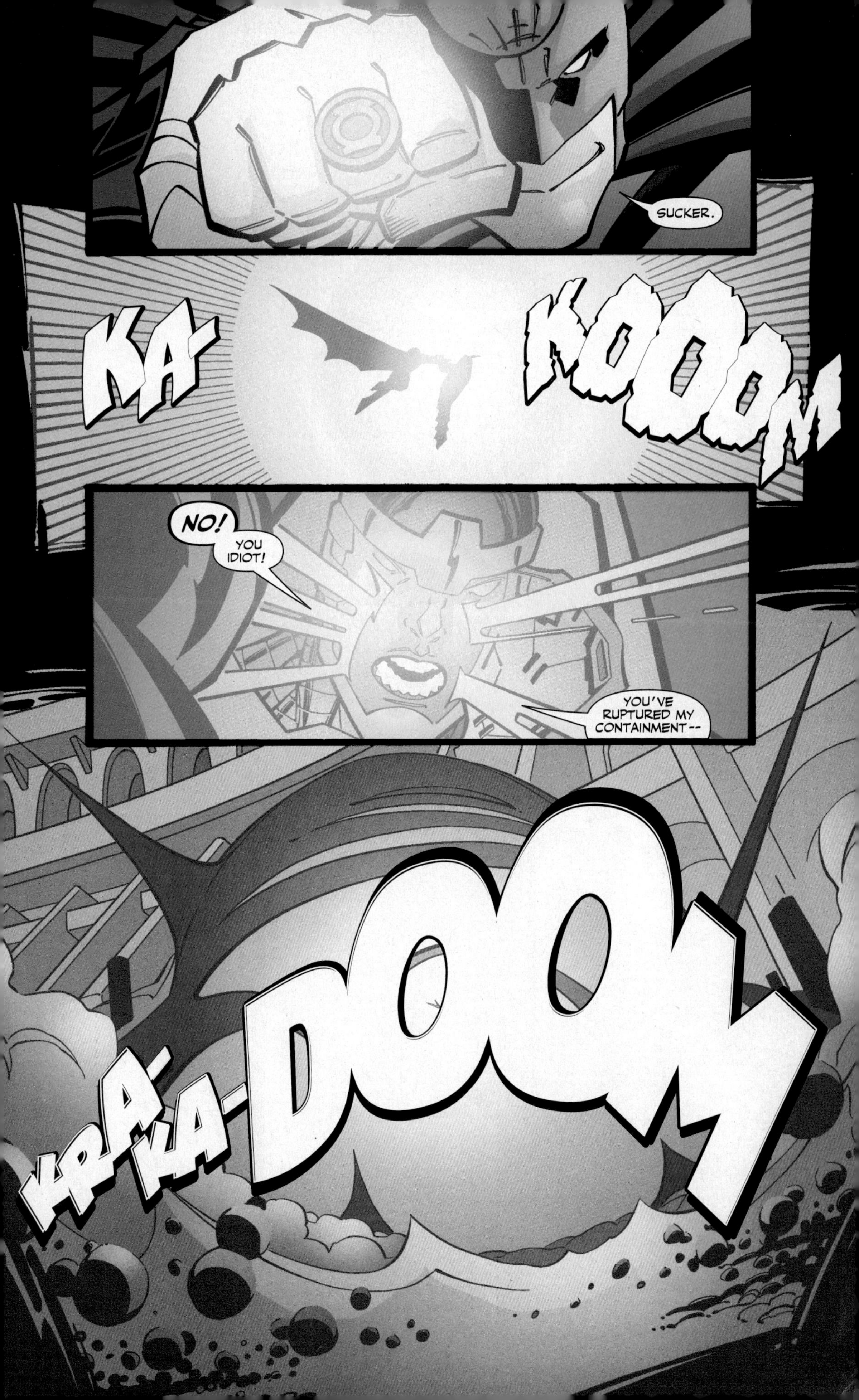
SUCKER.
KA-KOOOM
NO! YOU IDIOT!
YOU'VE RUPTURED MY CONTAINMENT--
KRA-KA-DOOM

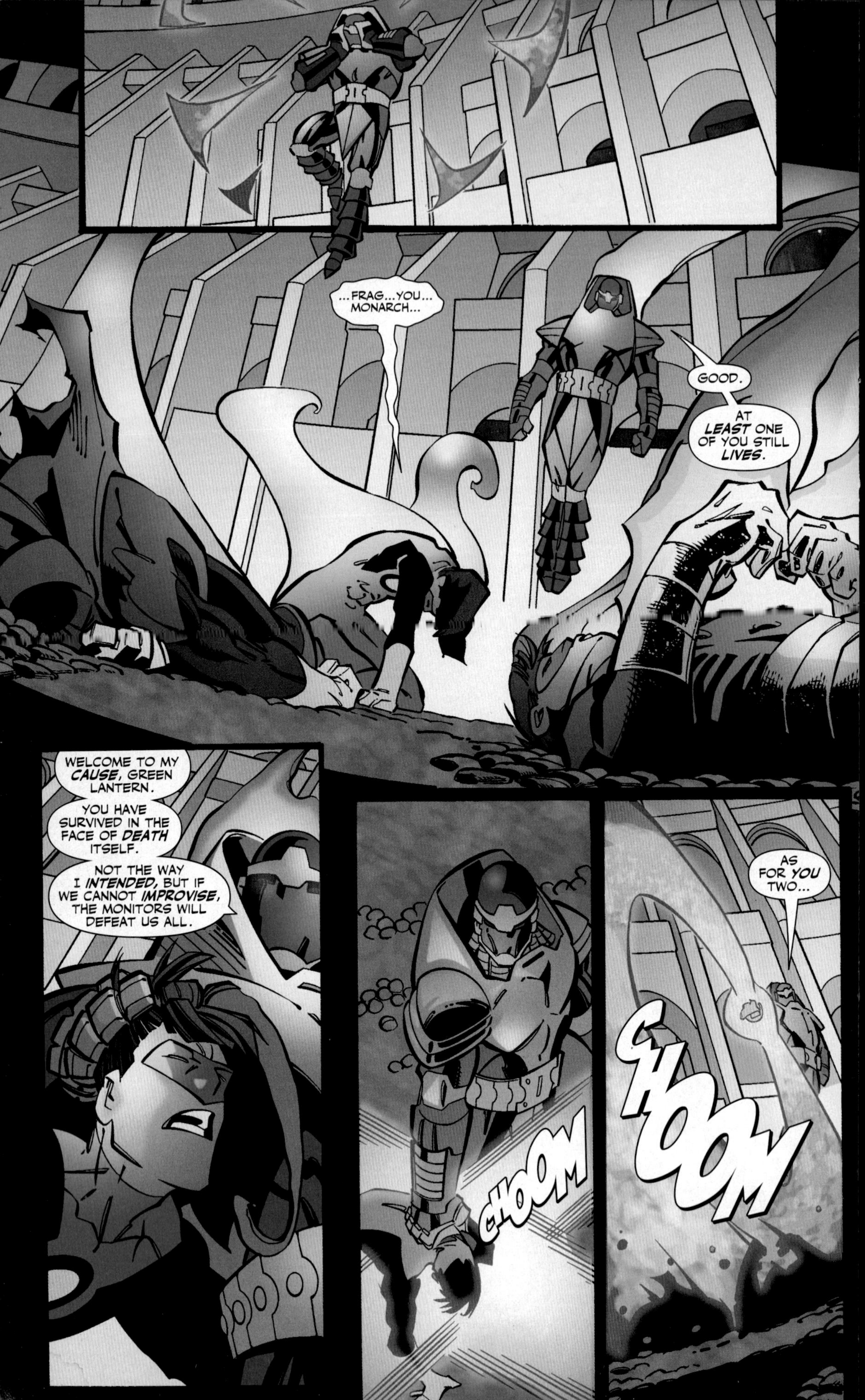
...FRAG...YOU... MONARCH...
GOOD.
AT *LEAST* ONE OF YOU STILL *LIVES*.
WELCOME TO MY *CAUSE*, GREEN LANTERN.
YOU HAVE SURVIVED IN THE FACE OF *DEATH* ITSELF.
NOT THE WAY I *INTENDED*, BUT IF WE CANNOT *IMPROVISE*, THE MONITORS WILL DEFEAT US ALL.
CHOOM
AS FOR *YOU* TWO...
CHOOOM

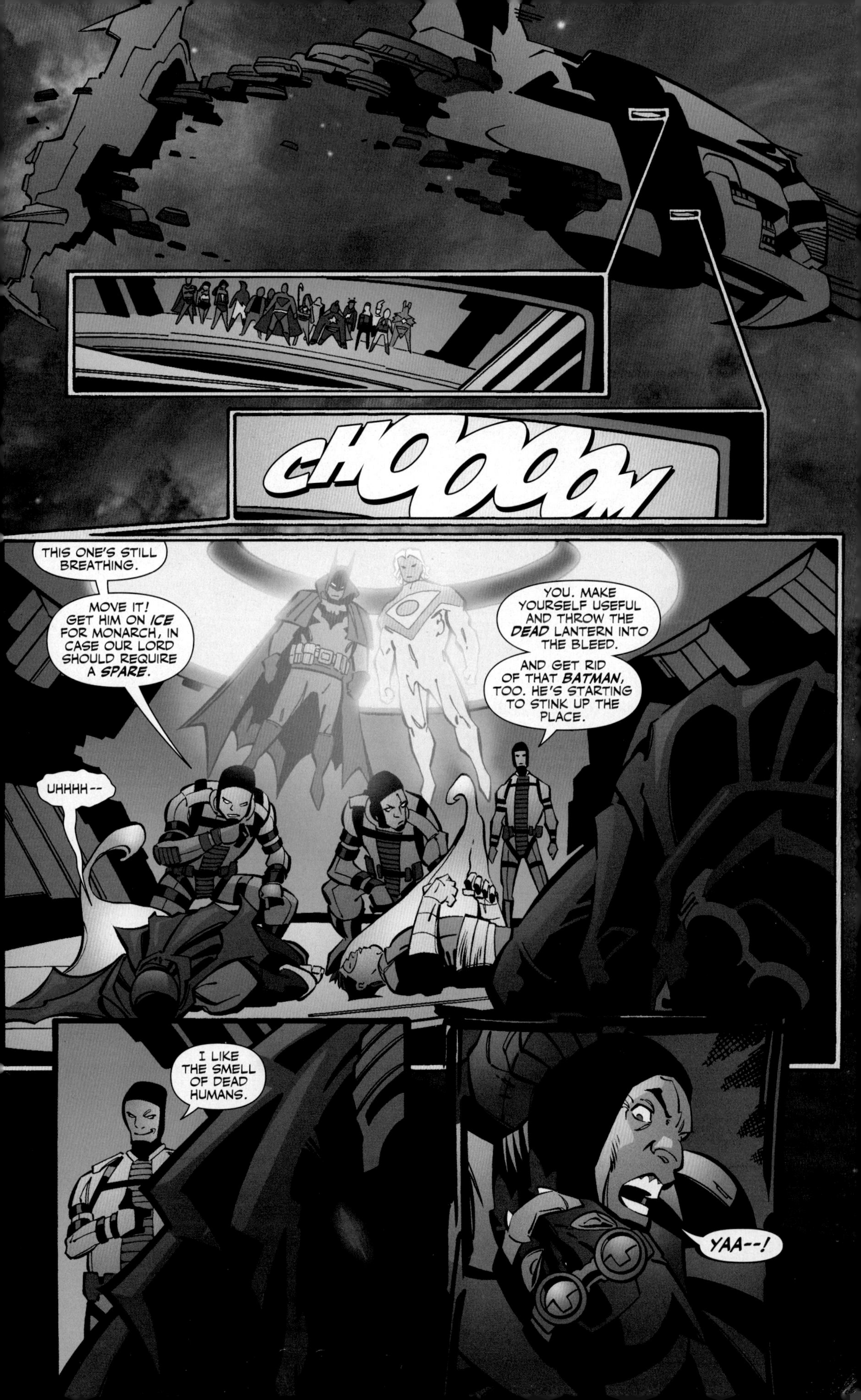
CHOOOOM
THIS ONE'S STILL BREATHING.
MOVE IT! GET HIM ON ICE FOR MONARCH, IN CASE OUR LORD SHOULD REQUIRE A SPARE.
YOU. MAKE YOURSELF USEFUL AND THROW THE DEAD LANTERN INTO THE BLEED.
AND GET RID OF THAT BATMAN, TOO. HE'S STARTING TO STINK UP THE PLACE.
UHHHH--
I LIKE THE SMELL OF DEAD HUMANS.
YAA--!

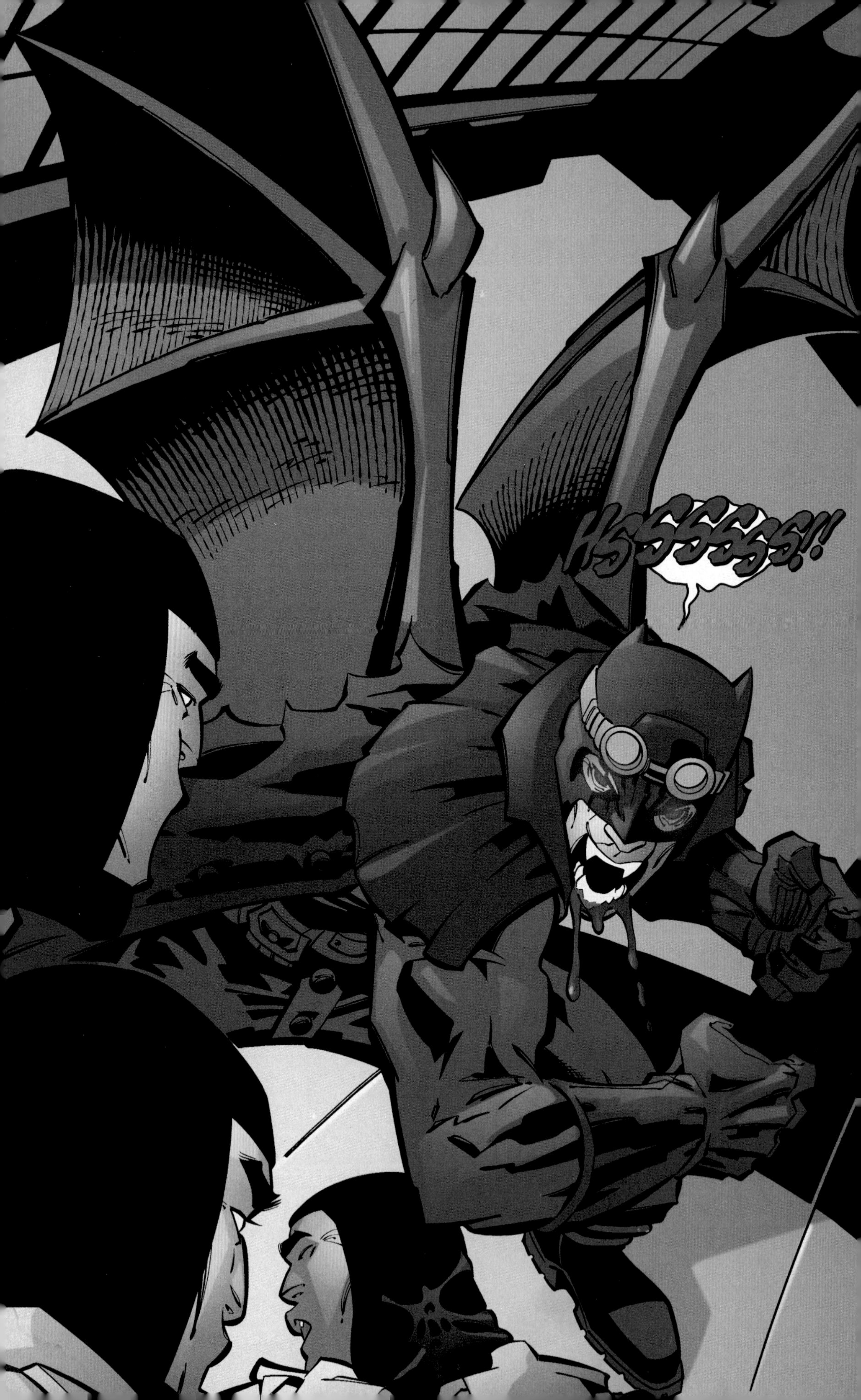
HSSSSSS!!

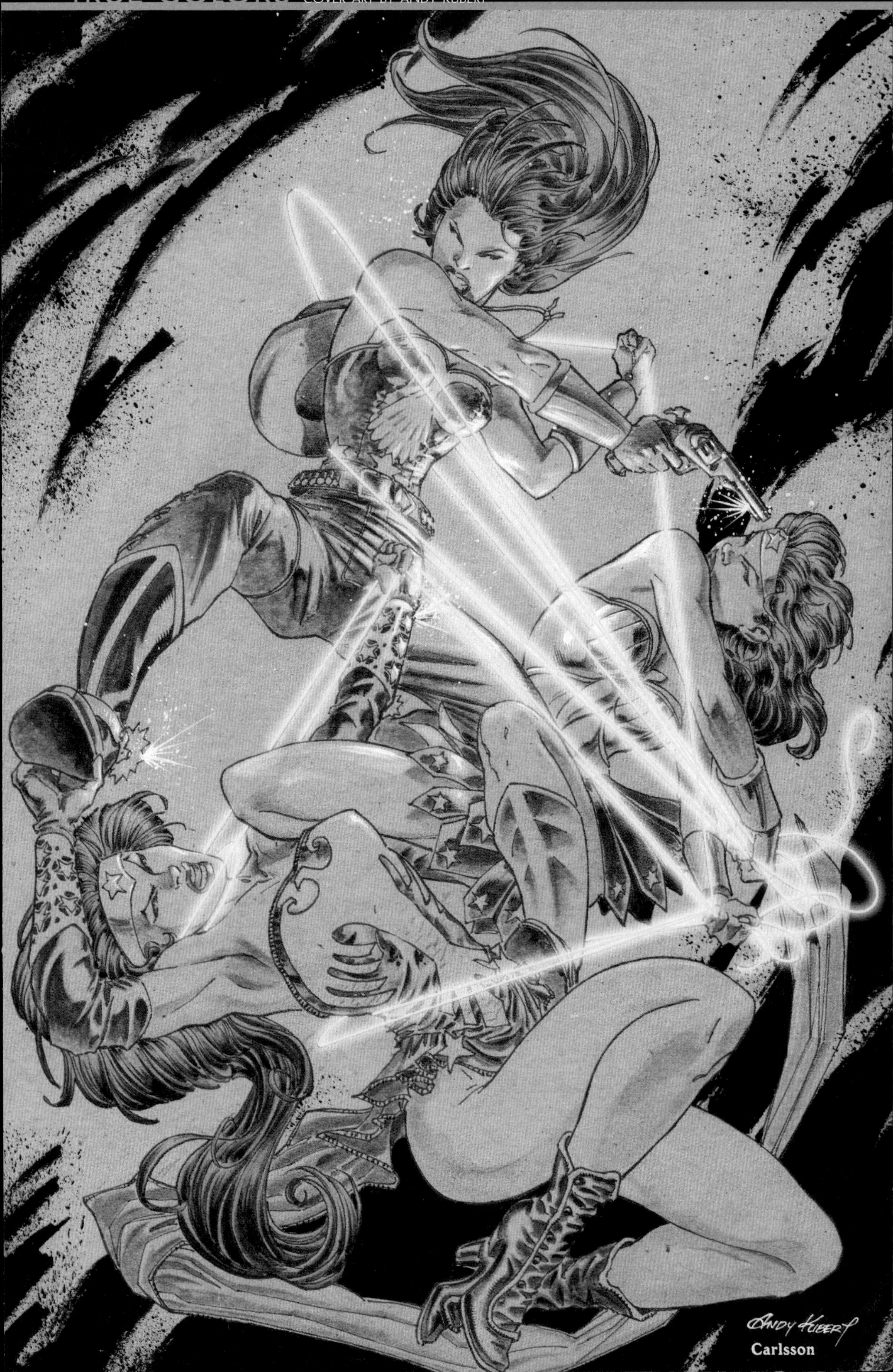
ANDY KUBERT
Carlsson

VARIANT COVER ART BY DALE EAGLESHAM & ANDY LANNING

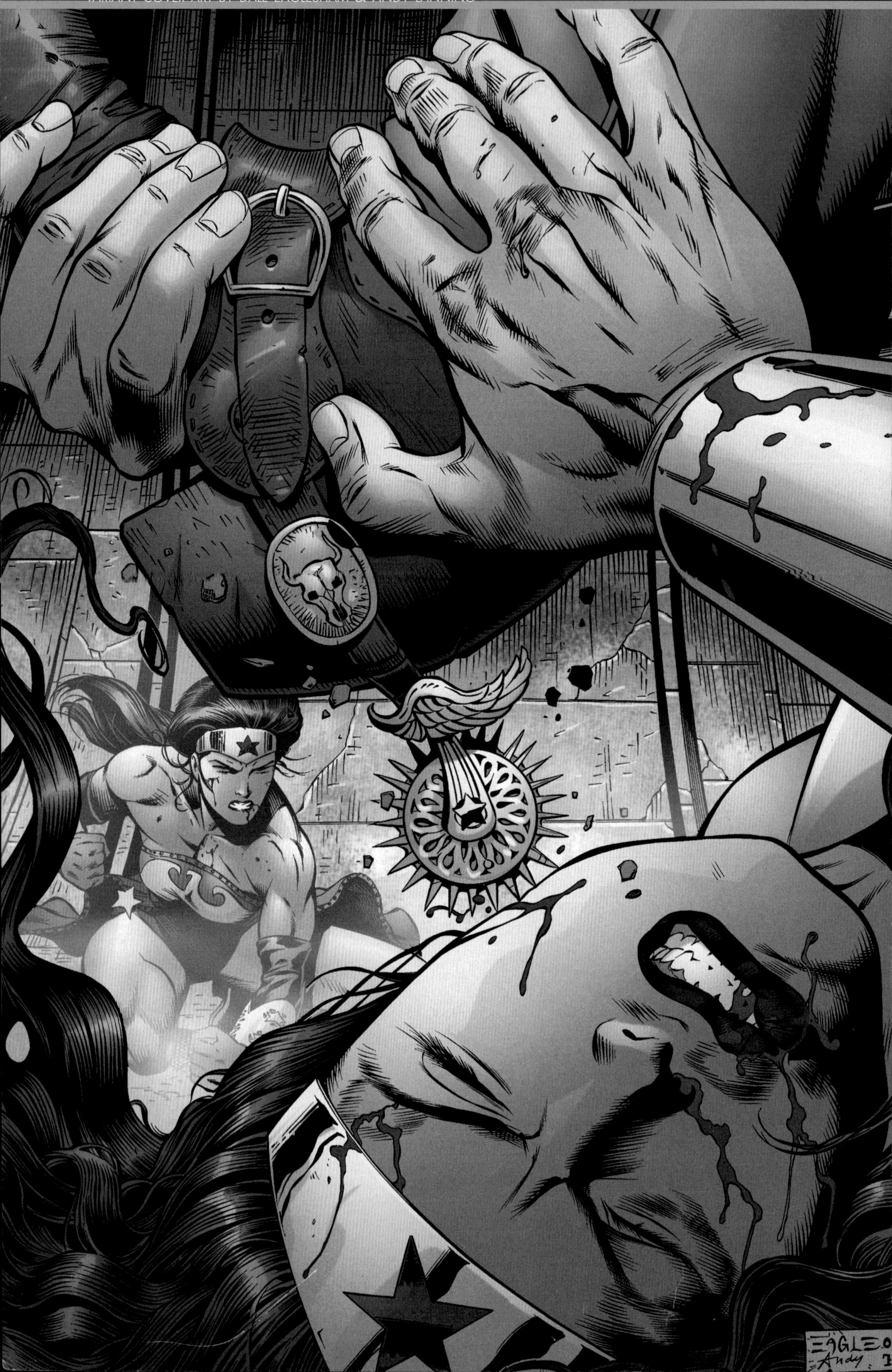

EAGLE
Andy

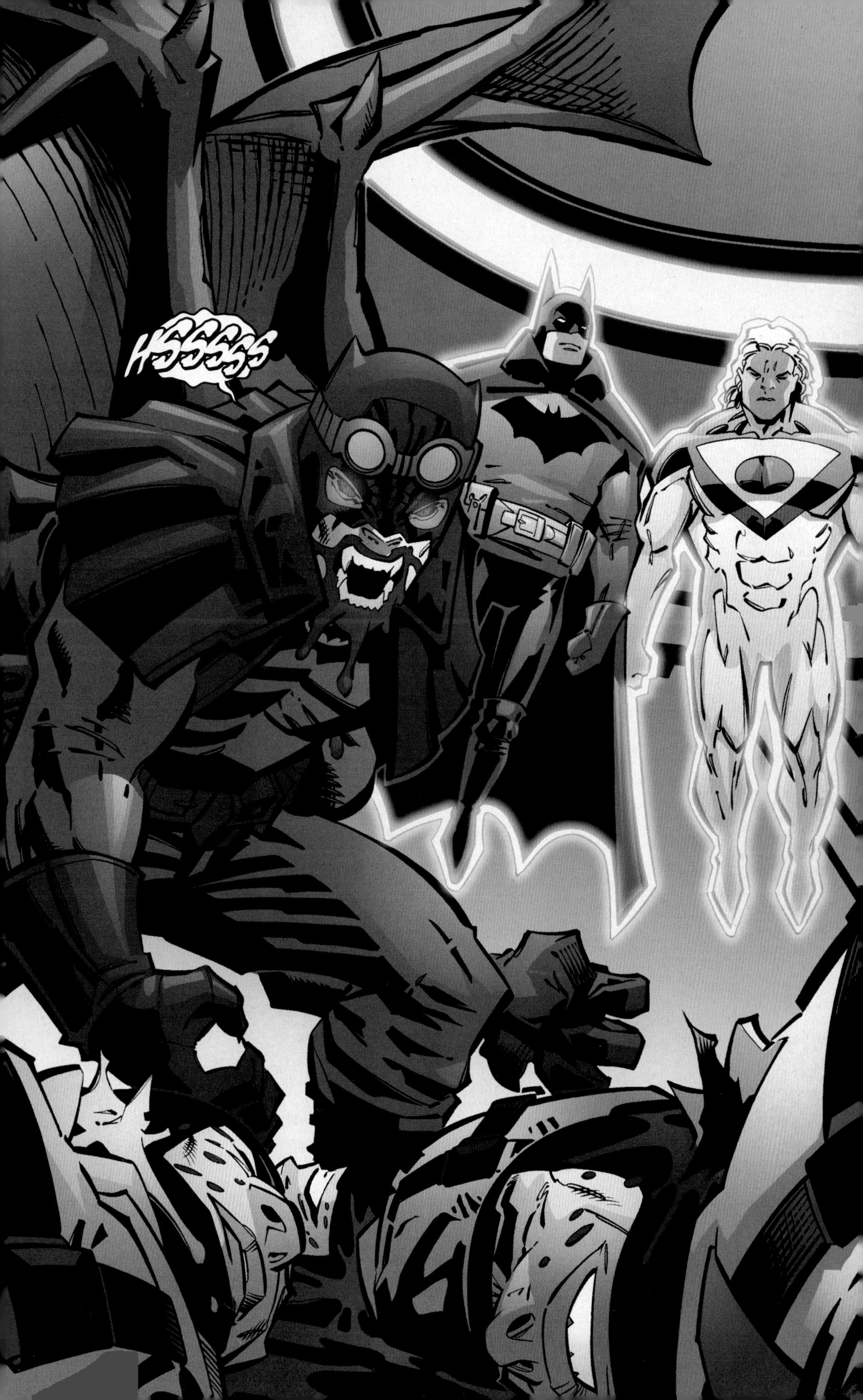
HSSSSSS

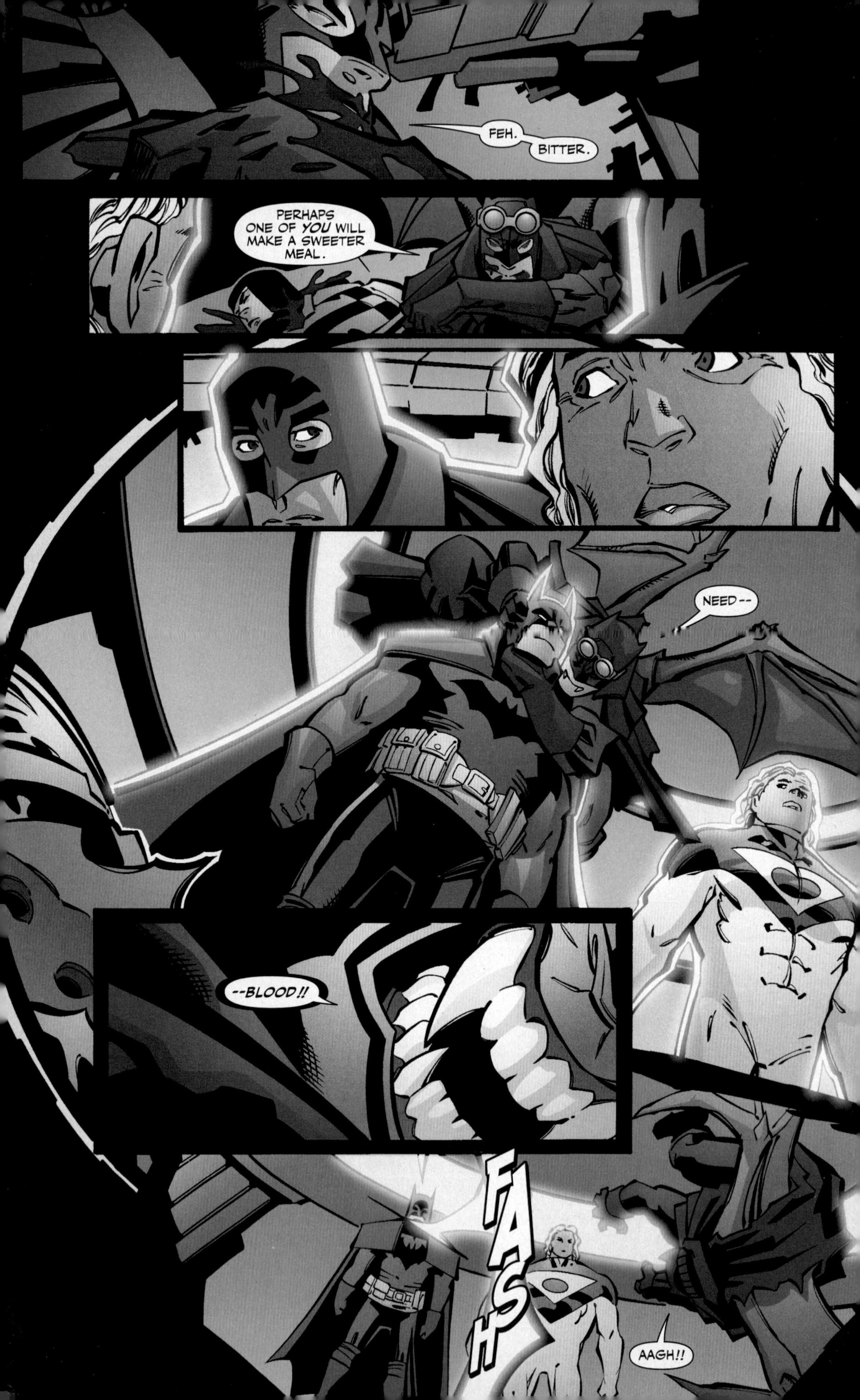
FEH.
BITTER.
PERHAPS ONE OF YOU WILL MAKE A SWEETER MEAL.
NEED--
--BLOOD!!
FASH
AAGH!!

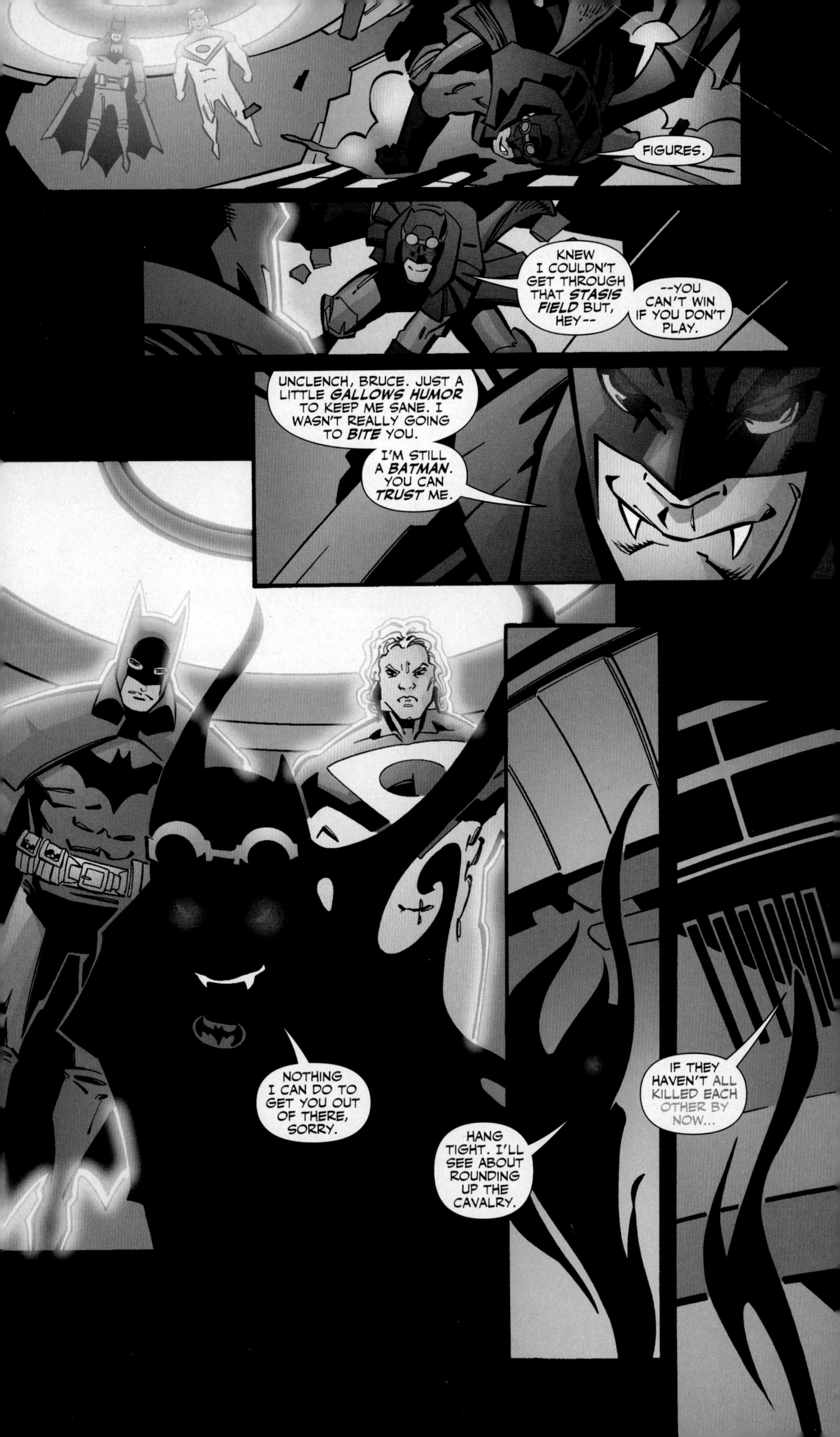
FIGURES.
KNEW I COULDN'T GET THROUGH THAT STASIS FIELD BUT, HEY--
--YOU CAN'T WIN IF YOU DON'T PLAY.
UNCLENCH, BRUCE. JUST A LITTLE GALLOWS HUMOR TO KEEP ME SANE. I WASN'T REALLY GOING TO BITE YOU.
I'M STILL A BATMAN. YOU CAN TRUST ME.
NOTHING I CAN DO TO GET YOU OUT OF THERE, SORRY.
HANG TIGHT. I'LL SEE ABOUT ROUNDING UP THE CAVALRY.
IF THEY HAVEN'T ALL KILLED EACH OTHER BY NOW...

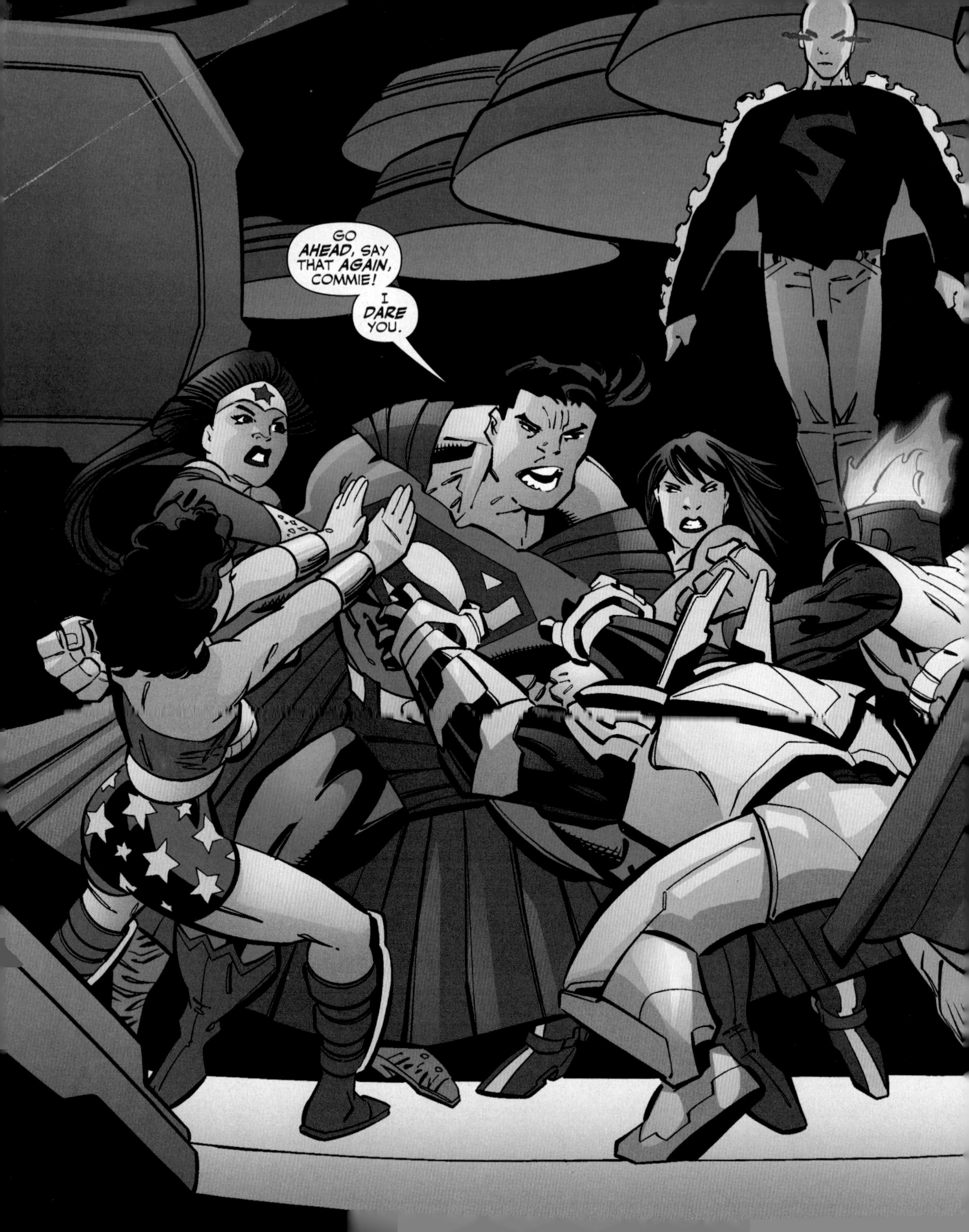
GO AHEAD, SAY THAT AGAIN, COMMIE!
I DARE YOU.

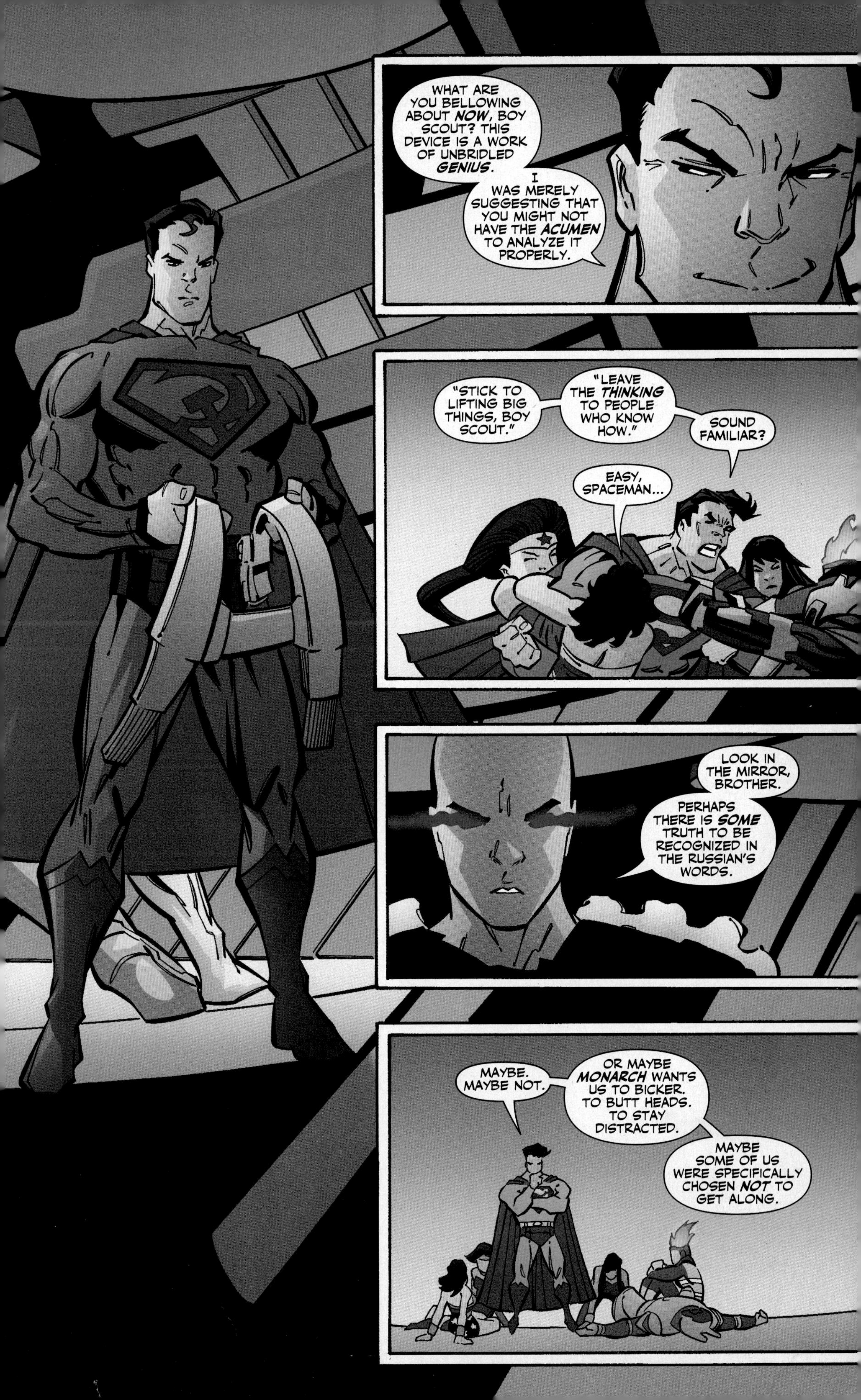

WHAT ARE YOU BELLOWING ABOUT NOW, BOY SCOUT? THIS DEVICE IS A WORK OF UNBRIDLED GENIUS.
I WAS MERELY SUGGESTING THAT YOU MIGHT NOT HAVE THE ACUMEN TO ANALYZE IT PROPERLY.
"STICK TO LIFTING BIG THINGS, BOY SCOUT."
"LEAVE THE THINKING TO PEOPLE WHO KNOW HOW."
SOUND FAMILIAR?
EASY, SPACEMAN...
LOOK IN THE MIRROR, BROTHER.
PERHAPS THERE IS SOME TRUTH TO BE RECOGNIZED IN THE RUSSIAN'S WORDS.
MAYBE. MAYBE NOT.
OR MAYBE MONARCH WANTS US TO BICKER. TO BUTT HEADS. TO STAY DISTRACTED.
MAYBE SOME OF US WERE SPECIFICALLY CHOSEN NOT TO GET ALONG.

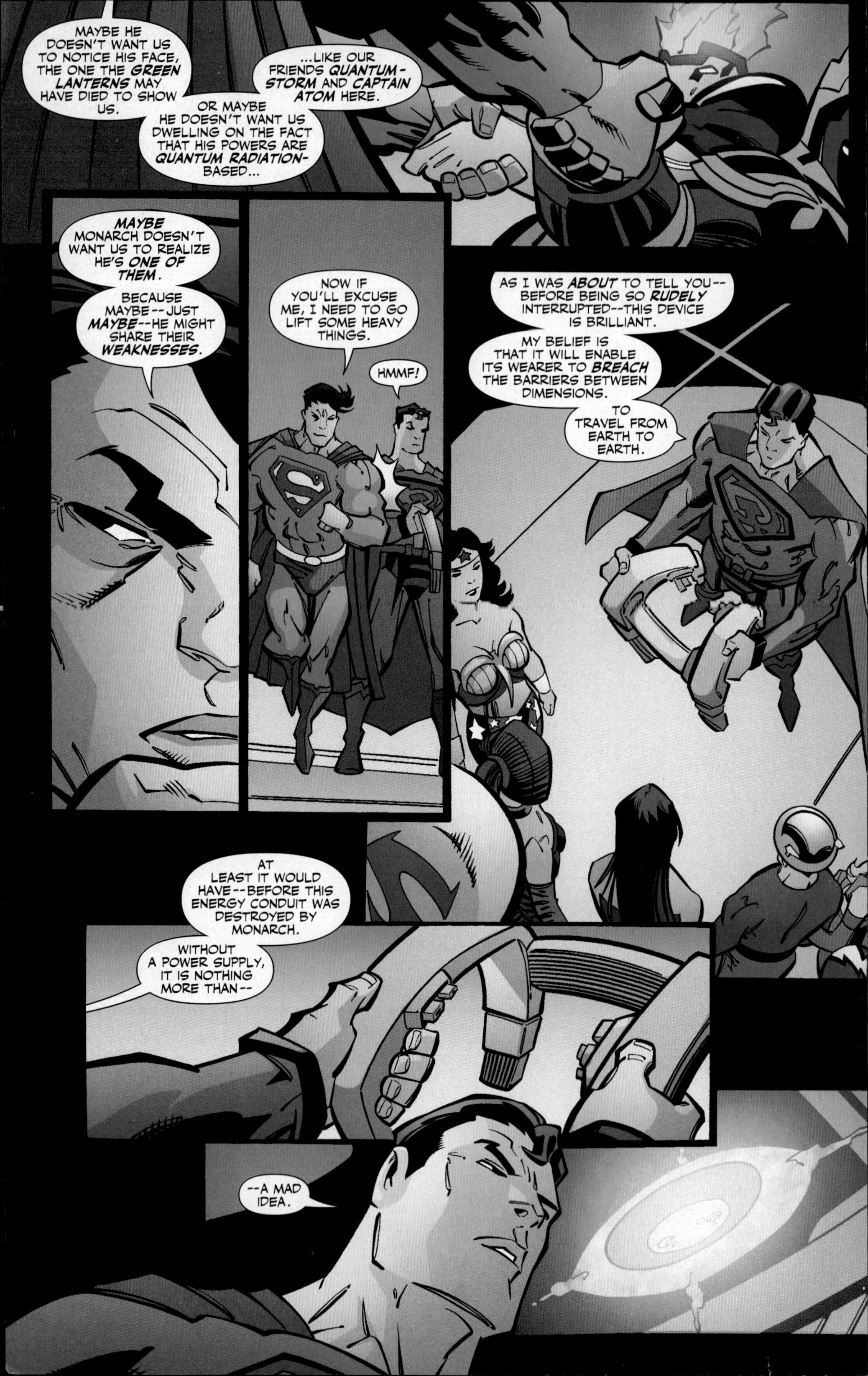
MAYBE HE DOESN'T WANT US TO NOTICE HIS FACE, THE ONE THE GREEN LANTERNS MAY HAVE DIED TO SHOW US.
OR MAYBE HE DOESN'T WANT US DWELLING ON THE FACT THAT HIS POWERS ARE QUANTUM RADIATION-BASED...
...LIKE OUR FRIENDS QUANTUM-STORM AND CAPTAIN ATOM HERE.
MAYBE MONARCH DOESN'T WANT US TO REALIZE HE'S ONE OF THEM.
BECAUSE MAYBE--JUST MAYBE--HE MIGHT SHARE THEIR WEAKNESSES.
NOW IF YOU'LL EXCUSE ME, I NEED TO GO LIFT SOME HEAVY THINGS.
HMMF!
AS I WAS ABOUT TO TELL YOU--BEFORE BEING SO RUDELY INTERRUPTED--THIS DEVICE IS BRILLIANT.
MY BELIEF IS THAT IT WILL ENABLE ITS WEARER TO BREACH THE BARRIERS BETWEEN DIMENSIONS.
TO TRAVEL FROM EARTH TO EARTH.
AT LEAST IT WOULD HAVE--BEFORE THIS ENERGY CONDUIT WAS DESTROYED BY MONARCH.
WITHOUT A POWER SUPPLY, IT IS NOTHING MORE THAN--
--A MAD IDEA.

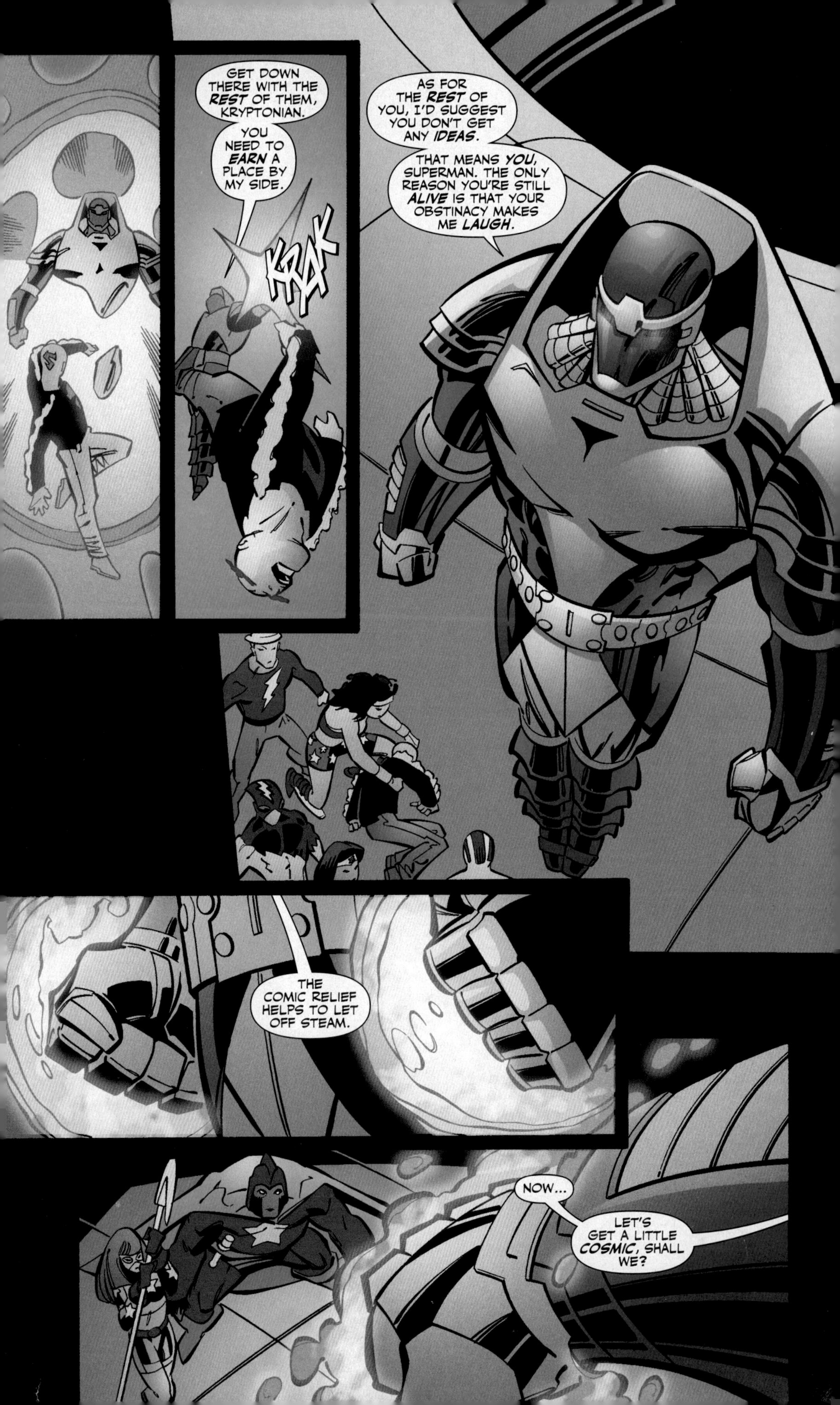

GET DOWN THERE WITH THE REST OF THEM, KRYPTONIAN.
YOU NEED TO EARN A PLACE BY MY SIDE.
KRAK
AS FOR THE REST OF YOU, I'D SUGGEST YOU DON'T GET ANY IDEAS.
THAT MEANS YOU, SUPERMAN. THE ONLY REASON YOU'RE STILL ALIVE IS THAT YOUR OBSTINACY MAKES ME LAUGH.
THE COMIC RELIEF HELPS TO LET OFF STEAM.
NOW...
LET'S GET A LITTLE COSMIC, SHALL WE?

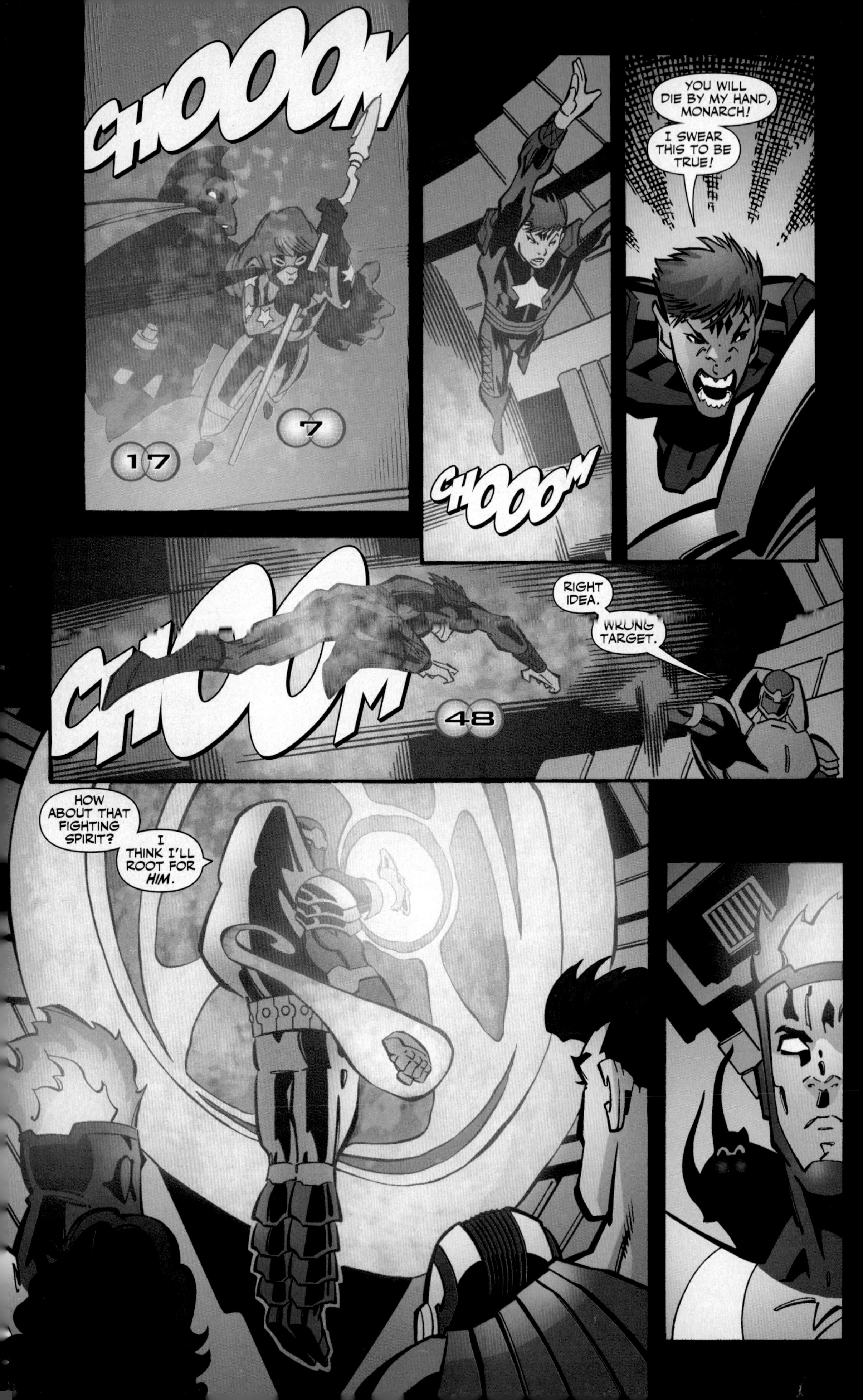
CHOOOM
17
7
CHOOOM
YOU WILL DIE BY MY HAND, MONARCH!
I SWEAR THIS TO BE TRUE!
CHOOOM
48
RIGHT IDEA.
WRONG TARGET.
HOW ABOUT THAT FIGHTING SPIRIT?
I THINK I'LL ROOT FOR *HIM*.

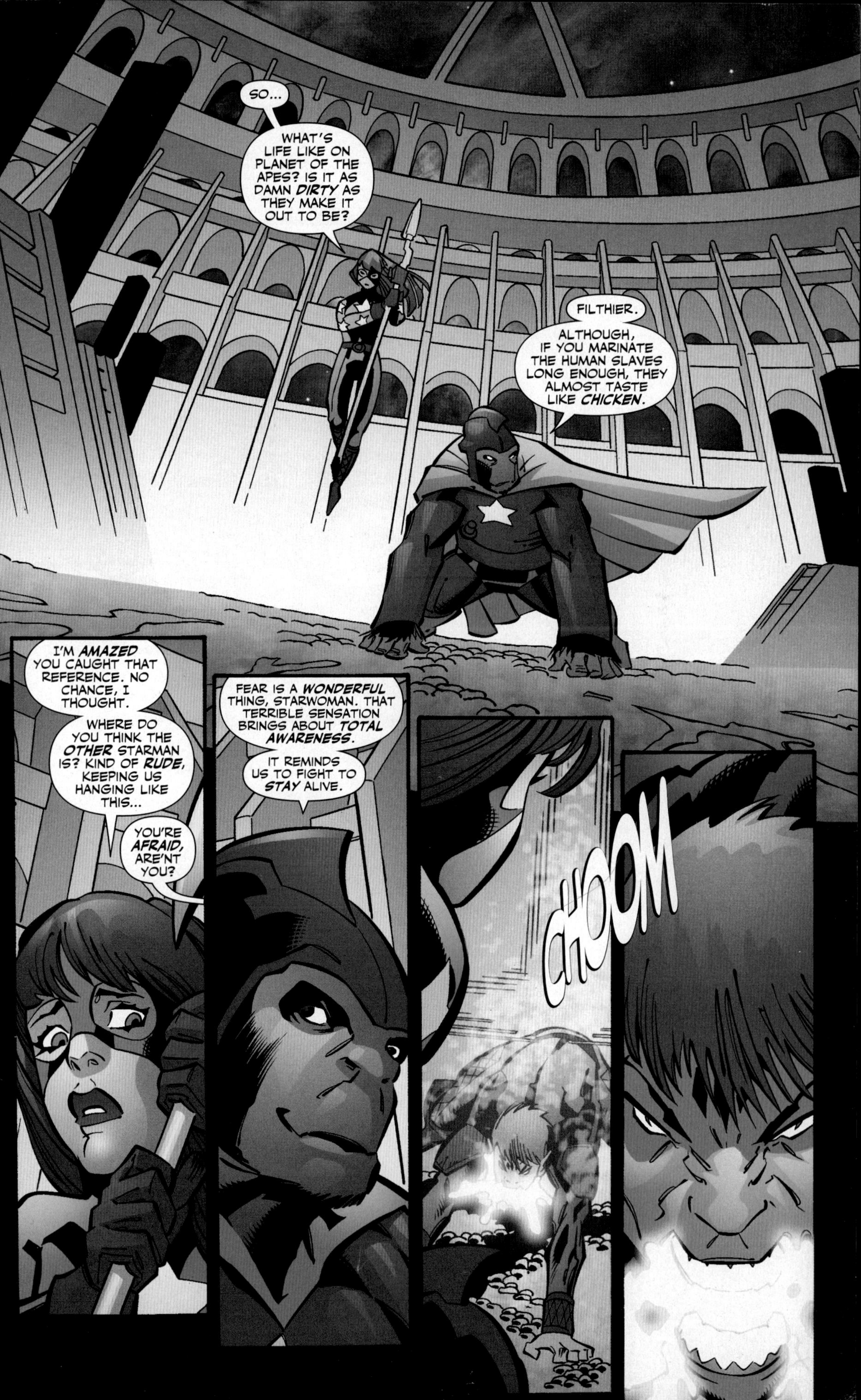
SO...
WHAT'S LIFE LIKE ON PLANET OF THE APES? IS IT AS DAMN DIRTY AS THEY MAKE IT OUT TO BE?
FILTHIER.
ALTHOUGH, IF YOU MARINATE THE HUMAN SLAVES LONG ENOUGH, THEY ALMOST TASTE LIKE CHICKEN.
I'M AMAZED YOU CAUGHT THAT REFERENCE. NO CHANCE, I THOUGHT.
WHERE DO YOU THINK THE OTHER STARMAN IS? KIND OF RUDE, KEEPING US HANGING LIKE THIS...
YOU'RE AFRAID, ARE'NT YOU?
FEAR IS A WONDERFUL THING, STARWOMAN. THAT TERRIBLE SENSATION BRINGS ABOUT TOTAL AWARENESS.
IT REMINDS US TO FIGHT TO STAY ALIVE.
CHOOM

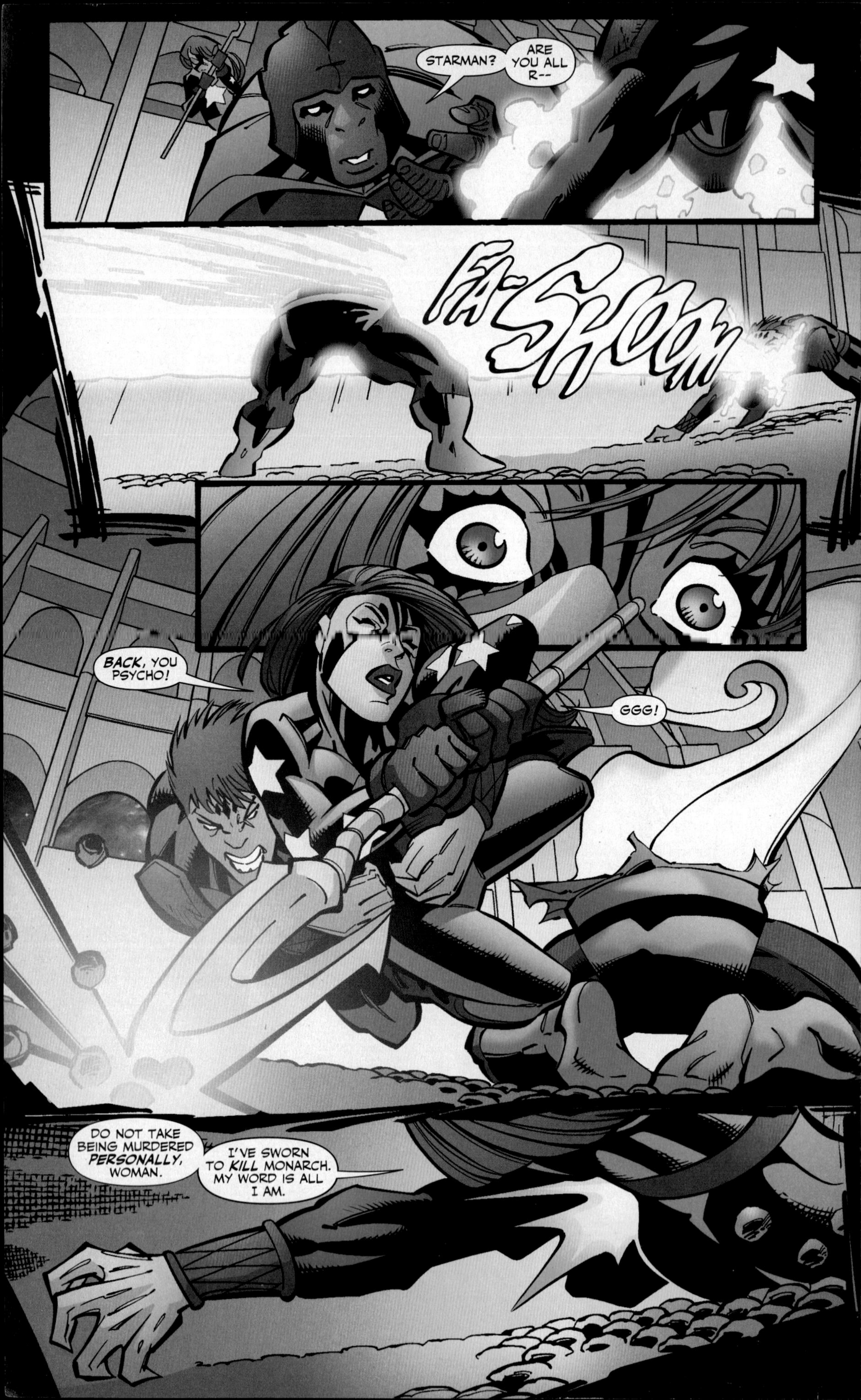
STARMAN?
ARE YOU ALL R--
FA-SHOOM
BACK, YOU PSYCHO!
GGG!
DO NOT TAKE BEING MURDERED PERSONALLY, WOMAN.
I'VE SWORN TO KILL MONARCH. MY WORD IS ALL I AM.

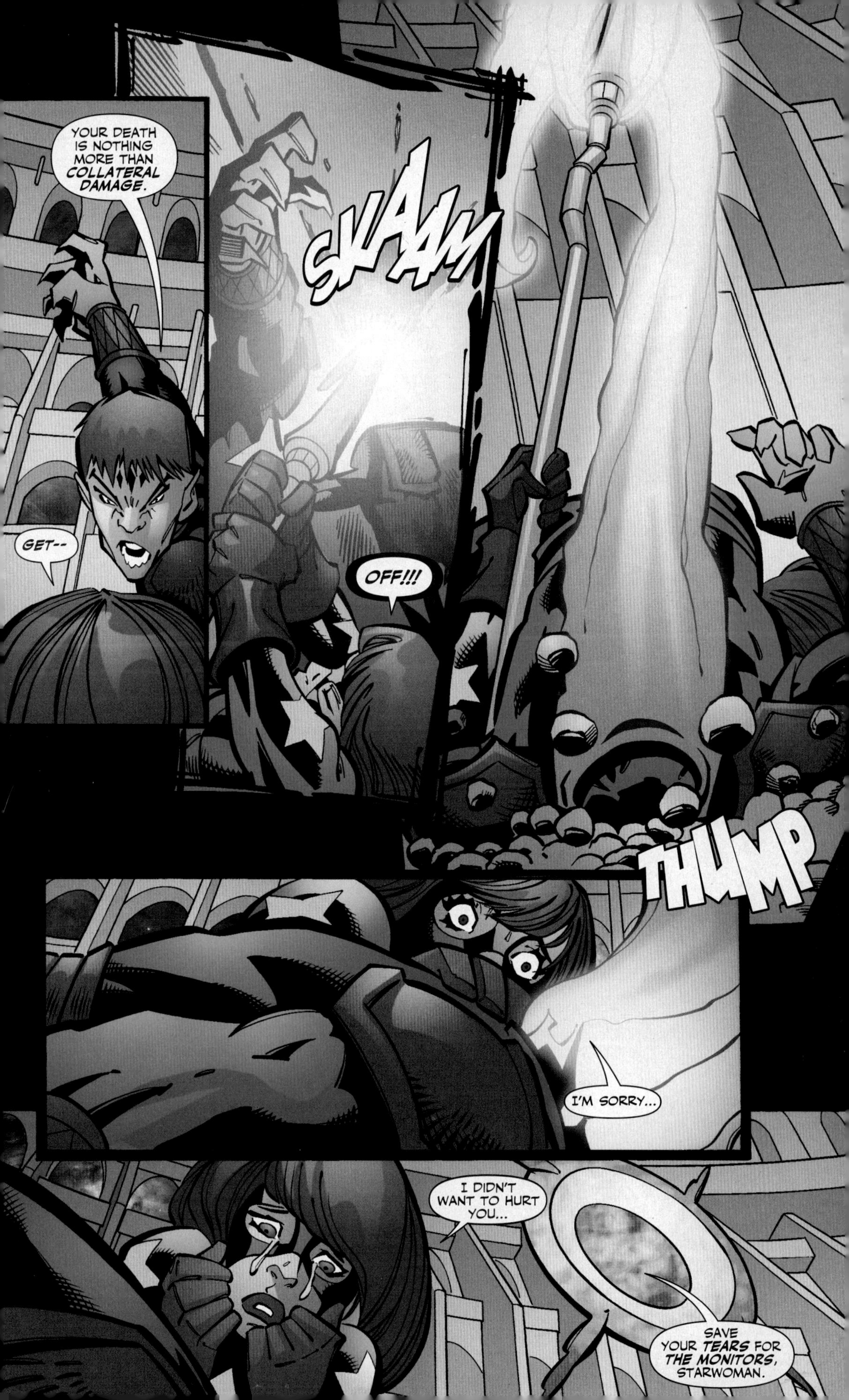
YOUR DEATH IS NOTHING MORE THAN *COLLATERAL DAMAGE.*
SKAAM
GET--
OFF!!!
THUMP
I'M SORRY...
I DIDN'T WANT TO HURT YOU...
SAVE YOUR *TEARS* FOR *THE MONITORS,* STARWOMAN.

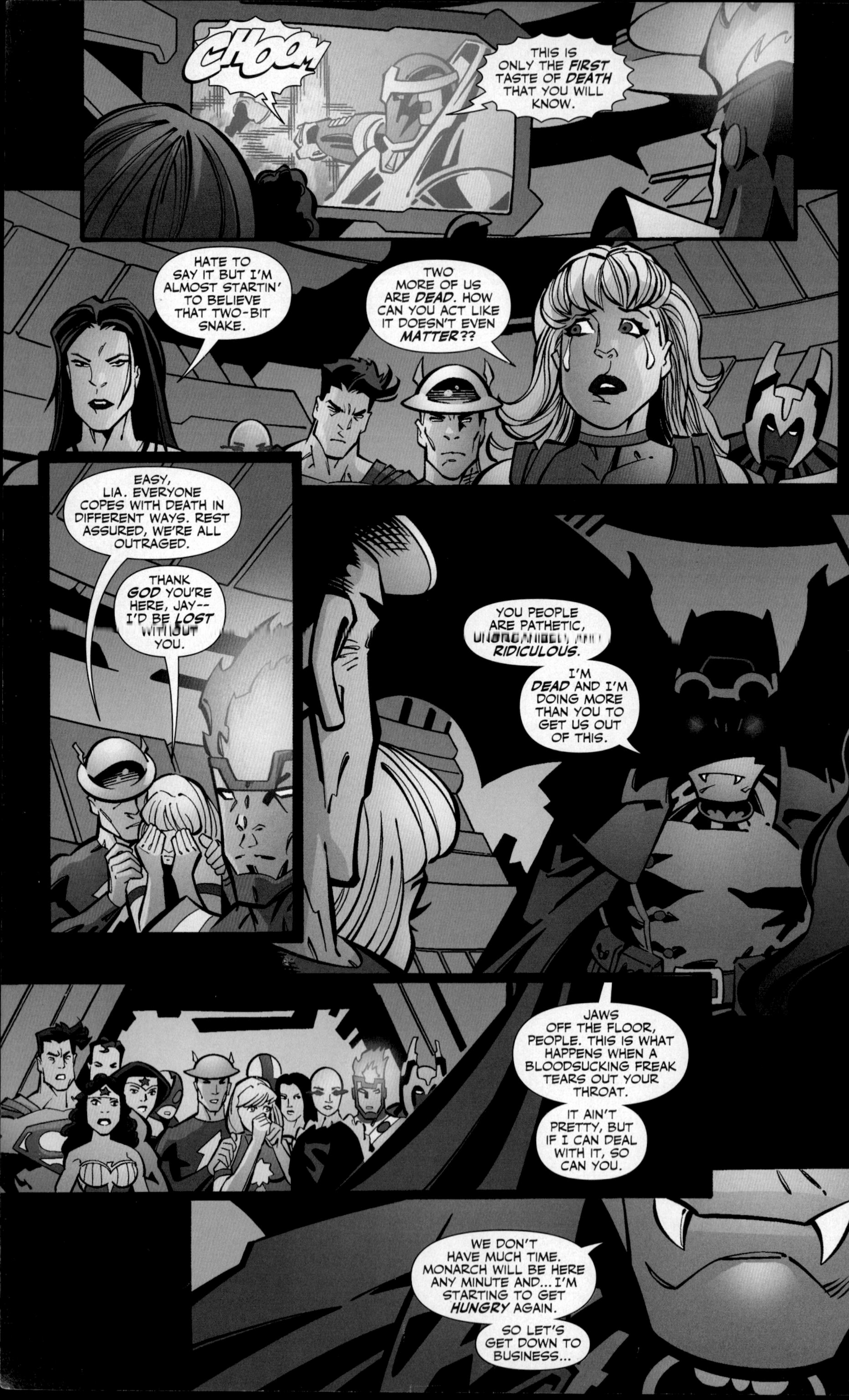
CHOOM
THIS IS ONLY THE FIRST TASTE OF DEATH THAT YOU WILL KNOW.
HATE TO SAY IT BUT I'M ALMOST STARTIN' TO BELIEVE THAT TWO-BIT SNAKE.
TWO MORE OF US ARE DEAD. HOW CAN YOU ACT LIKE IT DOESN'T EVEN MATTER??
EASY, LIA. EVERYONE COPES WITH DEATH IN DIFFERENT WAYS. REST ASSURED, WE'RE ALL OUTRAGED.
THANK GOD YOU'RE HERE, JAY-- I'D BE LOST WITHOUT YOU.
YOU PEOPLE ARE PATHETIC,
RIDICULOUS.
I'M DEAD AND I'M DOING MORE THAN YOU TO GET US OUT OF THIS.
JAWS OFF THE FLOOR, PEOPLE. THIS IS WHAT HAPPENS WHEN A BLOODSUCKING FREAK TEARS OUT YOUR THROAT.
IT AIN'T PRETTY, BUT IF I CAN DEAL WITH IT, SO CAN YOU.
WE DON'T HAVE MUCH TIME. MONARCH WILL BE HERE ANY MINUTE AND... I'M STARTING TO GET HUNGRY AGAIN.
SO LET'S GET DOWN TO BUSINESS...

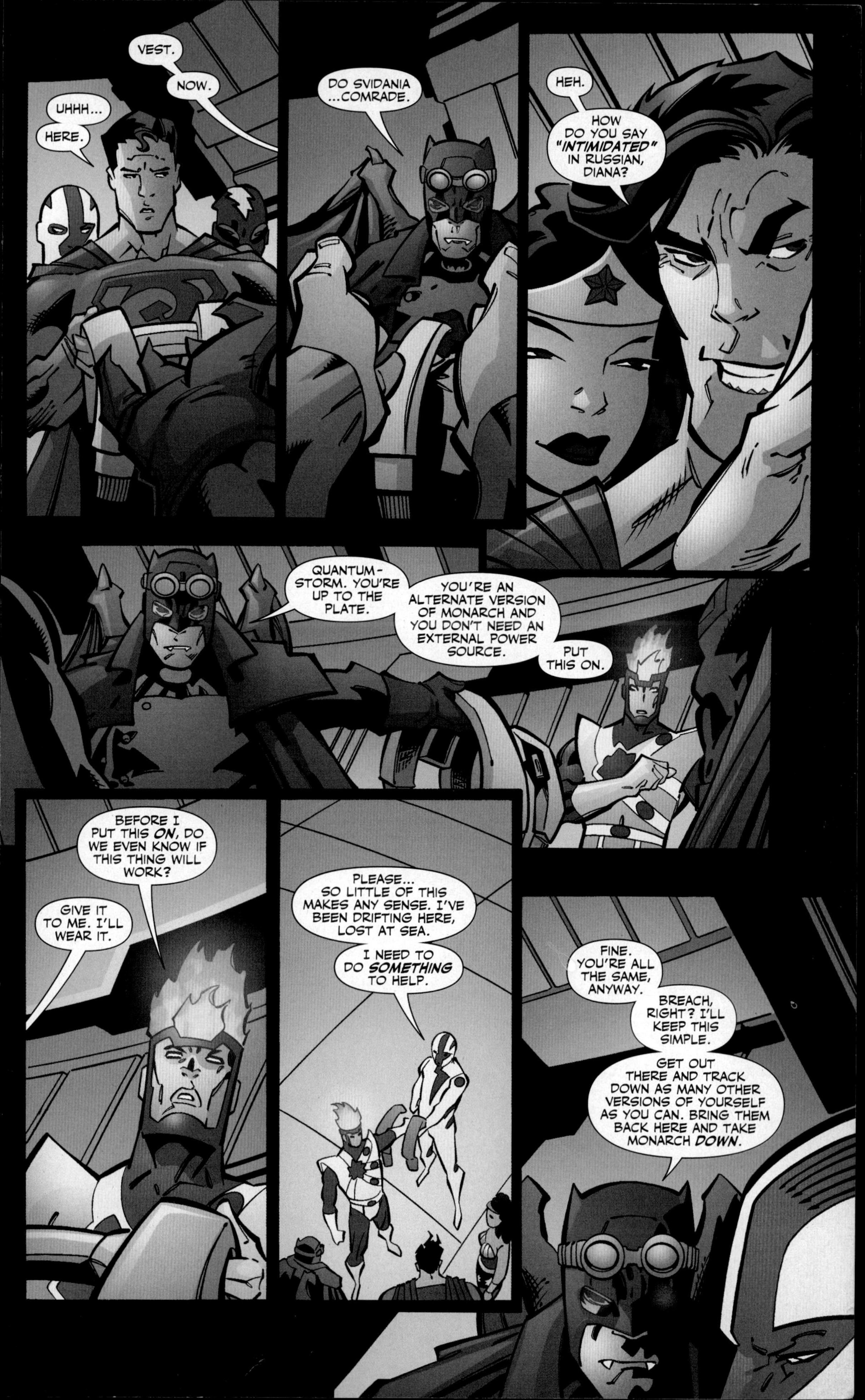
VEST.
NOW.
UHHH...
HERE.
DO SVIDANIA ...COMRADE.
HEH.
HOW DO YOU SAY "INTIMIDATED" IN RUSSIAN, DIANA?
QUANTUM-STORM. YOU'RE UP TO THE PLATE.
YOU'RE AN ALTERNATE VERSION OF MONARCH AND YOU DON'T NEED AN EXTERNAL POWER SOURCE.
PUT THIS ON.
BEFORE I PUT THIS ON, DO WE EVEN KNOW IF THIS THING WILL WORK?
GIVE IT TO ME. I'LL WEAR IT.
PLEASE... SO LITTLE OF THIS MAKES ANY SENSE. I'VE BEEN DRIFTING HERE, LOST AT SEA.
I NEED TO DO SOMETHING TO HELP.
FINE. YOU'RE ALL THE SAME, ANYWAY.
BREACH, RIGHT? I'LL KEEP THIS SIMPLE.
GET OUT THERE AND TRACK DOWN AS MANY OTHER VERSIONS OF YOURSELF AS YOU CAN. BRING THEM BACK HERE AND TAKE MONARCH DOWN.

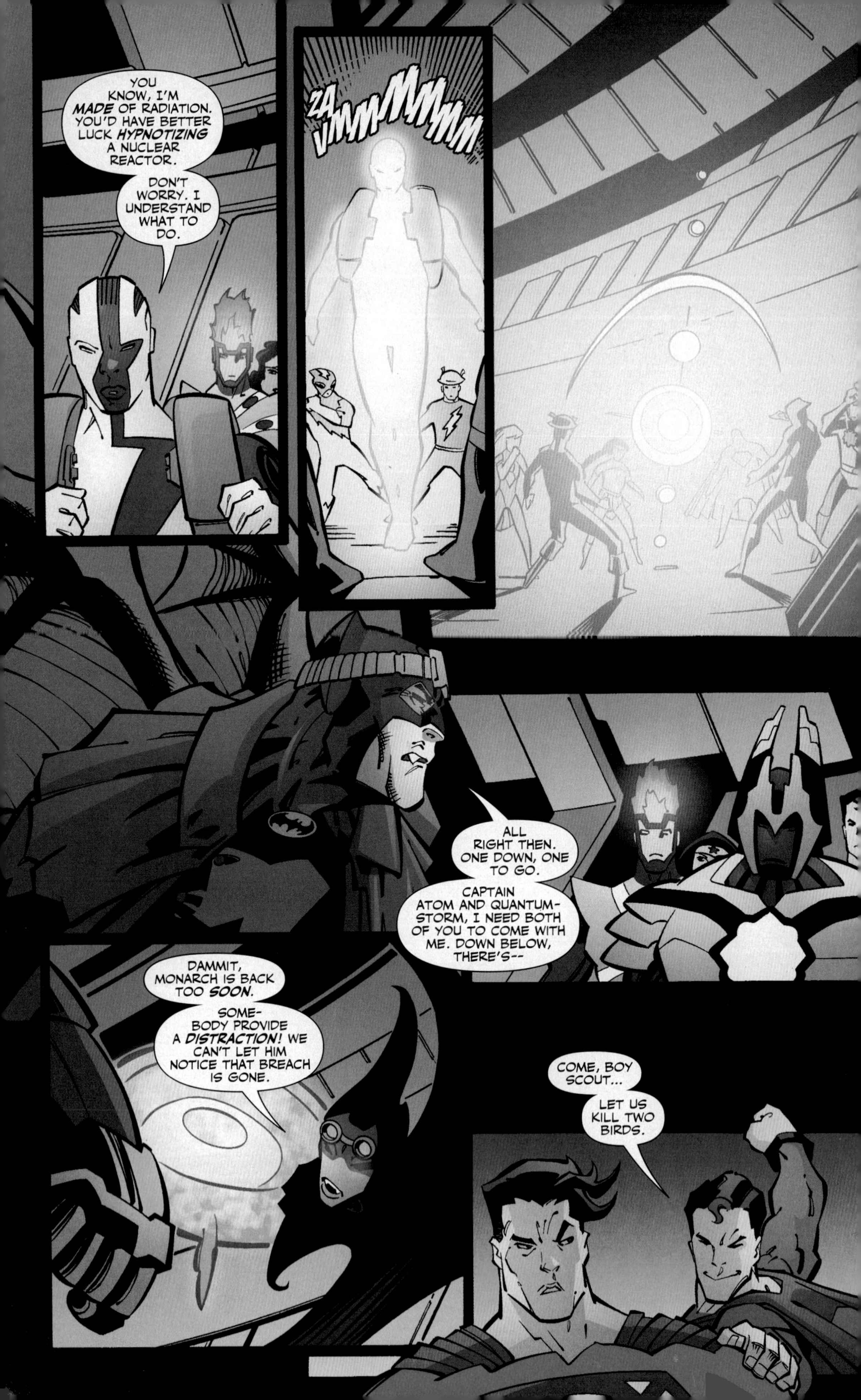

YOU KNOW, I'M MADE OF RADIATION. YOU'D HAVE BETTER LUCK HYPNOTIZING A NUCLEAR REACTOR.
DON'T WORRY. I UNDERSTAND WHAT TO DO.
ZAVMMMMMMM
ALL RIGHT THEN. ONE DOWN, ONE TO GO.
CAPTAIN ATOM AND QUANTUM-STORM, I NEED BOTH OF YOU TO COME WITH ME. DOWN BELOW, THERE'S--
DAMMIT, MONARCH IS BACK TOO SOON.
SOME-BODY PROVIDE A DISTRACTION! WE CAN'T LET HIM NOTICE THAT BREACH IS GONE.
COME, BOY SCOUT...
LET US KILL TWO BIRDS.

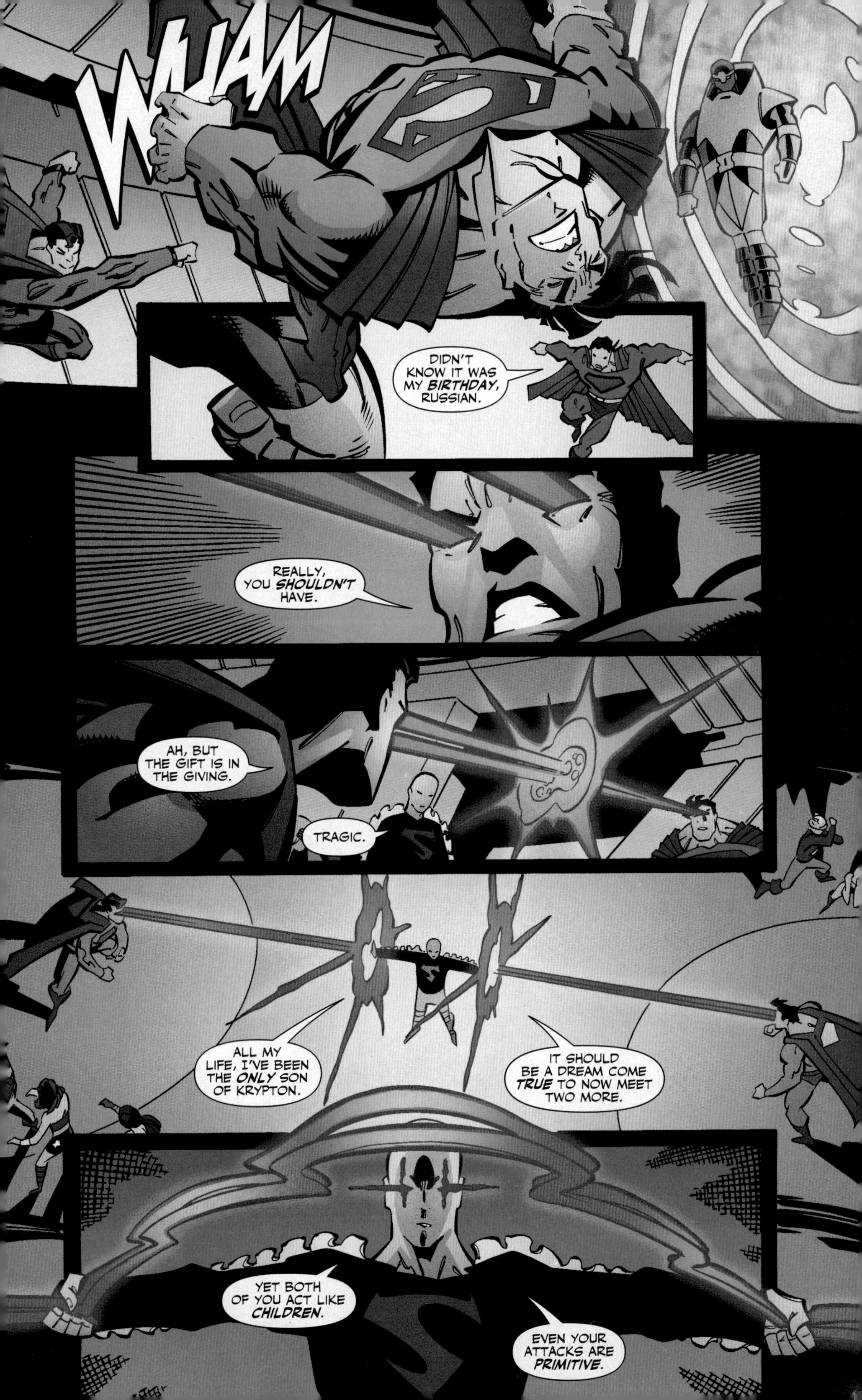
WHAM
DIDN'T KNOW IT WAS MY *BIRTHDAY*, RUSSIAN.
REALLY, YOU *SHOULDN'T* HAVE.
AH, BUT THE GIFT IS IN THE GIVING.
TRAGIC.
ALL MY LIFE, I'VE BEEN THE *ONLY* SON OF KRYPTON.
IT SHOULD BE A DREAM COME *TRUE* TO NOW MEET TWO MORE.
YET BOTH OF YOU ACT LIKE *CHILDREN*.
EVEN YOUR ATTACKS ARE *PRIMITIVE*.

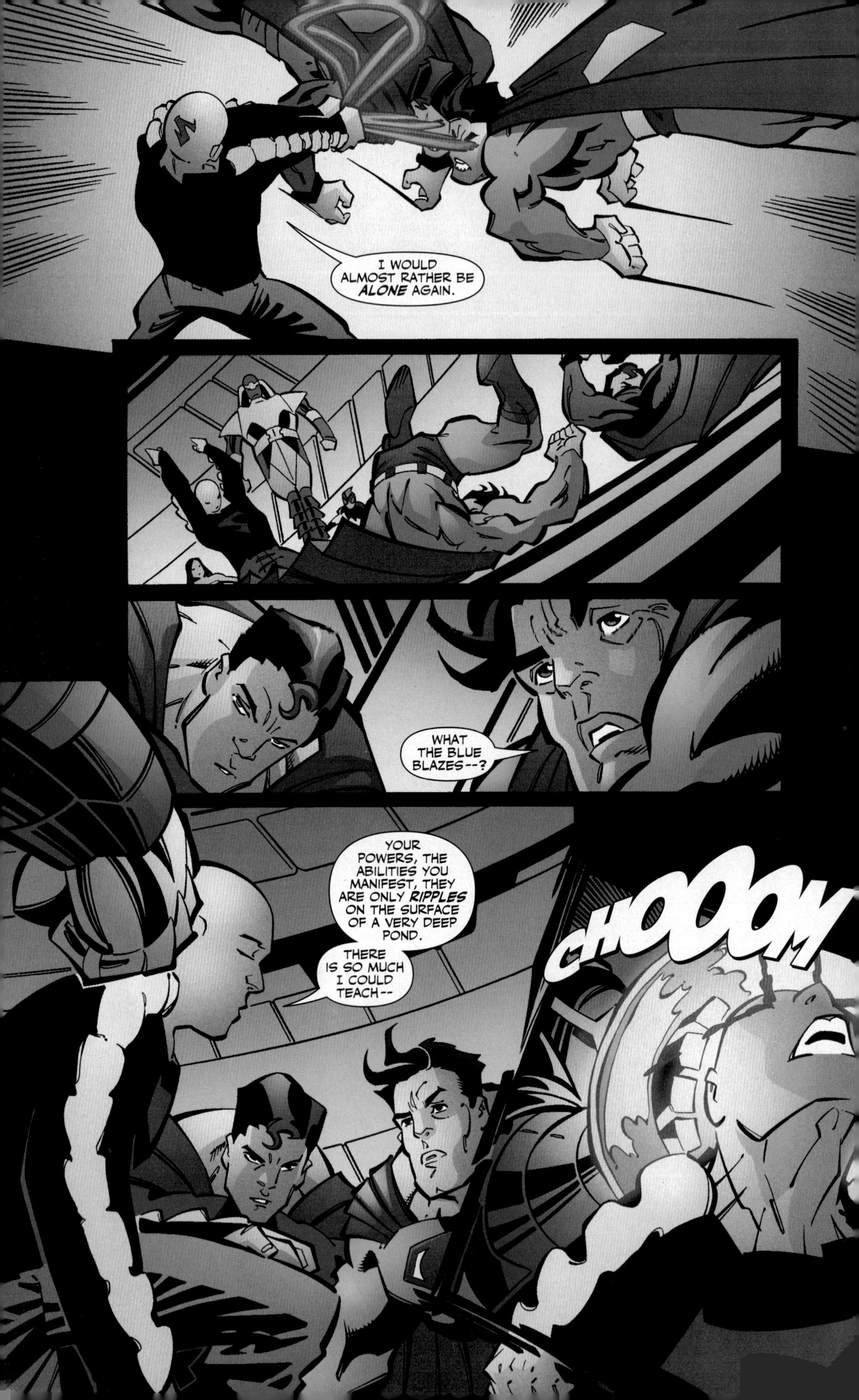
I WOULD ALMOST RATHER BE ALONE AGAIN.
WHAT THE BLUE BLAZES--?
YOUR POWERS, THE ABILITIES YOU MANIFEST, THEY ARE ONLY RIPPLES ON THE SURFACE OF A VERY DEEP POND.
THERE IS SO MUCH I COULD TEACH--
CHOOOM

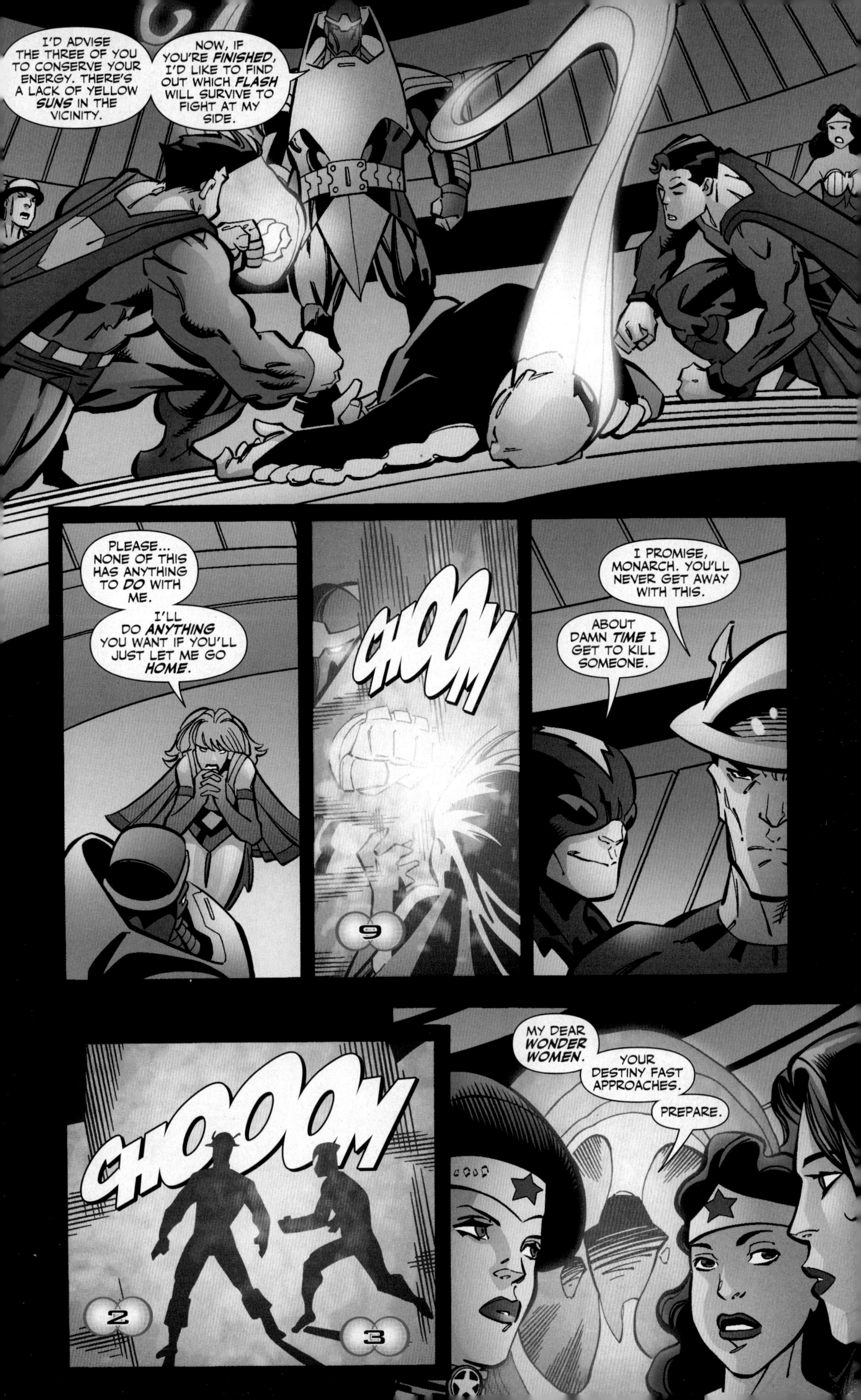
I'D ADVISE THE THREE OF YOU TO CONSERVE YOUR ENERGY. THERE'S A LACK OF YELLOW SUNS IN THE VICINITY.
NOW, IF YOU'RE FINISHED, I'D LIKE TO FIND OUT WHICH FLASH WILL SURVIVE TO FIGHT AT MY SIDE.
PLEASE... NONE OF THIS HAS ANYTHING TO DO WITH ME.
I'LL DO ANYTHING YOU WANT IF YOU'LL JUST LET ME GO HOME.
CHOOOM
9
I PROMISE, MONARCH. YOU'LL NEVER GET AWAY WITH THIS.
ABOUT DAMN TIME I GET TO KILL SOMEONE.
CHOOOOM
2
3
MY DEAR WONDER WOMEN.
YOUR DESTINY FAST APPROACHES.
PREPARE.

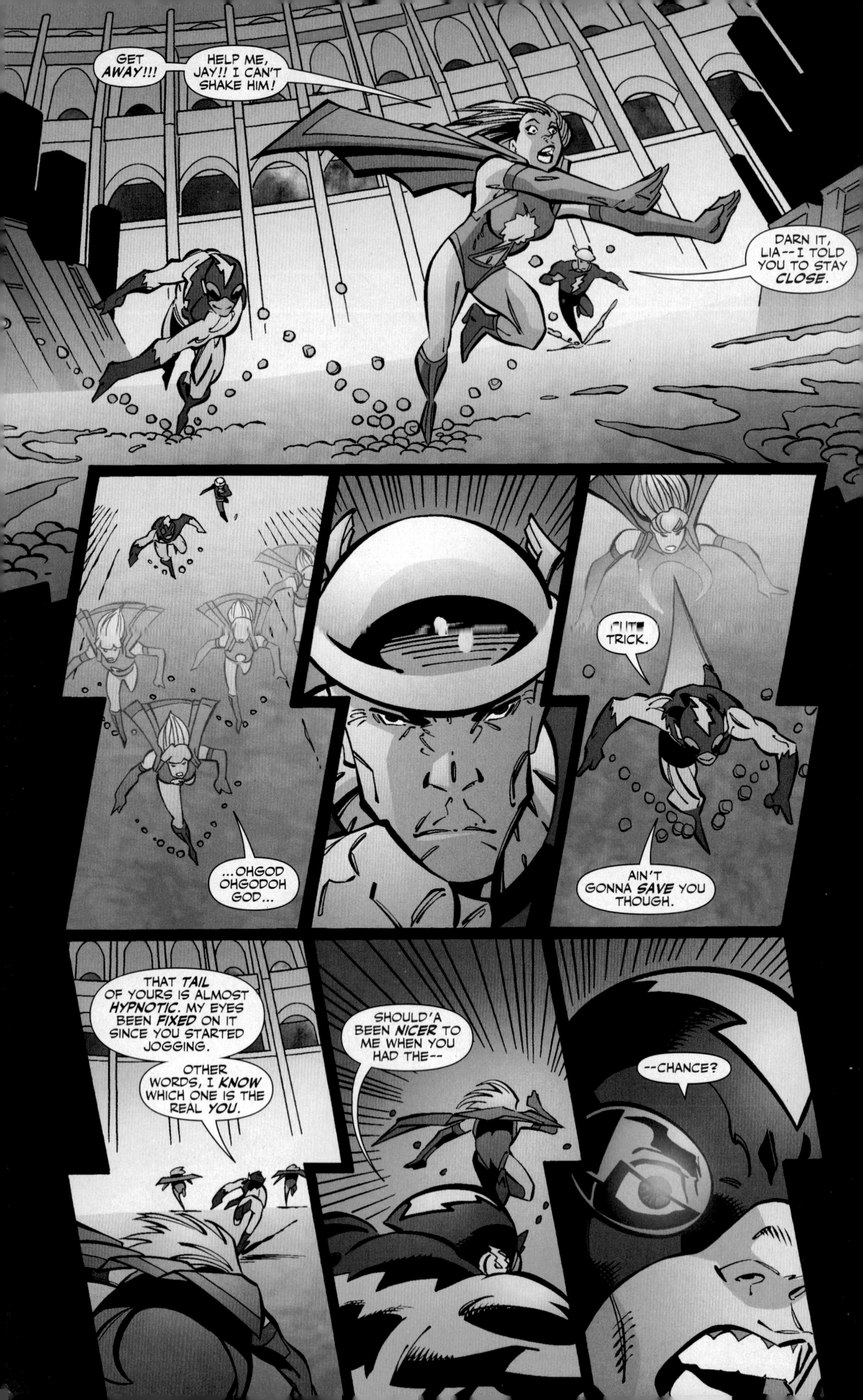
GET AWAY!!!
HELP ME, JAY!! I CAN'T SHAKE HIM!
DARN IT, LIA--I TOLD YOU TO STAY CLOSE.
...OHGOD OHGODOH GOD...
TRICK.
AIN'T GONNA SAVE YOU THOUGH.
THAT TAIL OF YOURS IS ALMOST HYPNOTIC. MY EYES BEEN FIXED ON IT SINCE YOU STARTED JOGGING.
OTHER WORDS, I KNOW WHICH ONE IS THE REAL YOU.
SHOULD'A BEEN NICER TO ME WHEN YOU HAD THE--
--CHANCE?

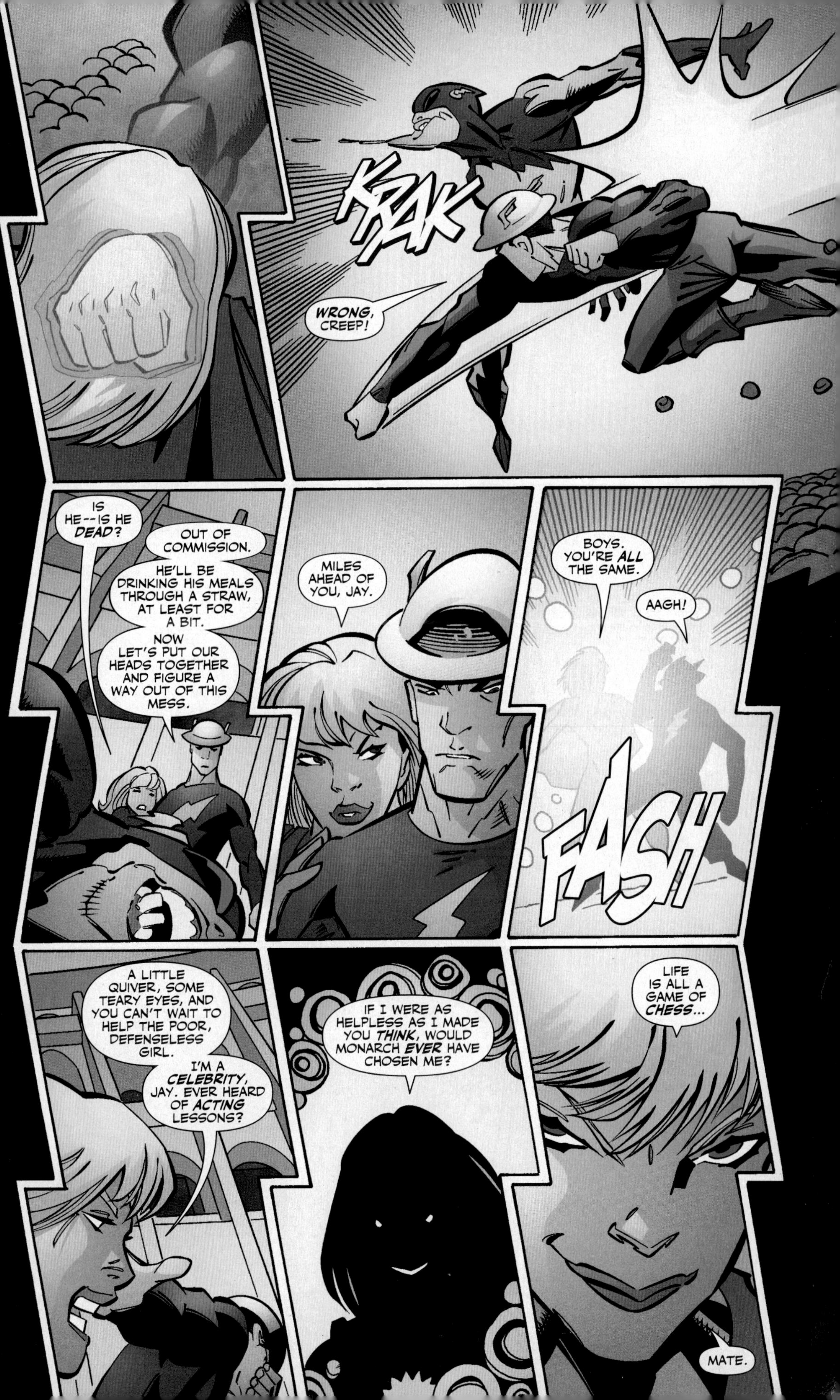

KRAK
WRONG, CREEP!
IS HE--IS HE DEAD?
OUT OF COMMISSION.
HE'LL BE DRINKING HIS MEALS THROUGH A STRAW, AT LEAST FOR A BIT.
NOW LET'S PUT OUR HEADS TOGETHER AND FIGURE A WAY OUT OF THIS MESS.
MILES AHEAD OF YOU, JAY.
BOYS. YOU'RE ALL THE SAME.
AAGH!
FASH
A LITTLE QUIVER, SOME TEARY EYES, AND YOU CAN'T WAIT TO HELP THE POOR, DEFENSELESS GIRL.
I'M A CELEBRITY, JAY. EVER HEARD OF ACTING LESSONS?
IF I WERE AS HELPLESS AS I MADE YOU THINK, WOULD MONARCH EVER HAVE CHOSEN ME?
LIFE IS ALL A GAME OF CHESS...
MATE.

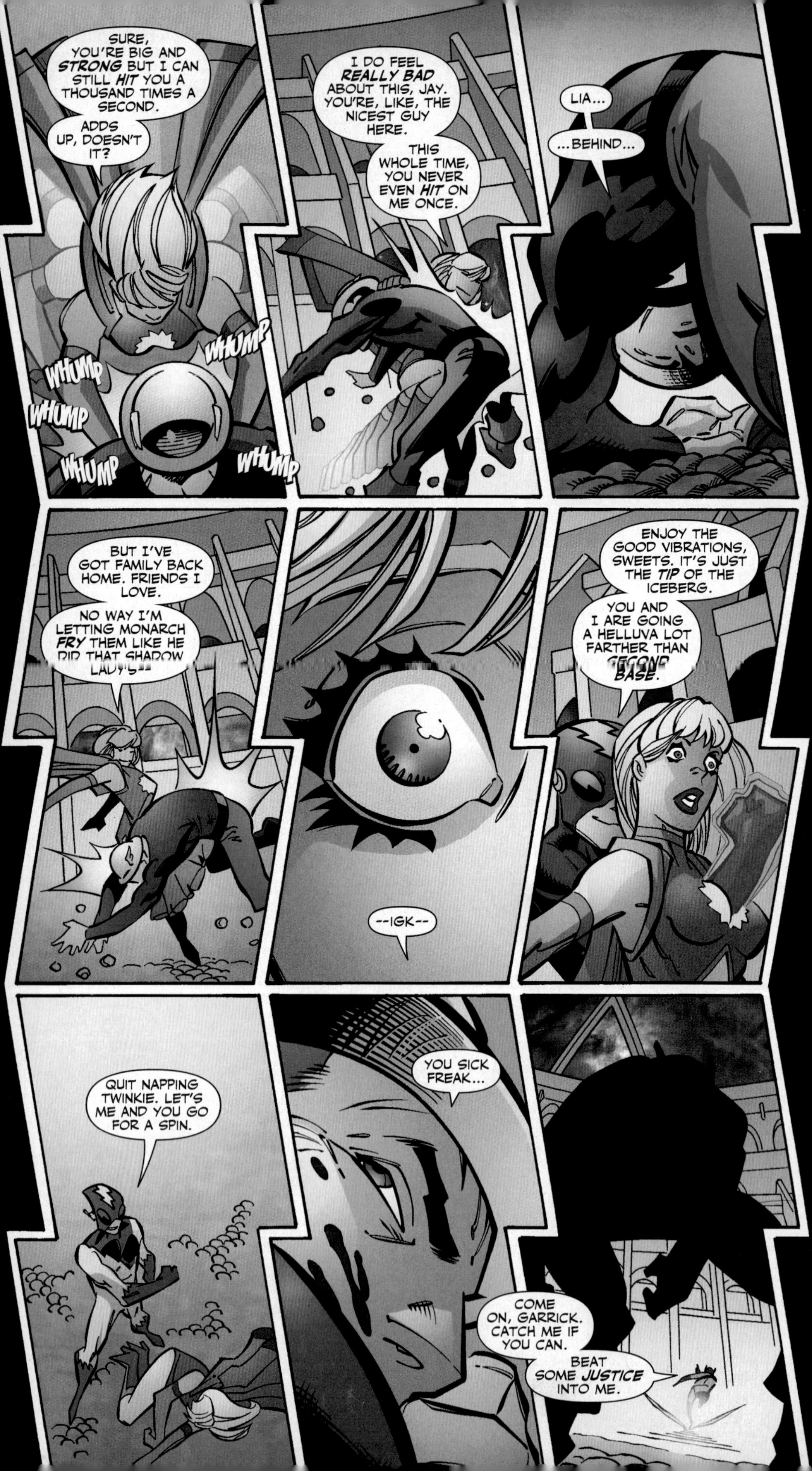
SURE, YOU'RE BIG AND STRONG BUT I CAN STILL HIT YOU A THOUSAND TIMES A SECOND.
ADDS UP, DOESN'T IT?
WHUMP
WHUMP
WHUMP
WHUMP
WHUMP
I DO FEEL REALLY BAD ABOUT THIS, JAY. YOU'RE, LIKE, THE NICEST GUY HERE.
THIS WHOLE TIME, YOU NEVER EVEN HIT ON ME ONCE.
LIA...
...BEHIND...
BUT I'VE GOT FAMILY BACK HOME. FRIENDS I LOVE.
NO WAY I'M LETTING MONARCH FRY THEM LIKE HE DID THAT SHADOW LADY'S--
--IGK--
ENJOY THE GOOD VIBRATIONS, SWEETS. IT'S JUST THE TIP OF THE ICEBERG.
YOU AND I ARE GOING A HELLUVA LOT FARTHER THAN SECOND BASE.
QUIT NAPPING TWINKIE. LET'S ME AND YOU GO FOR A SPIN.
YOU SICK FREAK...
COME ON, GARRICK. CATCH ME IF YOU CAN.
BEAT SOME JUSTICE INTO ME.

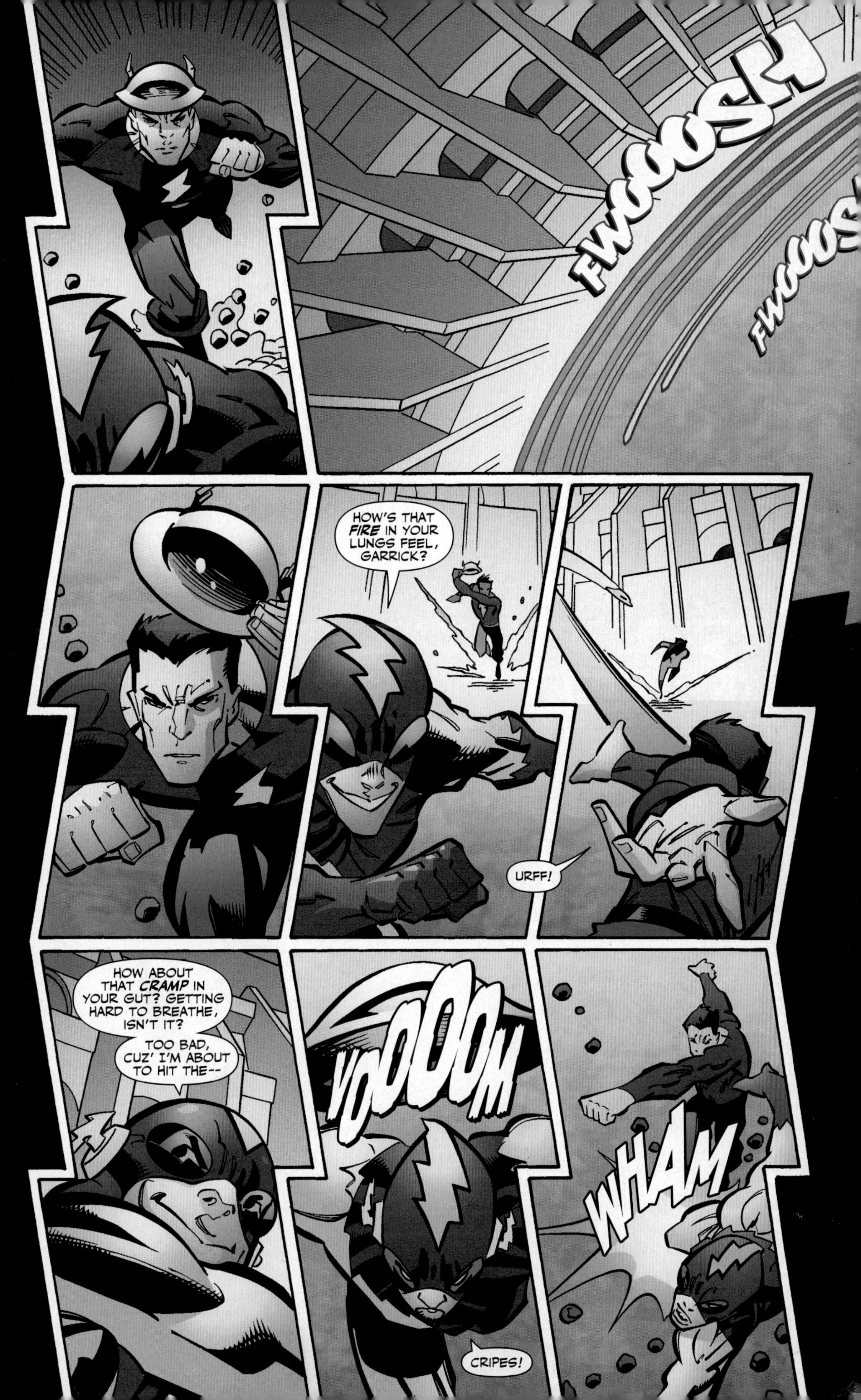
FWOOOSH
FWOOOSH
HOW'S THAT FIRE IN YOUR LUNGS FEEL, GARRICK?
URFF!
HOW ABOUT THAT CRAMP IN YOUR GUT? GETTING HARD TO BREATHE, ISN'T IT?
TOO BAD, CUZ' I'M ABOUT TO HIT THE--
VOOOOOM
CRIPES!
WHAM

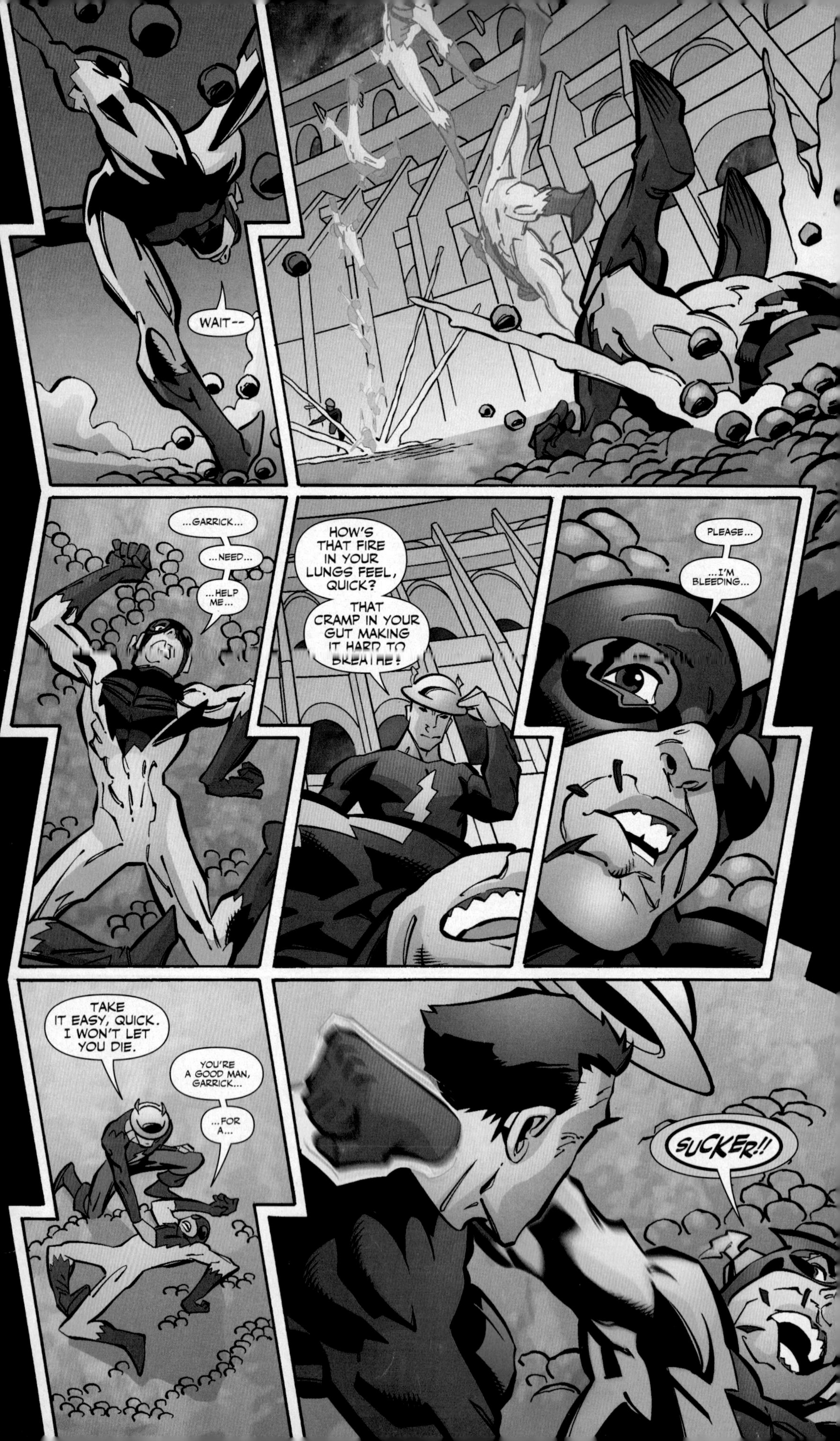
WAIT--
...GARRICK...
...NEED...
...HELP ME...
HOW'S THAT FIRE IN YOUR LUNGS FEEL, QUICK?
THAT CRAMP IN YOUR GUT MAKING IT HARD TO BREATHE?
PLEASE...
...I'M BLEEDING...
TAKE IT EASY, QUICK. I WON'T LET YOU DIE.
YOU'RE A GOOD MAN, GARRICK...
...FOR A...
SUCKER!!

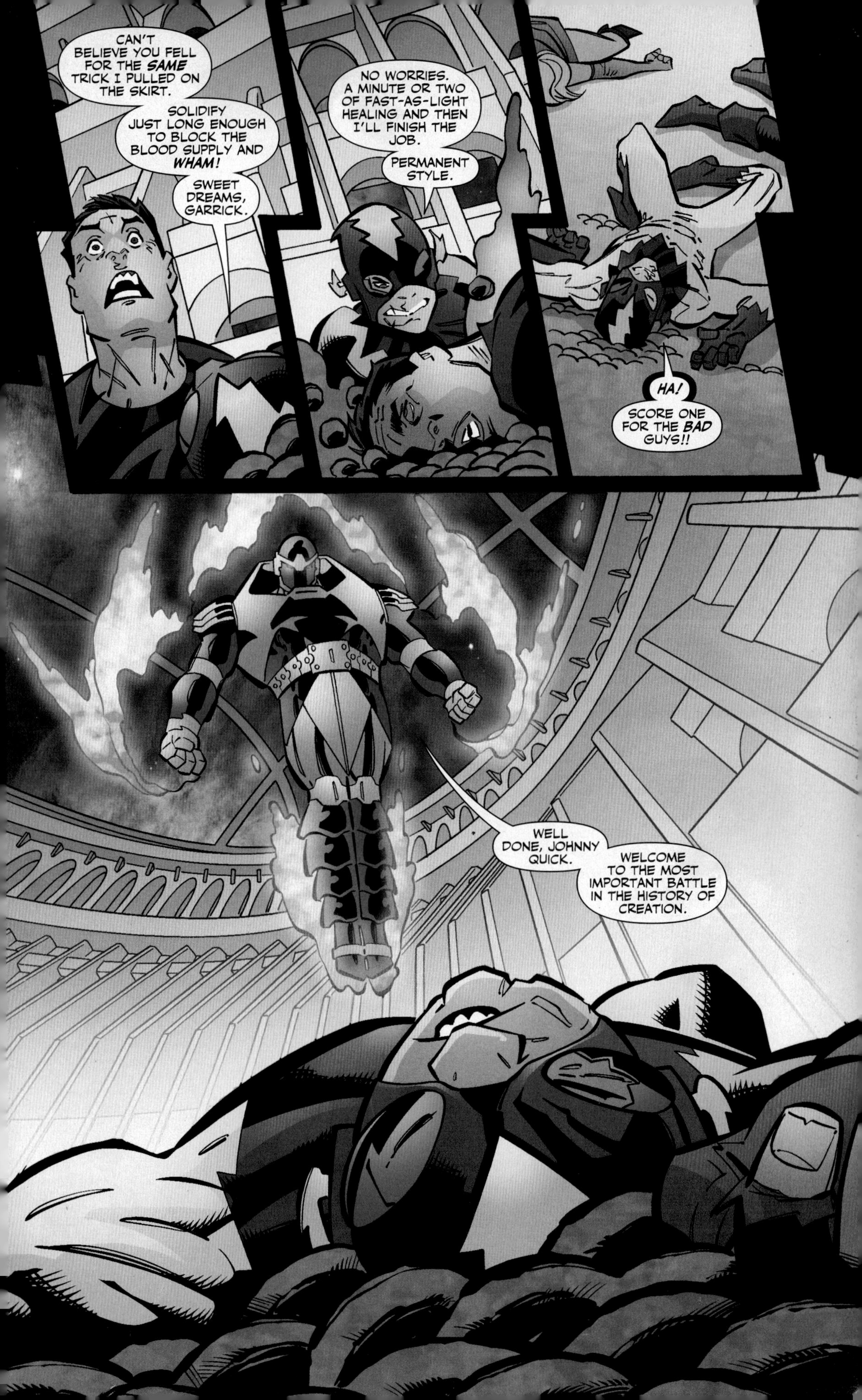
CAN'T BELIEVE YOU FELL FOR THE SAME TRICK I PULLED ON THE SKIRT.
SOLIDIFY JUST LONG ENOUGH TO BLOCK THE BLOOD SUPPLY AND WHAM!
SWEET DREAMS, GARRICK.
NO WORRIES. A MINUTE OR TWO OF FAST-AS-LIGHT HEALING AND THEN I'LL FINISH THE JOB.
PERMANENT STYLE.
HA!
SCORE ONE FOR THE BAD GUYS!!
WELL DONE, JOHNNY QUICK.
WELCOME TO THE MOST IMPORTANT BATTLE IN THE HISTORY OF CREATION.

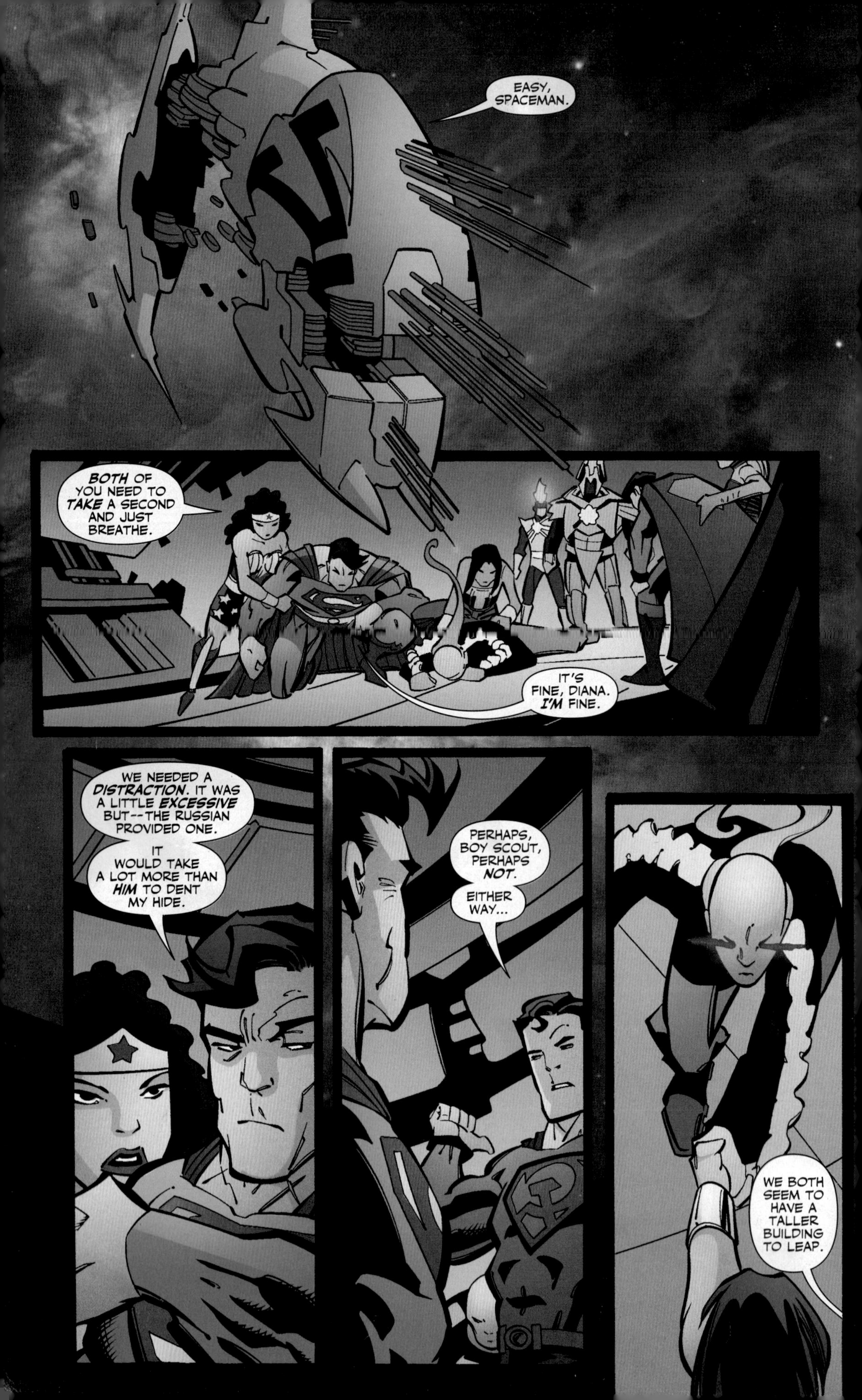
EASY, SPACEMAN.
BOTH OF YOU NEED TO TAKE A SECOND AND JUST BREATHE.
IT'S FINE, DIANA. I'M FINE.
WE NEEDED A DISTRACTION. IT WAS A LITTLE EXCESSIVE BUT--THE RUSSIAN PROVIDED ONE.
IT WOULD TAKE A LOT MORE THAN HIM TO DENT MY HIDE.
PERHAPS, BOY SCOUT, PERHAPS NOT.
EITHER WAY...
WE BOTH SEEM TO HAVE A TALLER BUILDING TO LEAP.

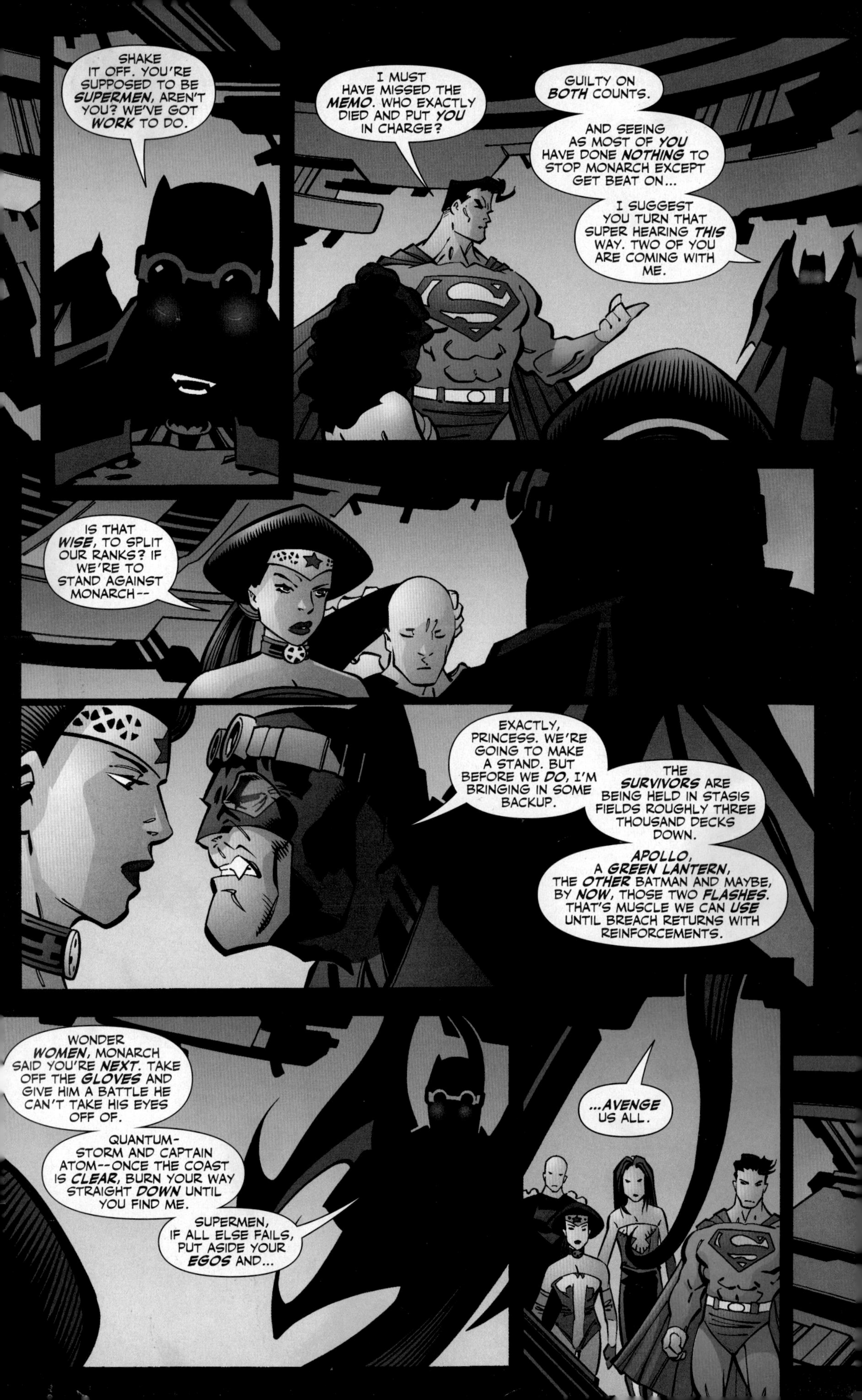
SHAKE IT OFF. YOU'RE SUPPOSED TO BE SUPERMEN, AREN'T YOU? WE'VE GOT WORK TO DO.
I MUST HAVE MISSED THE MEMO. WHO EXACTLY DIED AND PUT YOU IN CHARGE?
GUILTY ON BOTH COUNTS.
AND SEEING AS MOST OF YOU HAVE DONE NOTHING TO STOP MONARCH EXCEPT GET BEAT ON...
I SUGGEST YOU TURN THAT SUPER HEARING THIS WAY. TWO OF YOU ARE COMING WITH ME.
IS THAT WISE, TO SPLIT OUR RANKS? IF WE'RE TO STAND AGAINST MONARCH--
EXACTLY, PRINCESS. WE'RE GOING TO MAKE A STAND. BUT BEFORE WE DO, I'M BRINGING IN SOME BACKUP.
THE SURVIVORS ARE BEING HELD IN STASIS FIELDS ROUGHLY THREE THOUSAND DECKS DOWN.
APOLLO, A GREEN LANTERN, THE OTHER BATMAN AND MAYBE, BY NOW, THOSE TWO FLASHES. THAT'S MUSCLE WE CAN USE UNTIL BREACH RETURNS WITH REINFORCEMENTS.
WONDER WOMEN, MONARCH SAID YOU'RE NEXT. TAKE OFF THE GLOVES AND GIVE HIM A BATTLE HE CAN'T TAKE HIS EYES OFF OF.
QUANTUM-STORM AND CAPTAIN ATOM--ONCE THE COAST IS CLEAR, BURN YOUR WAY STRAIGHT DOWN UNTIL YOU FIND ME.
SUPERMEN, IF ALL ELSE FAILS, PUT ASIDE YOUR EGOS AND...
...AVENGE US ALL.

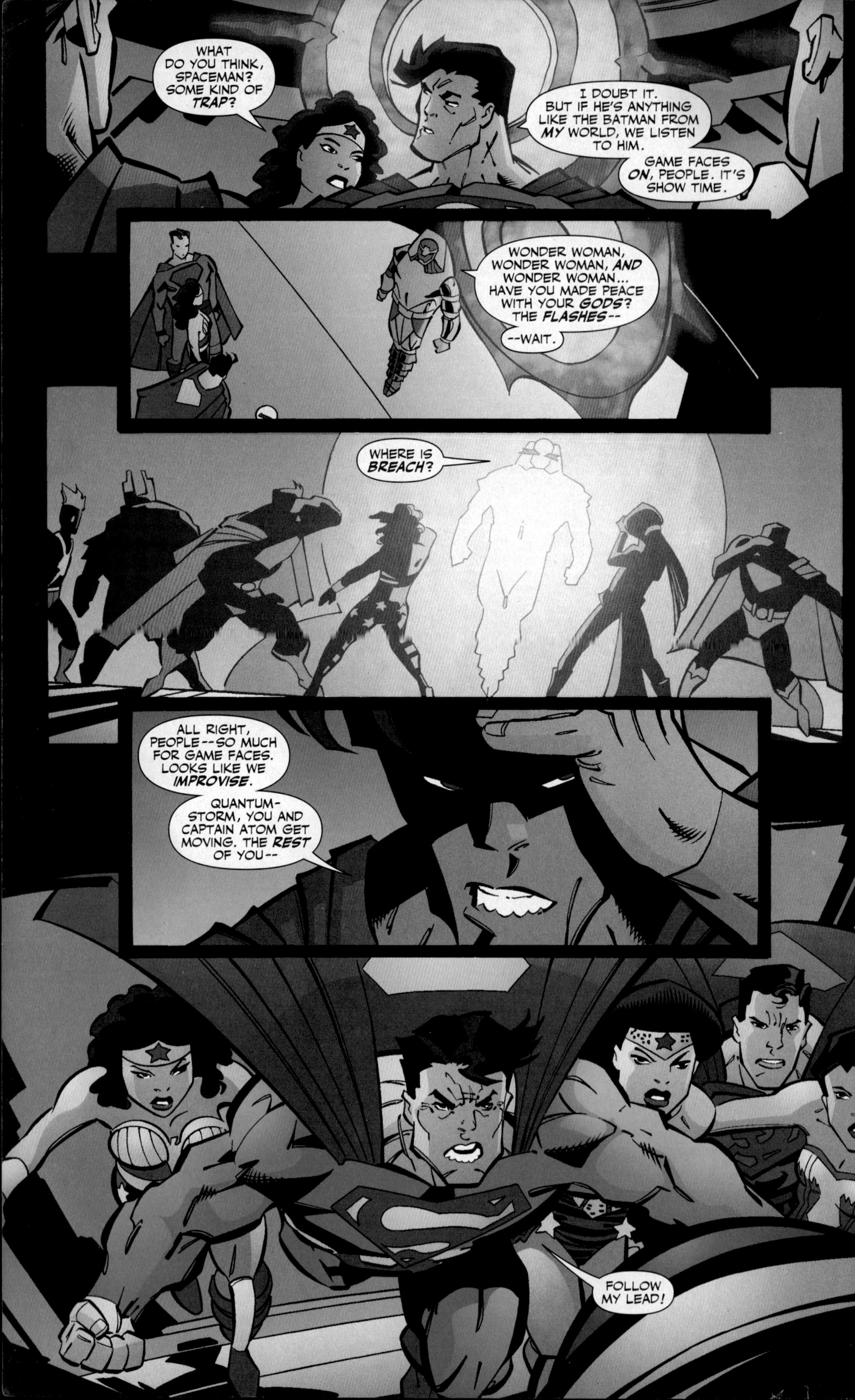
WHAT DO YOU THINK, SPACEMAN? SOME KIND OF TRAP?
I DOUBT IT. BUT IF HE'S ANYTHING LIKE THE BATMAN FROM MY WORLD, WE LISTEN TO HIM.
GAME FACES ON, PEOPLE. IT'S SHOW TIME.
WONDER WOMAN, WONDER WOMAN, AND WONDER WOMAN... HAVE YOU MADE PEACE WITH YOUR GODS? THE FLASHES--
--WAIT.
WHERE IS BREACH?
ALL RIGHT, PEOPLE--SO MUCH FOR GAME FACES. LOOKS LIKE WE IMPROVISE.
QUANTUM-STORM, YOU AND CAPTAIN ATOM GET MOVING. THE REST OF YOU--
FOLLOW MY LEAD!

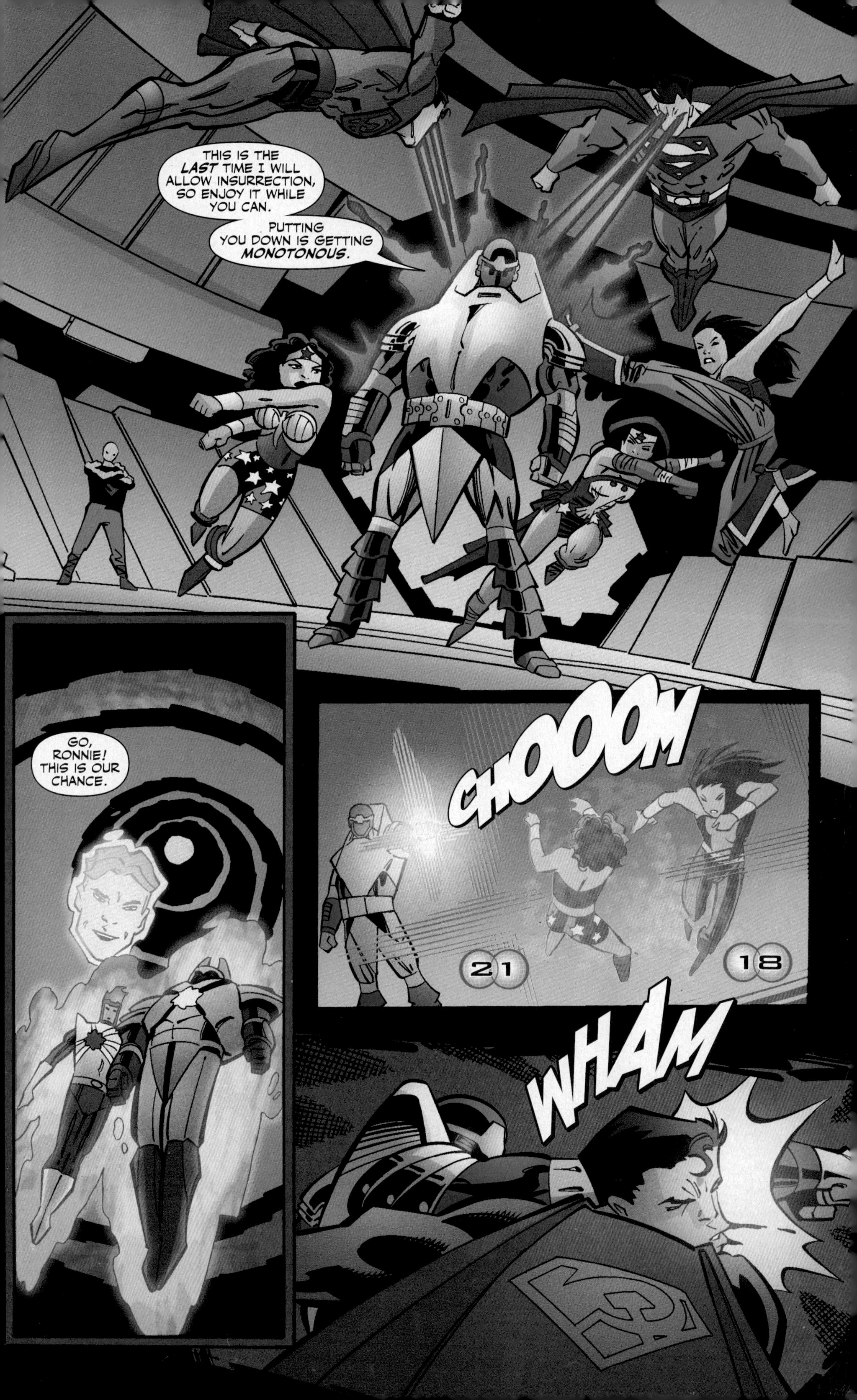
THIS IS THE LAST TIME I WILL ALLOW INSURRECTION, SO ENJOY IT WHILE YOU CAN.
PUTTING YOU DOWN IS GETTING MONOTONOUS.
GO, RONNIE! THIS IS OUR CHANCE.
CHOOOM
21
18
WHAM

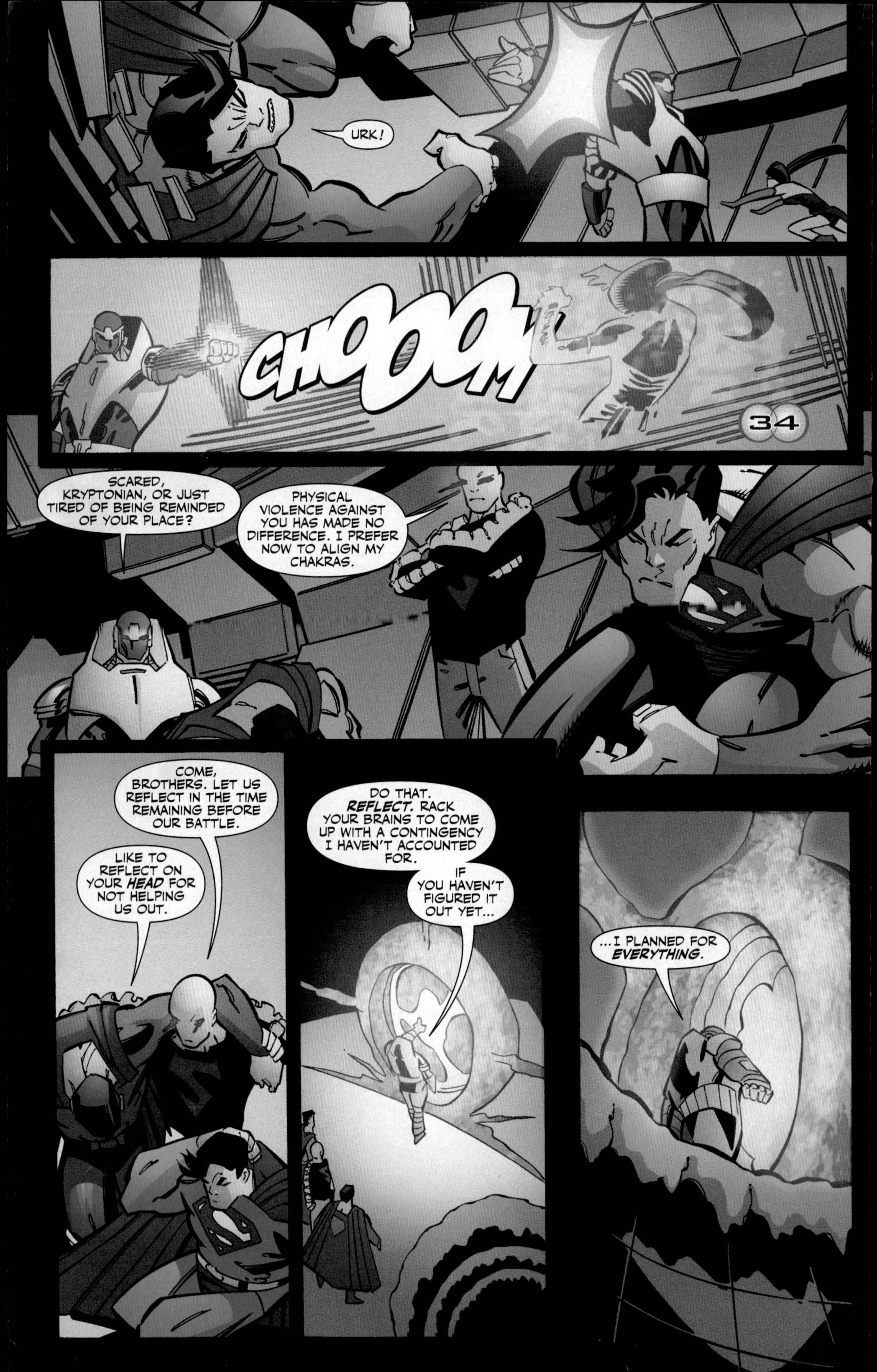
URK!
CHOOOM
34
SCARED, KRYPTONIAN, OR JUST TIRED OF BEING REMINDED OF YOUR PLACE?
PHYSICAL VIOLENCE AGAINST YOU HAS MADE NO DIFFERENCE. I PREFER NOW TO ALIGN MY CHAKRAS.
COME, BROTHERS. LET US REFLECT IN THE TIME REMAINING BEFORE OUR BATTLE.
LIKE TO REFLECT ON YOUR HEAD FOR NOT HELPING US OUT.
DO THAT. REFLECT. RACK YOUR BRAINS TO COME UP WITH A CONTINGENCY I HAVEN'T ACCOUNTED FOR.
IF YOU HAVEN'T FIGURED IT OUT YET...
...I PLANNED FOR EVERYTHING.

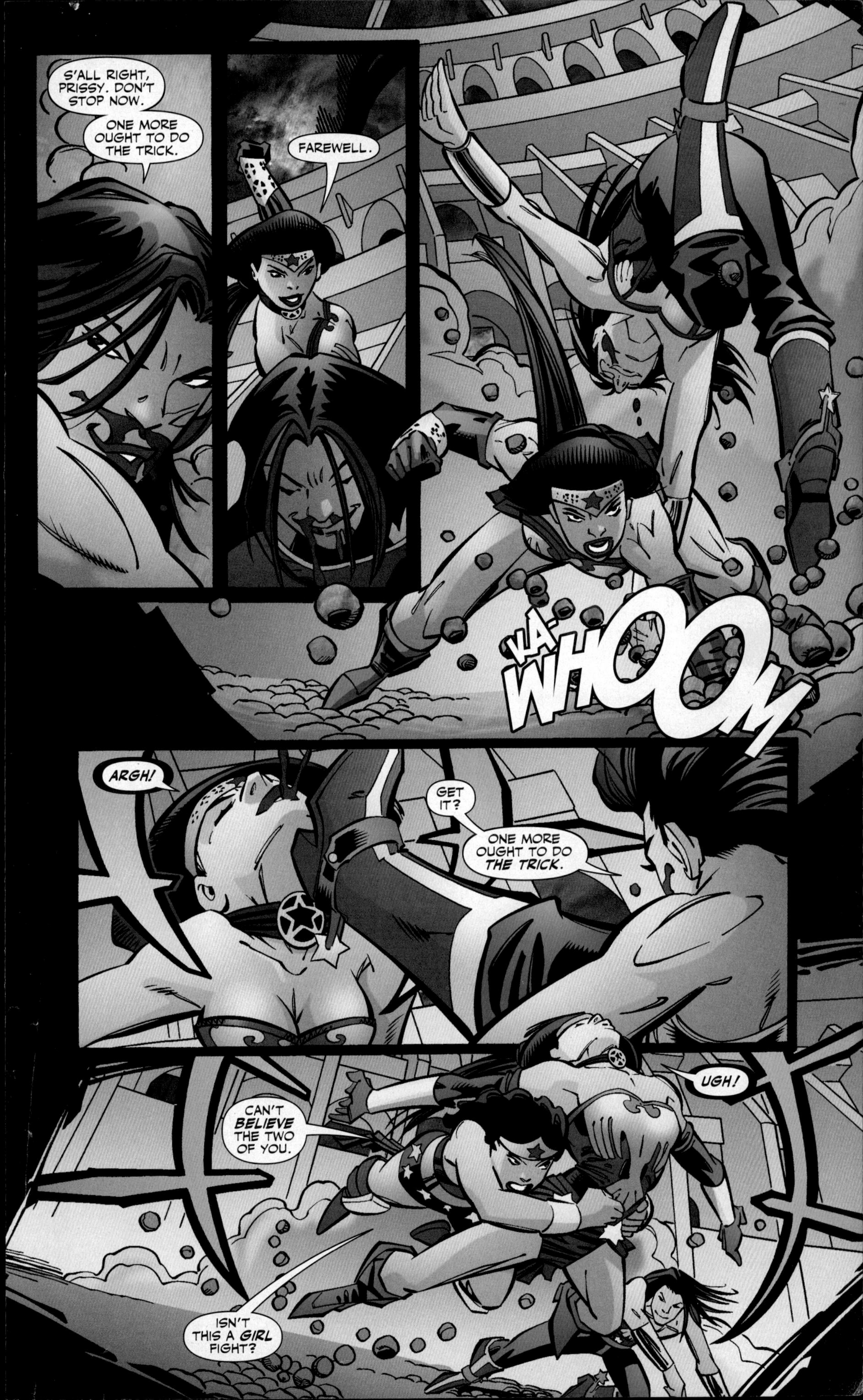
S'ALL RIGHT, PRISSY. DON'T STOP NOW.
ONE MORE OUGHT TO DO THE TRICK.
FAREWELL.
KA-WHOOOM
ARGH!
GET IT?
ONE MORE OUGHT TO DO *THE TRICK*.
UGH!
CAN'T *BELIEVE* THE TWO OF YOU.
ISN'T THIS A *GIRL* FIGHT?

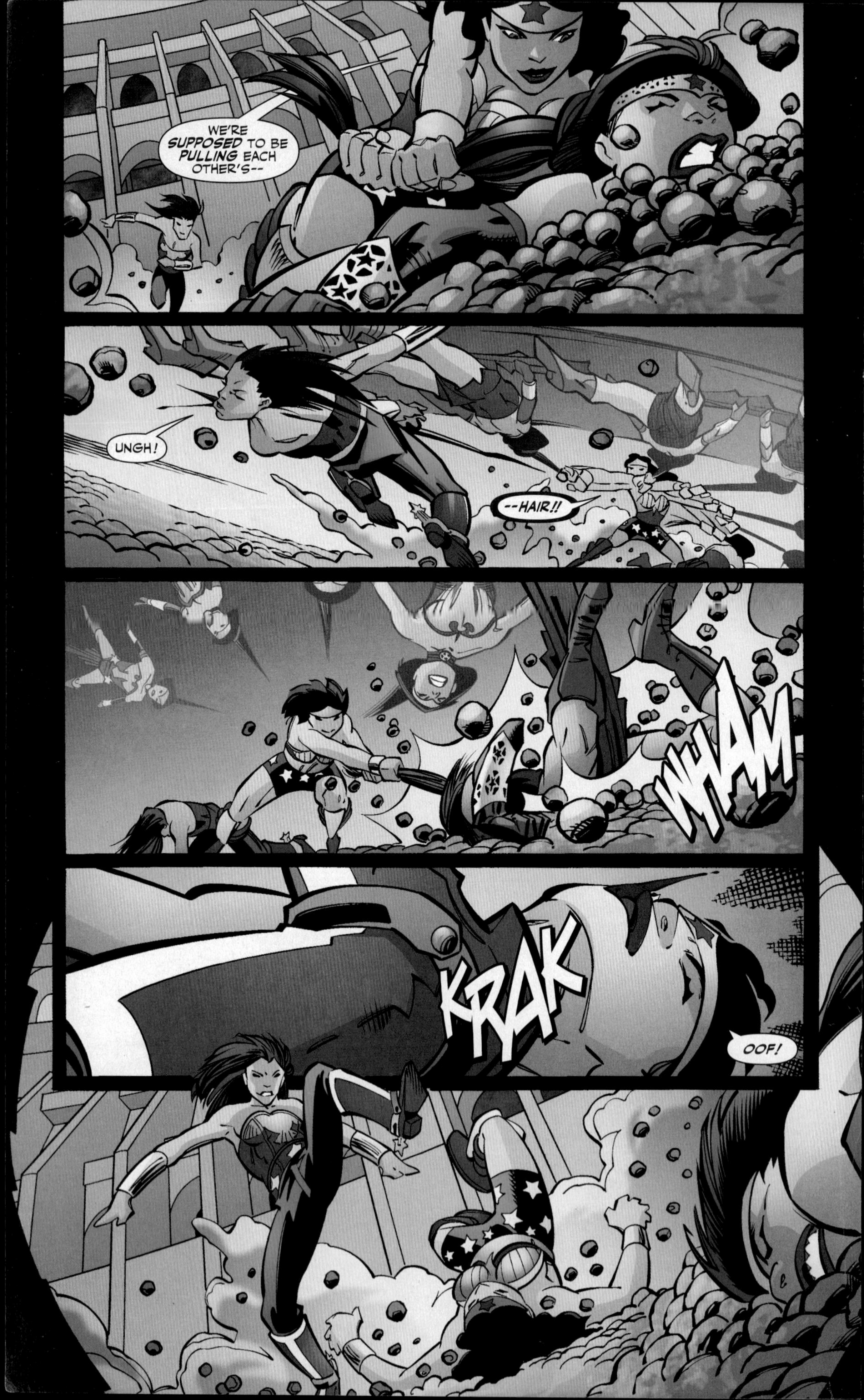
WE'RE SUPPOSED TO BE PULLING EACH OTHER'S--
UNGH!
--HAIR!!
WHAM
KRAK
OOF!

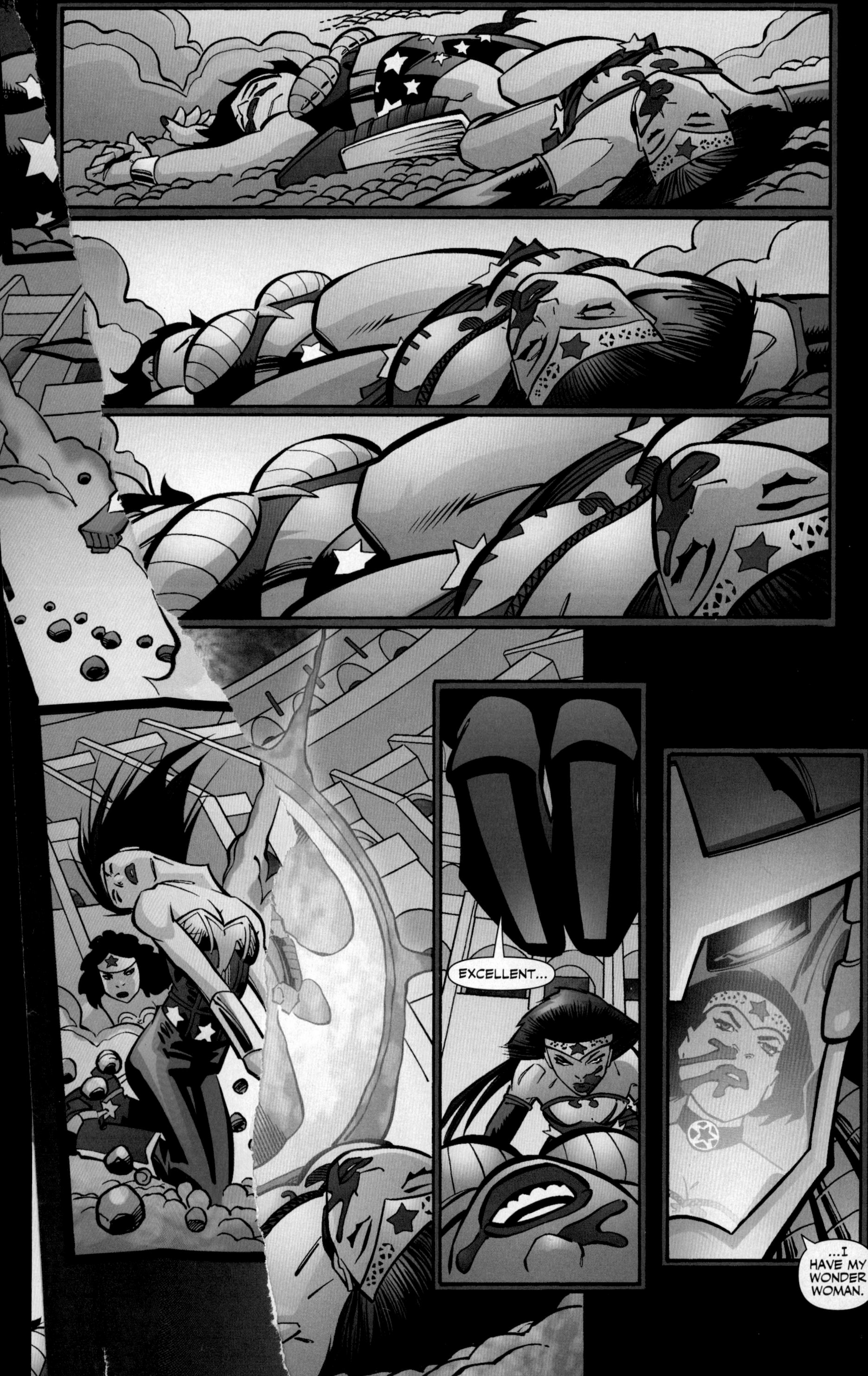
EXCELLENT...
...I HAVE MY WONDER WOMAN.

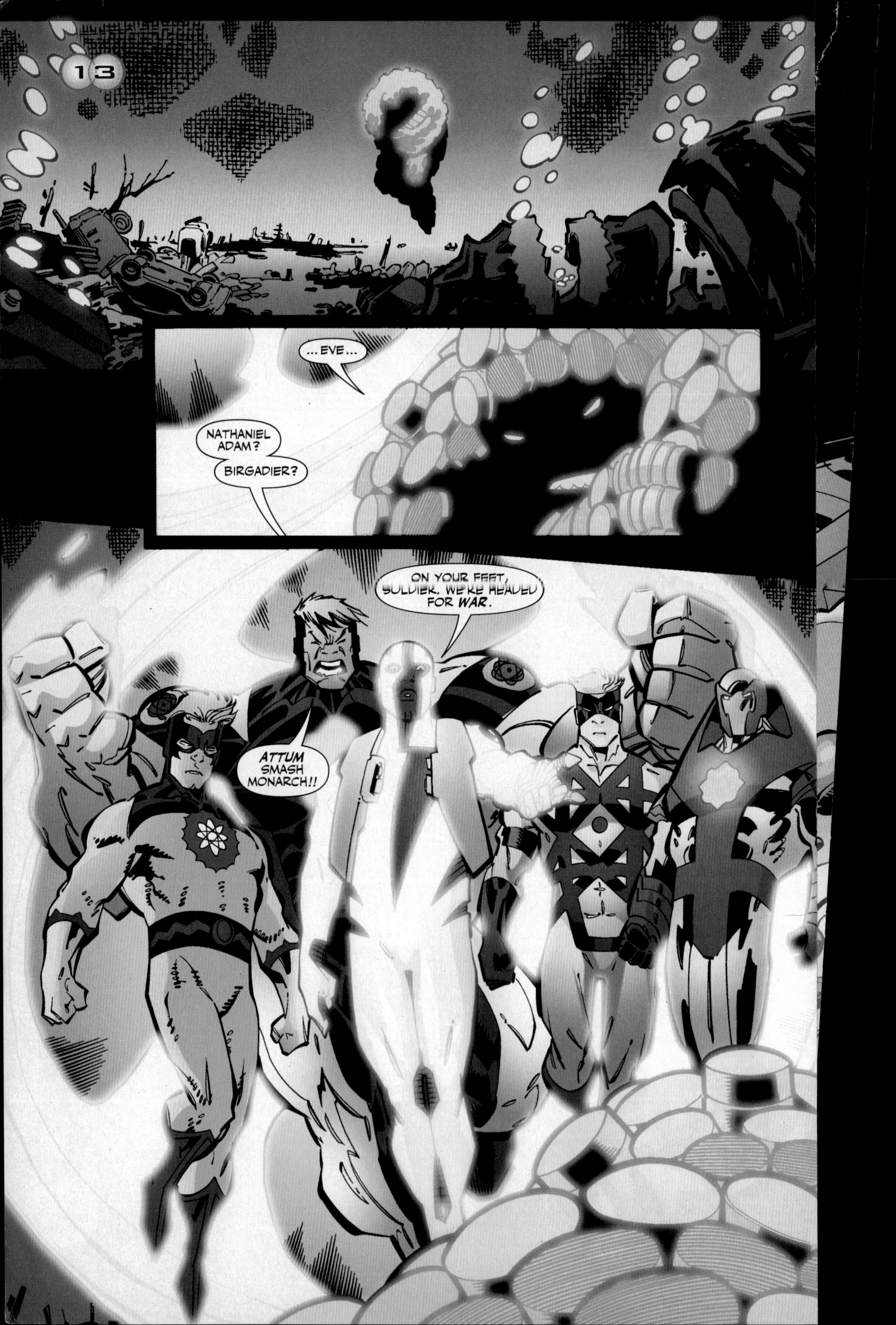
...EVE...
NATHANIEL ADAM?
BIRGADIER?
ON YOUR FEET, SOLDIER. WE'RE HEADED FOR WAR.
ATTUM SMASH MONARCH!!

ALL FALL DOWN COVER ART BY ANDY KUBERT

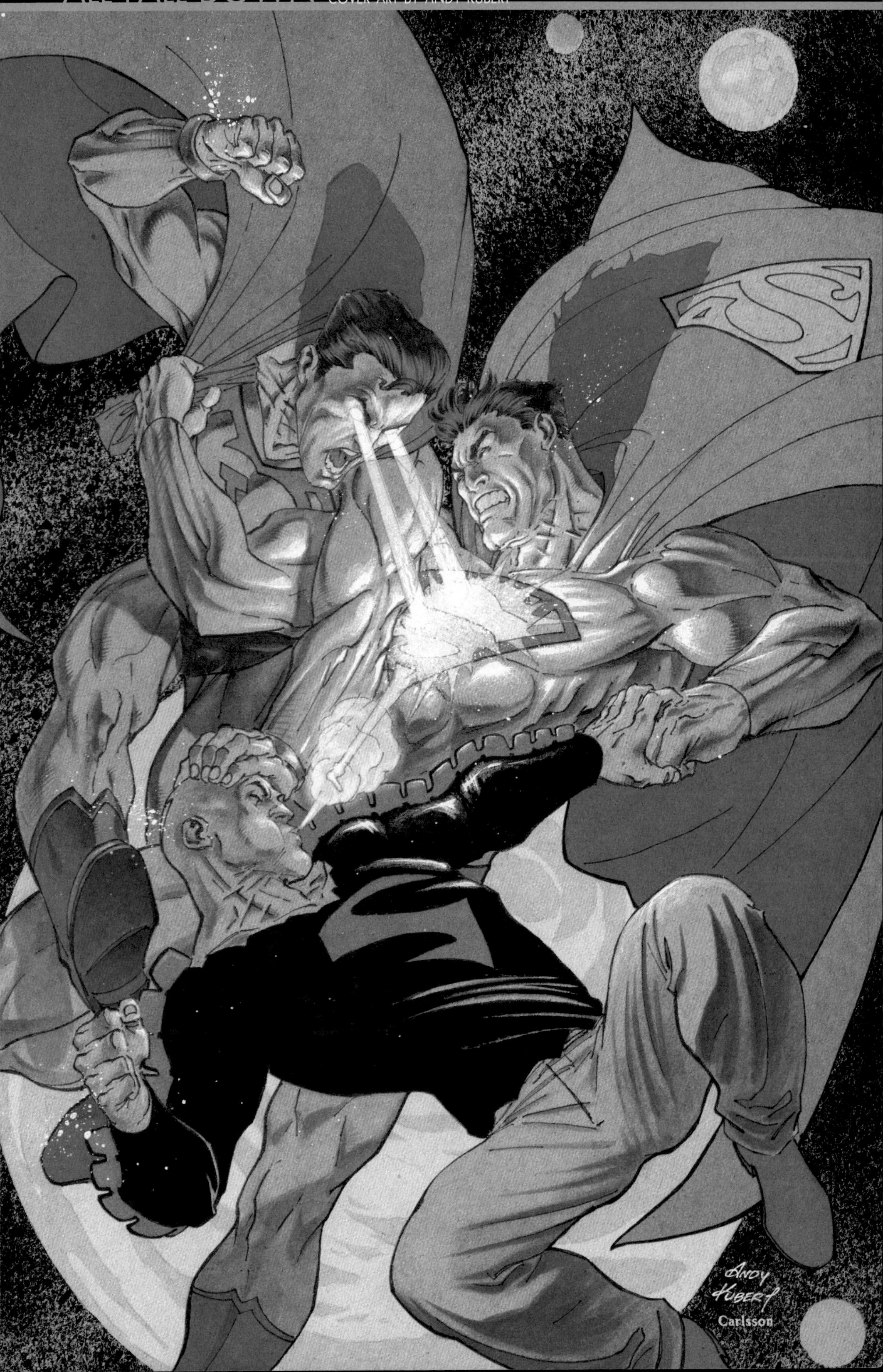
ANDY KUBERT
Carlsson

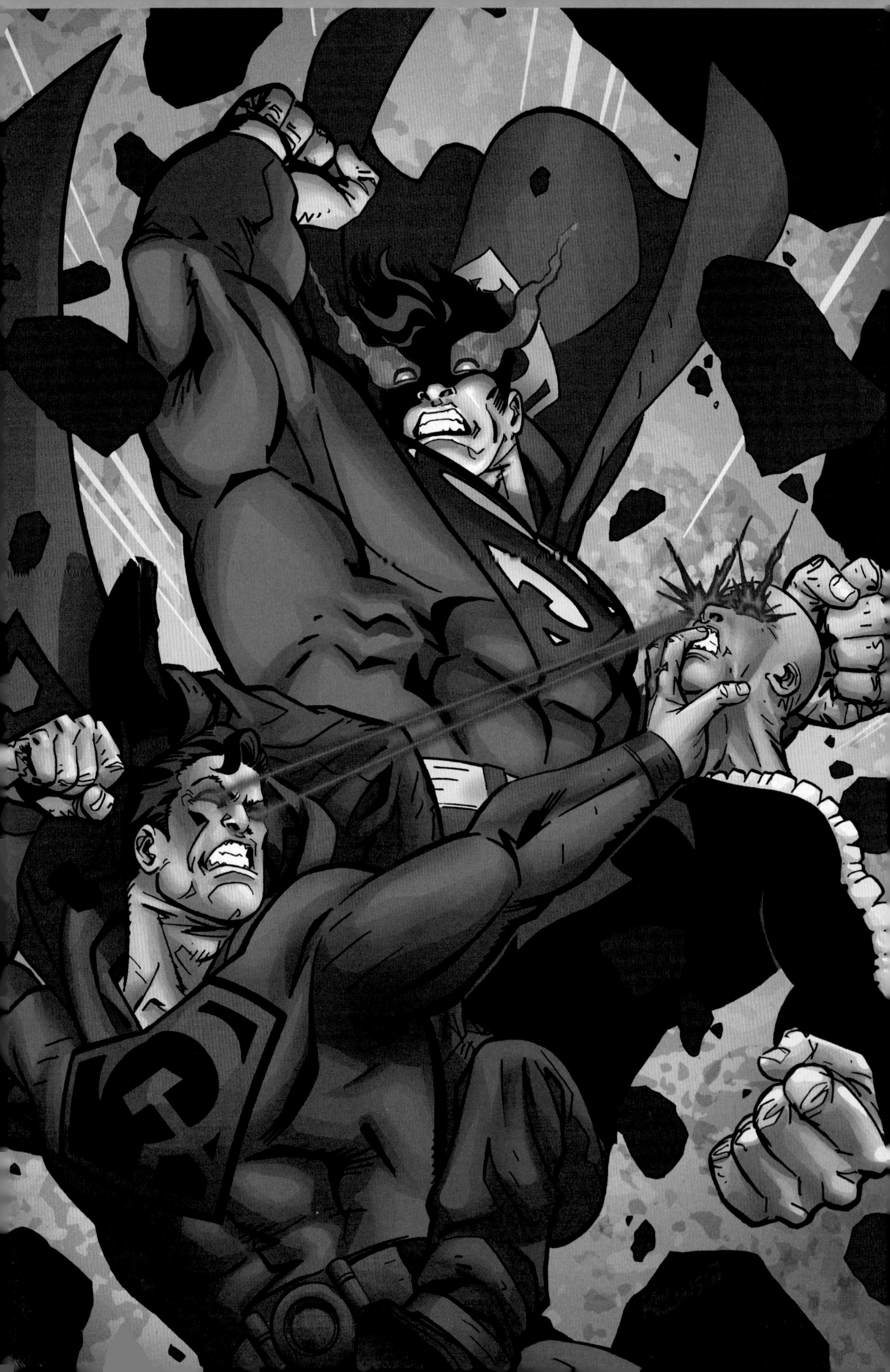

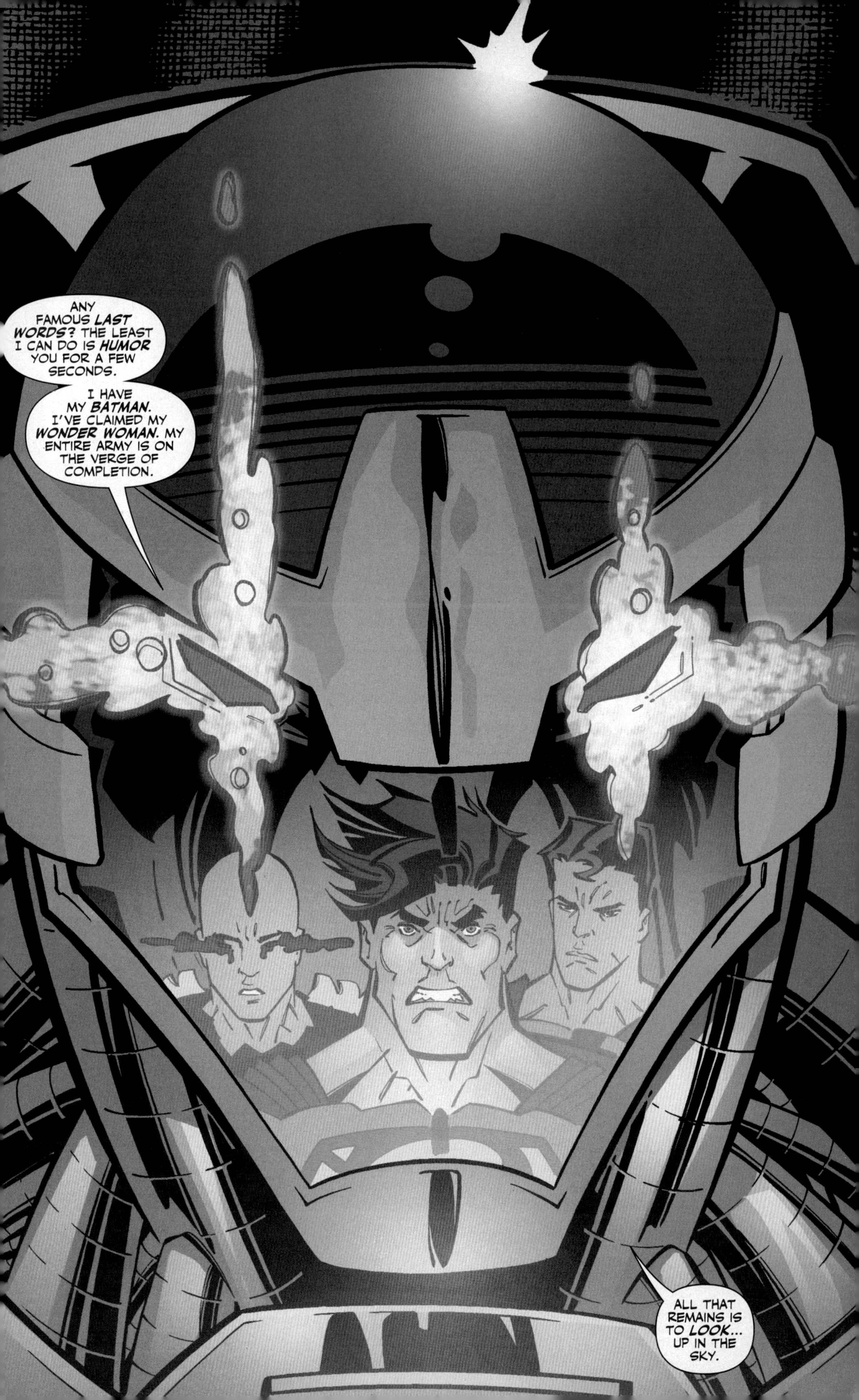
ANY FAMOUS LAST WORDS? THE LEAST I CAN DO IS HUMOR YOU FOR A FEW SECONDS.
I HAVE MY BATMAN. I'VE CLAIMED MY WONDER WOMAN. MY ENTIRE ARMY IS ON THE VERGE OF COMPLETION.
ALL THAT REMAINS IS TO LOOK... UP IN THE SKY.

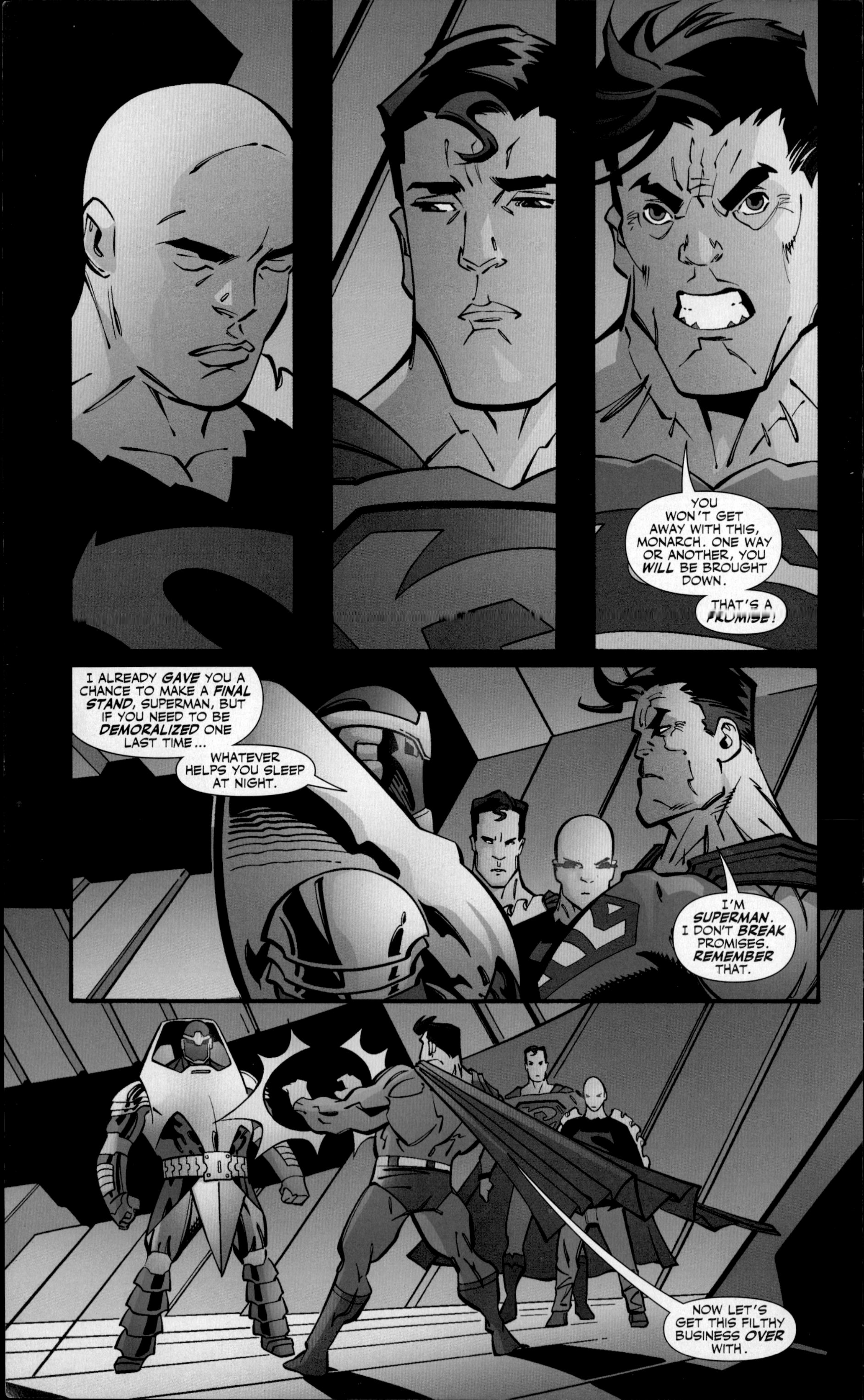
YOU WON'T GET AWAY WITH THIS, MONARCH. ONE WAY OR ANOTHER, YOU *WILL* BE BROUGHT DOWN.
THAT'S A *PROMISE*!
I ALREADY *GAVE* YOU A CHANCE TO MAKE A *FINAL STAND*, SUPERMAN, BUT IF YOU NEED TO BE *DEMORALIZED* ONE LAST TIME...
WHATEVER HELPS YOU SLEEP AT NIGHT.
I'M *SUPERMAN*. I DON'T *BREAK* PROMISES. *REMEMBER* THAT.
NOW LET'S GET THIS FILTHY BUSINESS *OVER* WITH.

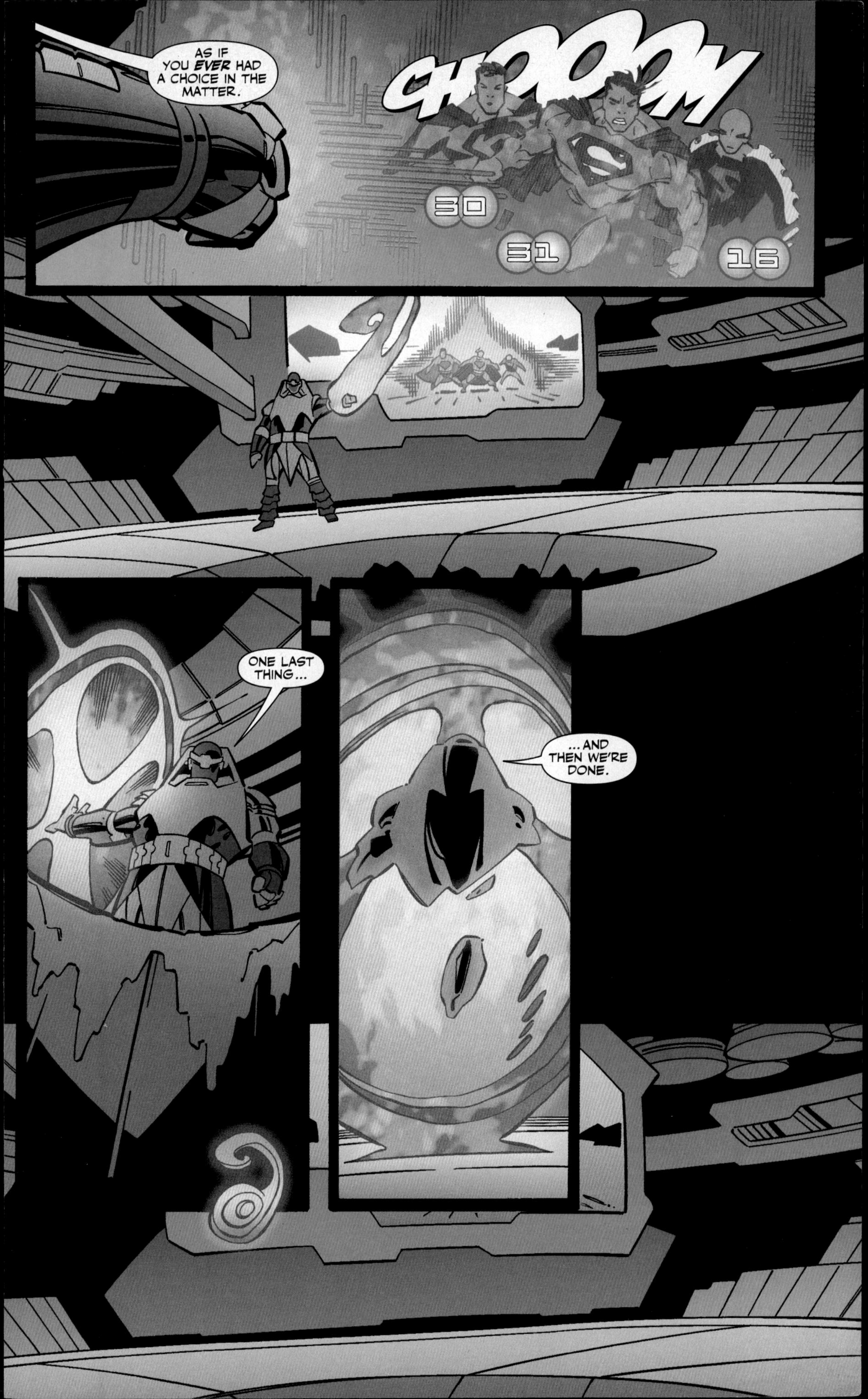
AS IF YOU EVER HAD A CHOICE IN THE MATTER.
CHOOOOM
30
31
16
ONE LAST THING...
...AND THEN WE'RE DONE.

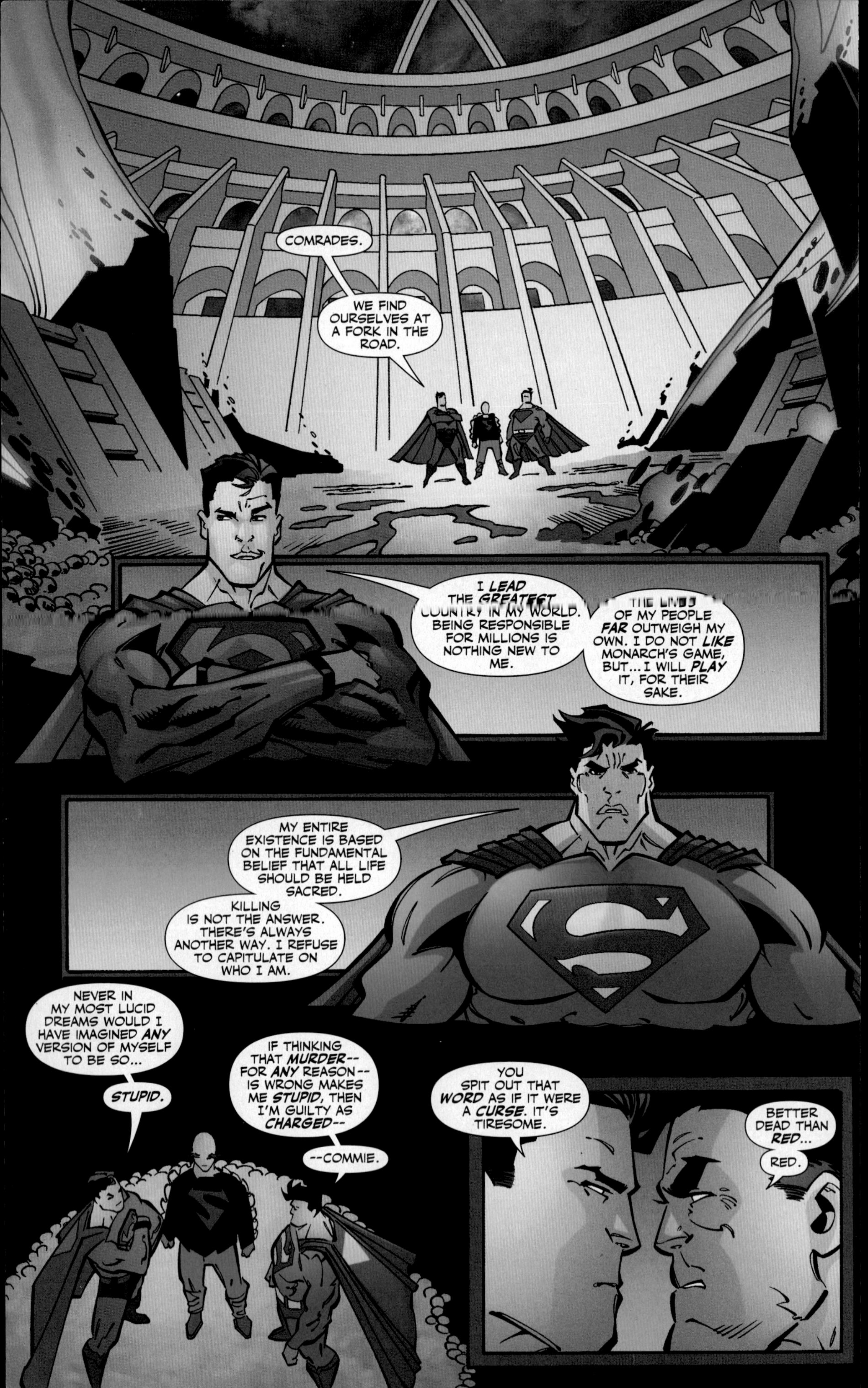
COMRADES.
WE FIND OURSELVES AT A FORK IN THE ROAD.
I LEAD THE GREATEST COUNTRY IN MY WORLD. BEING RESPONSIBLE FOR MILLIONS IS NOTHING NEW TO ME.
THE LIVES OF MY PEOPLE FAR OUTWEIGH MY OWN. I DO NOT LIKE MONARCH'S GAME, BUT... I WILL PLAY IT, FOR THEIR SAKE.
MY ENTIRE EXISTENCE IS BASED ON THE FUNDAMENTAL BELIEF THAT ALL LIFE SHOULD BE HELD SACRED.
KILLING IS NOT THE ANSWER. THERE'S ALWAYS ANOTHER WAY. I REFUSE TO CAPITULATE ON WHO I AM.
NEVER IN MY MOST LUCID DREAMS WOULD I HAVE IMAGINED ANY VERSION OF MYSELF TO BE SO...
STUPID.
IF THINKING THAT MURDER--FOR ANY REASON--IS WRONG MAKES ME STUPID, THEN I'M GUILTY AS CHARGED--
--COMMIE.
YOU SPIT OUT THAT WORD AS IF IT WERE A CURSE. IT'S TIRESOME.
BETTER DEAD THAN RED...
RED.

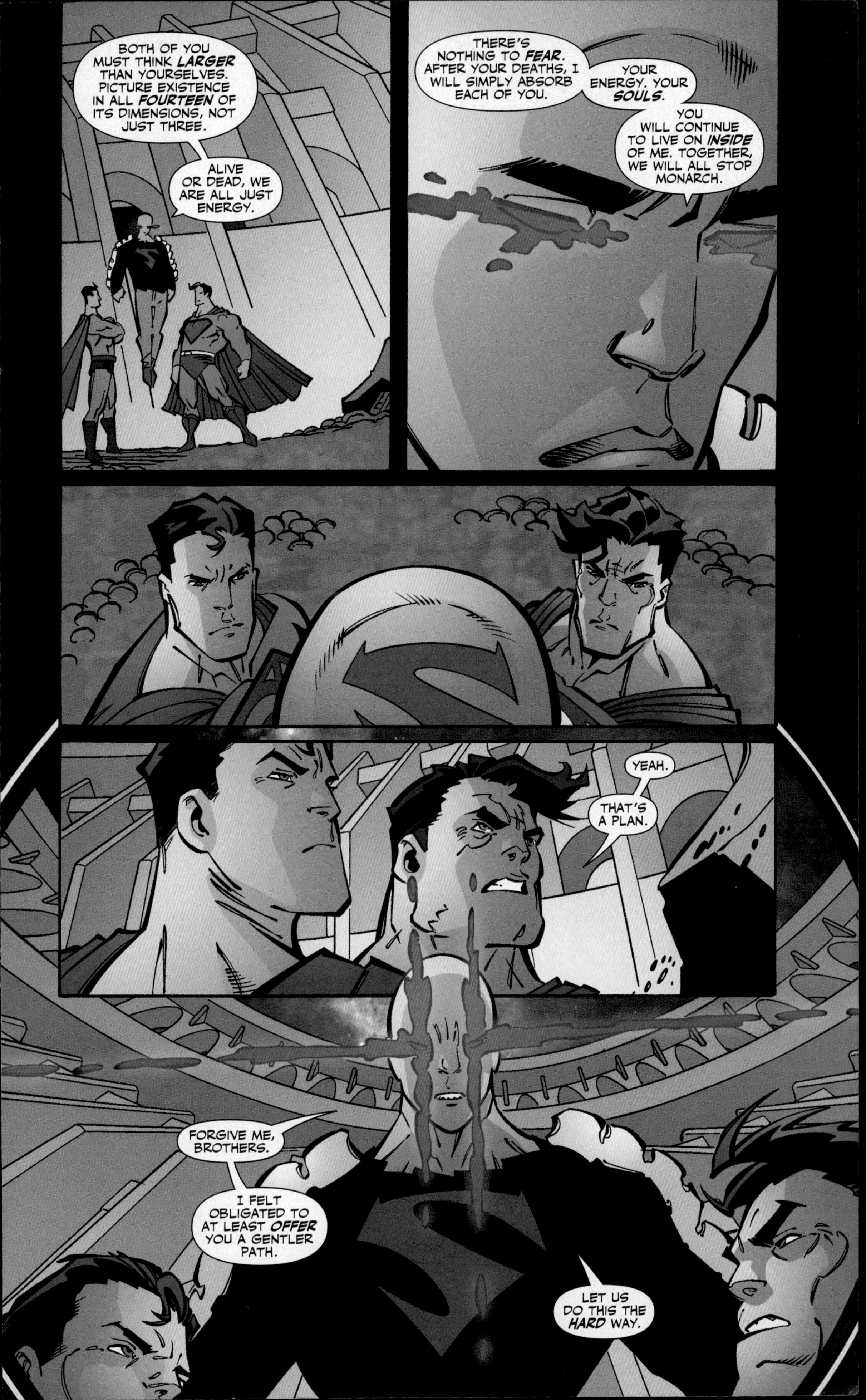
BOTH OF YOU MUST THINK LARGER THAN YOURSELVES. PICTURE EXISTENCE IN ALL FOURTEEN OF ITS DIMENSIONS, NOT JUST THREE.
ALIVE OR DEAD, WE ARE ALL JUST ENERGY.
THERE'S NOTHING TO FEAR. AFTER YOUR DEATHS, I WILL SIMPLY ABSORB EACH OF YOU.
YOUR ENERGY. YOUR SOULS.
YOU WILL CONTINUE TO LIVE ON INSIDE OF ME. TOGETHER, WE WILL ALL STOP MONARCH.
YEAH.
THAT'S A PLAN.
FORGIVE ME, BROTHERS.
I FELT OBLIGATED TO AT LEAST OFFER YOU A GENTLER PATH.
LET US DO THIS THE HARD WAY.

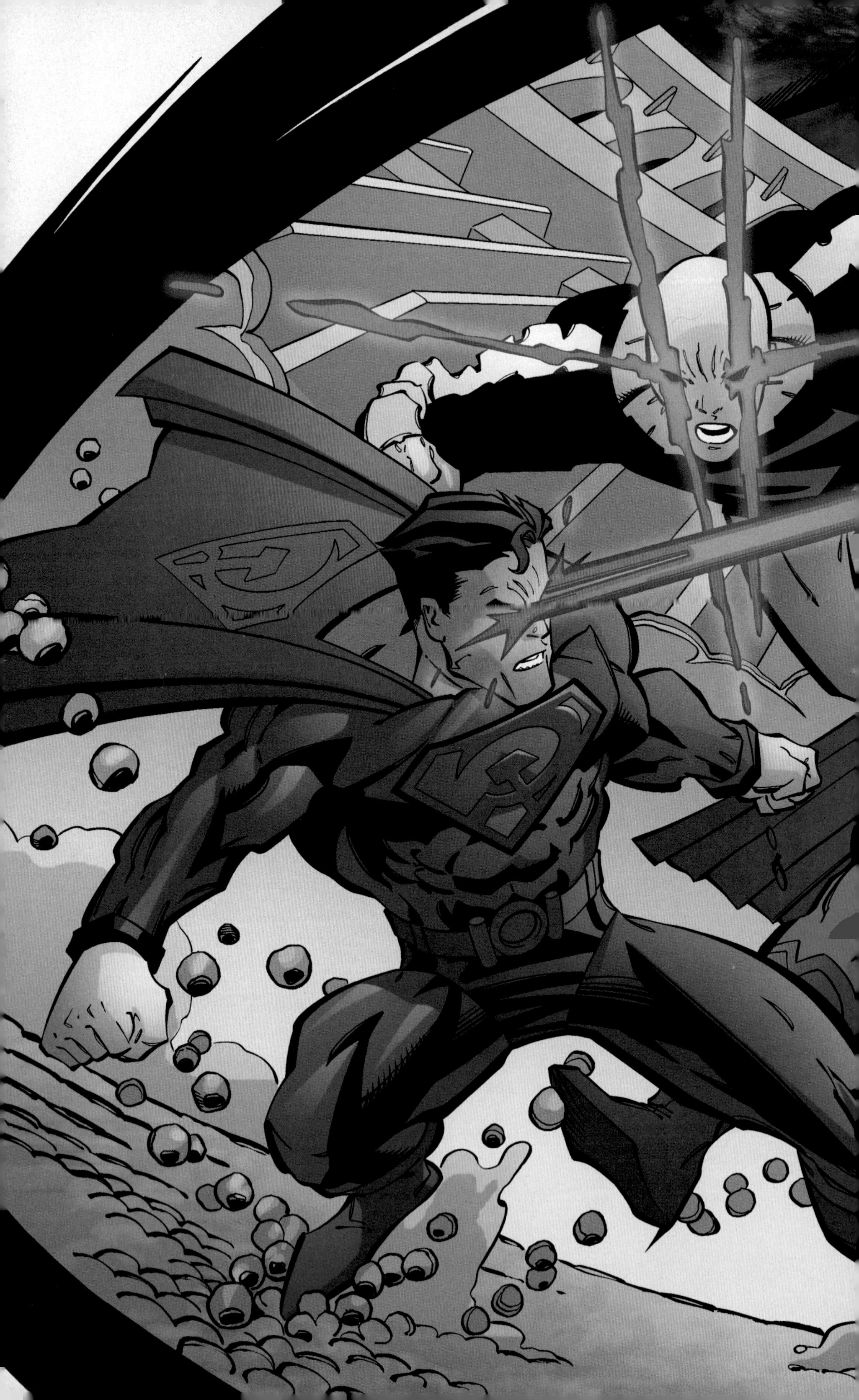

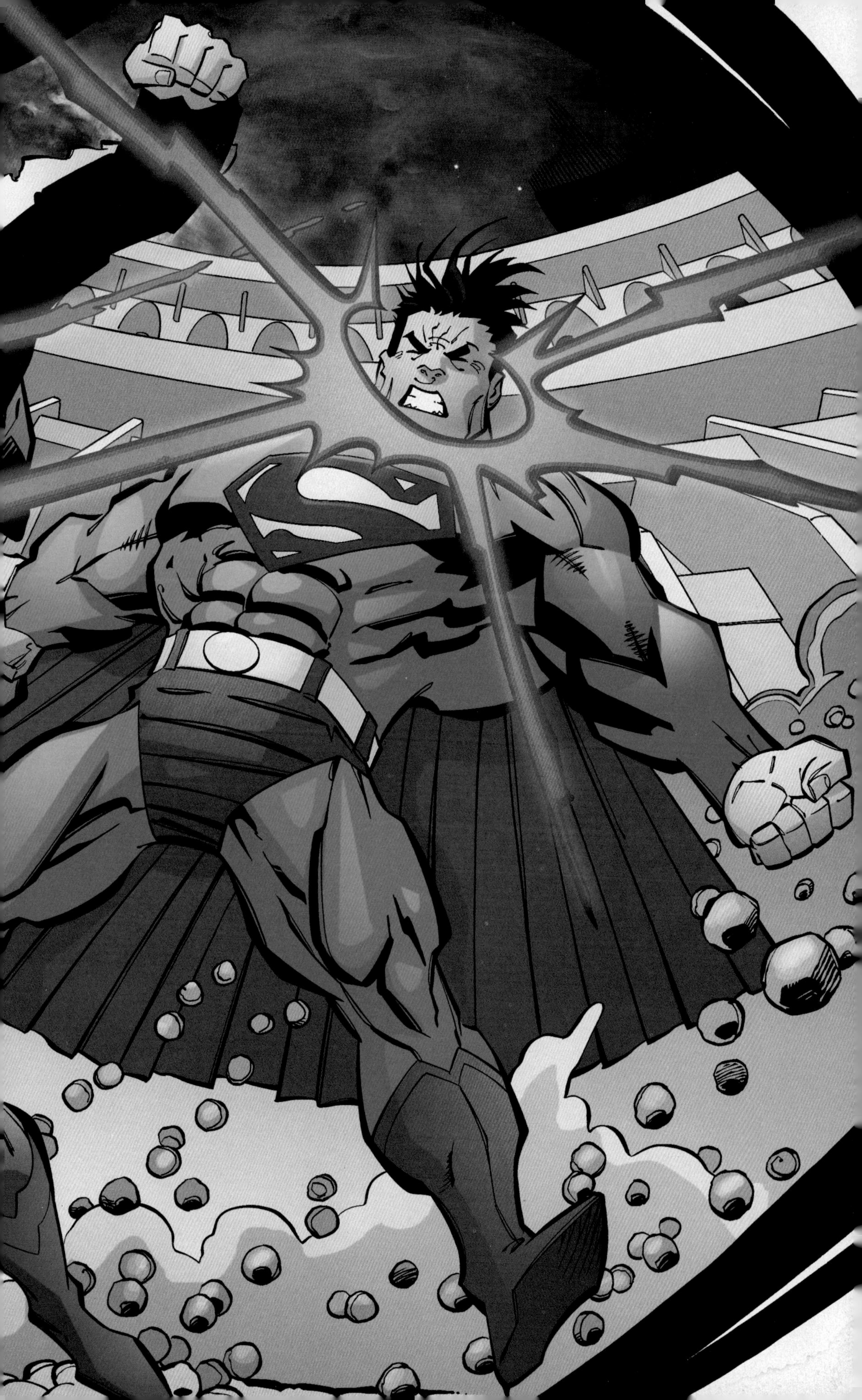

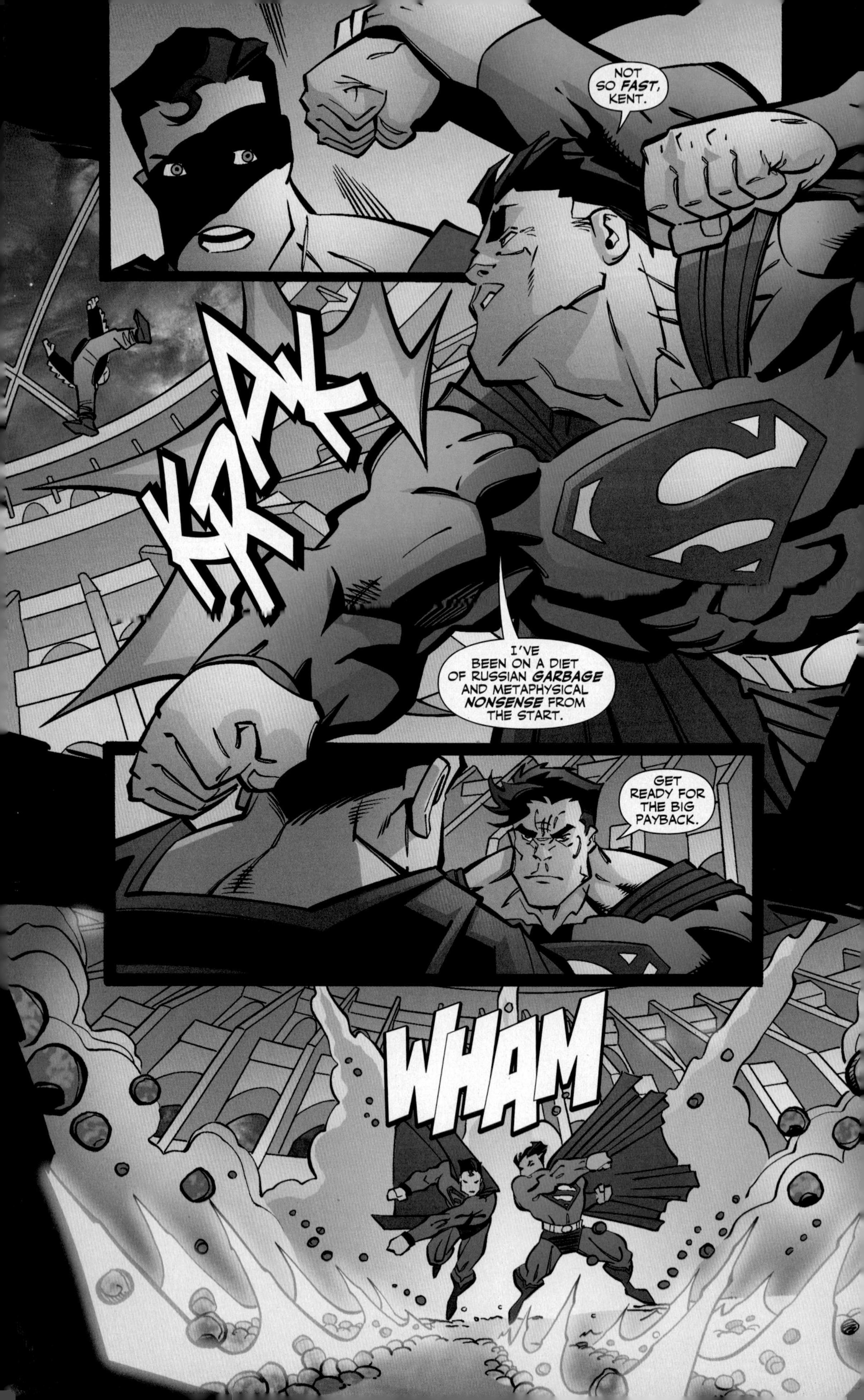
NOT SO FAST, KENT.
KRAK
I'VE BEEN ON A DIET OF RUSSIAN GARBAGE AND METAPHYSICAL NONSENSE FROM THE START.
GET READY FOR THE BIG PAYBACK.
WHAM

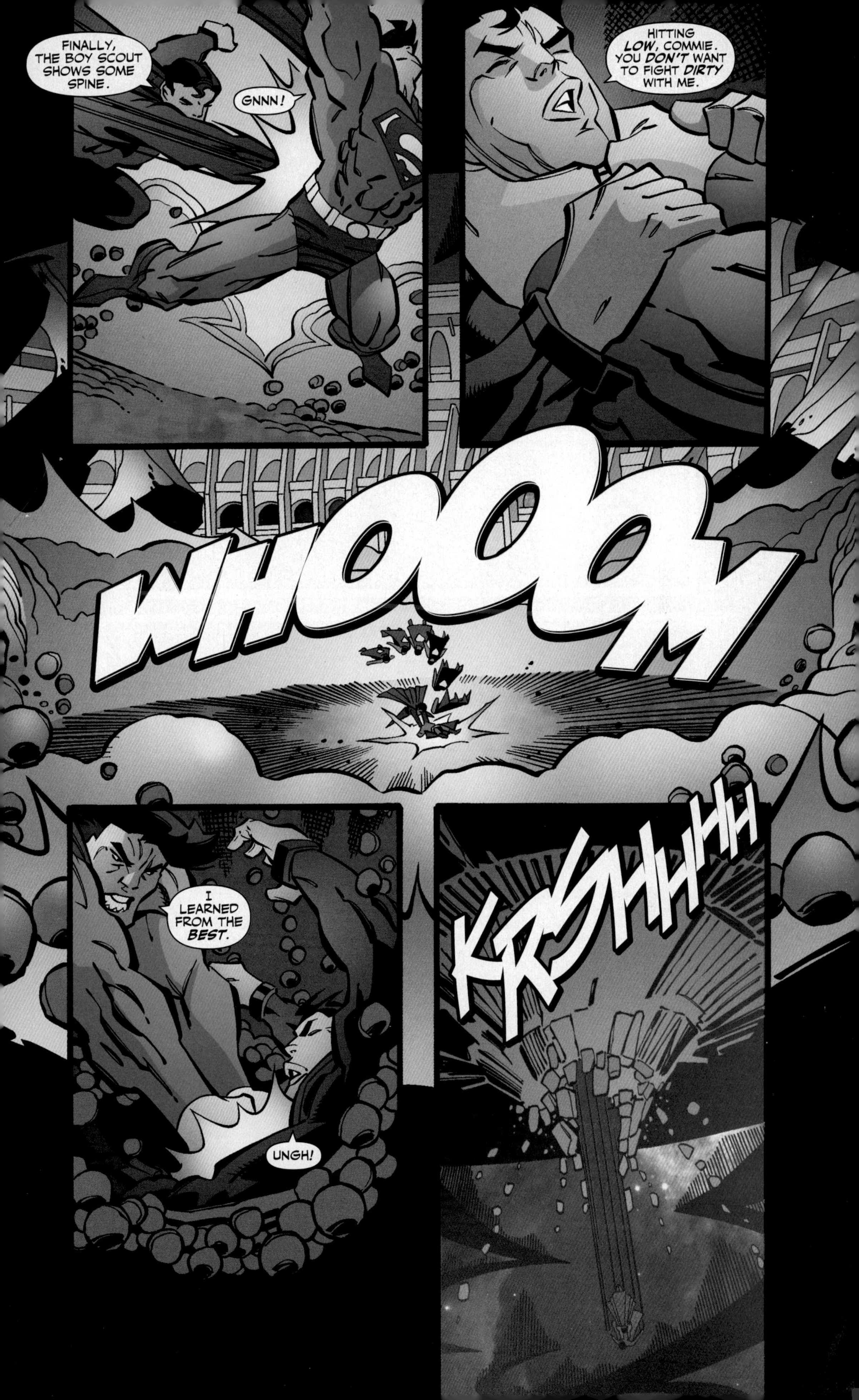
FINALLY, THE BOY SCOUT SHOWS SOME SPINE.
GNNN!
HITTING LOW, COMMIE. YOU DON'T WANT TO FIGHT DIRTY WITH ME.
WHOOOM
I LEARNED FROM THE BEST.
UNGH!
KRSHHHH

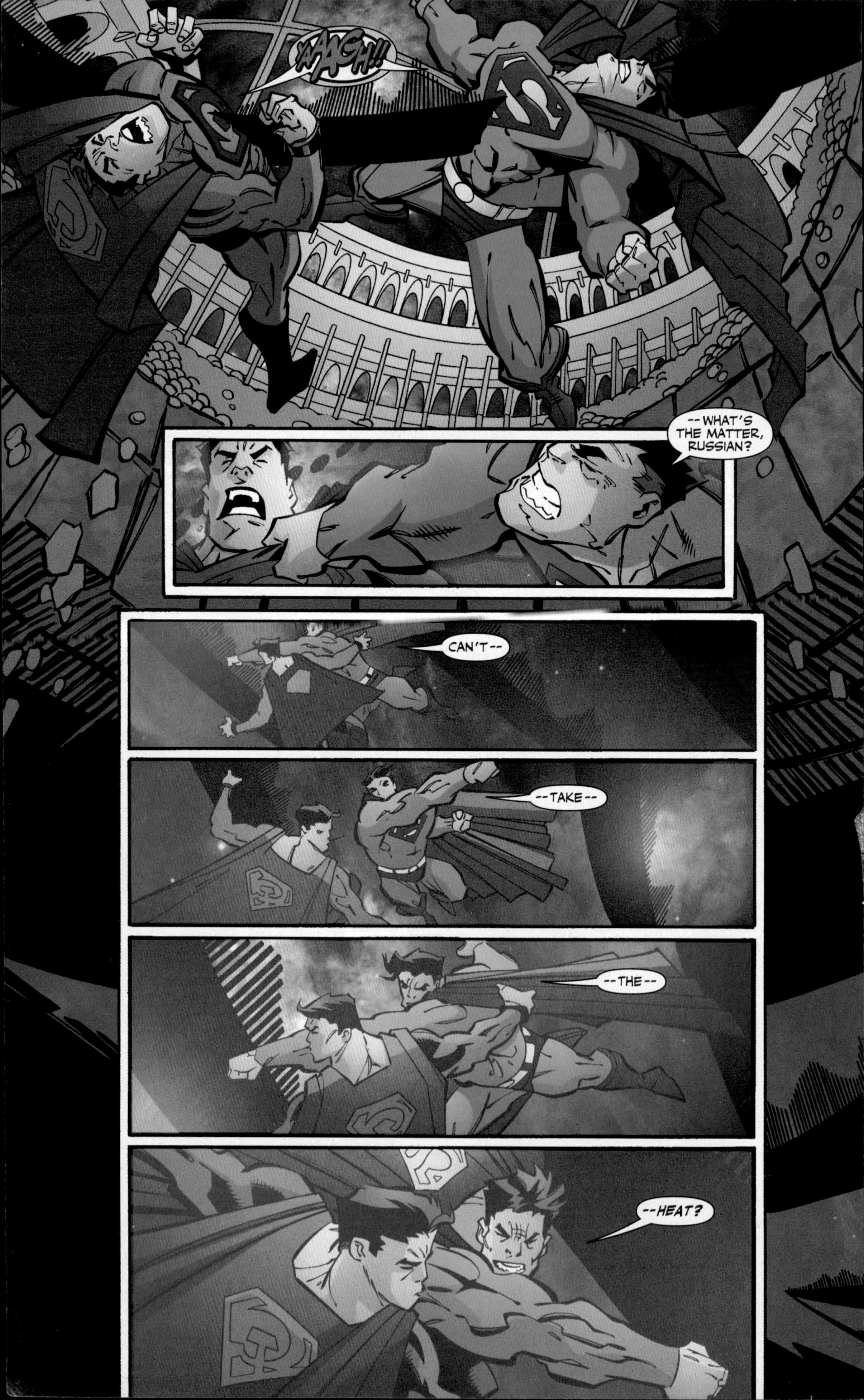
YAAGH!!
--WHAT'S THE MATTER, RUSSIAN?
CAN'T--
--TAKE--
--THE--
--HEAT?

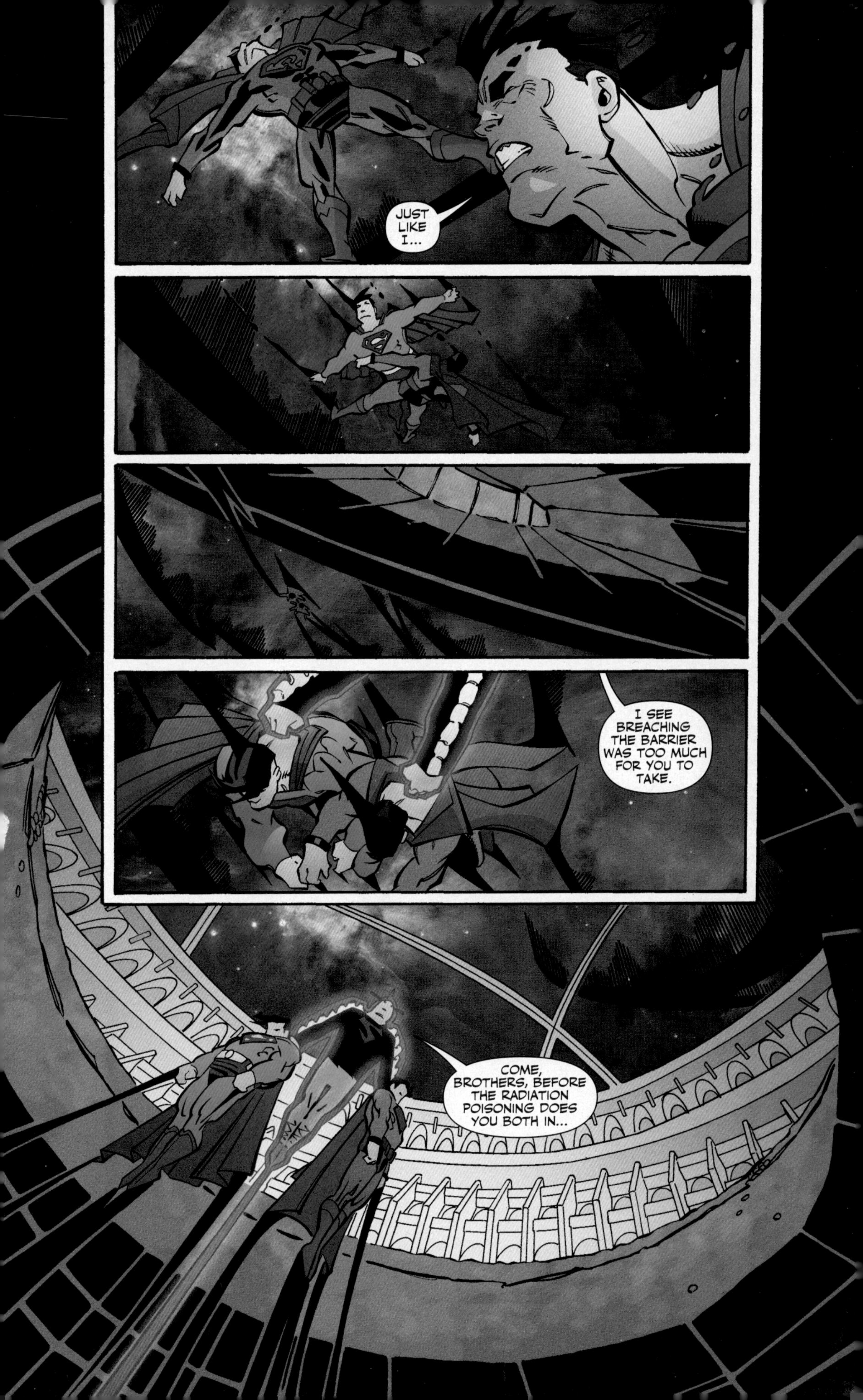
JUST LIKE I...
I SEE BREACHING THE BARRIER WAS TOO MUCH FOR YOU TO TAKE.
COME, BROTHERS, BEFORE THE RADIATION POISONING DOES YOU BOTH IN...

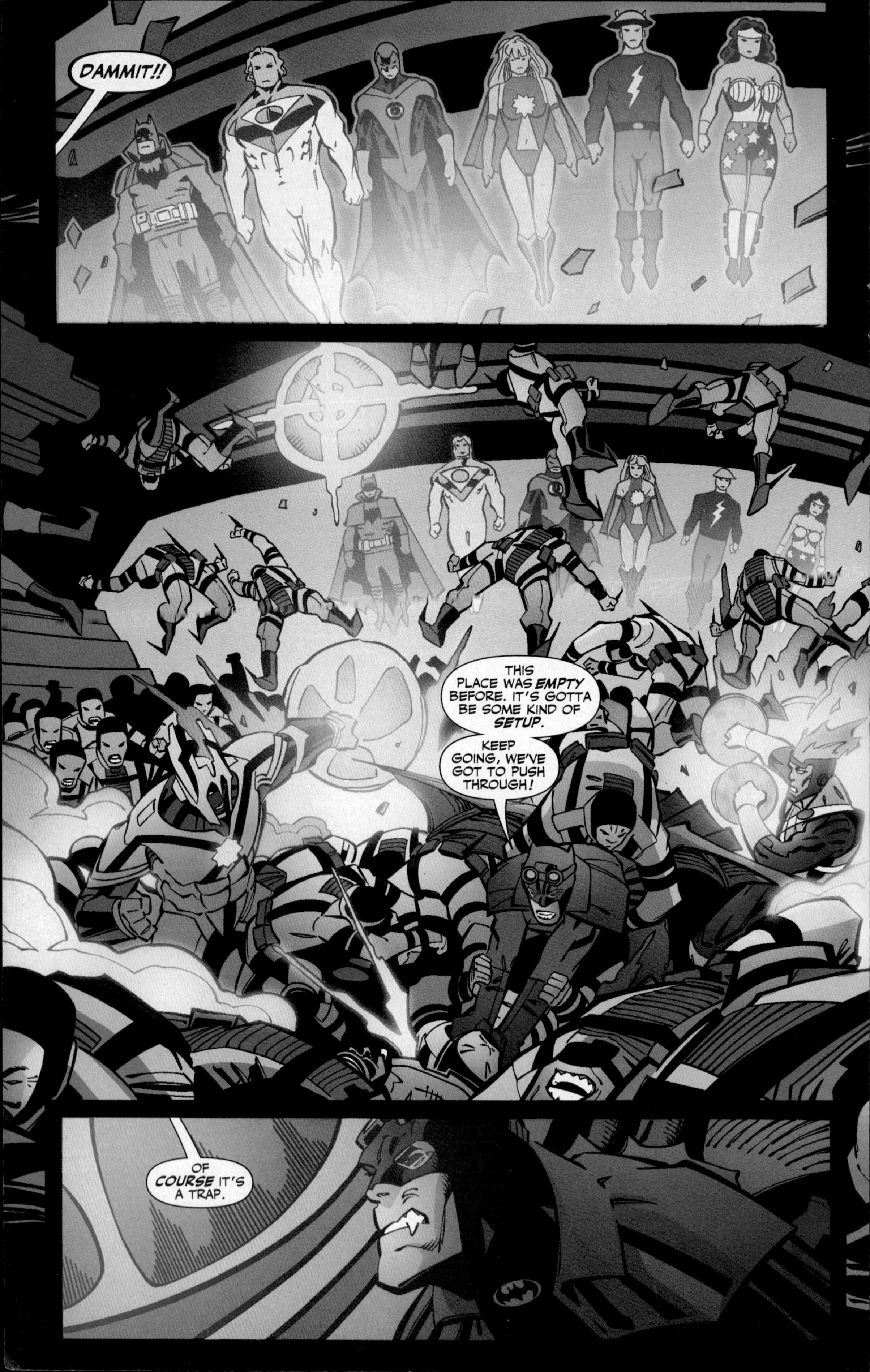
DAMMIT!!
THIS PLACE WAS EMPTY BEFORE. IT'S GOTTA BE SOME KIND OF SETUP.
KEEP GOING, WE'VE GOT TO PUSH THROUGH!
OF COURSE IT'S A TRAP.

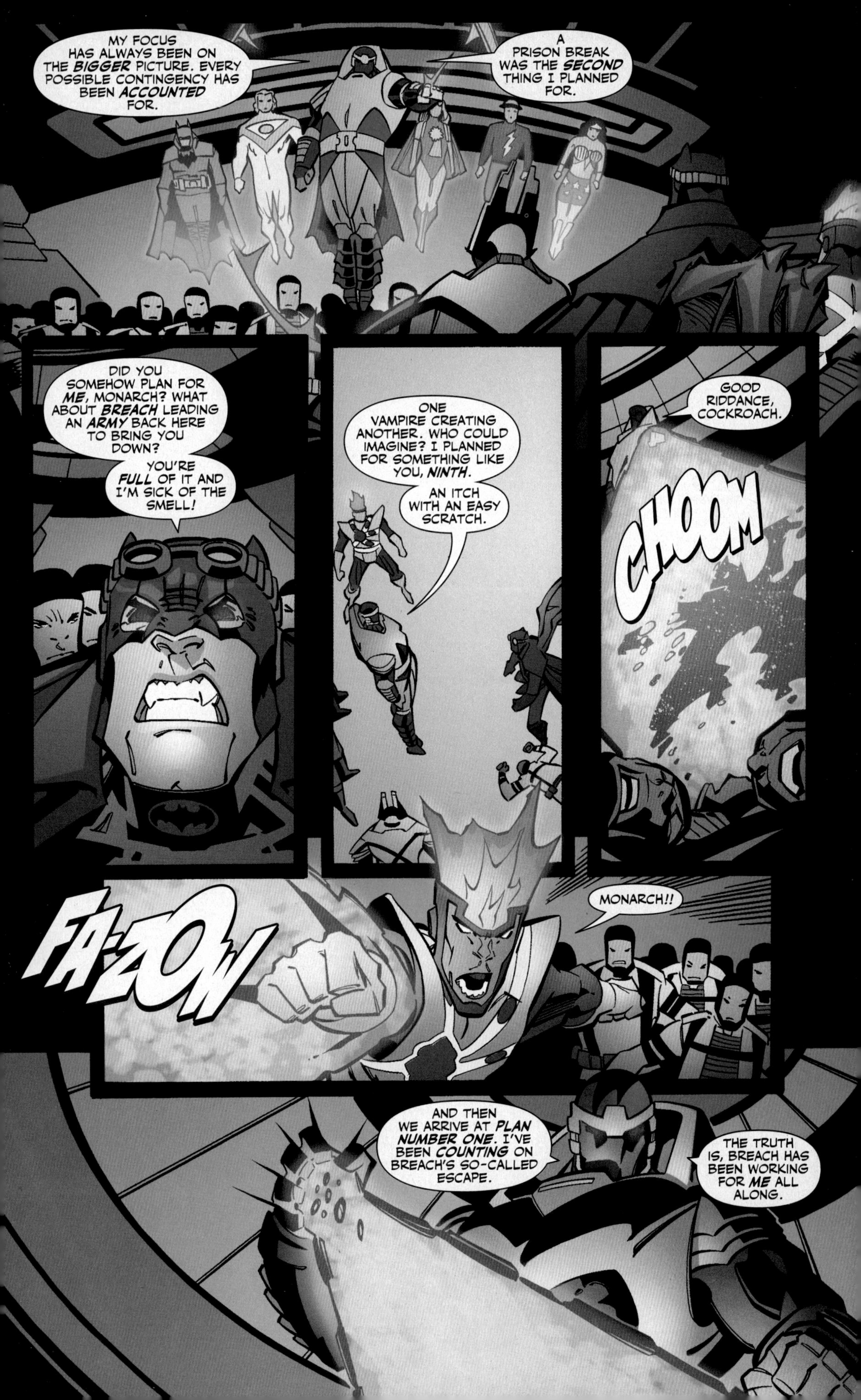
MY FOCUS HAS ALWAYS BEEN ON THE BIGGER PICTURE. EVERY POSSIBLE CONTINGENCY HAS BEEN ACCOUNTED FOR.
A PRISON BREAK WAS THE SECOND THING I PLANNED FOR.
DID YOU SOMEHOW PLAN FOR ME, MONARCH? WHAT ABOUT BREACH LEADING AN ARMY BACK HERE TO BRING YOU DOWN?
YOU'RE FULL OF IT AND I'M SICK OF THE SMELL!
ONE VAMPIRE CREATING ANOTHER. WHO COULD IMAGINE? I PLANNED FOR SOMETHING LIKE YOU, NINTH.
AN ITCH WITH AN EASY SCRATCH.
GOOD RIDDANCE, COCKROACH.
CHOOM
FA-ZOW
MONARCH!!
AND THEN WE ARRIVE AT PLAN NUMBER ONE. I'VE BEEN COUNTING ON BREACH'S SO-CALLED ESCAPE.
THE TRUTH IS, BREACH HAS BEEN WORKING FOR ME ALL ALONG.

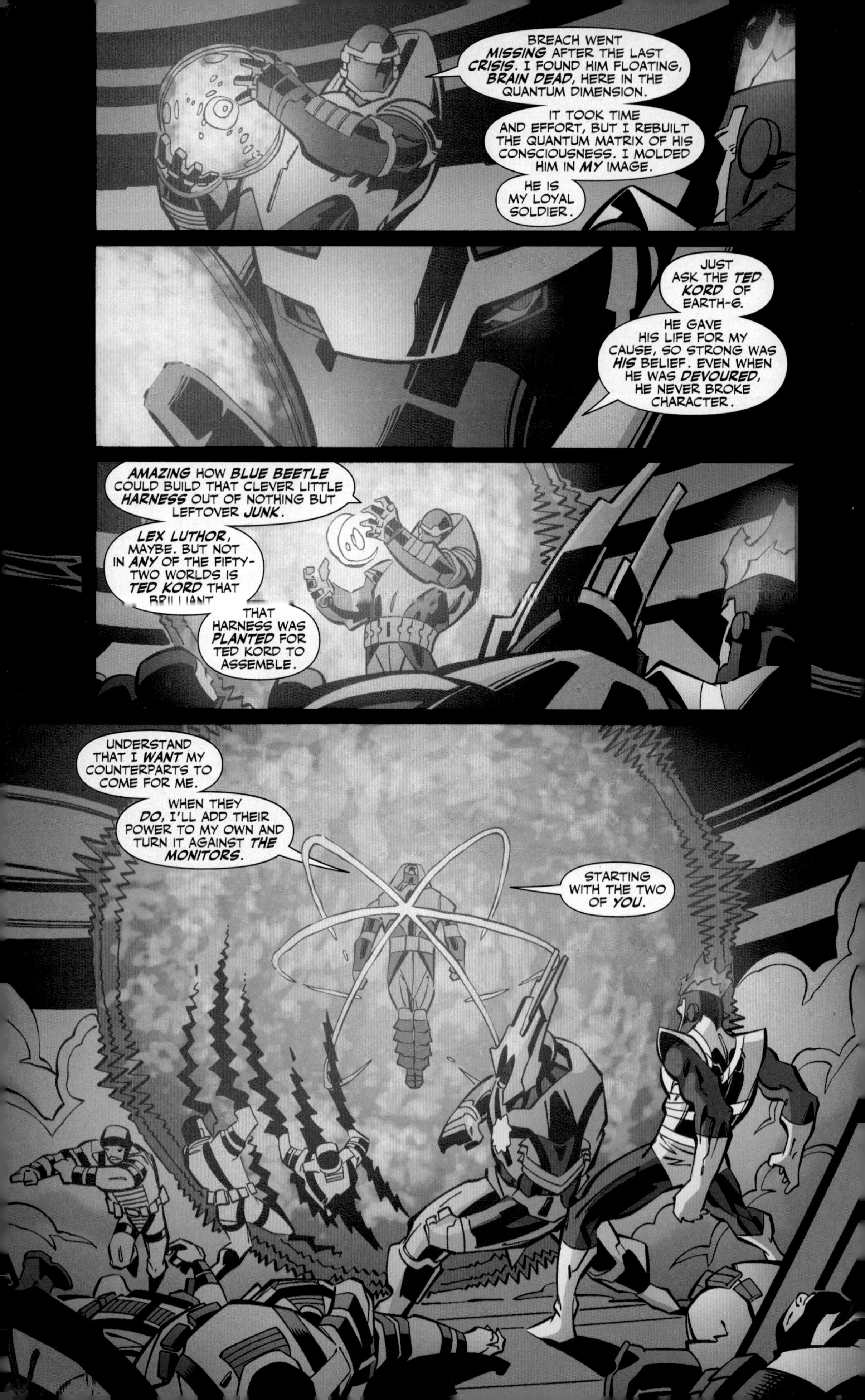
BREACH WENT MISSING AFTER THE LAST CRISIS. I FOUND HIM FLOATING, BRAIN DEAD, HERE IN THE QUANTUM DIMENSION.
IT TOOK TIME AND EFFORT, BUT I REBUILT THE QUANTUM MATRIX OF HIS CONSCIOUSNESS. I MOLDED HIM IN MY IMAGE.
HE IS MY LOYAL SOLDIER.
JUST ASK THE TED KORD OF EARTH-6.
HE GAVE HIS LIFE FOR MY CAUSE, SO STRONG WAS HIS BELIEF. EVEN WHEN HE WAS DEVOURED, HE NEVER BROKE CHARACTER.
AMAZING HOW BLUE BEETLE COULD BUILD THAT CLEVER LITTLE HARNESS OUT OF NOTHING BUT LEFTOVER JUNK.
LEX LUTHOR, MAYBE. BUT NOT IN ANY OF THE FIFTY-TWO WORLDS IS TED KORD THAT BRILLIANT.
THAT HARNESS WAS PLANTED FOR TED KORD TO ASSEMBLE.
UNDERSTAND THAT I WANT MY COUNTERPARTS TO COME FOR ME.
WHEN THEY DO, I'LL ADD THEIR POWER TO MY OWN AND TURN IT AGAINST THE MONITORS.
STARTING WITH THE TWO OF YOU.

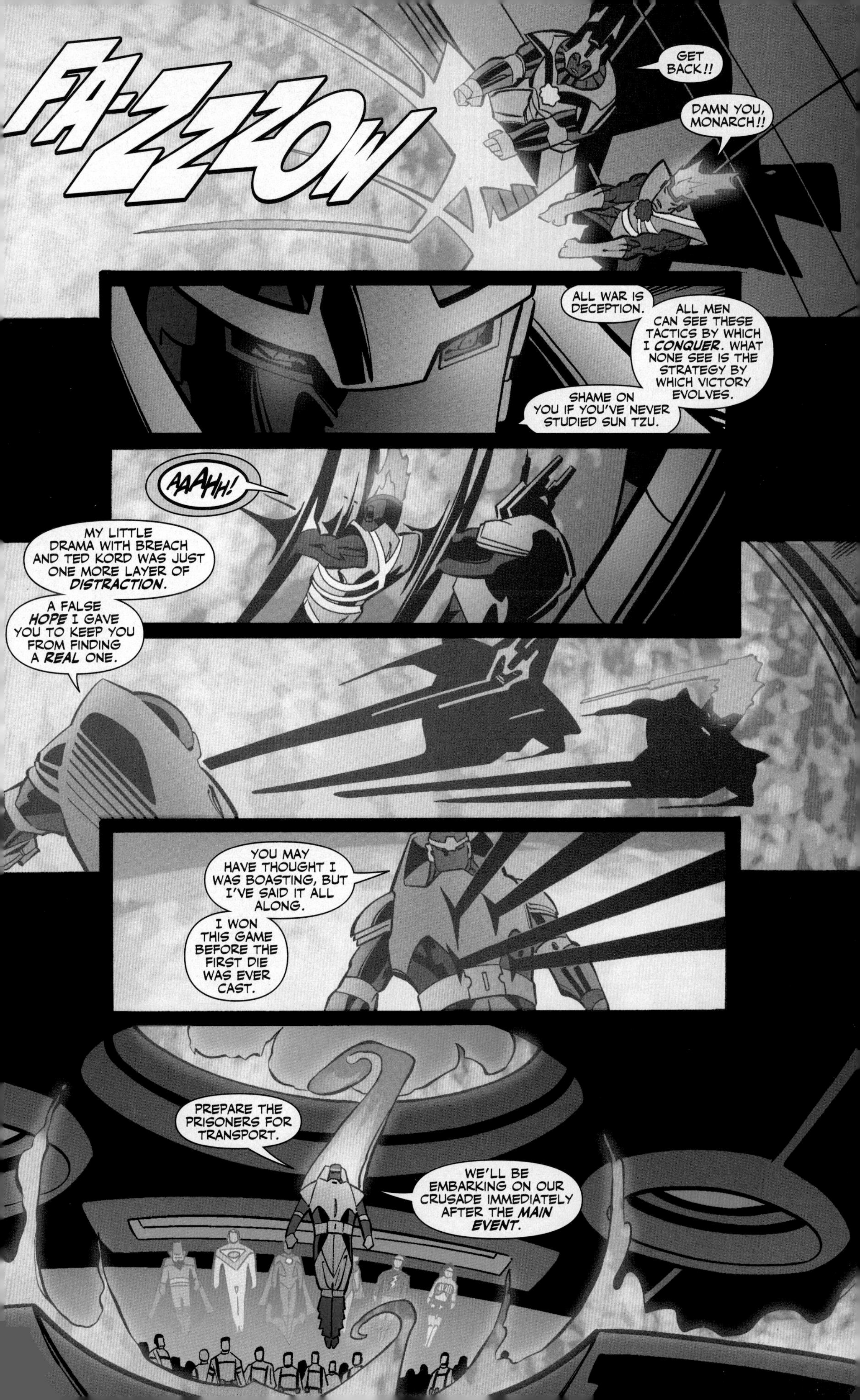
FA-ZZZOW
GET BACK!!
DAMN YOU, MONARCH!!
ALL WAR IS DECEPTION.
ALL MEN CAN SEE THESE TACTICS BY WHICH I CONQUER. WHAT NONE SEE IS THE STRATEGY BY WHICH VICTORY EVOLVES.
SHAME ON YOU IF YOU'VE NEVER STUDIED SUN TZU.
AAAHH!
MY LITTLE DRAMA WITH BREACH AND TED KORD WAS JUST ONE MORE LAYER OF DISTRACTION.
A FALSE HOPE I GAVE YOU TO KEEP YOU FROM FINDING A REAL ONE.
YOU MAY HAVE THOUGHT I WAS BOASTING, BUT I'VE SAID IT ALL ALONG.
I WON THIS GAME BEFORE THE FIRST DIE WAS EVER CAST.
PREPARE THE PRISONERS FOR TRANSPORT.
WE'LL BE EMBARKING ON OUR CRUSADE IMMEDIATELY AFTER THE MAIN EVENT.

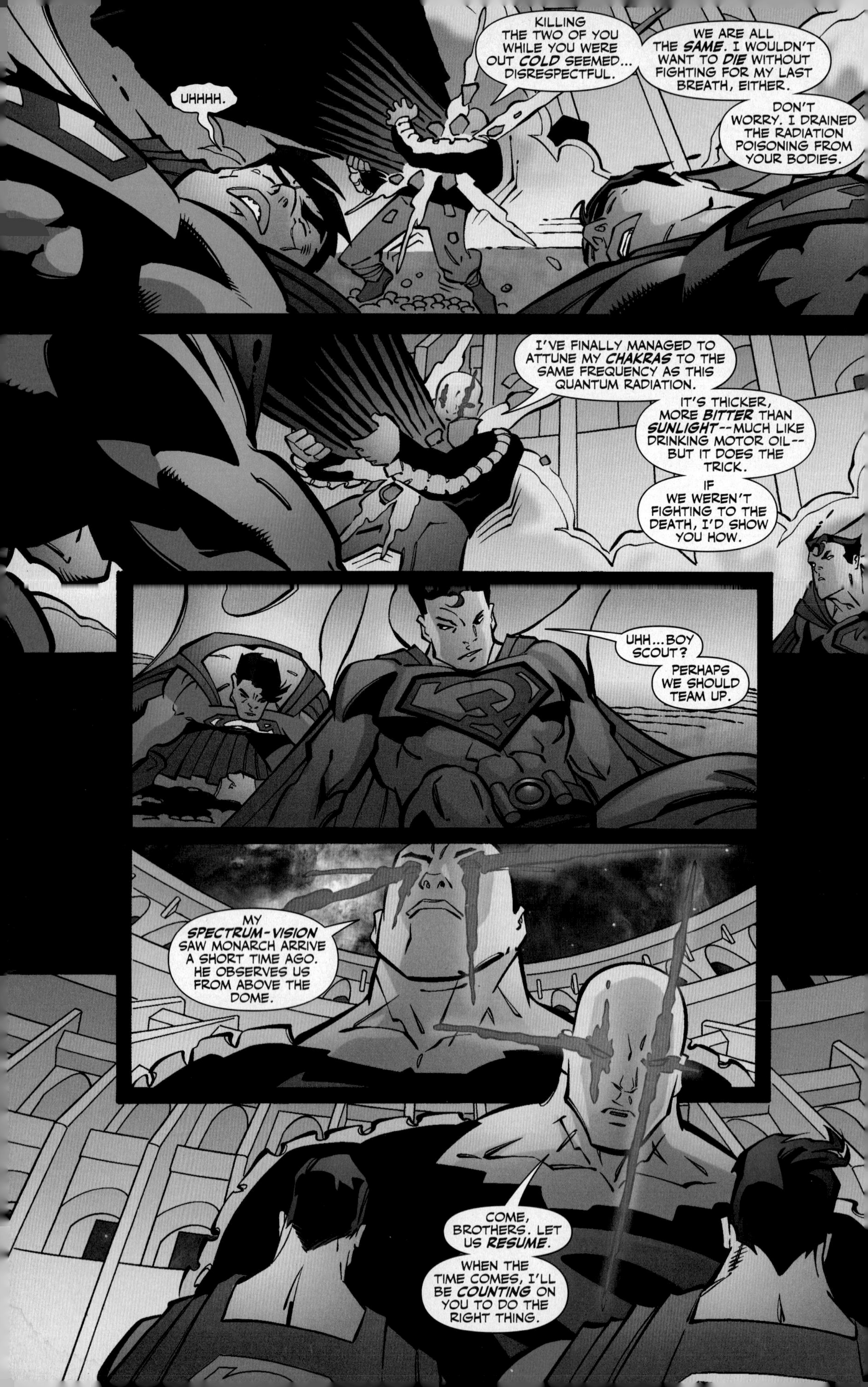
UHHHH.
KILLING THE TWO OF YOU WHILE YOU WERE OUT COLD SEEMED... DISRESPECTFUL.
WE ARE ALL THE SAME. I WOULDN'T WANT TO DIE WITHOUT FIGHTING FOR MY LAST BREATH, EITHER.
DON'T WORRY. I DRAINED THE RADIATION POISONING FROM YOUR BODIES.
I'VE FINALLY MANAGED TO ATTUNE MY CHAKRAS TO THE SAME FREQUENCY AS THIS QUANTUM RADIATION.
IT'S THICKER, MORE BITTER THAN SUNLIGHT--MUCH LIKE DRINKING MOTOR OIL--BUT IT DOES THE TRICK.
IF WE WEREN'T FIGHTING TO THE DEATH, I'D SHOW YOU HOW.
UHH...BOY SCOUT?
PERHAPS WE SHOULD TEAM UP.
MY SPECTRUM-VISION SAW MONARCH ARRIVE A SHORT TIME AGO. HE OBSERVES US FROM ABOVE THE DOME.
COME, BROTHERS. LET US RESUME.
WHEN THE TIME COMES, I'LL BE COUNTING ON YOU TO DO THE RIGHT THING.

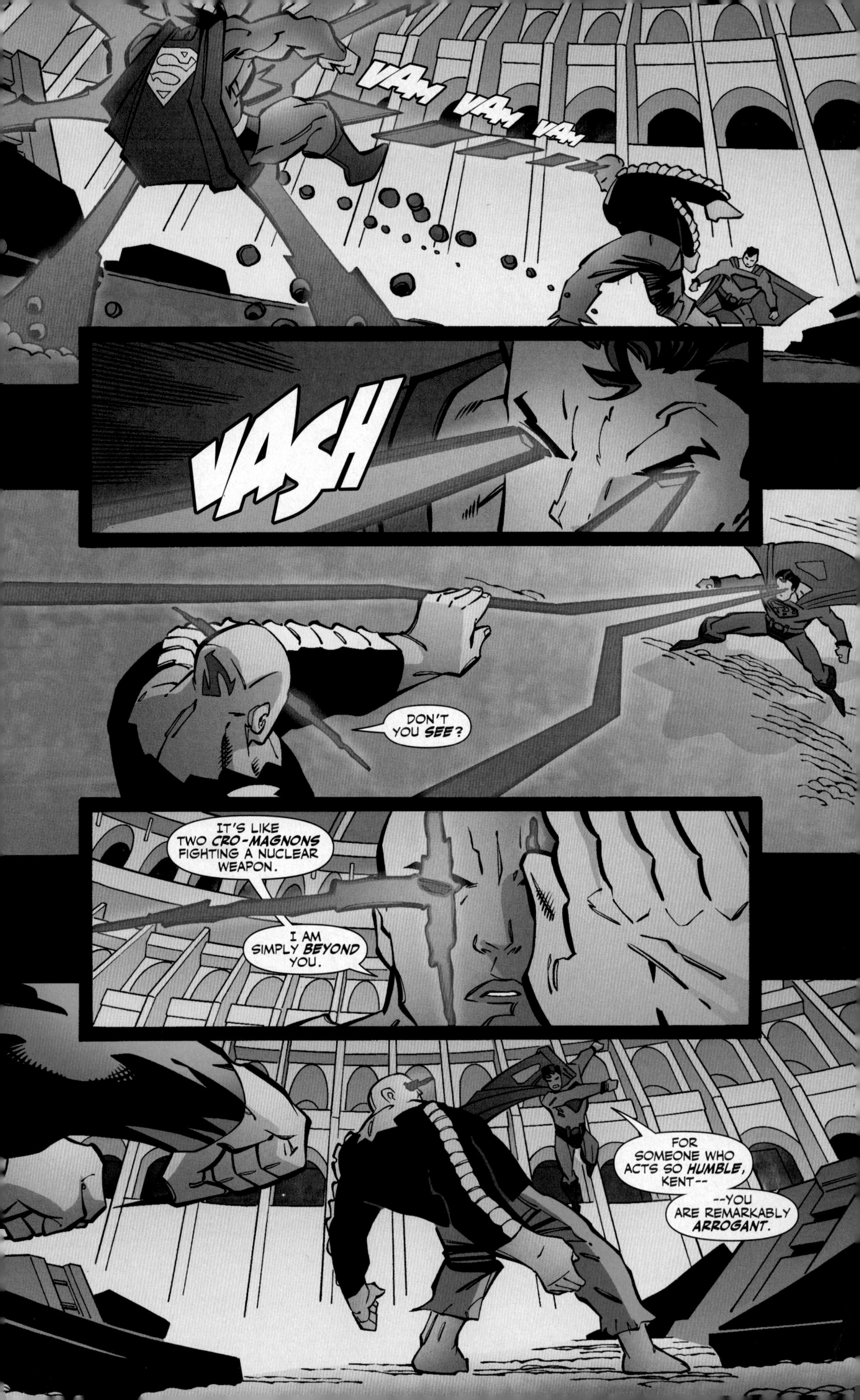
VAM VAM VAM
VASH
DON'T YOU SEE?
IT'S LIKE TWO CRO-MAGNONS FIGHTING A NUCLEAR WEAPON.
I AM SIMPLY BEYOND YOU.
FOR SOMEONE WHO ACTS SO HUMBLE, KENT--
--YOU ARE REMARKABLY ARROGANT.

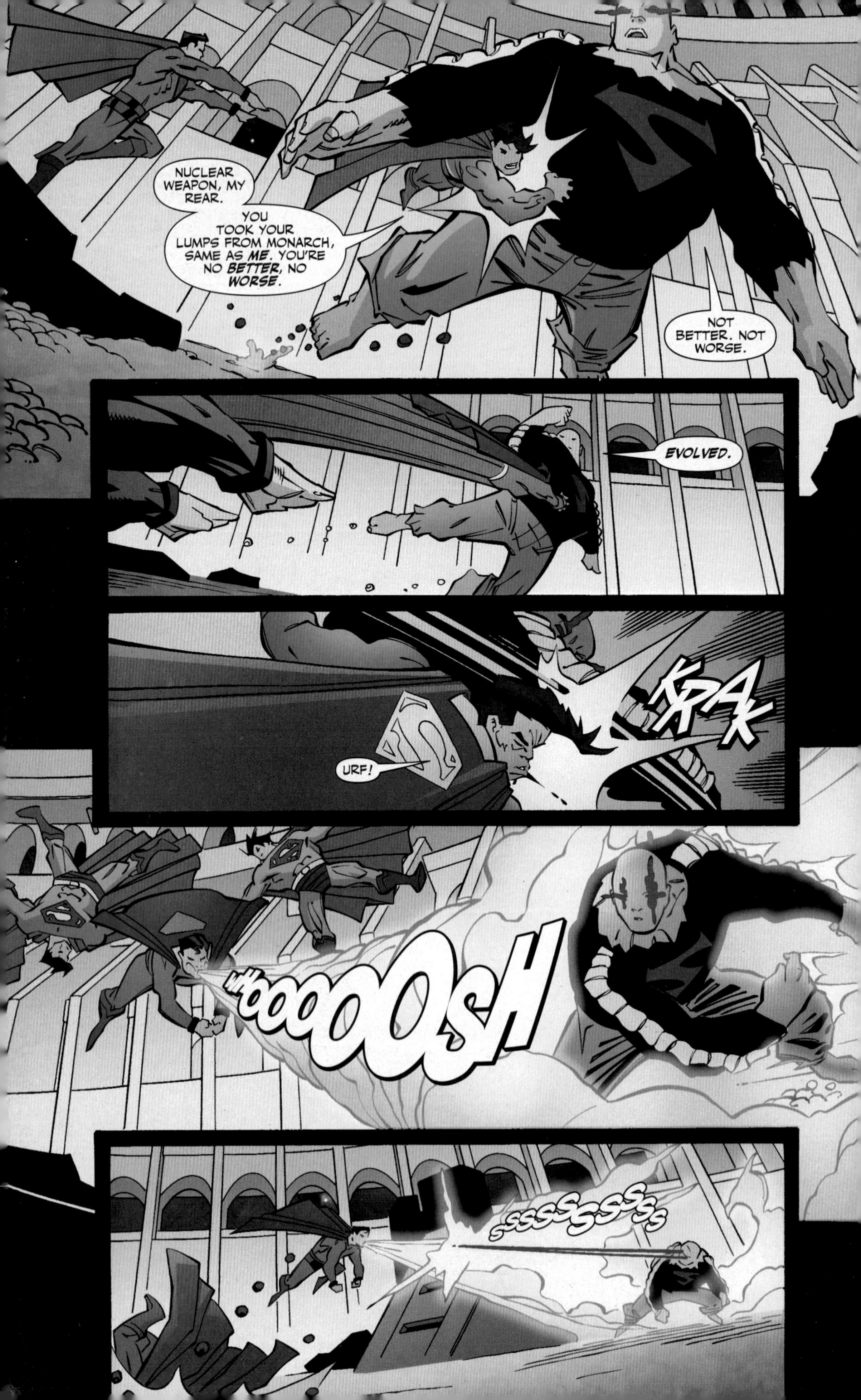
NUCLEAR WEAPON, MY REAR.
YOU TOOK YOUR LUMPS FROM MONARCH, SAME AS ME. YOU'RE NO BETTER, NO WORSE.
NOT BETTER. NOT WORSE.
EVOLVED.
KRAK
URF!
WHOOOOOOSH
SSSSSSSSSS

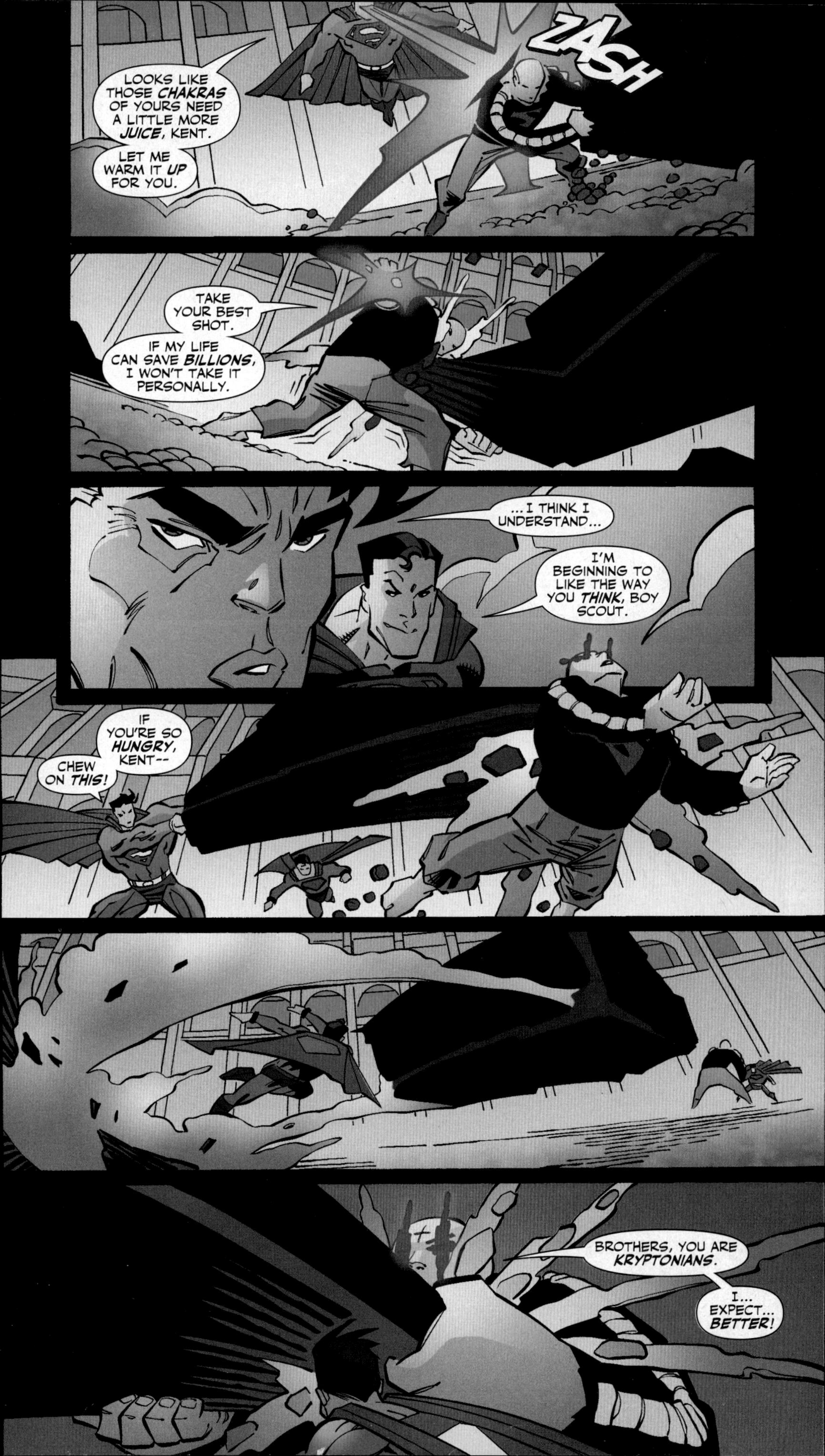
ZASH
LOOKS LIKE THOSE CHAKRAS OF YOURS NEED A LITTLE MORE JUICE, KENT.
LET ME WARM IT UP FOR YOU.
TAKE YOUR BEST SHOT.
IF MY LIFE CAN SAVE BILLIONS, I WON'T TAKE IT PERSONALLY.
...I THINK I UNDERSTAND...
I'M BEGINNING TO LIKE THE WAY YOU THINK, BOY SCOUT.
IF YOU'RE SO HUNGRY, KENT--
CHEW ON THIS!
BROTHERS, YOU ARE KRYPTONIANS.
I... EXPECT... BETTER!

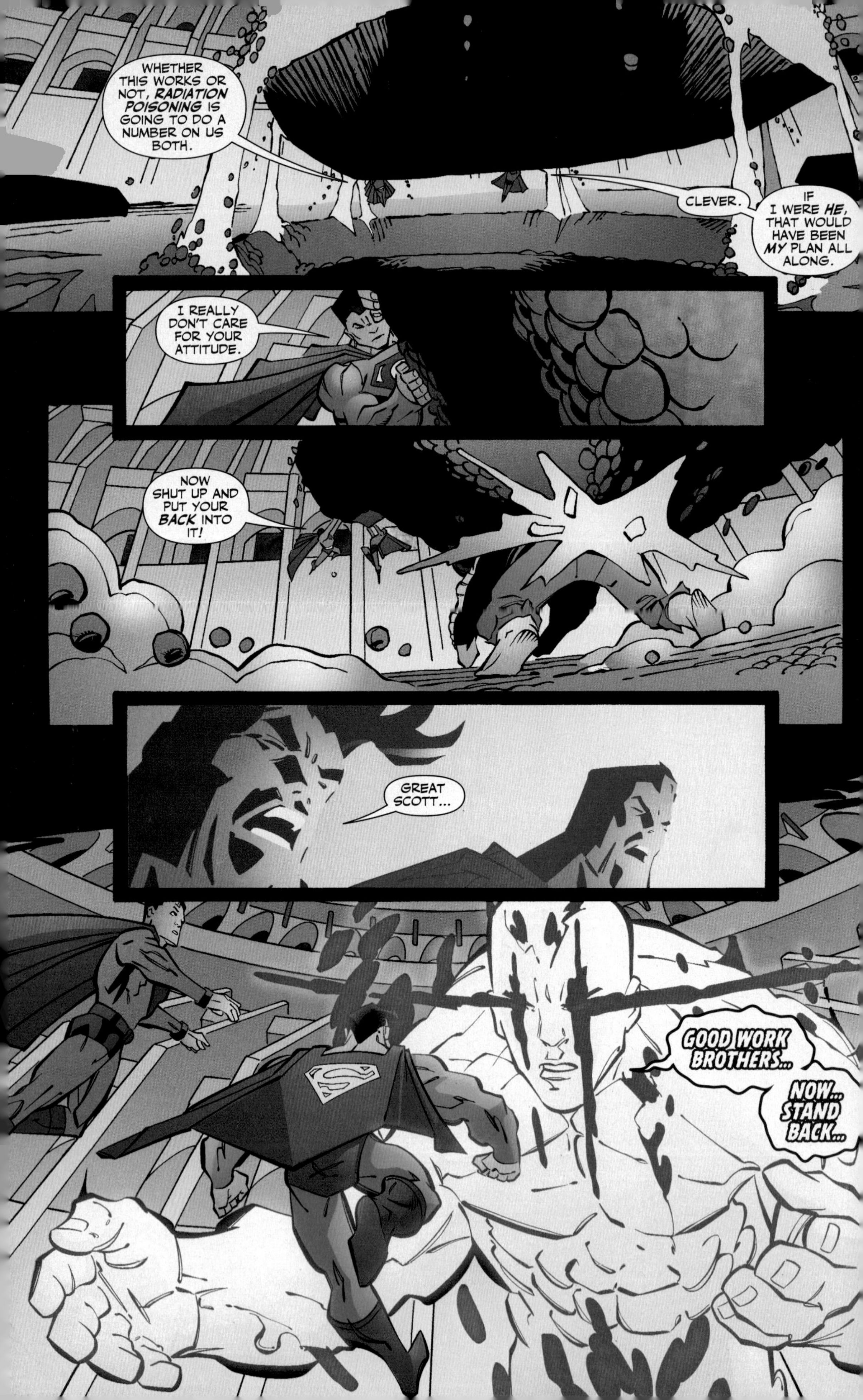
WHETHER THIS WORKS OR NOT, *RADIATION POISONING* IS GOING TO DO A NUMBER ON US BOTH.
CLEVER.
IF I WERE *HE*, THAT WOULD HAVE BEEN *MY* PLAN ALL ALONG.
I REALLY DON'T CARE FOR YOUR ATTITUDE.
NOW SHUT UP AND PUT YOUR *BACK* INTO IT!
GREAT SCOTT...
GOOD WORK BROTHERS...
NOW... STAND BACK...

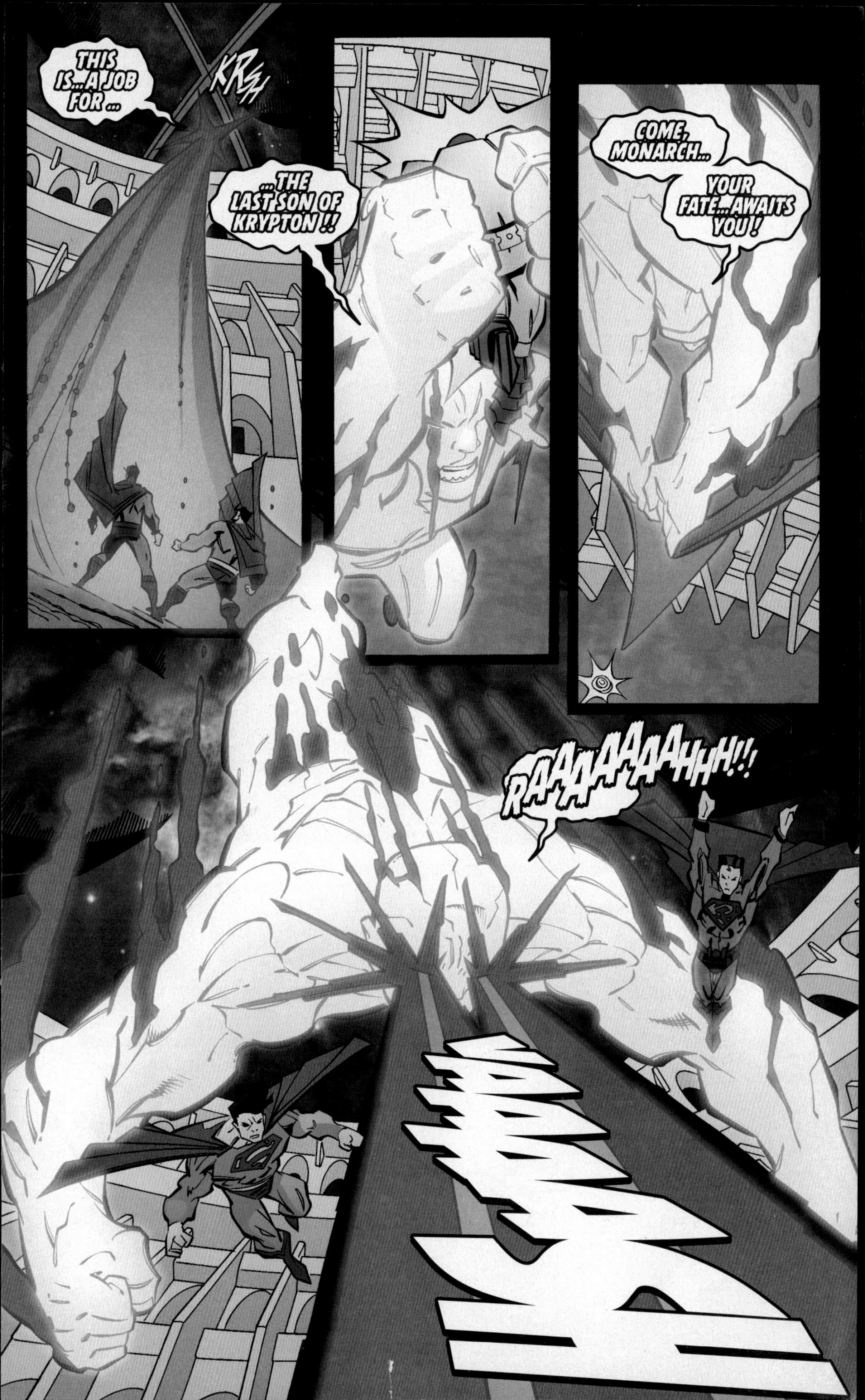
THIS IS...A JOB FOR...
KRSH
...THE LAST SON OF KRYPTON!!
COME, MONARCH...
YOUR FATE...AWAITS YOU!
RAAAAAAAHHH!!
WHAAAM

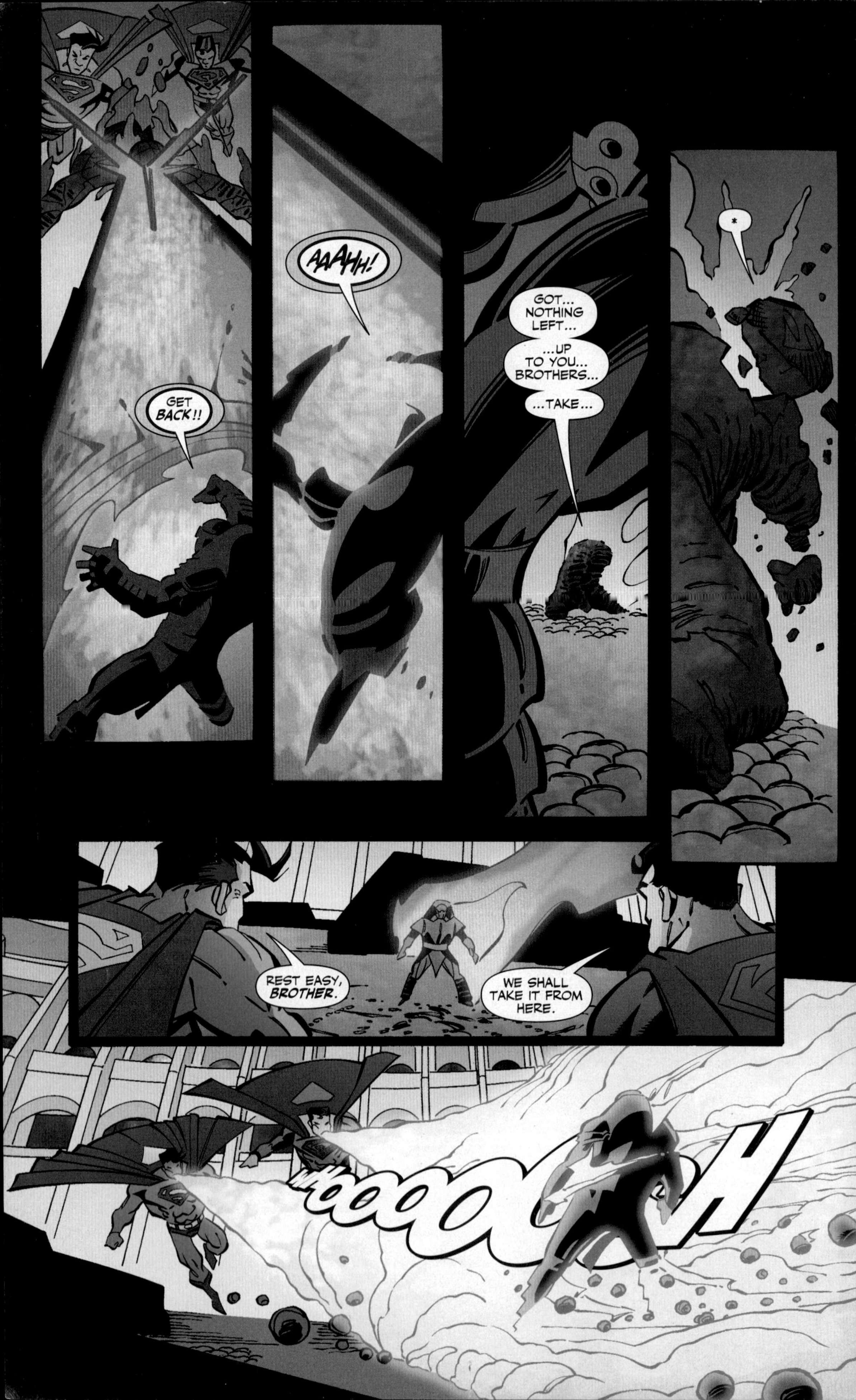
GET BACK!!
AAAHH!
GOT... NOTHING LEFT...
...UP TO YOU... BROTHERS...
...TAKE...
*
REST EASY, BROTHER.
WE SHALL TAKE IT FROM HERE.
WHOOOOOSH

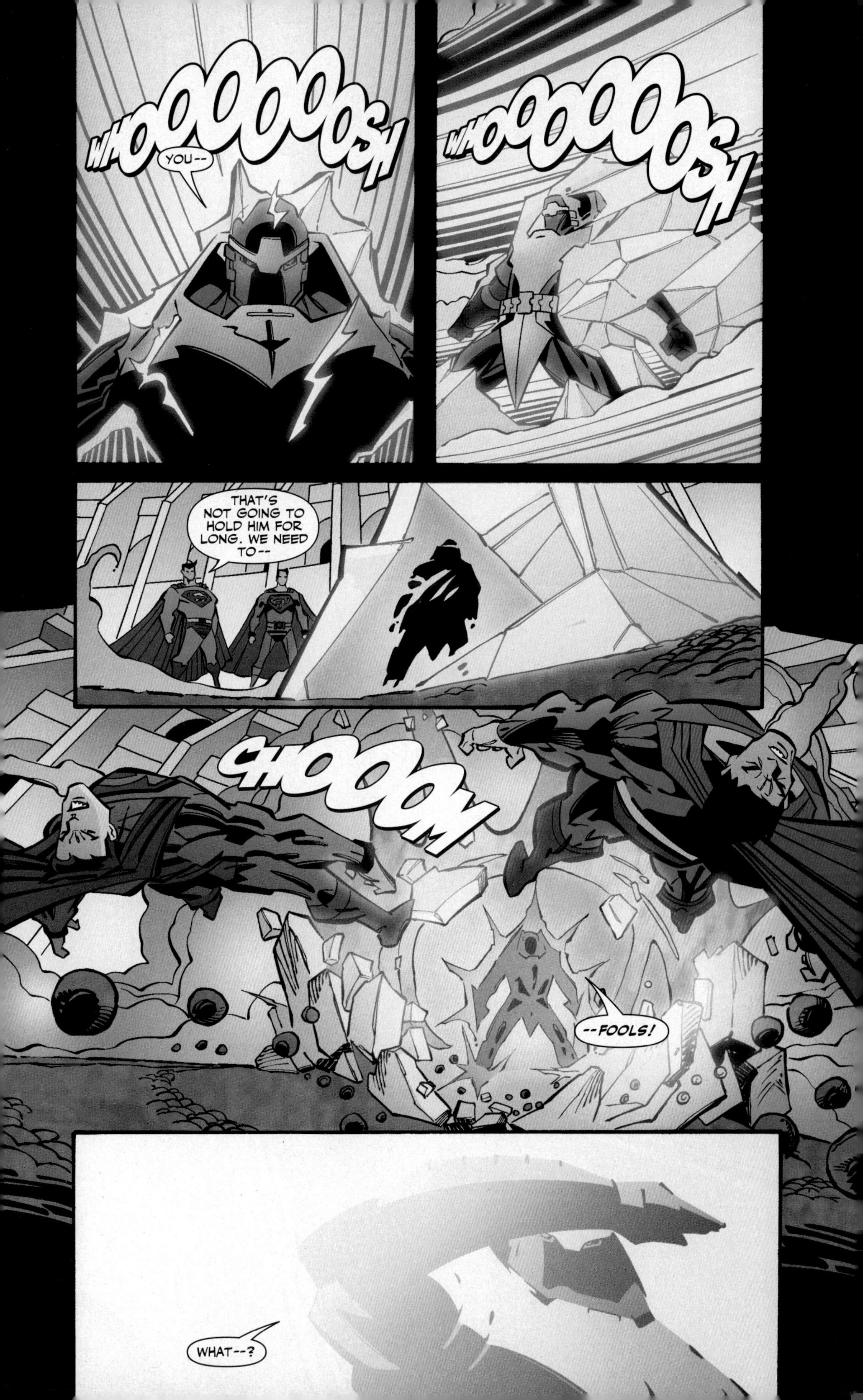
WHOOOOOOOSH
YOU--
WHOOOOOOOSH
THAT'S NOT GOING TO HOLD HIM FOR LONG. WE NEED TO--
CHOOOOM
--FOOLS!
WHAT--?

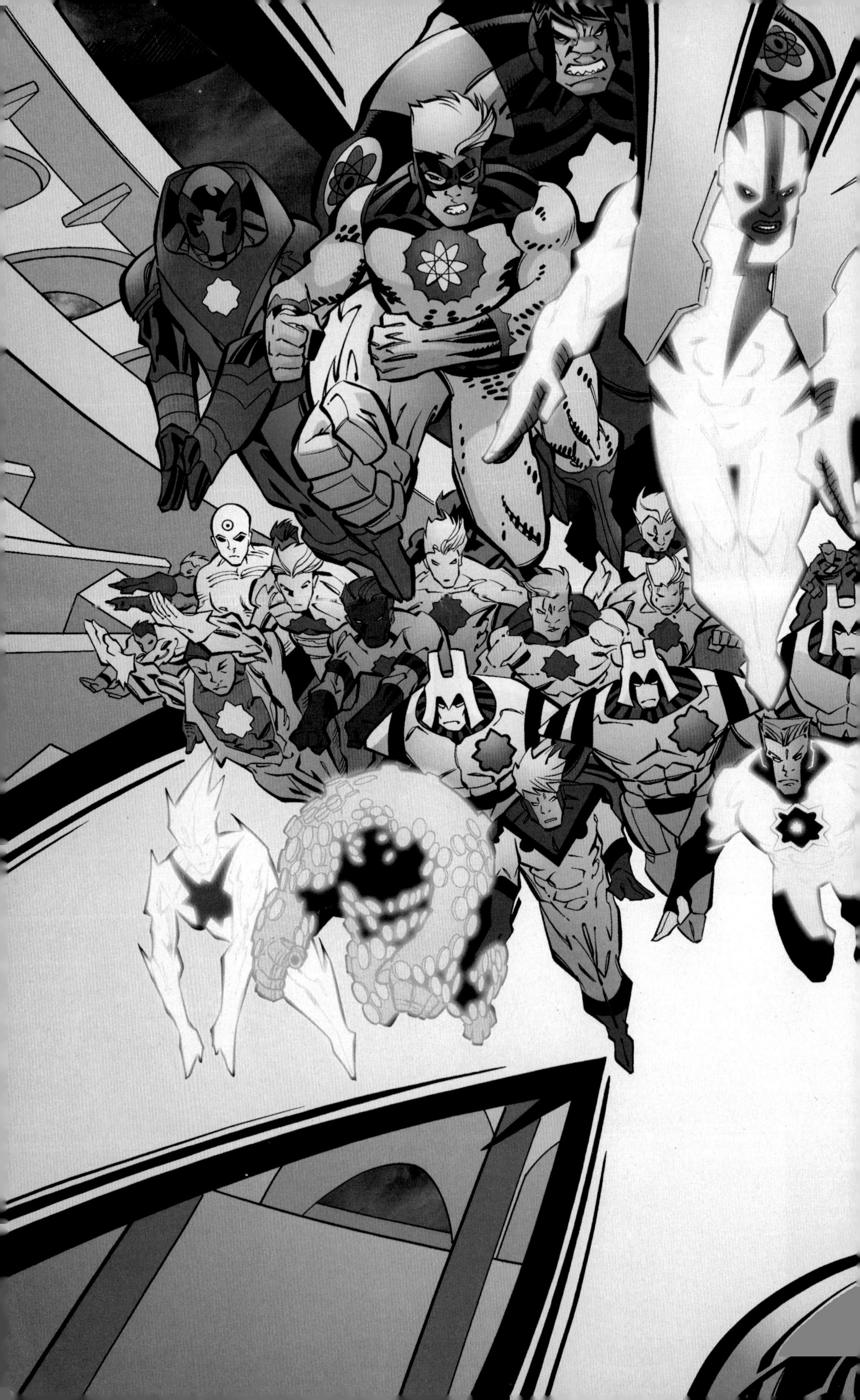

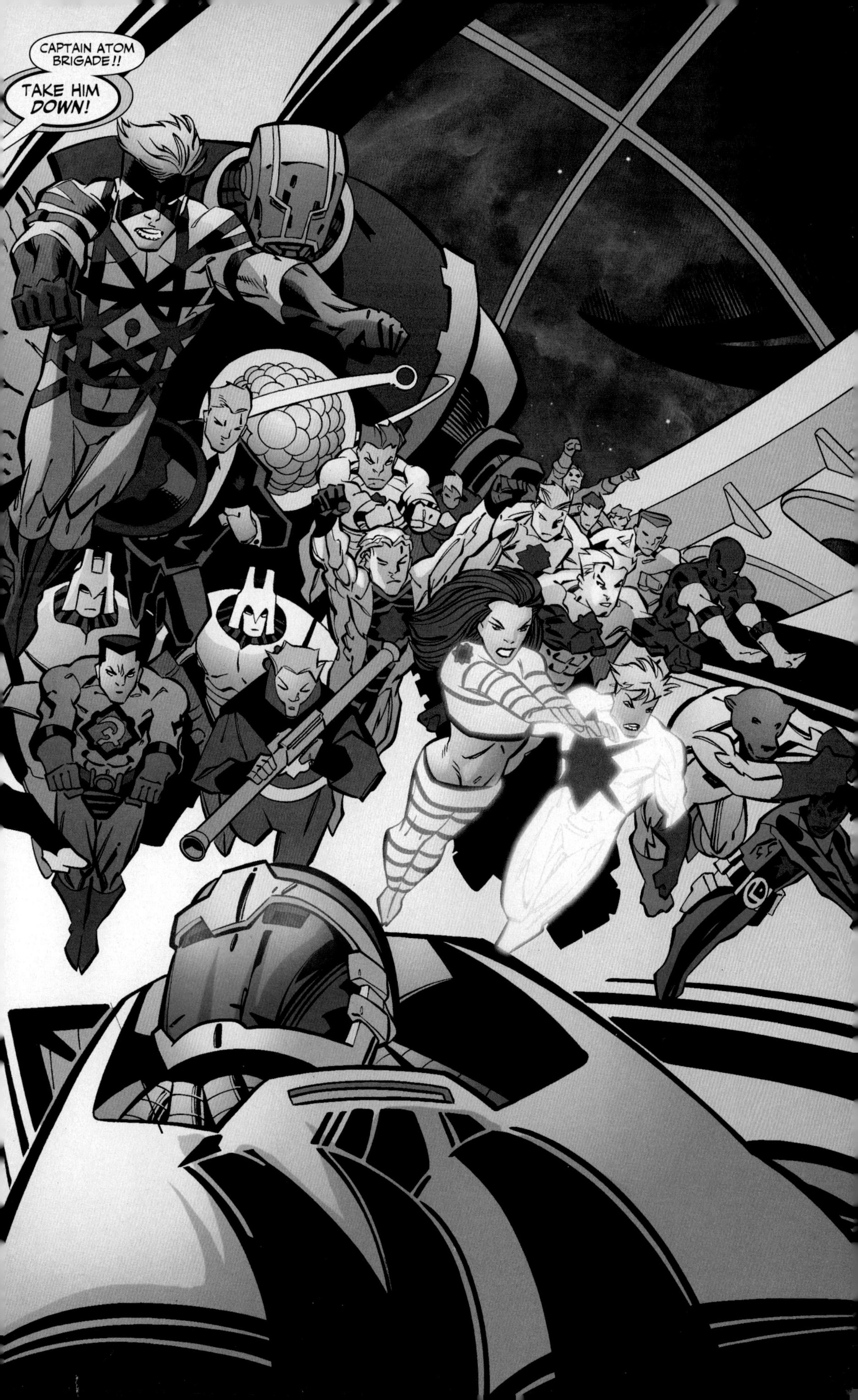
CAPTAIN ATOM BRIGADE!!
TAKE HIM DOWN!

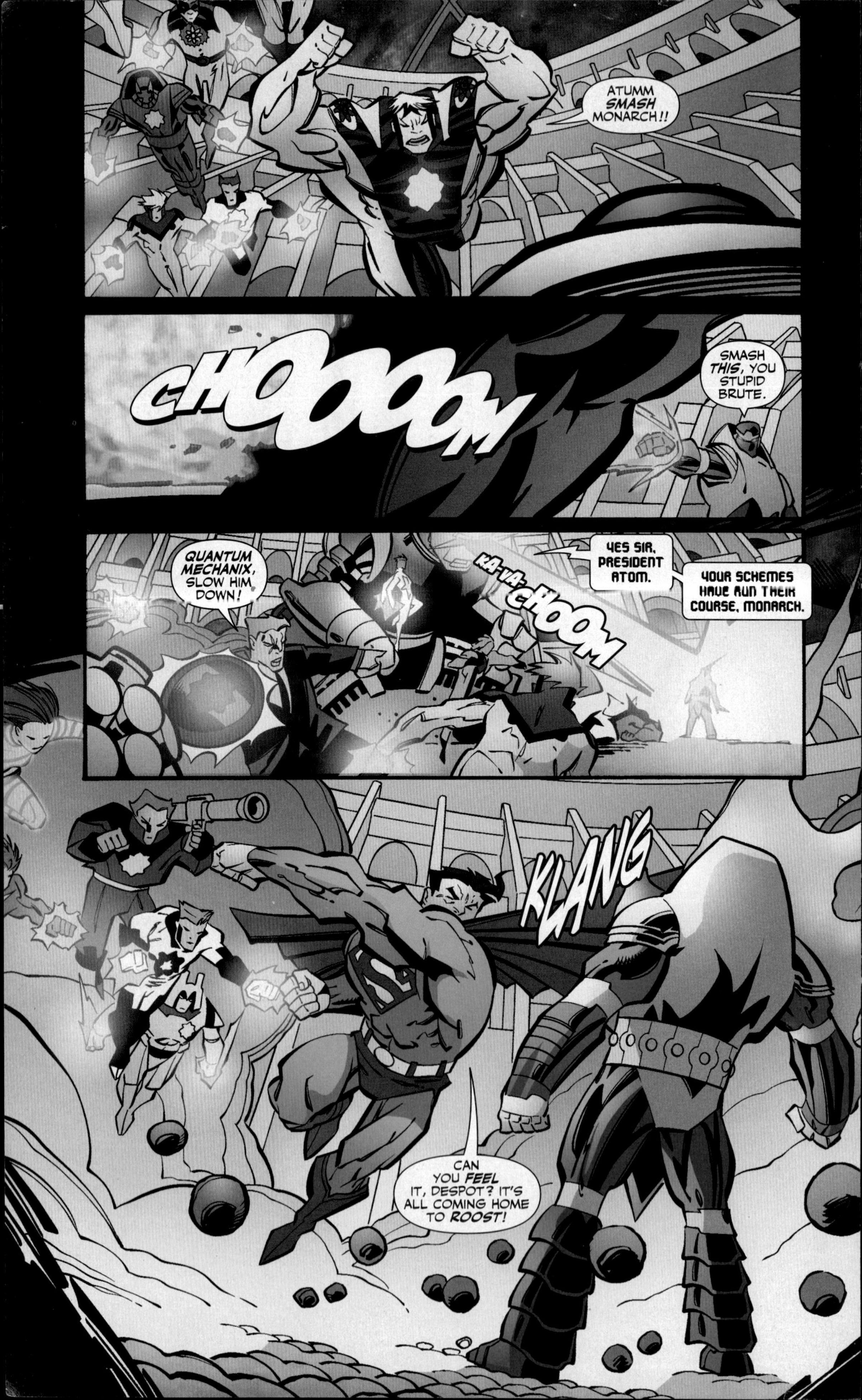
ATUMM SMASH MONARCH!!
CHOOOOM
SMASH THIS, YOU STUPID BRUTE.
QUANTUM MECHANIX, SLOW HIM DOWN!
YES SIR, PRESIDENT ATOM.
KA-VA-CHOOOM
YOUR SCHEMES HAVE RUN THEIR COURSE, MONARCH.
KLANG
CAN YOU FEEL IT, DESPOT? IT'S ALL COMING HOME TO ROOST!

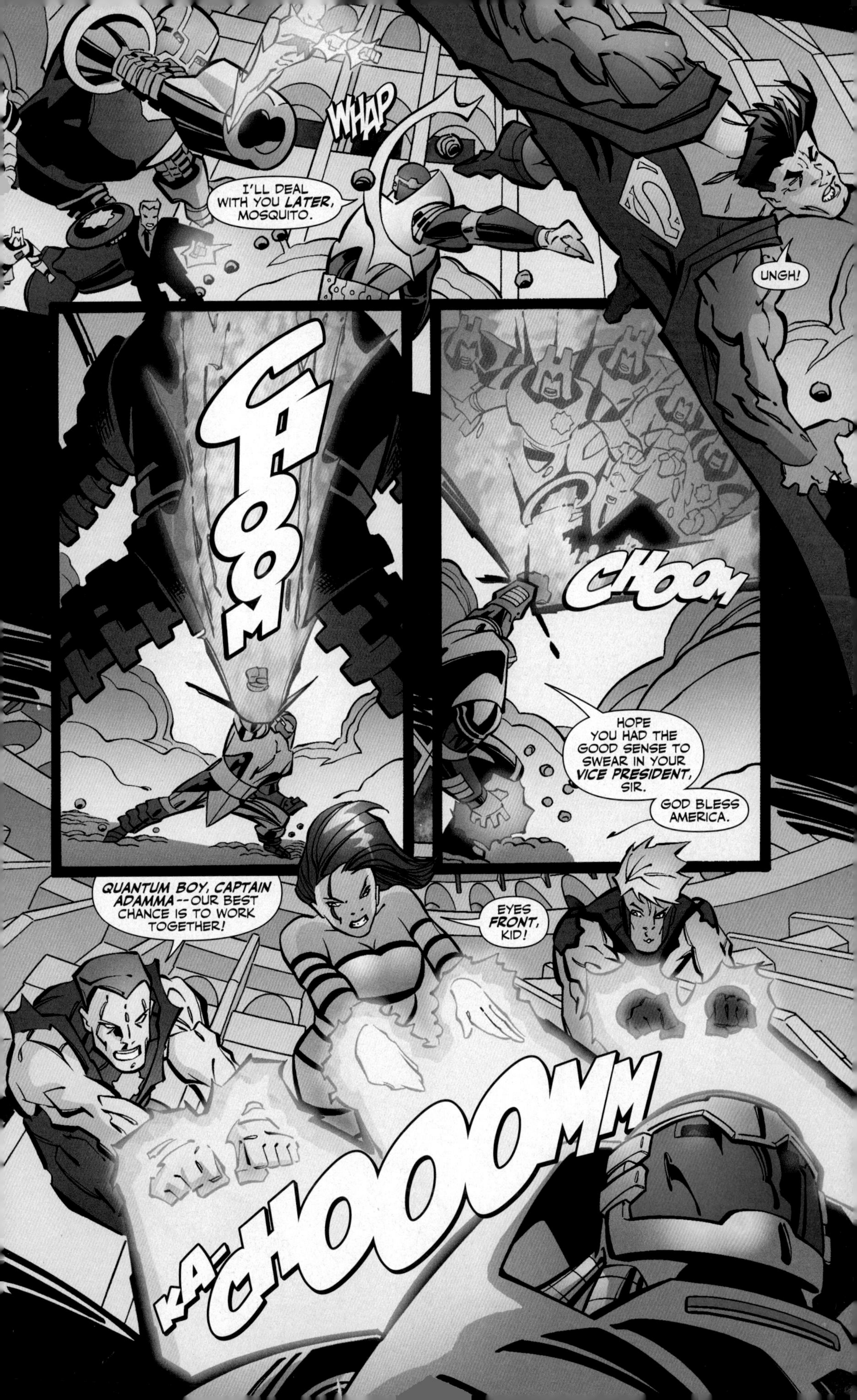
WHAP
I'LL DEAL WITH YOU *LATER,* MOSQUITO.
UNGH!
CHOOM
CHOOM
HOPE YOU HAD THE GOOD SENSE TO SWEAR IN YOUR *VICE PRESIDENT,* SIR.
GOD BLESS AMERICA.
QUANTUM BOY, CAPTAIN ADAMMA--OUR BEST CHANCE IS TO WORK TOGETHER!
EYES *FRONT,* KID!
KA-CHOOOMM

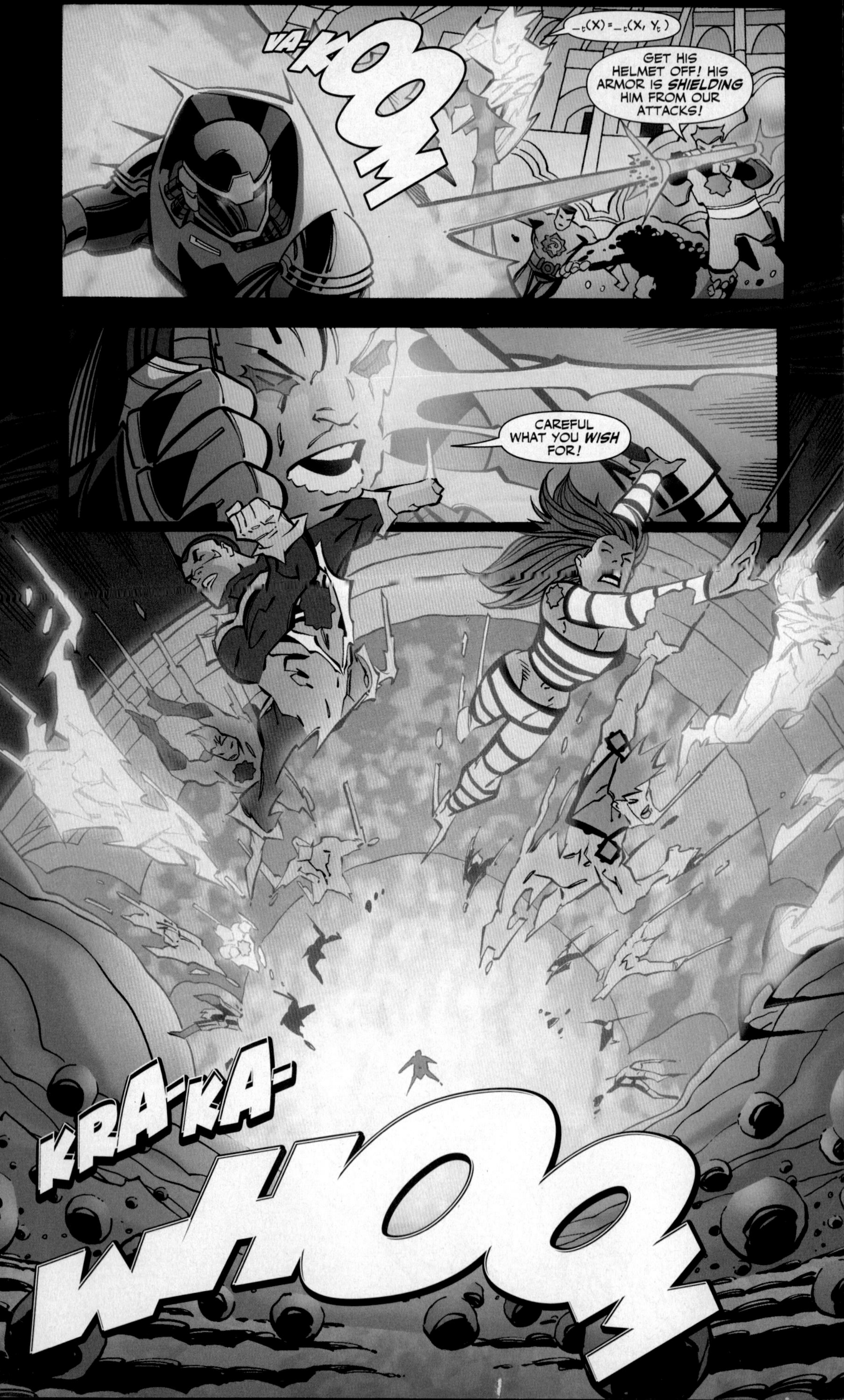
VA-KOOM
$_{t}(X) = _{t}(X, Y_t)$
GET HIS HELMET OFF! HIS ARMOR IS SHIELDING HIM FROM OUR ATTACKS!
CAREFUL WHAT YOU WISH FOR!
KRA-KA-WHOO

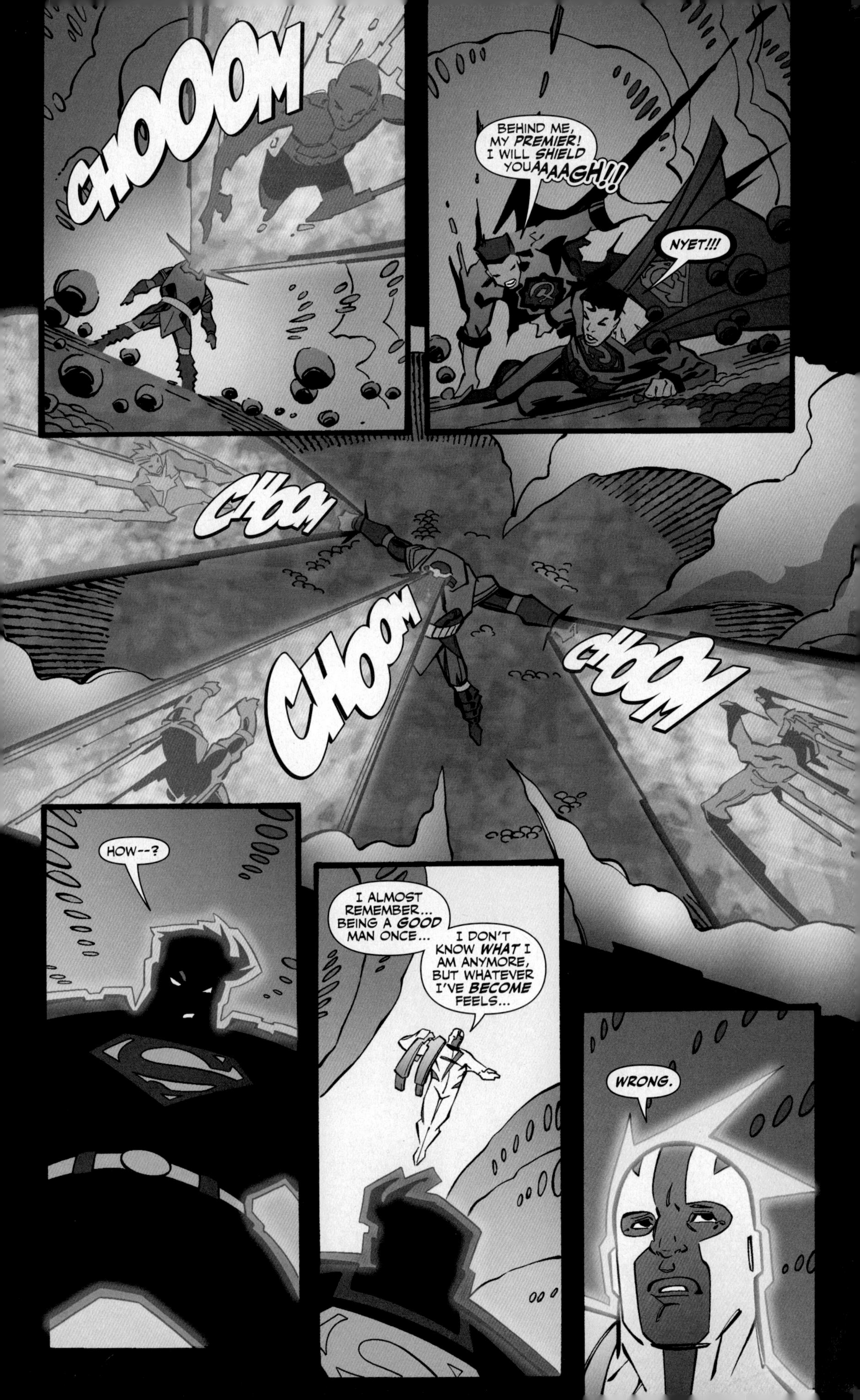
CHOOOM
BEHIND ME, MY PREMIER! I WILL SHIELD YOUAAAAGH!!!
NYET!!!
CHOOM
CHOOM
CHOOM
HOW--?
I ALMOST REMEMBER... BEING A GOOD MAN ONCE...
I DON'T KNOW WHAT I AM ANYMORE, BUT WHATEVER I'VE BECOME FEELS...
WRONG.

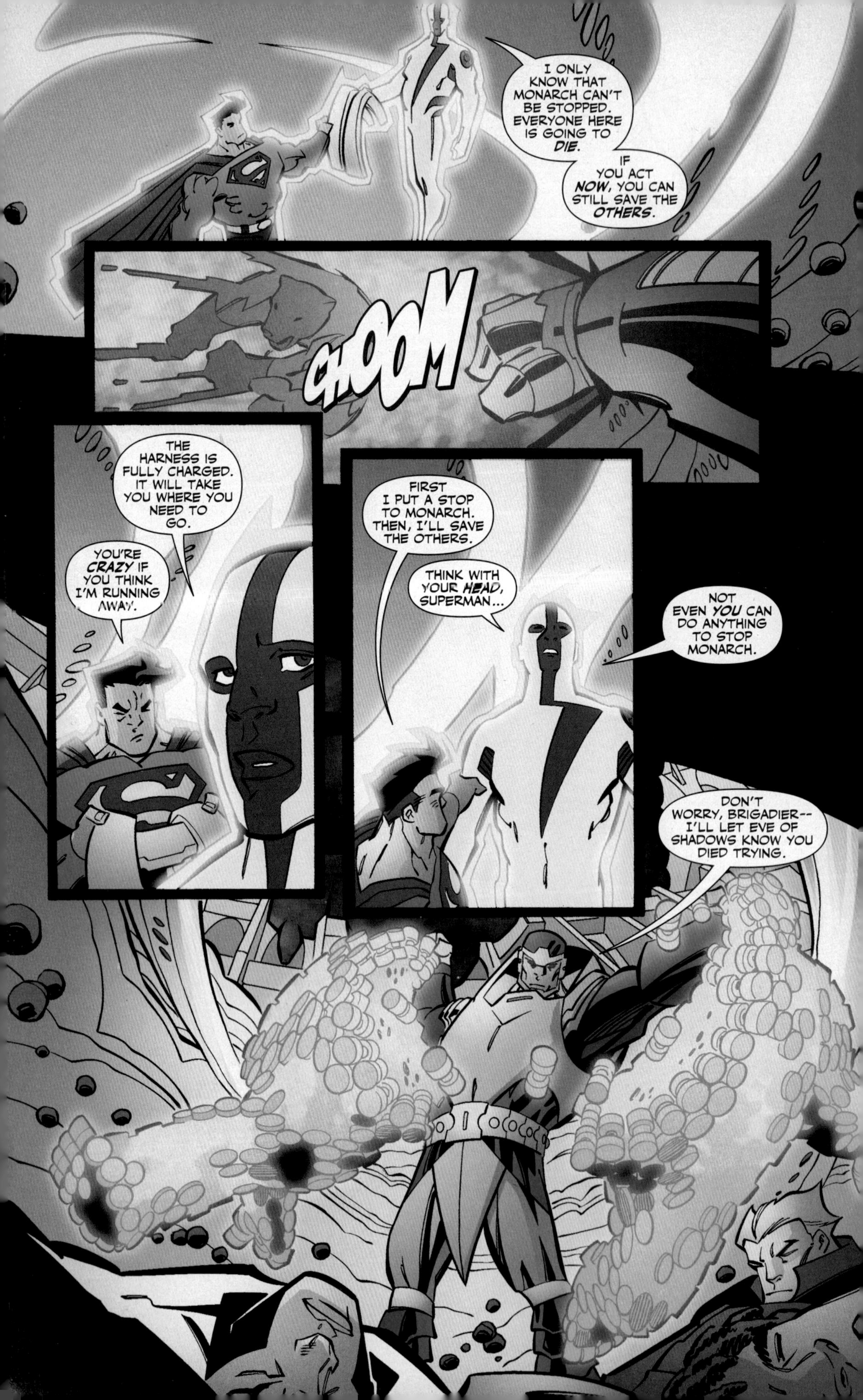
I ONLY KNOW THAT MONARCH CAN'T BE STOPPED. EVERYONE HERE IS GOING TO *DIE*.
IF YOU ACT *NOW*, YOU CAN STILL SAVE THE *OTHERS*.
CHOOM
THE HARNESS IS FULLY CHARGED. IT WILL TAKE YOU WHERE YOU NEED TO GO.
YOU'RE *CRAZY* IF YOU THINK I'M RUNNING AWAY.
FIRST I PUT A STOP TO MONARCH. THEN, I'LL SAVE THE OTHERS.
THINK WITH YOUR *HEAD*, SUPERMAN...
NOT EVEN *YOU* CAN DO ANYTHING TO STOP MONARCH.
DON'T WORRY, BRIGADIER-- I'LL LET EVE OF SHADOWS KNOW YOU DIED TRYING.

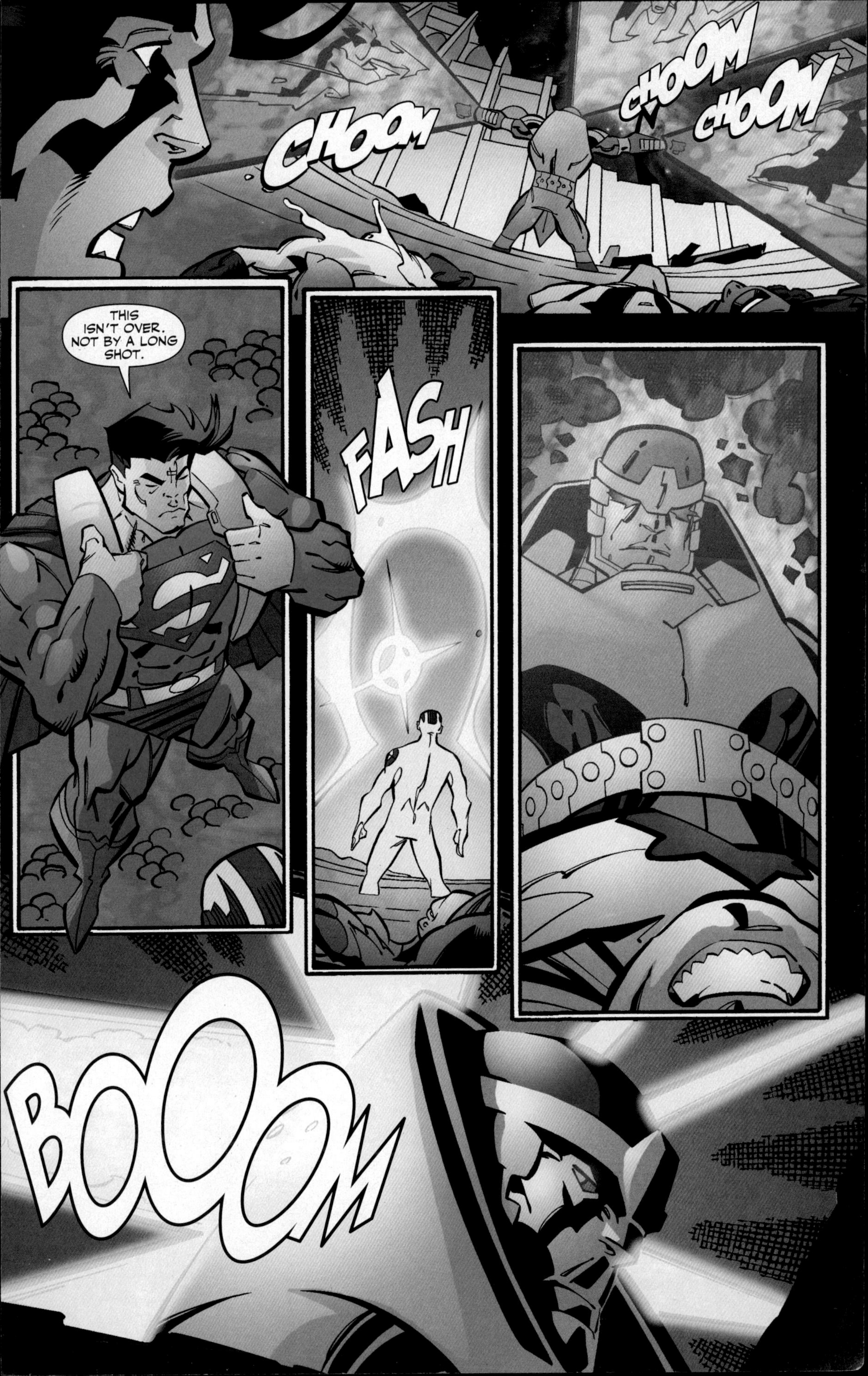

CHOOM
CHOOM
CHOOM
THIS ISN'T OVER. NOT BY A LONG SHOT.
FASH
BOOOOM

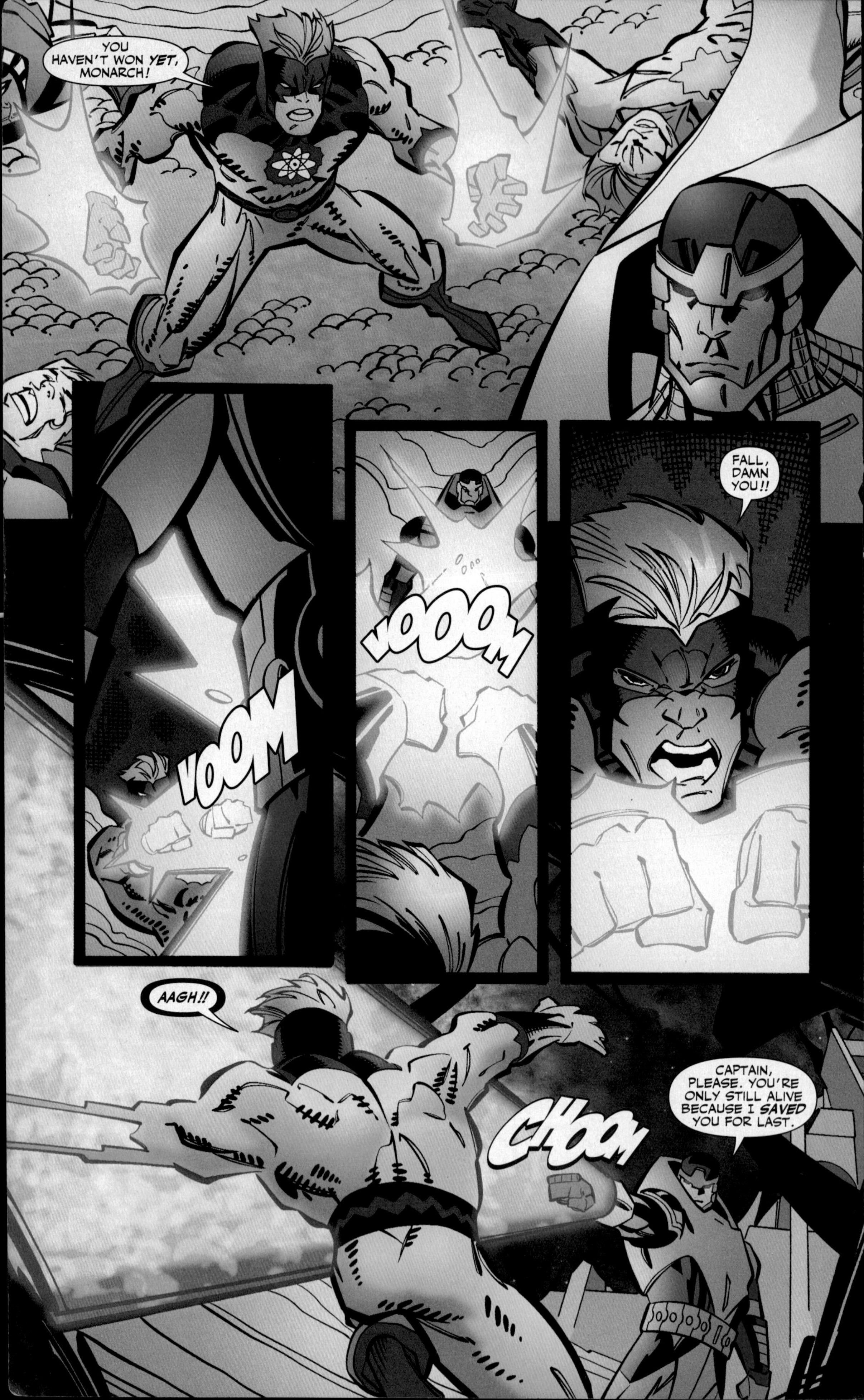
YOU HAVEN'T WON YET, MONARCH!
VOOM
VOOOM
FALL, DAMN YOU!!
AAGH!!
CHOOM
CAPTAIN, PLEASE. YOU'RE ONLY STILL ALIVE BECAUSE I SAVED YOU FOR LAST.

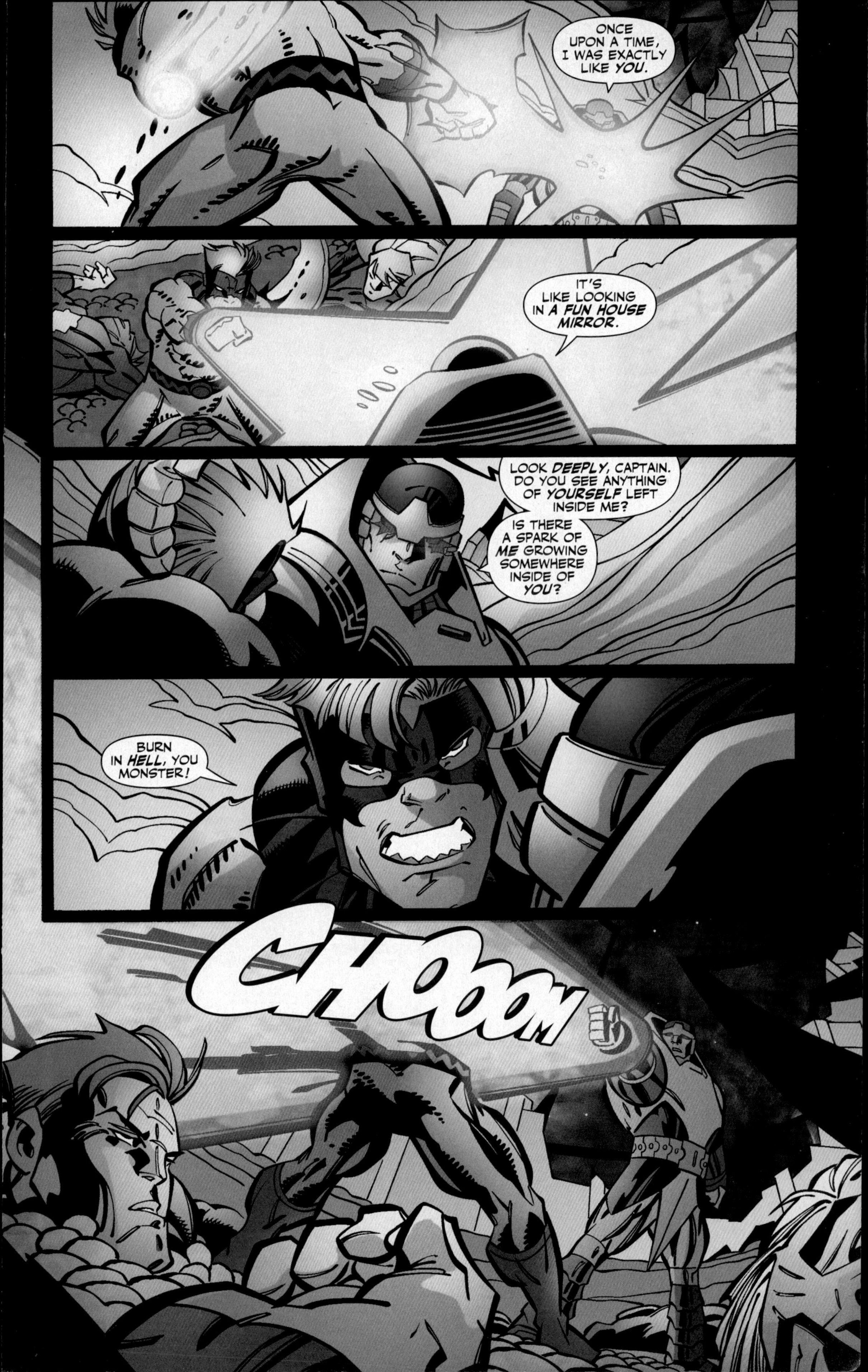
ONCE UPON A TIME, I WAS EXACTLY LIKE YOU.
IT'S LIKE LOOKING IN A FUN HOUSE MIRROR.
LOOK DEEPLY, CAPTAIN. DO YOU SEE ANYTHING OF YOURSELF LEFT INSIDE ME?
IS THERE A SPARK OF ME GROWING SOMEWHERE INSIDE OF YOU?
BURN IN HELL, YOU MONSTER!
CHOOOM

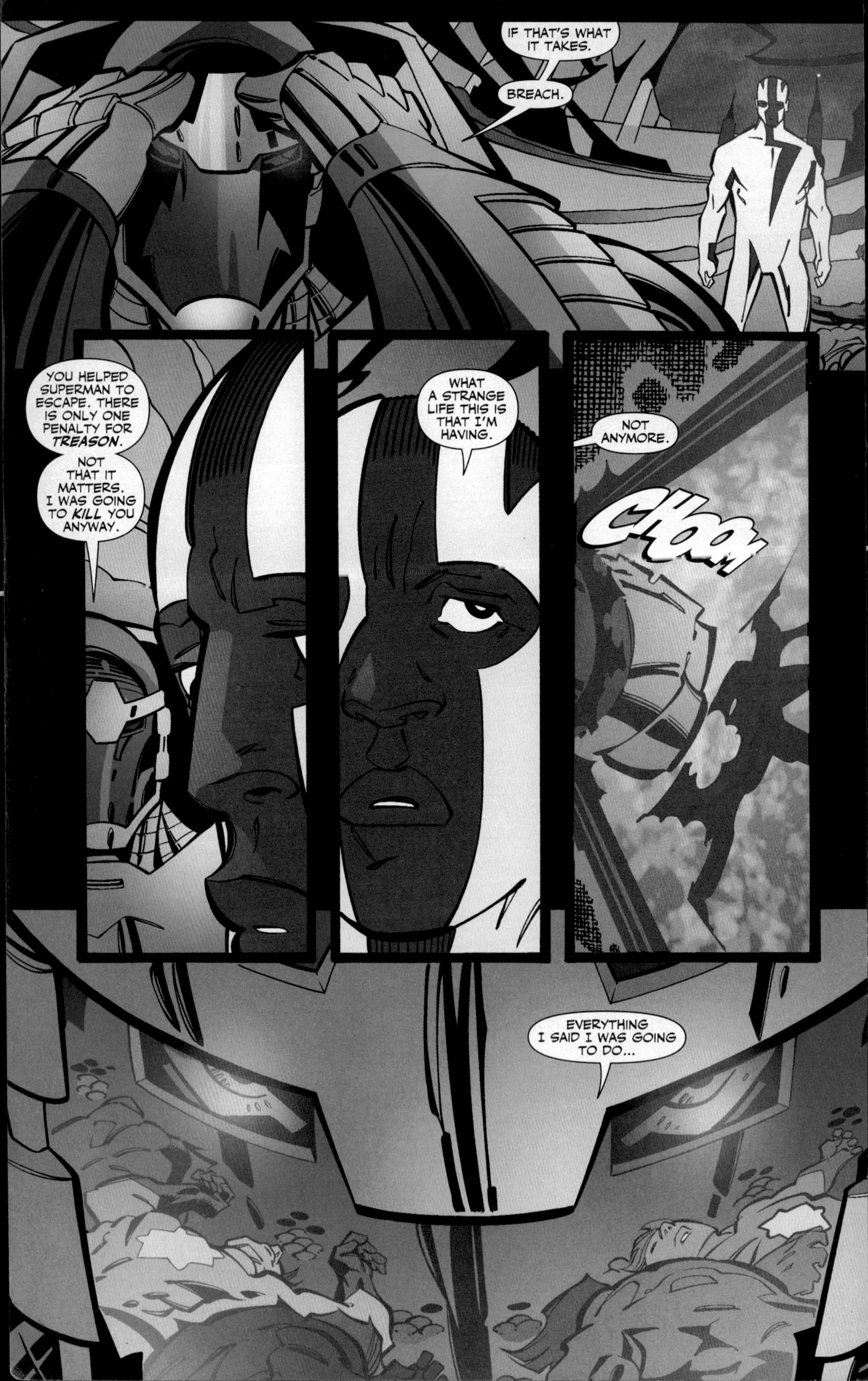
IF THAT'S WHAT IT TAKES.
BREACH.
YOU HELPED SUPERMAN TO ESCAPE. THERE IS ONLY ONE PENALTY FOR TREASON.
NOT THAT IT MATTERS. I WAS GOING TO KILL YOU ANYWAY.
WHAT A STRANGE LIFE THIS IS THAT I'M HAVING.
NOT ANYMORE.
CHOOM
EVERYTHING I SAID I WAS GOING TO DO...

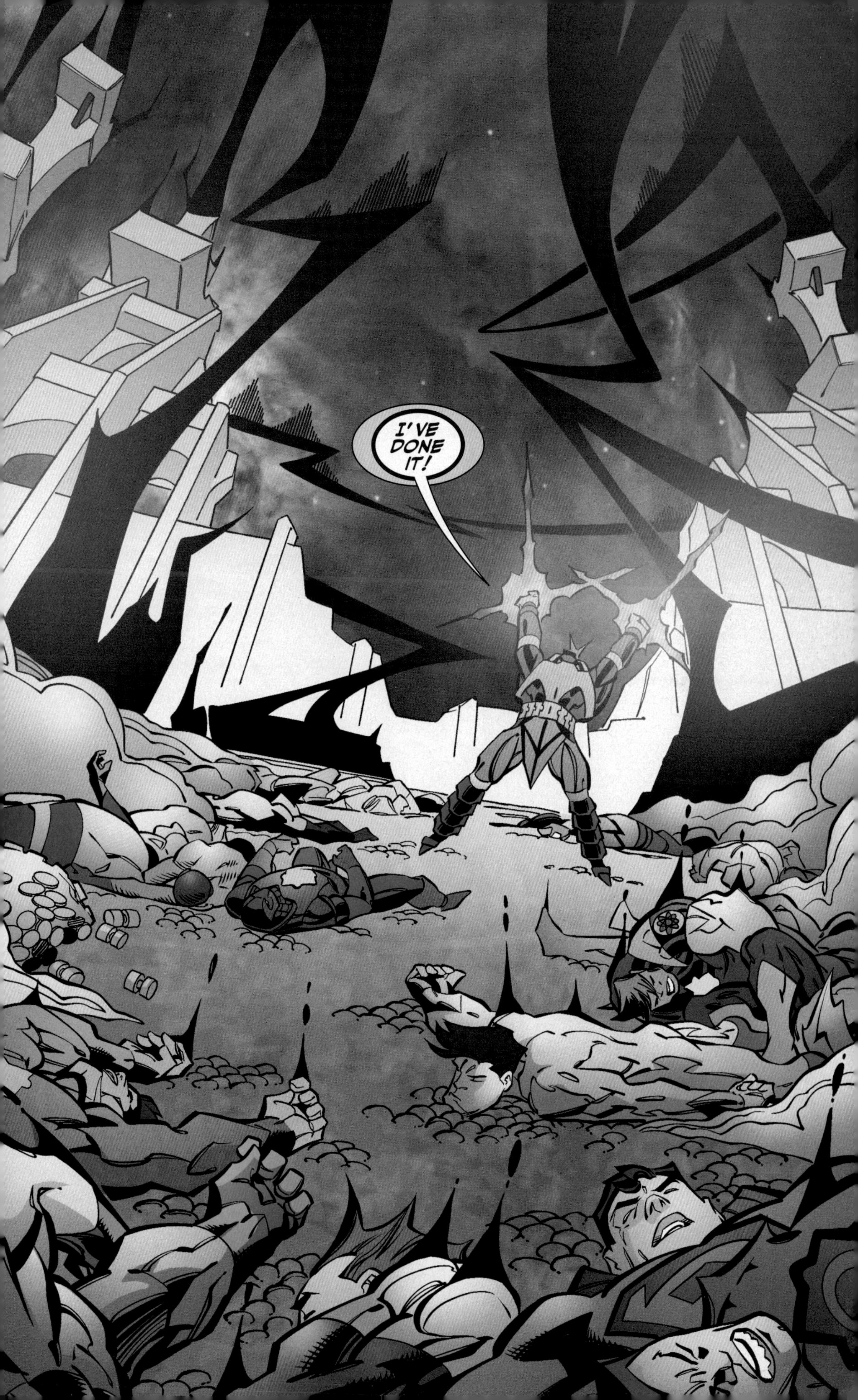
I'VE DONE IT!

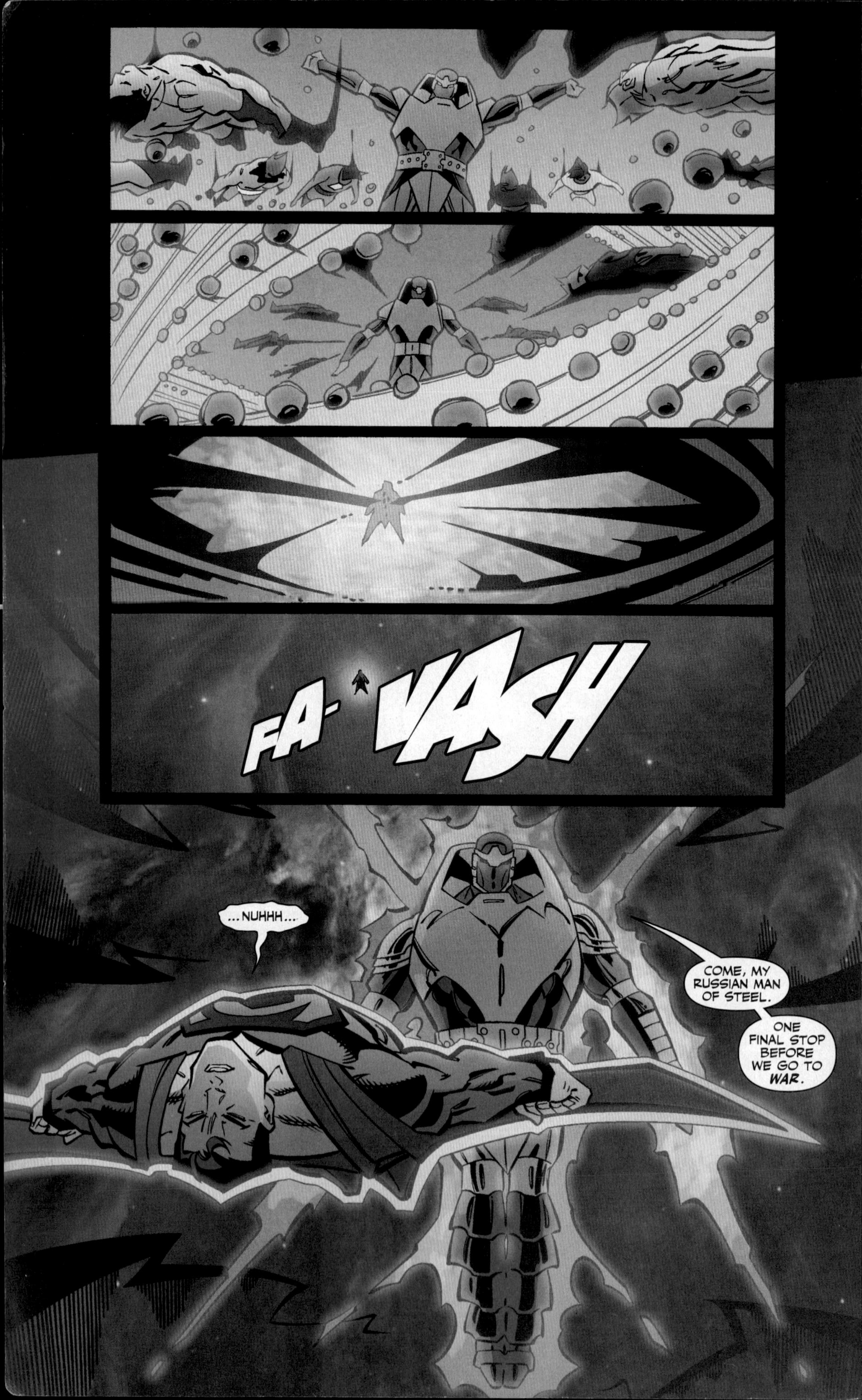
FA-VASH
...NUHHH...
COME, MY RUSSIAN MAN OF STEEL.
ONE FINAL STOP BEFORE WE GO TO WAR.

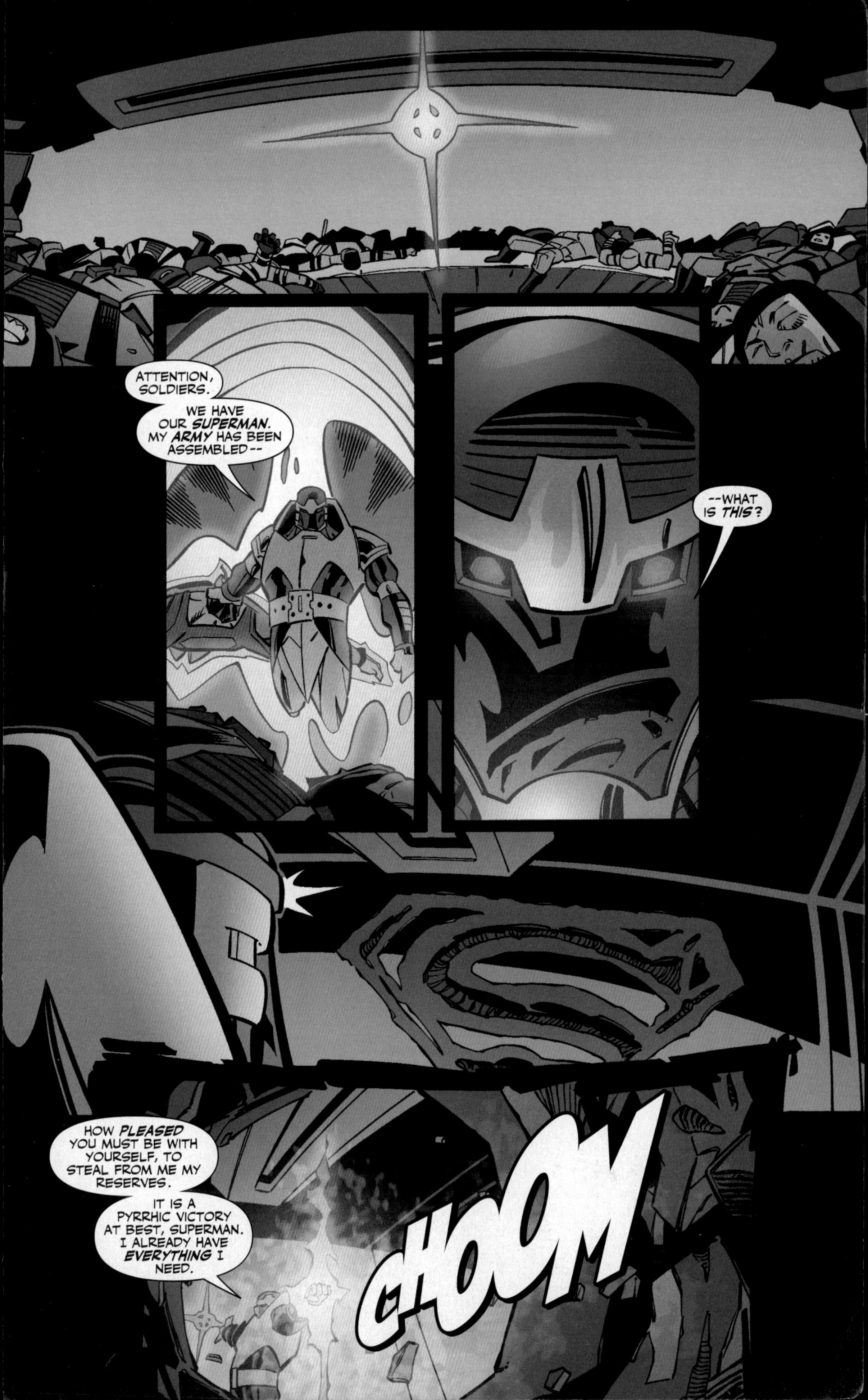
ATTENTION, SOLDIERS.
WE HAVE OUR SUPERMAN. MY ARMY HAS BEEN ASSEMBLED--
--WHAT IS THIS?
HOW PLEASED YOU MUST BE WITH YOURSELF, TO STEAL FROM ME MY RESERVES.
IT IS A PYRRHIC VICTORY AT BEST, SUPERMAN. I ALREADY HAVE EVERYTHING I NEED.
CHOOM

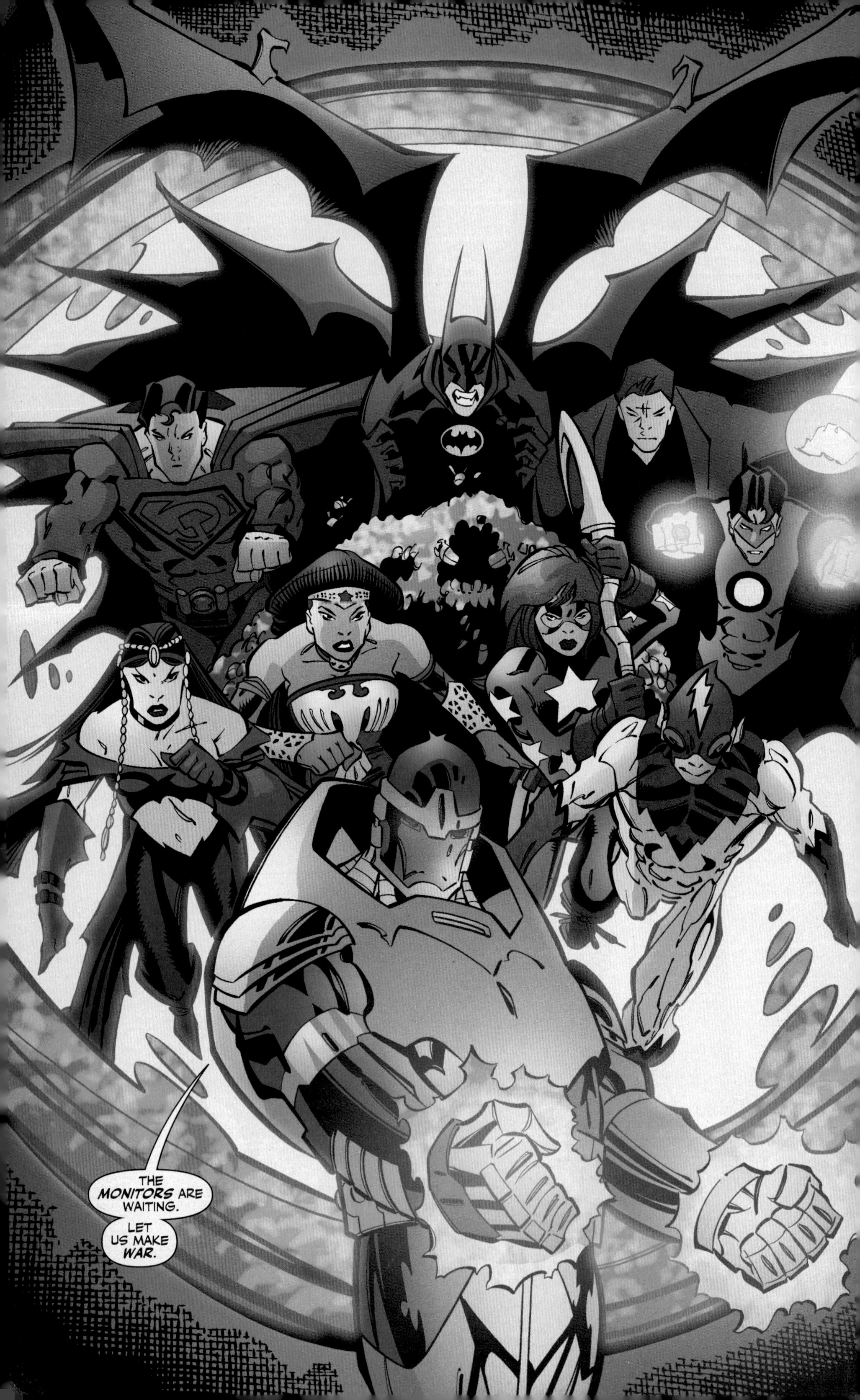
THE MONITORS ARE WAITING.
LET US MAKE WAR.

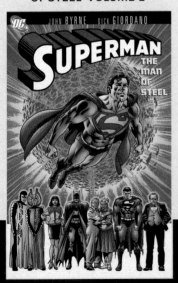

READ MORE ADVENTURES OF YOUR FAVORITE HEROES IN THESE COLLECTIONS FROM DC COMICS:

KINGDOM COME

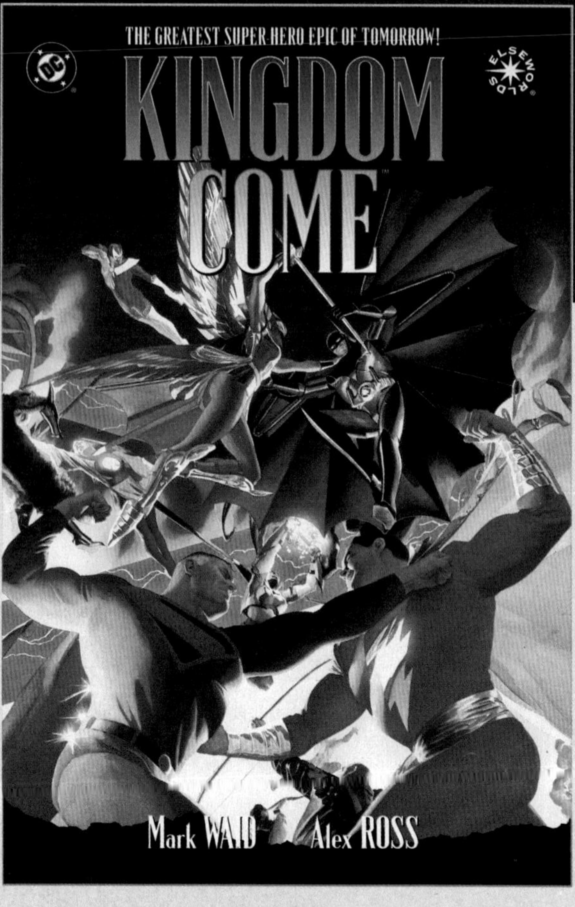
THE GREATEST SUPER-HERO EPIC OF TOMORROW!
KINGDOM COME
Mark WAID
Alex ROSS

Mark Waid and **Alex Ross** deliver a grim tale of youth versus experience, tradition versus change and what defines a hero. KINGDOM COME is a riveting story pitting the old guard — Superman, Batman, Wonder Woman and their peers — against a new uncompromising generation.

WINNER OF FIVE EISNER AND HARVEY AWARDS, INCLUDING BEST LIMITED SERIES AND BEST ARTIST

IDENTITY CRISIS

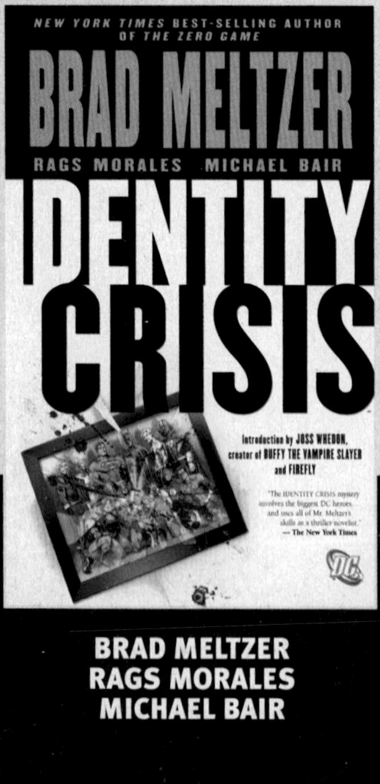
NEW YORK TIMES BEST-SELLING AUTHOR OF THE ZERO GAME
BRAD MELTZER
RAGS MORALES MICHAEL BAIR
IDENTITY CRISIS
Introduction by JOSS WHEDON, creator of BUFFY THE VAMPIRE SLAYER and FIREFLY

BRAD MELTZER
RAGS MORALES
MICHAEL BAIR

CRISIS ON INFINITE EARTHS

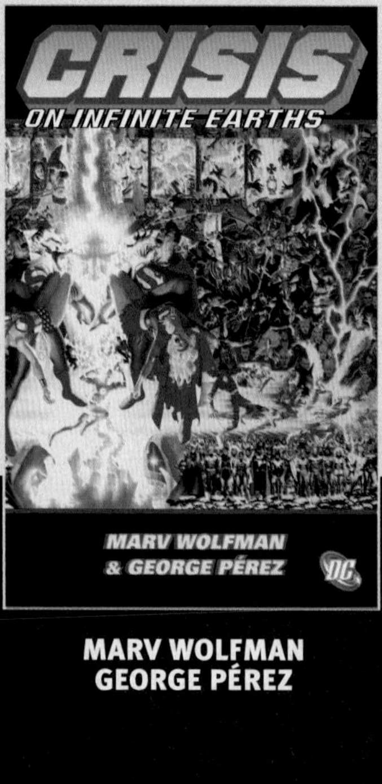
CRISIS
ON INFINITE EARTHS
MARV WOLFMAN
& GEORGE PÉREZ

MARV WOLFMAN
GEORGE PÉREZ

DC: THE NEW FRONTIER VOLUME 1

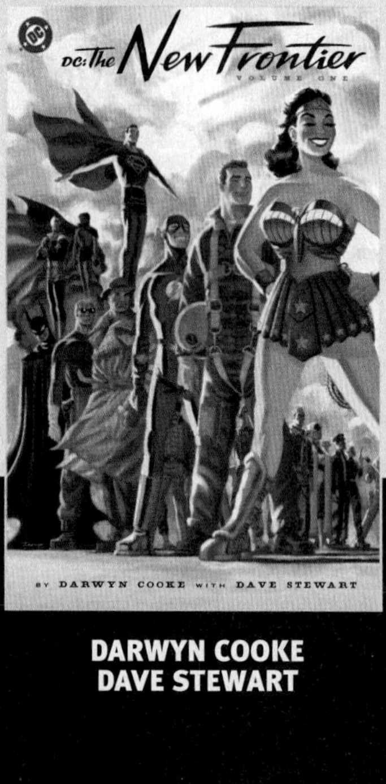
DC: The New Frontier
BY DARWYN COOKE WITH DAVE STEWART

DARWYN COOKE
DAVE STEWART

DON'T MISS THESE OTHER GREAT TITLES FROM AROUND THE **DCU!**

SUPERMAN:
BIRTHRIGHT

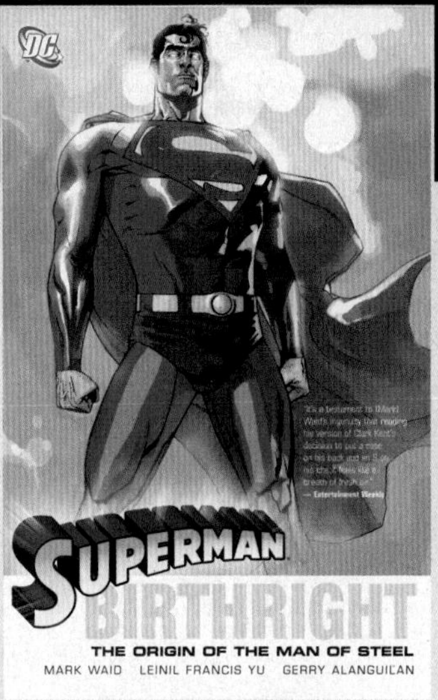
SUPERMAN
BIRTHRIGHT
THE ORIGIN OF THE MAN OF STEEL
MARK WAID LEINIL FRANCIS YU GERRY ALANGUILAN

MARK WAID
LEINIL FRANCIS YU
GERRY ALANGUILAN

BATMAN:
DARK VICTORY

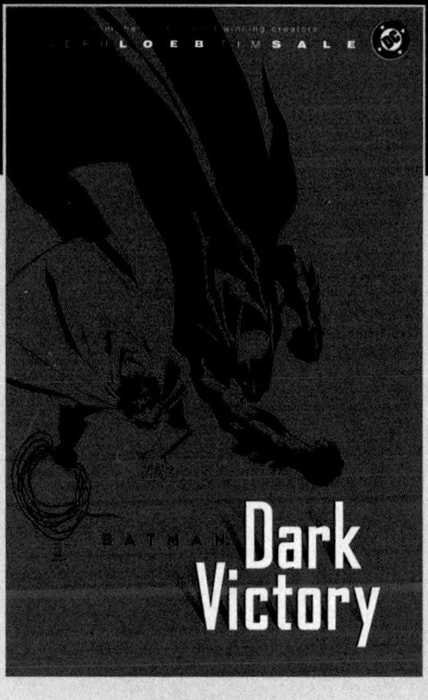
LOEB SALE
BATMAN
Dark Victory

JEPH LOEB
TIM SALE

WONDER WOMAN:
GODS AND MORTALS

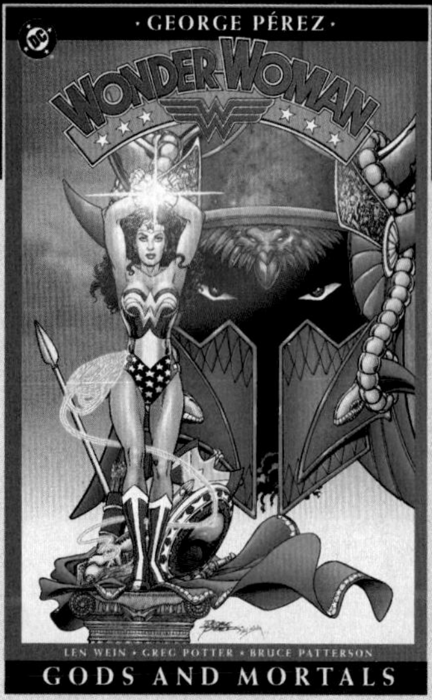
GEORGE PÉREZ
WONDER WOMAN
LEN WEIN • GREG POTTER • BRUCE PATTERSON
GODS AND MORTALS

GEORGE PÉREZ
LEN WEIN/GREG POTTER
BRUCE PATTERSON

GREEN LANTERN:
NO FEAR

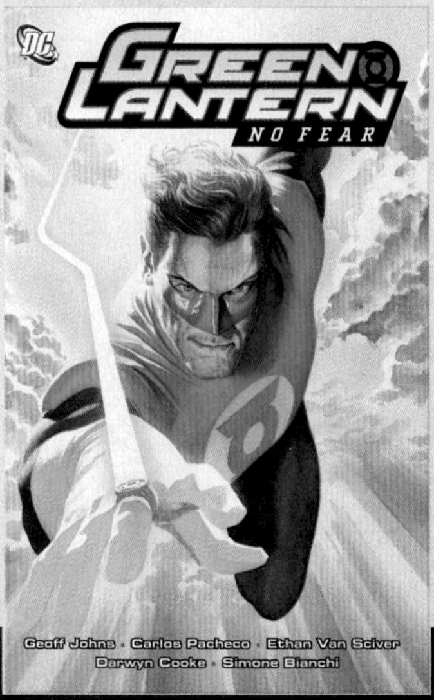
GREEN LANTERN
NO FEAR
Geoff Johns · Carlos Pacheco · Ethan Van Sciver
Darwyn Cooke · Simone Bianchi

GEOFF JOHNS
CARLOS PACHECO
ETHAN VAN SCIVER

GREEN ARROW:
QUIVER

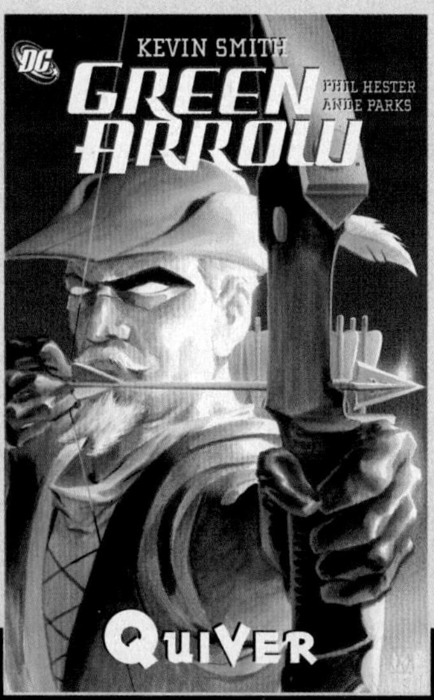
KEVIN SMITH
GREEN ARROW
PHIL HESTER
ANDE PARKS
QUIVER

KEVIN SMITH
PHIL HESTER
ANDE PARKS

TEEN TITANS:
A KID'S GAME

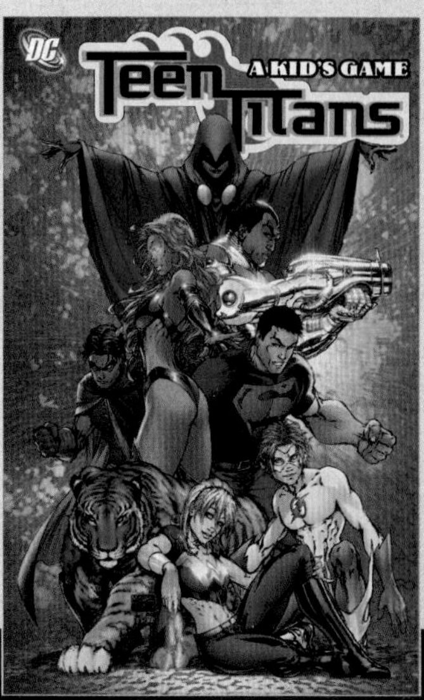
A KID'S GAME
Teen Titans

GEOFF JOHNS
MIKE McKONE

SEARCH THE GRAPHIC NOVELS SECTION OF
www.DCCOMICS.com
FOR ART AND INFORMATION ON ALL OF OUR BOOKS!